WHO FRAMED
COLIN WALLACE?

By the same author

The Politics of Harold Wilson
The Rise of Enoch Powell
Who Killed Hanratty?
Red Shelley
The Helen Smith Story
Murder at the Farm: Who Killed Carl Bridgewater?

Who Framed Colin Wallace?

Paul Foot

MACMILLAN
LONDON

First published 1989 by
MACMILLAN LONDON LIMITED
4 Little Essex Street, London WC2R 3LF
and Basingstoke

Associated companies in Auckland, Delhi, Dublin, Gaborone,
Hamburg, Harare, Hong Kong, Johannesburg, Kuala Lumpur,
Lagos, Manzini, Melbourne, Mexico City, Nairobi, New York,
Singapore and Tokyo

A CIP catalogue record for this book is available from
the British Library.

ISBN 0–333–47008–7

1001059281 T

Typeset by Macmillan Production Ltd

Printed by and bound in Great Britain by
Richard Clay Ltd, Bungay, Suffolk

Contents

Introduction

Shortly after I joined the *Daily Mirror* as a weekly columnist nearly ten years ago I was warned by a distinguished new colleague, Keith Waterhouse, about letters from *Mirror* readers. The problem, he said, was finding time to read them. I soon found out what he meant. Daily, piles of letters would be heaped up on one side as the weekly deadline approached, and left far too long unread. There was always the hope that the next pile would contain the secret document or the scoop. But as the Thatcher years went on, the piles were packed not so much with information as with long and desperate cries of distress. Reading them was not just wearisome, but also painful.

I got into the habit of taking letters home and slogging through them late at night. One midnight, somewhere in November 1986, I came, at the bottom of a bundle, to what looked like an interminable circular. It had no explanatory note, and was headed with the name of a solicitor in West Sussex. I glanced at it suspiciously, preparing to throw it into the bin. I stopped reading nearly three hours later, convinced that if half the document was true, it told one of the most extraordinary stories of postwar Britain.

It was written by Fred Holroyd, a former captain in Military Intelligence. It was an account of an injustice suffered by a former colleague and new friend of his, Colin Wallace. Wallace could not tell his story himself, since he was in prison.

A few weeks later he came out of prison, and gave an interview to the BBC which was summarily 'withdrawn' on the orders of the Director-General's office. I saw an illicit video of this interview. I was surprised when a glib and talkative Ulsterman started by saying how much he had enjoyed the company of his fellow prisoners and how many decent people there were among them. I couldn't recall anyone else making such a point in public on emerging from prison. The message from someone who looked and sounded cold, clinical and distant was curiously warm.

I didn't meet Colin Wallace until early April 1987 when he was regularly appearing on television. I got on well with him, but was extremely cautious. Nothing terrifies a journalist as much as an accomplished deceiver. Colin had been a professional deceiver, paid for his abilities as deceiver by the British Army, and unrivalled in his field.

On my return to London, I phoned the Ministry of Defence. Was it true, I asked, that Colin Wallace had served in a special unit of the Ministry of Defence press office in Northern Ireland and dealt in 'psychological operations'? Was it true that he had been engaged in a propaganda war against terrorism which had sometimes involved the circulation of entirely false information? Had he been removed from his post when he refused to take part in political dirty tricks? And was it true that he had served for a short time with the SAS? Back, quick as a flash, came the replies. No, no, no and no. Wallace had been an information officer in the press office. He had had nothing to do with psychological operations. He had not been sacked, he had resigned. He certainly had never served with the SAS.

That seemed to be that. I had wasted a journey to Arundel. I rang Wallace and told him as politely as I could that the whole of his story was bunk, and the Ministry of Defence had flatly and categorically denied each and every one of his suggestions.

Within hours Colin brought me a formal statement made in 1974 by the head of the Ministry of Defence Information Department in Northern Ireland, a Mr Peter Broderick. This stated quite clearly that Colin Wallace had been transferred to a separate unit in the information department; that he had a job description which was false; and that he dealt with psychological operations. As for the SAS, 'Ask them about Operation Bayleaf in New Zealand,' Colin suggested.

I phoned the Ministry of Defence again. What had they to say about their own former head of department apparently contradicting the denial they had just given me? Could they tell me whether Colin was attached to the SAS during Operation Bayleaf in New Zealand? Was it true that Colin had 'resigned' after initially being sacked, on the suggestion of the Civil Service Appeals Board, and, if so, why wasn't I told that after my first inquiry?

I was promised a reply, but I never got one. Since I have an answerphone in my office which Ministry of Defence press officers have telephoned many times before and since, it was clear that the silence from that quarter was not the result of some accident. When I printed the discrepancy between what I was told and what was fact, there was no response from the ministry.

I checked further. Colin had mentioned his department's leaks against the government it was allegedly serving in Northern Ireland. I found the leaks in the newspapers as he described. He was not always exactly right to the day or even (in one case) the month. But the information checked out. Merlyn Rees, former Secretary of State for Northern Ireland, could not refute it. Nor could his Under-Secretary at the time, Roland Moyle.

Ever since, I have been pursuing two lines of inquiry. First, does what Colin say check out with any known facts? Where the answer to that is yes, as it often is, a further question arises. Why do the authorities go to astonishing lengths to pretend that everything he says is false?

Since I first became hooked on this story, I have been intrigued by the degree and spread of official hostility to Colin Wallace and to Fred Holroyd. On the left, where I stand, people have warned me to have nothing to do with this former agent of the 'Lisburn lie machine'; this agent of British imperialism in Northern Ireland. On the right, Colin has been denounced to me as a 'traitor' and as a fantasist who has relentlessly pursued a deranged obsession with tricking journalists.

I have always been interested in people who stick to principles which have come down to them from on high, from God, from Queen, from Boss, from Country, but who find that by behaving according to those principles they have invoked the wrath of God, Queen, Boss and Country. Colin's political ideas and my own conflict all down the line. I have long since lost faith in the ruling hierarchies of society. He grew up with nothing but faith in them, and still retains that faith. I once listened to him and Fred Holroyd discussing what they wanted to do 'when all this is over'. Both agreed, in Colin's words, 'that all we really want is for them to give us a shovel and a sandbag and tell us to get back digging slit trenches'. My two years in the Army were by far the worst in my life. Colin loved the Army. My view on Ireland is that the British Government has done nothing but harm there for six hundred years or so, and should clear out immediately. That is not Colin's view, though he is reluctant to discuss these matters. I thrive on controversy, Colin is embarrassed by it. He is a genial, clubbable, loyal, conservative man who thinks and hopes that people should get on with one another. The more he has been rebuffed by the people he has admired, the more his geniality, clubbability, loyalty and conservatism has turned him into a far more dangerous and ferocious opponent of those who rebuff him than I can ever be.

After I had met him and Fred Holroyd several times, I suggested tentatively that if they wanted to set their story down in a book, I hoped they would consider me as author.

I warned them that I was a poor choice from their point of view, because of my strong (and extreme) political views. It was Fred who first brushed this aside, and asked me if I would like to write a book. We agreed the terms in the late summer of 1987. I would write the book and have complete control over it. They would make available all their material. I would start with Colin, and go on to Fred. An important condition was that if ever I had cause to disbelieve either man, I would drop the story at once.

Colin insisted that we go to Northern Ireland to visit what remains of his family, and his former friends.

I agreed reluctantly. We flew to Aldergrove and drove straight into the heart of the Protestant areas round Randalstown and Ballymena, where he was born and bred. As we approached a hamlet which Colin told me (apparently not in jest) was called Ballywatermoy, we came across a man in gumboots slapping a cow in the middle of the road. 'That,' said Colin, ' is the Mayor of Ballymena.' It was indeed Sandy Spence MBE, who greeted Colin like a long lost son, and urged us to go in for tea. I demurred, embarrassed, and not a little scared. Colin's total lack of embarrassment about my identity or my politics astonished me. He introduced me openly, almost proudly, to the friends of his youth – Orangemen, former B Specials and Paisleyites, people about whom I had fostered only dark and hostile images. His aim, which he triumphantly achieved, was to *prove* his background. He had been what he said he'd been, a canoeing, orienteering, adventuring, Duke-of-Edinburgh-Award-winning, mountaineering, gung-ho enthusiast for any kind of sport or challenge which was on offer.

When some weeks later he showed me a newspaper cutting to the effect that the Mayor of Ballymena had met Colin Wallace and wished him every good fortune in his campaign, I reflected on the curious contradictions of a part of the world of which I had talked a lot, and experienced nothing.

As the months went on I grew not just to trust Colin but also to like him, to feel sorry for him and admire him. It seemed (and seems) to me that he has been the victim of the most foul injustice, far worse than any normal 'miscarriage' which can be put down to the legal system or the judiciary. He was been wronged by all society and especially by the people whom he holds in the highest regard. His letters, for instance, to the Prime Minister in 1984 onwards are notable not only for their forcefulness but also for their respectful tone. He has always wanted to believe that the society and the Army he loved would suddenly realise he had been the victim of a mistake and sort things out for him. He still hopes that. But every time he is kicked in the teeth, he develops a renewed determination; a deep and lasting wrath.

Fred Holroyd dropped out of our project quite soon. We all agreed that the stories each man tells, though they have a lot in common, are essentially different; and to try to tell them both in one volume would be unnecessarily long and complicated. I stuck with Colin, meeting and talking to him with increasing frequency on endless journeys to Arundel. The whole of this book depends, as the jury in his trial depended, on a judgement about him. I believe him. Wherever I have been able to I have checked what he has told me. Nine times out of ten it has been confirmed and the tenth time has proved simply that his formidable memory is not infallible.

For one mighty flaw in this book I apologise, though it is not my fault. I discovered to my horror that the transcript of Colin's 1981 trial was destroyed in 1986, before I had come across him, or even heard of him. The shorthand writers at the trial assure me that this is routine. Their records of criminal trials where leave to appeal has been rejected are shredded after five years. It seems incredible to me that the record of such a controversial trial should not be available for ever, but I am assured that that is the case. Only about two days of the trial still survive in transcript, together with the judge's summing up. I have therefore had to pick my way through that part of the story with a (complete) copy of all the statements made to the police, and with the daily (and excellent, though by their nature cursory) reports in the Portsmouth *Evening News* and the Brighton *Evening Argus*.

Fred Holroyd has been of enormous assistance. He can be rung up at any time of the day or night and he will still give his cheerful opinion. His own book, though quite different from this one, badly needs and deserves a publisher. James Morgan-Harris, Colin's solicitor, twice gave up a valuable afternoon to allow me to plunder his memory and his files. He is plainly convinced of Colin's innocence, and has travelled many unpaid miles and devoted many unpaid hours to assisting his unusual client. 'In all the time I've known him I've never heard a single lie from Colin Wallace,' he tells me. That is also my experience.

As I tried to check out Colin's life in the British Army, I moved in unaccustomed military circles. Tony Staughton, former head of the public relations department in Northern Ireland, saw me in his home. So did Tony Yarnold. Mike Taylor, a friend and associate of Colin's, gave up time for me in Birmingham. All three men remain staunchly loyal to Colin and are convinced he has been wronged. My thanks, too, to Robin Ramsay, a journalist who prefers investigations in the sub-world of intelligence to making the good living which his talent could provide. He really should have written this book himself, since it was he, in the specialist and poverty-stricken *Lobster* magazine, who started the Colin Wallace story. My thanks to other journalists who have stood by Colin, or helped me: Barrie Penrose of the *Sunday Times*; Duncan Campbell of the *New Statesman*; and Christopher Hird who made the first television programme about Fred Holroyd; Richard Norton-Taylor of the *Guardian*; Bob Parker of *Channel Four News*; Liam Clarke, a freelance in Belfast; Stephen Dorril, co-editor of *Lobster*; Kevin Dowling, now of Central Television; Julian Hendy of Yorkshire Television; Chris Moore of BBC Northern Ireland; Robin Alp of the *West Sussex Gazette* and *Portsmouth Evening News* who stuck by Colin even when all other journalists seemed against him; Philip Colley, formerly of the Bognor Regis *Observer*; Ed Moloney of the Dublin *Sunday Tribune*, who with Andy Pollak published so much unpopular material about the Kincora Boys' Home in the *Irish Times* in the early 1980s. Moloney, like many of his contemporaries, still remains deeply sceptical about Colin Wallace but has never refused to talk about him. Neil Grant, Ken Livingstone's dogged researcher, has hardly ever been off the telephone.

I tried, twice, to speak to Jane Lewis and her family. I wrote them long letters, begging for an interview. They made it clear, politely, that they didn't want to talk to anyone.

The library staff of the *Irish Times* in Dublin and in Belfast have been specially good to me. As always I have depended on the magnificent cuttings library at the *Daily Mirror*, so carefully nurtured by the people who work there. Richard Stott, the *Daily Mirror* editor has once again generously indulged me in my obsession with a story he never fully believed in. Perhaps this will change his mind.

I was lucky, for the third time in a row, to have the book edited by Jane Heller, who spent the usual sleepless nights making bricks out of straw. Philippa Harrison took this on for Macmillan with characteristic enthusiasm and Adam Sisman persuaded me that the ridiculous speed he proposed for publication was (just) humanly possible. Indeed, the circumstances in which this book has been published have required superhuman efforts from three members of Macmillan's staff: Tracy Florance, Jayne Jenkinson and Hazel Orme.

My thanks, finally, to Eileen Wallace. Her calm certainty about her husband's innocence at a time when she had good reason to conclude otherwise was as persuasive as any other aspect of the story. There was never a time when I didn't feel welcome in her home. Arundel will always be a creepy place for me because of what I believe happened there but the Wallace household is quite a different matter.

Paul Foot, 31 March 1989

CHAPTER ONE

The Weasels in the Woods

Colin Wallace was born in June 1943 in Randalstown, a small town between Antrim and Ballymena in the Orange heartland of Northern Ireland. His father, John, a Scottish Presbyterian, was in the RAF. Colin has only one fleeting memory of his father carrying him upstairs. In the last throes of the war in Italy, John Wallace was injured. He died from his injuries soon after he was brought home to Randalstown in 1946.

Deprived of all income, Colin's mother got a job at once in Gallaher's cigarette factory in Ballymena. She rented a small terraced house in the town and left Colin with her parents who lived in a cottage near Randalstown. Colin grew up in what he describes as 'the sort of environment any kid would love'. There was an orchard at the back of the cottage and a stream running through it. As soon as he could ride a bike, he was off each morning to a farm a mile or so away which had been bought by his mother's sister, Rose, and his uncle, Isaac.

Idyllic and pastoral it certainly was; the shores of Lough Neagh were only a few fields away and there was plenty of fishing, hunting and farming to keep a child amused. None of Colin's family had any money. The men and women were all working in labouring jobs at low wages and, throughout his schooldays, Colin was always one of the poorest boys in his class. At a tiny school in Randalstown he was enthused by a teacher who excited him with readings from books about Irish history, in particular *My Lady of the Chimney Corner* by Alexander Irvine. Irvine's house at Antrim is now a museum in which the author and his belongings are immortalised. The book and its author are cherished in the area. 'My Lady' herself, the mother of a poverty-stricken working-class family and the heroine of the book, seems to worship an entirely different God from the one celebrated by Protestant supremacists who called for hellfire to consume the heathens of Rome.

Alexander Irvine himself was hostile to religious bigotry. His travels took him to the United States of America, where he became a socialist and a militant trade unionist. He was on the 'hit list' of the gangs employed by the big American trusts to rid themselves of militants. He himself would have been most indignant that any of his works and his

memory should be embalmed by Orange supremacists and passed on to
different generations of Northern Irish schoolchildren as though it were
the word of One (Orange) God.

This was certainly how the book was received in Colin Wallace's family.
His mother's family tree went all the way back to the sixteenth-century
'plantation' of the north-east of Ireland with Protestants from Scotland –
a plantation which led to four hundred years of sectarian warfare between
Roman Catholics and Protestants. Colin remembers the influences on his
childhood as being his Church, his Country (Britain) and the Armed
Forces.

The Old Congregation Presbyterian Church at Randalstown was the
centre of his existence. From it sprang the Boys' Brigade, and the sports
and the recreation in which he took an active part. Sundays were days of
discipline. 'The only things we were allowed to read were the *Christian
Herald* and the *Sunday Companion*.' There was Sunday school for the
children in the morning, followed by ordinary morning church, followed
by more Sunday school in the afternoon, and then, as they got a bit
older, an evening service. The no-nonsense, no-flummery Presbyterian
approach kept the services lean and lively, and Colin Wallace doesn't
remember being bored. Most of his family were paid-up members (and
sometimes senior officials) of the Orange Order or the Royal Black
Institution. All the talk at his grandparents' house was of the history
of the fight of Protestant people in Ireland to keep Republicans at bay.
History started when King William won the Battle of the Boyne in 1690.
Most of his uncles and great-uncles had all been active in the B Specials,
the heavily armed special Protestant-only police.

The strongest of the influences was patriotism. Every political discussion
started from the eminence of the British Crown, and the importance of
defending it against its enemies. Colin's grandmother was born in 1888
and recalled the notorious 'Black and Tans' who waged a dirty and violent
campaign in Ireland against Republicans in the years after the First World
War. The greatest upholder of the British Crown was the British Army.
The annual holiday celebrations and parades which marked the Orange
year always start on 1 July – to celebrate the Battle of the Somme when
thousands of young men from the 36th Ulster Division were cut down
fighting for the British Crown. Colin's grandmother eagerly followed
the progress of the various Ulster regiments through the Empire. She
embroidered handkerchiefs with pictures of King William of Orange, and
sent them to soldiers in the Ulster regiments serving in the trenches in
France during the First World War. Her walls were covered with framed
names of members of the family who had died for Britain in the Great War.
She was herself a crack shot, and would have volunteered her services as
a gunwoman if there were any IRA snooping about. As for the Catholic
population of the same island, Colin doesn't remember having contact with

any of them during the whole of his childhood. Everybody was Protestant. The 'enemy' lurked like weasels in the wood, unseen and undiscovered except perhaps to be shot at by a B Special patrol. He could see the hamlets where they lived from the high ground above Toomebridge and Moneyglass, but he never went near them. 'I grew up to believe above all else in the importance of loyalty to the Crown and service to my country,' Colin recalls. 'The attitude of complete, unswerving loyalty to the British sovereign state shaped the whole way I thought and behaved.'

All this changed only slightly when Colin, against the expectations of many children of similar background, passed the eleven plus and went to Ballymena Academy, a stern, masculine school whose alumni included many top Northern Ireland politicians, soldiers, sportsmen and businessmen.

The Academy, which had few Catholic pupils, was run on the traditions of the British public school. Sport and military training were considered crucial to the proper development of the young Protestant men.

As soon as he left the Academy in 1960, he looked for work. His mother's lungs and glands had been infected with tobacco poison at her workplace. Colin went to work for a Ballymena pharmaceutical company, J. A. Woodside, where he started as an apprentice working in the manufacturing of chemicals and drugs. His mother remarried and she and Colin went to live with her new husband in a much bigger house at Ballywatermoy on the outskirts of Ballymena. In 1963, his grandmother died. In 1964, the house was sold and the family moved to another bungalow in Ballymena. Then, in sad succession, Colin's mother's new husband died in 1965 and his mother died of cancer in 1966. His grandfather, who had come to look after the sick woman, died in 1973. Though not yet thirty, Colin had no parents or grandparents.

While at Woodside, he became an active officer of the Territorial Army Volunteer Reserve, into which he was commissioned in 1961. He was in charge of cadet adventure training, and used his skills as an instructor to involve boys and young men all over his home territory in adventure training. David Jamieson, who was captain of the Randalstown Boys' Brigade in the mid-1960s, persuaded Colin to supervise adventure training and canoeing courses for his members. What struck him about Colin was his readiness always to take a lead. 'If the boys had to climb a mountain, he climbed the mountain. If they had to stay all night in a trench, he stayed all night in a trench,' he told me when I interviewed him in December 1987. The Ballymena Royal Ulster Rifles Detachment had more boys winning the Duke of Edinburgh Award in 1964 than did any other group in the entire British Commonwealth, a proud record which its members still today ascribe to the detachment's award organiser, Colin Wallace. His unit also specialised in shows and displays throughout the area.

As if he were not doing enough in what was left of his spare time, Colin joined the notorious Ulster Special Constabulary – the B Specials – in 1966 and soon qualified as one of their marksmen. He was persuaded to do so by the growing (and groundless) anxiety, widely expressed in the Protestant community, that the IRA would start a violent campaign to coincide with the fiftieth anniversary of the Easter Rising in Dublin in 1916. His friend at the time, Robert Mooney, who was both a sergeant instructor in Colin's TAVR unit and a member of the same B Special platoon, recalls that Colin Wallace was always the volunteer for the most amount of work, and the least amount of credit. By 1968, he was one of the youngest and most active of the Territorial Army officers in Northern Ireland. His commitment to voluntary work, especially among the youth, was prodigious. He was also a highly competent shot. His Royal Ulster Rifles cadet detachment, with Colin as captain, won the *News of the World* shooting trophy in 1965.

In 1967, Colin was approached by the Chief of Staff of the Regular Army of Northern Ireland. 'With the amount of time you're giving to the Army part-time,' he said, 'why not come and work for us full time?'

Colin replied that he had always wanted to be a regular soldier – all his aspirations and upbringing pointed to that. He had, however, missed the chance, since he had been forced to get a job in Ballymena to look after his mother. The Chief of Staff mentioned that Lieutenant Colonel Jack Gracie, the deputy to the Public Relations Officer at Lisburn barracks, headquarters of the British Army in Northern Ireland, was retiring – why didn't Colin apply for the job? Colin was taken aback. He was, he thought, entirely unqualified for such a high-sounding job. Yet his relatives were now all dead, and here was a marvellous opportunity for a career of which every one of them would have approved.

He went into Lisburn barracks as Assistant Command, Public Relations Officer for the Army in Northern Ireland on 1 May 1968. He was a civil servant, with an equivalent Army rank of major; and of course he kept his commission in the TAVR, where he was now training Irish Guards cadets. He was also commissioned as a captain in the Ulster Defence Regiment.

Proud as Colin felt on the first morning he walked into the Army headquarters, even he would not have argued that the job he had just won would test him too severely. Lisburn barracks, Northern Ireland, was known in the British Army at that time as Happy Valley. It was a pasture for old warhorses who had not quite reached retiring age. The much feared IRA campaign had fizzled out, after almost total failure, in 1962. The IRA itself seemed to exist only in name, a pathetic organisation which sang songs to itself about its brave and bloody past. What was left of Republican activism could be left to the B Specials and the Royal Ulster Constabulary, who knew how to sniff out recalcitrant Republicans and deal with them. The underlying causes of the violence which had wracked the north-east of Ireland over the centuries were still there, but at the beginning of 1968, the effects seemed to have disappeared. The 'Protestant state for the Protestant people', as its first Prime Minister called it, seemed to be lying doggo, not even licking its wounds. The electoral system was rigged, the police force was sectarian, the whole state was founded on discrimination against two fifths of the population, but no one seemed to care very much. The only real role for the British garrison was to recruit from the ever willing populace more troops for more regiments (though no home-grown regiments were allowed to serve in Northern Ireland for fear that their religious loyalties might interfere with their patriotic ones).

The role of the public relations officers was perhaps more important than that of anyone else at 'Happy Valley'. They at least had something to do: athletic achievements of soldiers in Northern Ireland needed to be reported in English local newspapers. Jovial Father Christmases had to be found for children's functions; voluntary activities 'showing the flag' were in high demand. They were Colin Wallace's speciality. He started to organise a free-fall parachute display team. He threw himself into all sorts of games, stunts and sports to promote the Army. One day he would be writing a bromide speech for the General; the next he would be falling out of an aeroplane; the next he would be assisting a repertory company with a production of *Oh What a Lovely War*. He was the happiest man in Happy Valley and his colleagues noticed at once that he was always the first to volunteer to do anything, however unpleasant.

Colin's boss, who had the rather grand title of Command, Public Relations Officer, was Tony Staughton. He had started as a regimental soldier in the South Staffordshire Regiment and had served in many different parts of the world as regimental officer, staff officer and press officer. He had dealt with the press in Germany, Korea, Singapore, and Cyprus where he had worked at the start of the emergency.

In 1962 he left the Army and became a civilian information officer for the Army in the five Midland counties. In 1964 he was transferred to Northern Ireland to run the public relations unit there. The unit consisted of himself, an assistant and a secretary. 'I felt,' he says, 'that the new job was a reward due to me.' He quickly settled into the easy routine of Happy Valley.

When his assistant left in 1968, he attended the selection board for a successor with an officer from the Ministry of Defence and interviewed Colin Wallace. He was at once impressed with him and argued for his appointment. Within weeks of Colin's move to Lisburn – he had a room of his own at the back of the barracks – Tony Staughton was delighted with his choice.

'I found him remarkable in many ways,' he says. 'He had absolutely no conception of the limits of work. He was prepared to do a job at any time of the day or night.

'It became clear at once that he was in love with the Army. He kept proving himself excellent in many, many ways, and he was always going off for some entirely voluntary military activity of one kind or another. I liked him, and my wife liked him very much indeed. He was a tremendous person to have in the barracks. We came to look on him almost as a son.

'He was absolutely first class with the press from the beginning. He didn't believe in deceiving people at all, and he won the journalists' respect and trust right from the outset. We were extremely lucky to have found him. I would say about the whole period I knew him that he was the best thing that ever happened to public relations for the Army in Northern Ireland.' (Interview with the author, 10 October 1987.)

The turbulence of 1968 in other parts of the world seemed to be passing Northern Ireland by. The nearest thing to any action in the summer of that year was a vast NATO exercise, including members of the SAS, in the Mountains of Mourne. Colin was greatly excited by this, and threw himself into it. He was only mildly daunted when the centrepiece of the exercise, the cruiser HMS *Fearless*, was suddenly plucked away for a few days to accommodate the British Prime Minister, Harold Wilson, and the leader of the Rhodesian white rebellion, Ian Smith, for abortive talks in the Mediterranean.

Then suddenly that October, when Colin had been at Lisburn less than six months, the whole atmosphere changed. A demonstration demanding civil rights for the Catholic minority in Northern Ireland was broken up with savage force by the Royal Ulster Constabulary. Suddenly, Northern Ireland was in the news. Journalists flooded in from all over the world to re-open the age-old controversies. Colin Wallace at first thought nothing of it. All his adult life there had been scares about a reawakening of old hostilities, but they had always proved illusory. The B Specials had gone in, a shot or two was fired, an angry word or two printed in the Catholic press and then comfortable complacency returned. When Tony Staughton remarked one day late in 1968: 'Thousands will be killed here,' Colin scoffed at his English pessimism. Tony Staughton, however, read some of the same signs which he had read before, in Malaya and especially in Cyprus.

It didn't take Colin long to change his mind. It was not merely that the civil rights movement grew in influence, nor that their marches continued to be insulted and physically attacked by the very forces of law and order in which Colin himself had served. It was the effrontery of the new movement which shook him into the realisation that something momentous was happening.

He was sitting in his office on 14 August 1969 when Tony Staughton came in with astonishing news. 'The government's sending troops into Derry,' he said. 'You'd better go with them.' Riots in Derry had unleashed a violent backlash by B Specials and RUC, which threatened an outbreak of civil war. The Army went in to 'keep the peace'. Colin travelled to Derry in a four-ton truck which was full of barbed wire. He went straight with the first troops to be deployed to the Bogside, which was cordoned off by barricades. There he remembers a discussion between the officer commanding the Derry forces and a Queen's University student, Bernadette Devlin. He remembers a telephone call from Ulsterbus demanding the return of a bus which had been used for barricades. He negotiated with the demonstrators who said he could have the bus back if the Army would rebuild their barricade. 'We did just that,' he says. 'We built their barricade.' No wonder, on that first day, that the British troops were so popular with the Bogsiders.

The following day, he was whisked down by helicopter to Belfast, the scene of some of the worst rioting in the history of that city. As he tried to organise a press visit into the gutted Catholic areas in the Lower Falls, he remembers an object flying through the air at him. It was a medal case enclosing an MBE – a protest from an old warrior such as the ones for whom his grandmother had embroidered handkerchiefs, outraged that the British Army should be seen to be helping Catholics. 'My memory of the Falls that day is very clear,' says Colin. 'There were whole streets gutted, empty buildings everywhere, a huge linen factory burnt to the ground. I just couldn't believe the scale of the devastation. The normal cheerful atmosphere of the place had been replaced by a sullen resentment. It was quite obvious that something very serious was happening, something quite different from anything that had ever happened while I'd been alive.'

The 'sullen resentment' which Colin noticed in the Falls that August afternoon brooded over Northern Ireland in the ensuing months. For a brief period, many people on the scene believed that the 'August troubles' might well be just a flash in the pan, and that the uneasy peace which had prevailed ever since the 1930s would return. In fact, however, the old battle-lines were re-emerging. Sections of the Catholic minority were no longer prepared to accept a system of government which discriminated against them forever because of their religion. To begin with, this resistance and determination had shown itself in groups such as the People's Democracy, which had organised a long march from Belfast to Derry and which had been met with the sticks and stones of the upholders of Protestant law and Protestant order. Bernadette Devlin quickly emerged as a new leader, unsectarian in her attitude to Protestants, but uncompromising in her demands for an end to the Orange state. She was elected as an independent MP for Mid-Ulster in April 1969.

In a sense these political developments obscured what was really happening – namely a revival of the old religious confrontations, and of the old armies. In the weeks immediately following the troops' intervention in Belfast and Derry, the Catholic population were inclined to look at the troops as their saviours. Certainly if the troops had not intervened in Belfast there would have been something approaching a pogrom in the Catholic areas and there were many in those areas who greeted the troops with open enthusiasm.

But the enthusiasm quickly faded. If the British authorities did not want a pogrom and were prepared to use their troops to stop one, neither did they want to fan the flames of revolt among the minority. Increasingly, therefore, in the months following the summer riots of 1969, the British troops began to adopt a new role: isolating and controlling the outbursts of resistance in the Catholic population, and doing so in collaboration with the authorities in the Six Counties: authorities which were by their nature organised and constituted in the interests of the Protestant majority. Through 1970 and the early part of 1971, the troops came to be seen no longer as saviours but as upholders of the old plantation: the defenders of those in Ireland who saw themselves as 'British' against those who saw themselves as Irish. In turn, more and more people in the Falls Road in Belfast or in the Bogside in Derry felt the need for some reliable protection against Protestant attacks. What followed was the revival of the Irish Republican Army, which split into an Official section which talked in socialist and non-sectarian terms but did nothing, and the Provisionals which offered the military protection which was so badly needed.

This process did not evolve overnight. By 1971, however, there were two developments which made quite clear what was really happening. On 6 February, the first British soldier was shot in Northern Ireland – the first such life to be lost since the 1920s. Secondly, on 9 August, the British Conservative government sanctioned the right of the police and military authorities to intern dissidents without trial. Those interned included not just IRA suspects but many political dissidents as well, including Michael Farrell, the influential, non-sectarian leader of People's Democracy. Many of those arrested were tortured – as was later proved before, and denounced by, the European Court of Human Rights.

Colin Wallace recalls that the British Army command was strongly opposed to internment. The General Officer Commanding Northern Ireland, Sir Harry Tuzo, he remembers, was 'against it totally'. He argued that the authorities in the Six Counties did not then have the necessary intelligence to carry out an effective internment operation, and that therefore the exercise would be botched and would rebound.

These predictions were handsomely vindicated. Internment itself was hopelessly bungled. But the dictatorial methods used, and the 'inhuman and degrading treatment', as the European Court of Human Rights put it, helped to persuade large numbers of the more beleaguered of the

Catholic population that the British authorities were propping up the Orange supremacy; and that the only effective protection for them was the armed militia – the Provisional IRA. Thus the two chief events of 1971 – the killing of the first British soldier and internment – led to a rapid growth in the influence and military effectiveness of the Provisional IRA; and in turn convinced the British and Northern Irish authorities that they were in for a long period of civil war.

Suddenly, the garrison at Lisburn was transformed from being the least important and most neglected of all the British Army headquarters to the most important and the best supplied. Happy Valley became Siege City. Every branch of activity there had to change, none more drastically than information and public relations.

In the lull immediately after the summer of 1969, the changes were minimal. Tony Staughton stayed in control, with Colin Wallace as his assistant. In 1969, on the very day of the Bogside riots, they were joined by Major Tony Yarnold, a military public relations man of enormous experience. He had served in Egypt, Cyprus, Malaya and Hong Kong where he had run the Press Office during the communist insurgency.

Tony Yarnold immediately overhauled the system of collecting information. He called in more clerks and secretaries. He supervised a round-the-clock, three-shift system for the Press Office. By 1971, there was a new dark room, a new printing press and a staff of at least forty. Staff officers were brought in from other regiments to sit in at the press desk and answer questions from journalists.

Looking back on his three years at Lisburn, Tony Yarnold has nothing but praise and admiration for Colin Wallace. 'Let's face it, Colin was the linchpin of the whole operation. He was terrific – way ahead of us all in his knowledge, his skill with the press and his readiness for work. Everyone wanted him all the time, and somehow he was always available,' he told me when I interviewed him in his home in January 1988. This view was shared by one of the few civilians to join the press desk staff at Lisburn. Michael Taylor, though born and bred in Birmingham, had been living almost without a break in Northern Ireland since he had done his National Service at RAF Aldergrove, near Belfast, in the mid-1950s. He had married a local woman from Antrim and had set up his own photographic agency there. Later he got a job as the Press Officer for the Ulster Museum in Belfast.

Taylor had met Colin Wallace at an officers' mess dance at Aldergrove in the early 1960s when Wallace was working at the Ballymena chemists, Woodside's. The two men became friends and Colin enticed Mike Taylor into his adventure training activities in the Territorial Army, which Taylor later joined. In 1971, he was encouraged to apply for a job in the Army Press Office, and did so. To his surprise he was almost instantly accepted for the job, and started work in the period immediately following internment.

The chief reason why he got the job was that he had been recommended by Colin Wallace. One of the first things he discovered once he took up his post was the enormous influence wielded by Colin throughout the Lisburn barracks. He told me: 'It quickly became apparent that Colin was the guru of the whole information branch; in terms of his knowledge, his background, his forward thinking. He lived on camp, he had his own room. He was a permanent fixture there. He seemed to have no other interest but the Army and its image. He was regarded by all the principal officers from the General downwards as being a person they should get advice from about Northern Ireland and the political and military situation there. He had a tremendous capacity for remembering facts and dates.'   (Interview with the author, 9 December 1987.)

Although he was of the same Civil Service rank as Colin, Mike Taylor appreciated at once that Colin was being treated as someone far more important than an information officer. 'I played golf with the General,' he says. 'That was an accident. Colin was *needed* by the General. Everyone needed him. They just could not do without him.'   (Interview with the author, 9 December 1987.)

Mike Taylor's assessment was made almost immediately on taking up his job at Lisburn. How had the keen, rather naive, young information officer who had proved so expert at facile public relations in the months before the troubles emerged as this information giant? Wallace's own rather modest view ascribes his rise to his background in Northern Ireland. 'I was the only indigenous officer in the whole barracks,' he explains. 'The only people working there who came from Northern Ireland were the clerks, cooks and support staff. Northern Ireland regiments never served in Northern Ireland – that was a firm policy which was never altered, certainly not after the troubles started. After fourteen weeks' square bashing at Ballymena, Northern Ireland soldiers were posted off abroad, never to return to duty near their home. So I was a novelty there, and when people were suddenly asking: "Apprentice Boys? Who the hell are the Apprentice Boys?" Someone else would say: "Go and ask that fellow Wallace. He lives here." I think that's why I suddenly became in demand.'

There was some truth in this. The engulfing ignorance about Ireland and its problems spread down from the top at Whitehall. Most people who remembered the 'troubles' of the early 1920s were dead – or senile. If anyone in government or the civil service knew anything about Ireland, they were probably noticing the great boom in trade between Britain and the South, and the corresponding and catastrophic fall in trade between Britain and the North. The very idea that the old antagonisms would re-emerge had not for a moment occurred to the Home Office or even to any of the junior ministers who then had responsibility for overseeing what was in theory a self-governing province within the overall control of the United Kingdom. So when Ireland suddenly shot onto the political stage, the presence at Lisburn of a home-grown Northern Ireland soldier, an alumnus of Ballymena Academy, who was born and went to church not twenty miles away from the barracks, was a godsend.

But that is only part of the picture. However home-grown he was, no mediocre information officer could have even started to cope with the new demands imposed on the job by the new political situation. A sleepy battalion drilling and recruiting in Happy Valley can be looked after by a third-rate information officer without undue difficulty. An army in the field against experienced fighting terrorists needs in its information department something quite different.

The new order was slowly, though reluctantly, recognised in Whitehall. In 1970, on the orders of the Ministry of Defence, the information department of the Army in Northern Ireland was reorganised. Tony Staughton remained in charge of public relations, with Colin and Colonel Yarnold in support. Side by side, a new unit was set up, entitled Information Liaison – later Information Policy – commanded by a military officer with the rank of lieutenant colonel. The first of these was Lieutenant Colonel Johnny Johnston. He was swiftly replaced by a hard-line paratroop officer, Colonel Maurice Tugwell. Information Policy was a separate unit working for the intelligence services but expected to operate under the cover of public relations. Its function was psychological warfare. The best definition of that comes from a Ministry of Defence document 'An Introduction to Psychological Operations' which was published in 1974.

> Psychological Operations (Psyops) is an all-embracing term defined by NATO as 'planned psychological activities in peace and war directed towards enemy, friendly and neutral audiences, in order to create attitudes and behaviour favourable to the achievement of political and military objectives' . . .
> Strategic psywar pursues long-term and mainly political objectives. It is designed to undermine an enemy or hostile group to fight and to reduce the capacity to wage war.
> It can be directed against the dominating political party, the Government and/or against the population as a whole, or particular elements of it. It is planned and controlled by the highest political authority.

The references to 'the Government' and the 'dominating political party' were directed of course to the country in which the psychological warfare was being waged, and not to the British government or the ruling party in Westminster. This 'psyops' was not something new to the 1970s. It had been a routine feature in the British military response throughout the empire in the years after the Second World War. As the 1974 document made clear, psyops had become part of the military strategy of NATO countries, especially the United States of

America where the techniques of psyops were developed throughout the
Vietnam war.

In Northern Ireland, the normal activities of Army PR officers
were left to the public relations department under Tony Staughton.
Information Policy had a rather different function, namely to use information and disinformation from Intelligence as one of the many weapons
in the war with the IRA. Tony Staughton describes the process. 'To start
with, in the early part of the troubles, 1968, 1969 and 1970, I had a clear
run in my department, and we did well against the IRA. I think we won
the propaganda battle in those years. The IRA used to complain bitterly
about us, but we had a really excellent record of getting stuff in the papers
which did them down. I had a fundamental rule which I never broke in
all my years of service – and I know that Tony Yarnold thought the same
way: never lie to the Press. We didn't lie, we just carried out normal public
relations from the Army side, and we had the better of the other side.

'All this changed with internment. Immediately after internment,
the IRA started to get the upper hand. And from that time on, the
Foreign Office and the Intelligence people insisted on much more say
in public relations. They sent a man over called Hugh Mooney – he was
from a department of the Foreign Office called the Information Research
Department (IRD). None of us ever knew what Mooney was about: who
he reported to or what he was entitled to. All we knew was that they gave
him a big house to live in and freedom to move at will throughout the
barracks and Stormont. There was another man called Clifford Hill – I
always imagined that he had something to do with Intelligence. None of
us knew precisely what he was up to either.

'It was the same with Information Policy. I don't remember them
being at all important until after internment. Then, after Maurice Tugwell
took over, they became more important than we were. I remember some
furious rows about who was responsible for what. It was always agreed that
although Maurice Tugwell and I were of the same rank, I was in charge of
public relations. Yet I remember at least one meeting at Stormont when it
was clear that the Ministry and the Army were seeing Maurice for a job
which was plainly part of my responsibilities.

'The ordinary chain of command seemed again and again to be
broken. People seemed to be doing what they wanted to do in
information – often very puerile things which in my view gravely set
us back.

'The main cause of disagreement was my principle that you don't
deceive people in the press – you tell them your side of the story, but
if they ask for facts which you have at your disposal, you give them to
them. If you want to tell them something else which you can't verify but
which you're certain is true, you give it to the press "off the record". But
the one thing you can't do is invent facts and stories, and pass them over

as truth. If that's what they meant by "psychological operations", as they always called it, I didn't see it as part of public relations: and I was always fighting them – more and more furiously until I finally dropped out with a coronary in 1973.'   (Interview with the author, 10 October 1987.)

One of the jobs of the new unit was constantly to 'brief' visiting journalists. The journalists who were by now arriving in Northern Ireland in droves were not all hacks who could be persuaded to publish favourable propaganda because some PR man was being polite to them. The best journalists in Britain (and many from every other part of the world) were spending long periods in Northern Ireland. The roll call of British journalists who covered Northern Ireland at the time reads like a citation at a British Press Awards ceremony: Robert Fisk of *The Times*; Simon Winchester of the *Sunday Times*; Simon Hoggart of the *Observer*; Mary Holland of the *Observer* – these and other journalists of the highest flight were increasingly asking awkward questions. Why internment? Why torture? Does the Army assassinate people? What kind of war is being fought here and why is the Army fighting it?

British journalism was not mealy-mouthed and sycophantic as it became ten or twenty years later. Investigative journalism was the fashion and journalists had a nasty habit of refusing to accept the official version. Even editors could not always be relied on to co-operate with the Army. Ancestral calls on the solidarity of hierarchy were not necessarily answered. Sometimes they stung editors into insubordination. Harry Evans, then editor of the *Sunday Times*, gave full rein to the Insight team, whose investigative journalists swarmed throughout Northern Ireland, and who, Colin Wallace remembers, 'were always really hard to persuade'. A good example of this was recounted by Simon Hoggart in *New Society* on 11 October 1973:

An indication of how the PR operation has now become more sophisticated is the way that the Army treats unsympathetic reporters. I can show this best by my own experience. Last year, my predecessor, Simon Winchester and I printed a run of three anti-Army pieces in one week, ending with Winchester narrating how soldiers had shot at him during Bloody Sunday. The three articles came together quite by chance but, not surprisingly, were seen as deliberate aggression by the Army. For about a fortnight we were given 'minimal co-operation' by Lisburn – curt, unwilling accounts of violence and no background or any information at all. It was an inconvenience, but no more, since we got the information from helpful colleagues and it ended after a fortnight, following discussion at the Ministry of Defence. A few months later, I published another, fairly similar story, saying that soldiers had been unnecessarily brutal in putting down a Protestant riot. This time the treatment was quite different. I was invited to Lisburn for lunch and drinks and shown papers which suggested that the soldiers might, to some extent, have been justified. I am sure the lunch and drinks had nothing to do with it, but if I am completely honest, I think the approach might have made me a little more cautious when writing about the Army.

The central figure in this new persuasive approach was Colin Wallace. The new 'briefings', like the 'briefing' of Simon Hoggart, required not just local knowledge which Colin had in abundance. It also required journalistic, public relations and political skills as well as access to top level intelligence information. Very quickly *everyone* who worked with Colin Wallace – his bosses, Tony Staughton and Tony Yarnold, his colleague Mike Taylor – everyone realised that they had in their barracks even before the troubles broke out a political and public relations operator of considerable skill and dedication.

One immediate result was that Colin was, in effect, though not in name, transferred out of public relations to Information Policy. Peter Broderick, who took over as head of the whole of Northern Ireland Army Information in 1973, explained this well:

> The Army by this time (1970) had become keen converts to the need for active public relations as an integral part of their operational capability, and became impatient with the Senior Information Officer (Tony Staughton) who was neither well enough nor personally trained for an operational role.
>
> Consequently, and with the full agreement of the Army in Whitehall, a separate military staffed unit was set up in Northern Ireland, literally on the other side of the corridor from Public Relations. Under the title of Information Policy, its brief was to use psychological means to assist operations strategically and tactically. It is a skill that requires sensitivity, political finesse and a thorough knowledge of the situation. The military approach – with officers who had a minimum of theoretical training and no practical experience – would have been doomed to embarrassing failure. They had forgotten the one basic essential – a channel of communications to enable them to transfer their thoughts and ideas into effective coverage of the press.
>
> Colin Wallace at first became a pawn in this game. Though on the staff of public relations, he was used by Information Policy as their outlet to the press. He also had a knowledge of the Irish situation which was totally unique in the headquarters and surpassed that even of most of the Intelligence Branch. As time progressed, he was not only the main briefer for the press, but also the adviser on Irish matters to the whole Headquarters and – because of his personal talents – contributed much creative thought to the Information Policy Unit. In order to do his job, he had constant and free access to information of the highest classification and extreme sensitivity.   (Peter Broderick's statement to Civil Service Appeal Board, October 1975.)

Tony Staughton confirms all this. 'It was fairly obvious to me from quite early on that Colin was getting drawn in on the FO/IRD side. A lot of people were soliciting his services. I'm sure the Intelligence people were.'   (Interview with author, 10 October 1987.)

Indeed, Colin Wallace was wanted far and wide throughout the Army in Northern Ireland. When top politicians came to Northern Ireland, the Army insisted that Colin was on hand to answer questions and help with briefings. When Edward Heath, the Prime Minister, visited Derry in 1972, Wallace was seldom more than a few yards away from him. When the Under-Secretary of State for the Army, Geoffrey Johnson Smith, came on an extended visit in 1973, Colin was permanently in attendance. When Harold Wilson made his first visit to the Province, Colin Wallace briefed him and arranged his press conference at RAF Aldergrove.

He was often seen on television. When James Burke, a popular presenter at the time, put on an hour-long programme about the arms trade, the man he quizzed about the arms (indeed the man who arranged for the arms to be shipped from Northern Ireland to the BBC headquarters) was Colin Wallace.

An indication of the importance attached to Colin by the Army authorities was his attendance at the tribunal, under Lord Chief Justice Widgery, into the killing of thirteen people by the Army after a civil rights' demonstration in Derry on 30 January 1972 – 'Bloody Sunday'. The outcry after the killings echoed all over the world. Critical journalists had a field day. The Army, and especially the Parachute Regiment (whose officers included Maurice Tugwell, then head of Information Policy) was at a low ebb. Enormous efforts were made by Information Policy to prove to the sceptics that the IRA had started the bloodbath. An impressive legal team was put together to represent the Army at the tribunal. It included Mr Brian Gibbens QC (later a judge), Michael Underhill QC (later a judge), Lieutenant Colonel Colin Overbury from the Army Legal Service and Major Henry Hugh-Smith, a staff officer in the Life Guards, sent over from Ministry of Defence headquarters to act as secretary to the legal team. Attached to this illustrious band, with full accreditation as though he himself were a barrister, was Colin Wallace. He attended every day at the inquiry, sat with the Army barristers and assisted them with the many inquiries which they put to him.

Colin was still a part-time captain in the UDR and kept up his training in the Territorial Army. When his TA regiment, the Royal Ulster Rifles, was amalgamated into the Royal Irish Rangers, he was affiliated to the lst Battalion of the Irish Guards.

The Guards welcomed him especially for his experience in parachuting. The regimental journal carried an article about the new Irish Guards cadet company, known as the 'Mini-Micks', including this tribute to a senior officer.

The second in command, Colin Wallace, whilst suffering slightly from 'Paramania' (he is a parachutist of international repute) performs most nobly for the Mick cause. He is a great training enthusiast and is never happier than

when he is on top of one 3000-foot peak busily engaged in plotting his hop to
the next one. Mr Wallace will eventually achieve great fame as he will, no
doubt, be the first Brigade officer to visit RHQ without getting a salute at
the main gate – as knowing him he will surely parachute in. (*Irish Guards
Association Journal*, February 1969, p. 35.)

In 1971, he went on attachment to the Irish Guards in Hong Kong to
take part in training and to carry out information work for the regiment.
A company from the battalion was sent that year to New Zealand, to take
part in a huge training exercise called Operation Bayleaf. The New Zealand
SAS had just come back from Vietnam and took part in the exercise with
the Irish Guards acting as 'enemy' against New Zealand Army troops.

How he found time for these exercises still puzzles his colleagues in
Lisburn at that time. Everyone who worked with him pays tribute not
just to his ability in the field, on paper and on the telephone, but to
his extraordinary sense of duty. 'There wasn't a night when he wasn't
off somewhere doing something: patrolling with the UDR or the TA,
or jumping out of the sky somewhere,' says Mike Taylor. 'If he wasn't
doing anything, he would put himself down for some voluntary duty or
another.' (Interview with author, 9 December 1987.)

Tony Staughton says: 'I once sat down and worked out what he
could claim in special payments for working nights and holidays and
things like that. It came to hundreds of pounds. I told him, Colin, this is
your money; it's owed to you.' But one way or another, he got his way.
He wouldn't accept it.' (Interview with author, 10 October 1987.)

Peter Broderick's report was more specific:

To my knowledge he worked at least 80 hours a week: coming to his desk
every day. He lived in the Officers' Mess and regarded himself as always on
duty. He has never claimed long hours' gratuity nor overtime as a matter of
principle . . . Upon my arrival, I found that he had taken virtually no leave
for six years except to attend his Territorial Army camp. For about two nights
every week, he served with the Ulster Defence Regiment which meant going
on armed patrol from 8 p.m. until dawn and getting no sleep.' (Broderick's
statement to Civil Service Appeal Board, October 1975.)

These opinions were not confined to the information branch. Each
year, the work of the people at Lisburn barracks was assessed by the Army
Chief of Staff. In 1971, the report on Colin concluded: 'This is an officer of
the highest calibre. Totally dedicated to the Army, he demonstrates this
by a devotion to duty that is truly remarkable.' The counter-signing officer
scribbled underneath: 'I heartily agree.' In 1972, the Chief of Staff recorded
that enthusiasm and dedication were not his only virtues. His abilities were
just as remarkable: 'Continues to demonstrate that his talents are of the

very highest standard.'   (Army reports submitted to Civil Service Appeal Board, October 1975.)

Before he finally left his post after his stroke in the spring of 1973, Tony Staughton twice recommended Colin Wallace, who was not yet thirty years old, for the MBE, and to this day cannot understand how and why the recommendations were turned down. 'I've never known such a deserving case,' he says. 'I had the champagne on ice.' He concludes that an MBE for a twenty-nine-year-old is so exceptional that even in this exceptional case the authorities could not stomach it. Another reason, perhaps closer to the mark, is suggested by a sentence in Peter Broderick's official report: 'Wallace's dual role was particularly resented in Whitehall, while highly valued by the operational commander in Northern Ireland.'   (Broderick's statement to Civil Service Appeal Board, October 1975.)

The dual role was soon made official. Peter Broderick took up the post of Head of Army Information Services in July 1973. He wrote in his report:

> One of my first actions was to legitimise the role of Colin Wallace and to allocate him firmly to Information Policy. As it involved an upgrading, we were put in a difficult position of having to trawl the post publicly to comply with civil service rules, and we could scarcely mention psychological warfare. A device was therefore agreed for a cover title as Head of Production Services – but the trawl did not mention briefing the press as an important function.   (Broderick's statement to Civil Service Appeal Board, October 1975.)

In other words, in order to comply with the strict rules in the Civil Service about advertising for jobs, and in order to ensure that Colin stayed ostensibly in a civilian role (and was therefore much more acceptable to journalists), Broderick, with the full agreement of his superiors, invented a job description which could be advertised without mentioning psychological warfare. You cannot advertise a post for a 'black propagandist', yet 'black propaganda' was what Colin was going to put out. He formally applied for the falsely-described post of Head of Production Services. In September 1974, he got the job, and was promoted to the rank of Senior Information Officer, a post which carried an equivalent rank of lieutenant colonel. Colin was just twenty-nine; the youngest man in the British Armed Services to hold such a senior rank.

Broderick's report sums up what Colin was now to do above board, in the open, in a new sound-proofed office with one-way glass in the windows across the corridor from the main press room.

> Wallace's primary job was to win friends among the press and to gain their total confidence as a reliable source of information. By agreement with Intelligence in each case, he was supplied with selected information about terrorists, their activities, their sources of money and arms at home

and overseas, of the allegiances of so-called innocents and such matters. This –
together with his long-term and intimate knowledge of the Irish scene – made
him an invaluable contact for the press. Almost all his background briefings he
gave non-attributably and it is a measure of his skill and the regard for him by
the press that I cannot recall a single occasion when any reporter, even from the
hostile papers, disclosed the source of the briefings.   (Broderick's statement to
Civil Service Appeal Board, October 1975.)

For any journalist arriving to report on the 'troubles' in Northern
Ireland after July 1973, the straightest and easiest road led to Colin
Wallace's office. There you were met by a man with an easy-going,
cheerful manner and a high regard for good journalism. Colin flattered
the journalists every bit as much as he used them. He knew they were
after information and he knew that most of them were too good to be
satisfied with silly public relations or blatantly false stories.

His skill in dealing with journalists was recognised by the best of
them. In his book *In Holy Terror*, Simon Winchester who reported on
the 'troubles' for the *Sunday Times*, wrote:

The Army have been of unique assistance. Not all who offered their help and
advice would wish to be identified, but of those who allow their names to be
published, Lieutenant Colonel Tony Yarnold and Colin Wallace must head the
list. (S. Winchester, *In Holy Terror: Reporting the Ulster Troubles*, London,
Faber & Faber, 1974, p. 9)

Most of the information which Colin provided was true – but
occasionally it was untrue. In this respect, he was breaching the rules
set out by Tony Staughton who insisted that no press or information
officer should ever divulge information which was false. Deceit of the
type in which Colin was engaged for the British Army from 1970 to at
least the end of 1973 was something he regarded as wholly justified. This
was because the deceit was aimed at what he regarded as the most deadly
enemy of his country: terrorism. The powerful patriotism of his youth was
by far the strongest of the forces which inspired him.

Peter Broderick's official report has a revealing sentence: 'He [Colin]
acted resolutely and to effect against anyone – Republican or Loyalist –
who was destroying his country.'   (Broderick's statement to Civil Service
Appeal Board, October 1975.)

This even-handedness was perhaps a little disingenuous. The real
enemies for Colin at that time were the same weasels in the woods
of his youth, the inhabitants of that undiscovered country down in the
valley near Toomebridge, the ancestral foe: the IRA. It was not until
1974 that the menace of Orange terrorism fully engaged him.

The purpose of the black propaganda which Colin Wallace put out
was to disorientate and discomfort the terrorists: chiefly the IRA, but

also Protestant terrorists. That, in his view, entirely justified the murky waters in which he was paddling.

'Only ill-informed people believe there can be a total military victory in Northern Ireland,' he says. 'All we could do was deal with terrorism: wean the terrorists away from the population, set them against one another, disorientate them and make their leaders unpopular both with their supporters and the population at large. That way, I believed we could isolate them, break them and return to peace, however uneasy that peace was – the peace I'd been used to in the past.'

'Black propaganda' or 'psychological operations' carries with it the suggestion that the information put out is necessarily false. But a lot of the work of Information Policy, and of Colin Wallace, was normal public relations. Campaigns, for instance, were run to stop people giving guns to their children for Christmas, for fear that the children might be shot by the Army if they went into the streets with their toy guns. There were also campaigns to stop people accepting gifts from strangers, since these 'gifts' might turn out to be terrorist bombs, handled by an innocent party. Such campaigns stemmed from genuine information and genuine fear, and were plainly unexceptionable. There were also 'deception operations' to which Colin contributed. A British Army 'laundry' was set up in the heart of the most militant Catholic area in Belfast. Clothes taken there were rushed back to Lisburn and tested for explosives, before being laundered elsewhere. Massage parlours were set up in which British Army and intelligence 'masseuses' picked up information from their clients.

Colin's expertise as an organiser of stunts and fake operations was put to good use by the Army, not just to disorientate the enemy but also to check on security. In 1973 he was asked to test the security of Belfast's Aldergrove Airport, where a major IRA offensive was suspected. Colin marshalled his team of 'terrorists' for the task and even recruited a journalist to assist. He himself dressed up as a vicar, on his way to conduct a service in Belfast. Mike Taylor drove with him in a battered old blue Mini which was packed with a mortar, explosives and other weapons, all obvious to the most cursory inspection. The Mini was stopped at each checkpoint, but sailed through after Colin's masterly explanation of his mission, delivered in his best Ulster brogue. The Mini was never once inspected. A 'TV team' with cameras (all part of Colin's group) managed to bluff its way through the guards and place an undetonated bomb in a desk drawer in the headquarters of an Army unit near the airport. Another bomb was put in a shoe box on a railway line near the airport by another of Colin's men, a photographer, allegedly on his way to a dinner dance. A journalist and another of Colin's recruits acting as weekend lovers sailed through the road blocks near the airport.

The operation was considered perhaps too outstanding a success by the Army authorities. The General was not a little distressed when he learnt that a bomb had been planted in an Army unit. The man ostensibly in charge of the Aldergrove Airport operation was then running the Operations Room at Army Headquarters in Lisburn, Major The Hon. Willie Rous. In 1987, *Channel Four News* asked the Ministry of Defence about the incident. The reply came back from Rous himself, who was then a brigadier and Director of Public Relations: 'I do not recall this incident.' Mike Taylor, however, recalls it very well. 'It was a tremendous achievement for Colin, which greatly tightened up security at the airport.'

Many of the stories which Colin planted in reputable newspapers did indeed help to disorientate and confuse the IRA. He had information from the most secret sources that IRA bombs were exploding early – killing the IRA men who were carrying them or planting them. The reason for this was their ultra-sensitive but unreliable timing devices. The Army was anxious that the IRA should not trace this source of the trouble so Information Policy leaked a series of stories that the reason the bombs were exploding early was that the IRA were using impure sodium chlorate for their bombs – imported from France.

Selected journalists, told of this 'unstable' source of IRA bombs, hurried into print. The *Guardian*'s report on 23 August 1972 was followed the next day by one in the *Daily Telegraph* which promoted the story to a page 2 lead under the headline FAULTY BOMB CHEMICALS USED BY THE IRA GANGS. Six weeks later the story ran in the *Observer*, headlined IRA USING FRENCH CHEMICALS. Colin was amused to find himself described in the second paragraph as 'an army chemical expert'. His time at Woodside's, the chemists, had served him well. The completely bogus story, he is certain, had its effect. The IRA *were* more careful about the use of chlorate of soda, especially if it was imported from France. And Colin heard in the ensuing weeks of their continuing difficulties in finding a substitute anywhere else. He was also delighted that the real cause of the premature explosions was not discovered for many months after his expert story appeared in the newspapers.

Another story with a similar thrust was what Colin wryly describes now as the 'big cancer scare'. This was floated in the same month (August 1972) as the 'sodium chlorate' spoof. The paper chosen for launch was the one which sold more copies in Northern Ireland than any other: the *Sunday Mirror*. On 13th August 1972, the *Sunday Mirror* lead front page story declared: POISON IN THE STREETS.

This referred to another ingredient of IRA bombs – nitrobenzine. It was poisonous, not just to the IRA but to everyone else. The story quoted an Army spokesman (Colin Wallace) saying: 'Symptoms of nitro-poisoning are difficult to spot. By the time they are visible it is too late to treat the victim. Vomiting and a coma follow and later the glands and liver break down.'

The same point was made in an enormous article the next day in the *Guardian*, entitled: WORRY OVER POISON IN IRA BOMBS, by Peter Chippindale and Derek Brown. This article quoted 'informed sources in Belfast' (Colin Wallace) highlighting the poisonous qualities of nitrobenzine. 'Children finding it stored in a derelict house or people forced to store it by the Provisionals could suffer from the poisoning.'

Colin Wallace watched in delighted amazement as the 'cancer scare' took off in press and television. Learned scientists were interviewed on television late into the night about the possibility that thousands of Belfast people might catch leukaemia or other cancers from the storing of nitrobenzine. Colin himself had none of the scientific knowledge which was now being daily made available to the public in support of the wild theory he had floated – with the single intention of making IRA men and women feel uneasy about their explosive materials. The story ran and ran. In September 1973, more than a year after Colin first floated his cancer scare, he was earnestly telling one of his most frequent visitors, Gerald Bartlett of the *Daily Telegraph*, of the threat of cancer from nitrobenzine. Bartlett duly obliged: LEUKAEMIA THREAT TO PROVOS.

> Dozens of Provisional IRA members in Northern Ireland are believed to have contracted blood disorders caused by fumes from their home-made bombs. Medical experts say the disorders could lead in some cases to leukaemia and aplastic anaemia. One senior Belfast provisional who recently died of leukaemia may have contracted it in this way.' (*Sunday Telegraph*, 9 September 1973.)

The article went on to say that several Provisionals may have died in this way, and quoted medical experts linking leukaemia deaths to nitrobenzine. The article ended: 'A leading leukaemia consultant said: "Certainly nitrobenzine poisoning can cause leukaemia. But I am not aware of any cases." '

Late in 1972, the Army heard of a new consignment of Russian rocket launchers which had been supplied to the IRA. The rocket launchers themselves presented a serious threat, since the screens necessary to protect armoured cars and police stations from such rocket launchers had not yet been installed. The Army needed time to install the screens and Information Policy was asked to help. From what he could find about the rocket attacks, Colin discovered that the IRA had been mishandling their weapons. The instructions were in Russian and the IRA did not fully understand them. Several rockets had been fired with the safety pins still in; others, which had been sent by the Russians to be used for training purposes only, had been used in action, and had not functioned properly. There was considerable disarray in the IRA about their much-vaunted new weapons and Colin Wallace set out to make it worse.

He chose perhaps the best journalist on station in Northern Ireland: Robert Fisk of *The Times*.

Fisk, who later won many awards all over the world (especially the Middle East), was no push-over. The piece he wrote after the conversation with Colin Wallace was cautious and named the source: IRA ROCKETS MADE IN RUSSIA ARE IN DANGEROUS CONDITION, ARMY BALLISTICS EXPERTS SAY. 'Army ballistics engineers at the Ministry of Defence,' wrote Fisk, 'believe that most of the Soviet-manufactured rockets held by the Provisional IRA are in a dangerous condition because the explosive charge inside the warheads has deteriorated through age.' (*The Times*, 29 December 1972.)

The article then referred to 'Cyrillic markings' on the rocket launchers which showed that they should have been used 'more than a year ago'. It was this, Fisk reported, which accounted for the 'remarkably low rate of success' of the IRA rocket launchers.

By focusing on the wrong reasons for that low rate of success, Information Policy hoped to distract the IRA from the real reasons they were failing with their rocket launchers and at the same time, strain their relations with their Soviet suppliers. To make sure, Colin also had a conversation with Derek Brown of the *Guardian*, which resulted in a substantial story on the same day (29 December 1972) under a headline: IRA ROCKETS 'ARE TOO OLD TO EXPLODE'. In this article the multi-talented source was described as 'Army munitions experts'.

In August 1973, Information Policy was presented with another problem. The IRA was using women to plant their bombs. This had led to a number of fruitless and quite roughly handled searches of innocent women in the streets of Belfast and Derry – which had got the Army a bad name. Was there anything which could be done to try to stop the use of women as bomb-carriers?

One faintly ridiculous answer appeared in the *Sunday Mirror* on 19 August 1973 – again after a discussion between its author, Kevin Dowling, and Colin Wallace.

DANGER IN THOSE FRILLY PANTIES was the catching headline. The story underneath it started with the bizarre proposition: 'Frilly nylon undies worn by IRA bomb girls may have helped to kill three of them.' That, disclosed the report, 'was the verdict of Army experts', one of whom was quoted directly as saying: 'It is probable that static electricity generated by the bombers' clothes is responsible for at least some of the deaths.'

Colin Wallace enjoyed that one, though he was sceptical enough even then to doubt how sensitive the hardened cadre of the IRA were to that kind of propaganda. Certainly, there was no appreciable decline in the use of the women bomb-handlers by the Provisionals.

As the IRA established itself in 1972, so the British Army became concerned to shut off its arms supply. Early intelligence reports suggested that the main source of arms for the IRA was the United States of America where the IRA still enjoyed support in the large American Irish community.

In October 1972, Colin Wallace built up a stack of captured weapons and paraded it for the press as though it were a secret hoard of weapons supplied by IRA supporters in the United States. It featured dramatically in the *Daily Mirror* of 11 October 1972, under the headline THE CLUES OF HARDWARE HILL. 'The location of the hill,' warned the *Daily Mirror*'s Joe Gorrod mysteriously, 'must remain secret.' The *Daily Express* followed with an enormous 'special investigation' headlined: WHERE THE IRA KILLERS GET THEIR GUNS. The information about the American sources of the weapons was exactly the same as in the *Daily Mirror*, and other papers, and was supplied to the newspaper, via British Intelligence, by Colin Wallace.

The point of these articles was to whip up hostility in the United States to the 'men of violence' who were being assisted by otherwise unexceptionable American arms traders. This effort was reinforced by an Information Policy campaign to link the IRA to American peaceniks and crypto-communists who had learnt how to fight in Vietnam and were using their skills to help the IRA.

There was very little evidence of any substance that there were any such Vietnam veterans in Northern Ireland and it therefore required considerable creativity on the part of Information Policy to 'interest' distinguished British journalists in this idea. Colin was specially delighted with an early success in this area, an article in the *Daily Express* on 30 March 1972 by 'Chapman Pincher, the man who gives you tomorrow's news today'.

'Tomorrow's news' on this occasion warned of the 'serious threat' from American ex-Vietnam soldiers being recruited to fight with the IRA 'as paid gunmen and saboteurs'. Pincher reported: 'There is no shortage of ex-Vietnam veterans – many of them Catholics of Irish origin – prepared to hire out their services.'

He could not, however, provide evidence of any one such veteran, nor even an incident in which any such gunmen had been involved. But he speculated: 'The move to employ them actively as gunmen seems to be linked with a drive by pro-Irish muggers in New York to steal the passports of British visitors.'

The notion of a combined campaign by former Vietnam war veterans and street muggers (all of them Irish and probably Catholic) let off a smell which delighted the boys at Information Policy. They felt with some reason that this story could run and run. And so it did. As late as February 1973, Gerald Bartlett of the *Daily Telegraph*, a regular visitor to Colin's office, was reporting in the *Sunday Telegraph*: US VIETNAM VETERANS TRAIN IRA TERRORISTS.

The story was very much the same as Pincher's the previous year, except that Gerald Bartlett was able to report: 'One of the first American instructors to be recruited by the Provisionals lost a leg when a bomb he was constructing exploded prematurely. He was, it is understood, given forged papers and flown to the Chelsea Naval Hospital, Boston, as a Vietnam casualty.'

How did Gerald Bartlett come across this bizarre incident, and how was he unable to name the soldier, or even to check the matter with the hospital in Boston? One answer is that the source for his story was Colin Wallace, who never went too far into details.

As the months wore on and the battle with the IRA turned into a war which the British Army seemed to have little hope of winning, the emphasis switched from the Americans to the Russians. In December 1972, for instance, the *News of the World* had an 'exclusive' on what it called the 'Emerald Isle Red Plot'. This was a remarkable story about 'three young intellectuals' – Trotskyists, apparently – who, in spite of the unpopularity which most Trotskyists encountered in Brezhnev's Russia, were lucky enough to have been smuggled into Ireland in a Russian submarine. All three, the story reported, died 'mysteriously'. Well, one of them, a young woman, died of cancer, but that could be put down to another of the stories manufactured by Information Policy – that IRA explosives can lead to cancer.

Colin chuckles today as he looks back on this 'exclusive', which was circulated to the *News of the World*'s sixteen million readers. He specially likes the pictures of the Soviet submarine with 'Russian markings' on its conning tower 'off the coast of Donegal'. 'It was probably off the coast of Finland,' says Colin drily. The story was bunkum from start to finish, but its purpose – to demonstrate that the IRA were a sinister bunch of communists with close links to the Russians and the KGB – was triumphantly achieved.

Colin recalls being a little bit concerned that the fantasy might have been carried too far. There was, after all, nothing directly true about any of this story, and it seemed to stretch the connection with the Russians almost beyond belief. But the enemy was the enemy whether in Belfast or in Moscow, and it seemed to everyone in Information Policy at the time that this was fair game.

This is a small sample of the press work in which Colin and his associates in Information Policy were engaged both before and after he was officially assigned to the group when Peter Broderick took charge of Army Public Relations in the summer of 1973. That summer and autumn seem to Colin, in retrospect, as the high point of his life. He was just thirty, yet he was one of the most important and sought-after people in the whole vast effort of the British Army and the British government.

He was able, popular, dedicated. He had discovered, almost by accident, that he was a master of communications. He was trusted by the journalists who printed his information and by the people who provided him with that information. The Army liked him. Civilians liked him. He got on particularly well with the intelligence community, which was then represented in Northern Ireland by MI6 and its officer in charge, Craig Smellie. He could look forward with confidence not simply to promotion, but also to decoration, since he had already (twice) been turned down for the MBE.

He was in his element, rushing from place to place, anxious to keep up his military training and expertise at the same time as he perfected his new skills in public relations. He felt himself the most fortunate man in all the British Army. He wanted nothing more than to 'carry on' as a good and loyal servant of the British Crown.

When the change came, it came quietly.

CHAPTER TWO

Clockwork Orange

The period from the end of 1973 until the middle of 1975 was the most volatile in postwar British history. For many months, 'society as we know it' was in peril.

The storm broke suddenly out of a clear sky. For most of 1973 it seemed that the 'U-turn' forced on the Heath Conservative government by its crushing defeat at the hands of the miners in 1972 had led to political success. The sudden respect for nationalised industries and the pumping of public money into them; the recognition of trade unions as part of the structure of the state; the effective abandonment of the anti-union Industrial Relations Act; the 'soft' approach to the welfare state – all these looked as though they were working. Nineteen seventy-three was a halcyon year. Unemployment dropped sharply to less than a half a million. All the talk in wise economic circles was of growth and expansion. Even the strikes which had dominated the industrial landscape in 1972 slowed down as trade union leaders urged a new respect for the Conservative government and their pay and prices 'norms'.

The bubble, for it was nothing more than that, burst in the late autumn. The immediate cause was the new-found confidence in the Arab world after the Yom Kippur war against Israel and the sudden surge in the price of oil. In November, the Chancellor of the Exchequer, Anthony Barber, who had promised that his boom was 'here to stay', slammed on the financial brakes. The miners, by a huge majority, voted for a new strike. Before the year was out, the Prime Minister had to announce that the New Year would start in conditions of austerity which had not been heard of for twenty years. The whole of British industry was put on short time – a three-day week.

The Labour Party, in its resolutions at its 1973 conference, moved marginally to the left. Further left, confidence rose higher. Even before the miners' strike started, the Vice-President of the National Union of Mineworkers, Michael McGahey, warned that troops might be used to help break the strike. He urged the soldiers not to fire on striking miners, who were 'your own people'. The declaration convinced the ever-apprehensive rich that Nemesis was at hand.

John Davies, Secretary of State for Trade and Industry in the Conservative government, gathered his children round him during the 1973 Christmas holiday and warned them of awful things to come. 'I deeply believed then,' he told two *Sunday Times* journalists, 'that it was the last Christmas of its kind that we would enjoy.' This apprehension was shared in the higher levels of the armed forces and in the intelligence services. More and more officers began openly to talk of the terrible danger of a Labour government.

While Edward Heath and his ministers were trying to grapple with the problems in a constitutional and Parliamentary way, a new right-wing alliance began to take shape. Its aim was to prevent at all costs the return of a Labour government and to dispense as soon as possible with the 'wet' Conservative leadership.

This group and its ideas had a specially strong influence on Army and Intelligence officers in Northern Ireland. They watched in horror as Harold Wilson for the Labour Party met IRA leaders in Dublin in 1972 and even the government (whose Secretary of State for Northern Ireland, William Whitelaw, met them in 1973) treated with the IRA while security collapsed. They suspected a link between 'appeasement' of the IRA and 'appeasement' of trade unions. The fact that Michael McGahey of the NUM was not prosecuted for his open appeal to the troops to disobey orders – a most obvious incitement to disaffection, and there was on the statute book an Incitement to Disaffection Act – seemed clear proof to the not entirely sophisticated brains at Lisburn that there was a conspiracy of leftists, which extended into the leadership of the Conservative Party.

While such views were commonplace in officers' messes everywhere, in Northern Ireland they carried with them a special urgency. As Colin Wallace put it: 'We were losing friends and colleagues almost every day to the IRA. When we felt, as many of us did, that these terrorists were being appeased by Conservative ministers, we were pretty sick. Even worse, when we thought there might be a change of government and a new set of ministers, some of whom seemed to us to be openly on the side of the terrorists, we became extremely disillusioned and anxious to do something about it.'

Colin himself, from 1973 officially ensconced in Information Policy, absorbed much of the political talk at Lisburn, and largely sympathised with it. He too had nothing but contempt for Labour or Tory politicians' meeting with the IRA. He felt that these meetings gave encouragement to the killers of his colleagues. Years later, he explained his political position as follows: 'Politically, I only knew what I had come across in the course of my work. My whole life was the Army and all my political knowledge, such as it was, came from the Army. My ideas were very firmly allied to the right, but I knew almost nothing about British politics. When it came to finding out what was happening, I took on trust what I was told.'

The chief source of 'inside information' for Colin, as for the whole of Information Policy, was Intelligence. Until 1973, Colin worked closely with MI6 (Secret Intelligence Service), the overseas arm of British Intelligence. Ever since the troubles began, MI6 had been in charge of intelligence in Ireland, because Southern Ireland was a foreign country and it was more convenient and efficient to have the same intelligence arm working North and South. During 1973, however, there was a decisive shift in the organisation of Intelligence in the North. At Stormont, the seat of Northern Ireland government which was controlled directly by Britain, a new post called 'Chief of Intelligence' was created and filled by a senior MI5 officer, Denis Payne. Soon afterwards, the MI6 officer at Lisburn, Craig Smellie, left Northern Ireland. He was replaced by an MI5 officer, Ian Cameron. Effectively, MI6 dropped out of the picture and intelligence in Northern Ireland became almost the exclusive preserve of MI5.

In his biography of Maurice Oldfield, who was appointed head of MI6 by Prime Minister Edward Heath early in 1973, Richard Deacon writes:

> Oldfield welcomed the replacing of some of MI6 by MI5, as he thought this made constitutional sense as well as preventing a lot of mistakes . . . Unfortunately, though these moves made sense and initially all went smoothly, much later MI5 also committed blunders in Ulster. (*'C': A Biography of Sir Maurice Oldfield*, London, Futura, 1985, p. 174.)

Sir Maurice's enthusiasm for the change, was probably not entirely unconditional. From the moment of his appointment at MI6, he laid down firm rules about the behaviour of his officers. Assassination, for instance, whether directly by the British security forces or in league with one or other of the extremist paramilitary groups, was firmly ruled out. MI6 officers, including Craig Smellie, responded positively to these rules. They were men and women who had served, and expected to serve, in many different countries, and their approach to their business depended on a relaxed, well-informed understanding of the political situation. Because by their nature they had to work as diplomats with foreigners, they were marginally less vulnerable to the cliquish, racialist and intrigue-ridden atmosphere – and the politics which thrived in such an atmosphere – which dominated MI5.

Not long after the change-over from MI6 to MI5 was completed, Colin was called to a high-level conference at Stormont. Senior MI5 officers were there, including Denis Payne. The subject for discussion was a new initiative to meet the deteriorating security crisis and to stem the rising tide of sectarian assassinations. A top secret information offensive was proposed. Its code name was to become 'Clockwork Orange'.

The documents which were filed under 'Clockwork Orange' were not generally available to anyone else in the Information Policy department, a fact which Mike Taylor, an ordinary Army Information officer, recalls very clearly.

'I was the branch security officer,' he says. 'It was my duty to check that all documents were in all the right files. I did see the "Clockwork Orange" file – but whenever I had it out for inspection, all the documents were taken out of it first. We were told that this was because of the very high confidentiality of the project.' (Interview with author, 9 December 1987.)

The Army's involvement in Clockwork Orange was approved early in 1974 by the Commander of Land Forces, Northern Ireland, Major General Peter Leng. Colonel Peter Goss, the senior Army Intelligence officer at Lisburn, was instructed to release to Colin secret information on terrorists. Captain 'Tim Perkins', another Intelligence officer, was appointed to do the basic research and supply Colin with the results.

Colin's instructions were to construct from Perkins' material, and from other information from Intelligence sources, four mythical stories from mythical people who had been involved in terrorism or sectarian politics. Colin was chosen for the job because of his mastery of the language and habits of the people of Northern Ireland.

Originally, the purpose of the new initiative seemed harmless, even mundane. It was to expose the personal vulnerabilities of the commanders of terrorist organisations, Orange and Green. Most of the material which came to Colin from Tim Perkins dealt with individual members of the IRA, the UDA or other similar organisations. Most of it was already known to Colin.

Very soon, however, Colin was inundated with scraps of information from other Intelligence sources in Northern Ireland and in London. Much of this was new to him. It concerned, in the main, British politicians, about whom Colin knew very little. But he shared the prevailing Army official view that one of the main reasons for the continued success of the terrorists was the succour they received from some politicians in London. He therefore wrote down the main features of the information in his Army-issue notebooks.

When he left Northern Ireland in 1975, Colin quickly bundled up his notes and private papers. They included most (though unfortunately not all) of the 'political notes' he made for the Clockwork Orange project.

Thirteen years later, these notes were submitted to Dr Julius Grant, one of Britain's top forensic experts in paper and in ink. Dr Grant was asked if he could fix a date when the notes were written. He replied in his report, dated 26 June 1987:

We have relied largely on the fibre furnish composition [of the notepaper]; and presence of starch and other additives consistent with 1974 rather than more recent times. We find nothing inconsistent with origin in 1974, and some features peculiar to that era. However, this does not entirely exclude the possibility that some mill somewhere was making this kind of paper after 1974. However 'balance of probabilities' are against this likelihood.

Turning to the ink used, Dr Grant reported:

It was found that the writing was made with a speciality blend of QUINK 'washable' ink, the dyestuff formula of which was changed in 1976.

Although it was still just possible that a skilful forger in the 1980s had arranged to get hold of paper which was special to 1974 and ink which went out of production in 1976, the professor himself was quite clear that the notes were not forged. 'In such circumstances, the forger would have had to know as much as I do about paper, and more than I do about inks,' he told Bob Parker of *Channel Four News*.

The inescapable conclusion was that the Clockwork Orange notes were written exactly when Colin Wallace said he wrote them: in the first six months of 1974.

The content of the notes also gives a clue to the time at which they were written. Early on, there is an analysis of three previous general elections – 1964, 1966 and 1970. The notes were clearly started before the February election of 1974, which returned a minority Labour government. They begin at page 121 (the numbers are printed on the regulation paper). On page 124, there is the first reference to the Labour government – so it is a fair deduction that the first two or three pages were written before 28 February 1974, polling day. The notes are obviously written at different times, sporadically, as a new piece of information or a new quotation came through. The first twelve pages, 119–30, are in sequence. There are then three pages, 135–37, then another gap until pages 145 to 146. The next page available is 151, on which starts a summary essay, entitled: 'Ulster – A State of Subversion'. This is continuous, and lasts for four pages to page 154. There are, in all, twenty-one pages of notes, with eleven pages apparently missing. Colin thinks that not all the missing pages included Clockwork Orange material, but there is clearly some of that missing. Colin can provide no reason for the missing pages, except that he may have taken them out when writing the concluding essay, and not collated them on his hurried departure.

The pages are divided into three. On the left is a margin which is blank throughout. In the main section in the centre are the basic notes. On the right margin, Colin has included, obviously at different times, further notes and additions which are, in his view, relevant to the main entry.

The chief source of the information in the notes, Colin believes, was MI5 in London. On one occasion, Colin travelled to London to pick up information from an MI5 officer. 'I met him at Charing Cross Underground station,' Colin recalls, with a chuckle. 'It was exactly like something out of a third rate spy novel. He was, I promise you, wearing one of those Russian style fur hats. He knew me; I didn't know him. We went for a coffee at a nearby café in Villiers Street and he handed me lots of the stuff about left-wing groups in Britain which eventually ended up in my notes.'

The notes are mainly smears and allegations, prepared without the slightest regard for the truth. They start with a series of statements in quotation marks.

POLITICAL NOTES, MISCELLANEOUS. – Themes, thoughts.

'In Northern Ireland, the largest category of TV and Radio is that devoted to the speeches and comments of people.'

'One of the disturbing features of the unrest is that the terrorists and their supporters have more in common than the moderates have with government policy.'

'Ministers live in a vacuum, cut off from life as it is.'

'Government policy over Ireland seems to be limited to a wish that Ireland and the Irish should go away and get lost.'

'The pathological ignorance of the Englishman is unsurpassable.'

'A brief examination of the Ulster scene makes it very clear that the Northern Ireland Office, the nominal seat of authority, is not the effective source of authority.'

'The weakness of present government policy is that it is addressed to the wrong problem and that it assumes conditions that do not exist in the Province.'

These seven quotations were written *while a Conservative government was in office*. This is quite clear, since in the middle of them, outside quotation marks, is the remarkable sentence: 'Damage caused to Conservative Party by Heath, Pym and Maudling.'

Edward Heath was Prime Minister, Francis Pym was appointed Secretary of State for Northern Ireland to succeed William Whitelaw in January 1974, and Reginald Maudling was deputy leader of the Tory Party. Maudling had resigned as Home Secretary (with responsibility for Northern Ireland) during the Poulson scandal in 1972.

The clearest message of the quotations is their challenge to government policy. Colin Wallace was employed by and directly responsible to that government. Yet every one of the opening quotes of his Clockwork

Orange notes is either a cliché or a direct assault on the government whose interests he was paid to propagate. Ministers were 'cut off'. They had more in common with terrorists than with moderates. Their own ministries were not in charge of events and their policies were fundamentally cynical and wrong-headed.

There then follows a brief analysis of the leadership of newspapers by party allegiance in the 1964 general election and a discussion of the media treatment of the two party leaders (Harold Wilson and Edward Heath) in the 1970 general election. This analysis led to the following conclusion:

> Given the foregoing, it is clear that the campaign for the next General Election will be heavily dominated by the personality factor, and every effort should be made to exploit character weaknesses in 'target' subjects and, in particular:–
> a). Financial misbehaviour.
> b). Sexual misbehaviour.
> c). Political misbehaviour.

Alongside this conclusion, in the right-hand margin, is written a series of names, as follows:

> Heath, Maudling (T. Dan Smith), Pym, Gilmore, St John Stevas, Van Straubenzee, Wilson, Rees, (suspicion), Benn, Mikardo, Owen D and Owen W, Hart/Stonehouse, Driberg etc. T Dan Smith, Short (also Poulson), Thorpe, Byers, Smith, Foot, Thomas, Wellbeloved, Heffer, Castle.

T. Dan Smith was a former leader of Newcastle City Council and a prominent Labour Party official who had been imprisoned for his part in the Poulson corruption scandal. Ian Gilmour (correct spelling) was a Tory minister, Norman St John Stevas was a prominent Tory backbencher and chairman of the Conservative Party's Northern Ireland Committee, William Van Straubenzee was Minister of State for Northern Ireland, Merlyn Rees was Labour's front bench spokesman on Northern Ireland, soon to be Secretary of State, Tony Benn and Ian Mikardo were leading Labour left-wingers, as were Tom Driberg, Judith Hart, Michael Foot, Eric Heffer and Barbara Castle. Ted Short was deputy leader of the Labour Party. George Thomas was a former Labour minister, soon to be Speaker of the House of Commons. John Stonehouse was a former Labour minister, imprisoned for multiple frauds after faking his disappearance on a Florida beach. Jim Wellbeloved was a stalwart right-wing Labour backbencher. David Owen was an up-and-coming right-wing Labour MP. Will Owen was also a Labour MP, who later resigned after it was shown he had close connections with the communist government of Czechoslovakia. Jeremy Thorpe was leader of the Liberal Party, who later resigned after a sex scandal. Lord Byers was leader of the Liberals in the House of Lords and Cyril Smith was a Liberal MP.

The inclusion of these names in this column could have had only one meaning: that every one of them were considered 'targets' for attack on account of alleged financial misbehaviour, sexual misbehaviour or political misbehaviour. That this was indeed the purpose of the notes becomes clearer as they proceeded.

The notes can best be explained by breaking them down into their separate 'target' areas. The chief among these – which became ever more prominent after 28 February when a Labour government took office – was the Labour Party and its leaders.

The tone of the Clockwork Orange notes on the Labour Party is well summarised in an introductory paragraph on the third page of the notes, on page 121. This page was probably written during the election campaign, and ran as follows:

> There is little doubt that the Labour Party are very vulnerable to the allegation of Communist or Left-wing infiltration. It is estimated that between 20 and 30 Labour MPs are members of the Communist Party, and that Wilson has bowed to this pressure by revoking the embargo on CP membership of the Labour Party.

Under this paragraph are written the names Scanlon, McGahey.

Was it possible that Labour MPs could be members of the Communist Party? The question goes back to the formation of the Communist Party in 1920, and the bitter arguments which broke out inside both parties on the subject of dual membership. Lenin urged the leaders of the Communist Party to try to play their part in the Labour Party and several attempts were made throughout the 1920s to persuade the Labour Party conference to agree to dual membership for Communist Party members. All these efforts were defeated by enormous majorities.

In June 1921, the Labour Party conference voted by 4,115,000 to 224,000 against Communist Party affiliation; in 1922, the vote was 3,086,000 to 261,000. In 1924, it was specifically resolved that no candidate for Parliament or local government could be a member of the Communist Party, and that a member of the Communist Party could not be a member of the Labour Party. This last point was agreed again by the Labour Party conference in 1925 by 2,870,000 to 321,000. The same conference appealed, again by a huge majority, to affiliated trade unions not to send Communist Party members as delegates to the Labour Party conference. In the 1930s the same argument arose over attempts by left-wingers to get the Labour Party to agree to a United Front for anti-fascist action with Communist Party members. This was turned down, year after year, by huge majorities. Even when the miners' union, in 1935, supported the idea of the United Front, the vote was 1,728,000 to 592,000. After the position had been made so very clear, even at the height of Communist Party influence, the matter was laid to rest. The plain fact (easily assessable by anyone who knew even the barest history of the Labour Party) was that it was *quite impossible* for any member of the Labour Party, let alone an MP, let alone twenty to thirty MPs to be members of the Communist Party.

In 1973/74, when Colin wrote his notes, the embargo on Communist Party membership had not just been 'revoked' by Harold Wilson, as the notes pretended. On the contrary, the embargo had just been reaffirmed. In the wake of Mick McGahey's 'appeal to the troops' speech before the miners' strike (which started in January 1974), the Labour leader issued a press statement dissociating himself from any suggestion that troops should not obey orders, or that there was any other authority in the land stronger than Parliament. In the same statement, Wilson took the opportunity to distance the Labour Party from the communists.

There was nothing at all odd about this since Harold Wilson, all his political life, was a bitter enemy of the Communist Party. At Oxford in the late 1930s he had never for a moment been part of the alliance between left Labour Party members and the Communist Party – the Popular Front. His lifelong hostility to the Communist Party came to the fore soon after his second election triumph in 1966 when, in the middle of the seamen's strike which started in April of that year, he gave two long House of Commons speeches branding the leaders of the strike as a 'tightly knit group of politically motivated men'.

The notion that Wilson would 'bow to pressure' and lift an embargo on Communist Party membership was absurd. What had happened was that the Labour Party had removed the blanket ban on 'proscribed organisations'. This 'proscribed list' had been drawn up in the years when Labour was obsessed that it was being taken over by the Communist Party and other socialist groups. It had produced a list of 'front organisations', whose meetings, rallies and discussions were forbidden to all members of the Labour Party because, it was alleged, the organisations were 'fronts' for the Communist Party. This arbitrary list had led to much resentment. The Labour Party conference of 1973 decided to abolish it.

Moreover, the Communist Party was in irreversible decline. Harold Wilson, in reply to a television interviewer, described it as 'arteriosclerotic'. He perceived, correctly, that the mantle of the old Communist Party was being discarded by its new theorists, and the new revolutionary parties in the Trotskyist tradition were growing as fast as the Communist Party was declining.

Apart from a list of names of such organisations which Colin Wallace dutifully wrote down, there is only one detailed reference to them in the notes. It is on page 123, and goes like this:

ERNEST MANDEL: Visited Dublin in November 1972, Flight 1645 ex-London. General Secretary of the Trotskyist Fourth International. Met Brendan Kelly, UCD, between 1800 to 1930 [hours] he met with members of the Irish section of the Fourth International at the Four Courts Hotel, Dublin. Mandel is a father figure for young Trotskyists. He is of Jewish origin and comes from Hamburg in West Germany. Was involved in the Algerian war of independence.

Against this altogether unexciting collection of facts was written in the margin the words 'Links with Lotta Continua', and another list of names of prominent Labour MPs: 'Foot, Thorne, Litterick, Maynard, Wellbeloved, McNamara, Lestor'. Stan Thorne was Labour MP for Preston, Tom Litterick for Birmingham, Selly Oak, Joan Maynard for Sheffield, Brightside, Joan Lestor for Eton and Slough, and Kevin McNamara for Hull North. Most were left-wingers (though Jim Wellbeloved certainly was not). None had any association whatever with Ernest Mandel, Lotta Continua, an Italian Trotskyist organisation, or the Fourth International.

At that time the British section of the Fourth International (a very small Trotskyist organisation) was extremely hostile to the social democratic parties of Europe and did not advocate 'entrism' into it (as another group, which ran the paper *Militant*, did). The hostility between the Labour Party and Trotskyist groups such as the International Marxist Group, which was associated with Ernest Mandel, was intense. The IMG did not try to join the Labour Party. If it had, the Labour Party would by a mighty majority have refused them entry. There is no way that Ernest Mandel, or his visit to Dublin in 1972, could have had the slightest connection with any of the MPs named, still less with the Prime Minister, whose name was added in the suggestive footnote: 'see links with Harold Wilson'. Yet here was this irrelevant incident, filed solemnly to Colin by Intelligence sources who were able to disclose the flight number of the plane, the time the man was met and by whom, and even his Semitic origin, but could not supply a single word or idea to link their man with any of the 'target' politicians they were after.

This brief reference to a Trotskyist, however, is the exception. The notes on Harold Wilson return again and again to the theme that he was being 'run' by the Communist Party and the Soviet secret service, the KGB.

The main references of this kind were as follows:

It can be shown that both Wilson and Heath are under Soviet control through Dick Vasgaukas (?) and Lord Rothschild. It can also be shown that Wilson has received about sixty thousand pounds from East German sources for campaign funds and that he has a friend in the Soviet Government.

Against this is written in the margin: 'see also KGB officers Victor Louis, Yuri Ustimenko, Nicolas Glavatsky, Yuri Yashnev', and against 'friend in the Soviet Government' is written 'FNU (first name unknown) Mikoyan'.

Most of the names which might confirm the remarkable allegation that the British Prime Minister was under the direct control of the Russian government were well known to intelligence experts in London. Vaygauskas – the correct spelling – was an official in the Russian Trade Delegation in London. He was probably working for the KGB – most trade officials were. He was friendly with a clothing manufacturer called Joseph Kagan. Kagan was indeed very close to the Prime Minister, who obliged him during the 1964 election by wearing a Gannex raincoat, manufactured by one of Kagan's clothing factories in Yorkshire. MI5 kept both men under the closest possible surveillance. No political link could be established with Vaygauskas or anyone else from the KGB.

In 1971, Vaygauskas was thrown out of Britain with 104 other Russian diplomats, all of whom were suspected by the Conservative Foreign Secretary, Sir Alec Douglas Home, of being spies. The 'Vaygauskas connection' was then raised by Harold Wilson himself who demanded of MI5 that nothing should be spared in an investigation of the connection between Kagan and Vaygauskas. All MI5 could come up with was that Kagan and Vaygauskas had played one or two games of chess. No warnings were given to Wilson about Kagan. The matter was dropped and Wilson was told it had been dropped. Yet here it was appearing in the lists against him in Colin Wallace's Clockwork Orange notes in 1974.

The other 'KGB officers' mentioned in the margin were all known figures in the spy world. Victor Louis was as well known as a KGB officer as he was as 'Russian correspondent' of the *Evening News*. None of the named 'officers' had any known connection with Harold Wilson or anyone else in the Labour Party hierarchy.

The rest of page 123 deals with various suggestions for 'proof' that the Labour Party and the trade unions were under the control of the KGB. There is a reference, without comment, to a 'visit to Labour officials' by the 'secretary of the Soviet Central Committee' I. V. Kapitonov, and four of his officials. Mr Kapitonov, who was in fact a junior official of the Central Committee of the Communist Party in Russia, did visit Britain as part of a delegation. They did indeed meet representatives of the Labour Party. They also met representatives from the Conservative Party, other political parties and senior officers in the armed forces.

There then appears this reminder:

Note: visits by Marcia Williams to Soviet Union, and Marcia Williams's refusal to be subjected to positive vetting.

Mrs Marcia Williams was Harold Wilson's secretary, and had been since 1956. As such, she had visited Russia with Wilson on more than one occasion. Wilson had business in Russia. From 1951, when he resigned from the Cabinet in protest against the Labour government's rearmament programme and the imposition of health charges, he had been a consultant to a timber company which exported to Russia.

The reference to Marcia Williams's 'refusal to be subjected to positive vetting' is extraordinary. A close study of newspaper cuttings in 1974 failed to reveal a single reference at that time to the suggestion that she had refused the standard 'positive vetting' procedures for 10 Downing Street staff.

The only public mention of anything of the kind came in a House of Commons question on 9 April 1974, from Mr Wyn Roberts, the Conservative MP for Conway, who asked about the new political unit set up by Prime Minister Harold Wilson under Dr Bernard Donoughue. When Wilson answered the question, Mr Roberts asked this supplementary:

'I am grateful to the Prime Minister for that reply. Are all members of the unit paid from public funds? Is this bill justified in view of the party political nature of their work? Have they all been positively vetted? How many members of the Prime Minister's personal political staff at Downing Street are not members of this unit, and have they been positively vetted?'

The Prime Minister replied:

'Regarding vetting, in 1964 I introduced the requirement that all members of the Prime Minister's staff, whether paid from public funds or not, must be positively vetted.' (House of Commons, Official Report, 9 April 1974).

That was the end of the matter for the time being. None of the reports of this question and answer suggested that Marcia Williams had refused positive vetting. In March 1976, Harold Wilson resigned as Prime Minister. Joe Haines, his Press secretary, left to join the *Daily Mirror* as chief leader writer. He wrote a book *The Politics of Power*, which was serialised in the *Daily Mirror* during February 1977. One of the many sensational revelations in these articles was that Mrs Williams (by now ennobled as Lady Falkender) had refused to be positively vetted when Labour returned to office in 1974. Joe Haines said that Mrs Williams *had* been positively vetted when she first went to Number 10 in 1964 but had refused to go through the procedure again in 1969. In 1974, when, Labour was again returned to office, according to Joe Haines, Marcia Williams had again refused to be positively vetted. Her reasons, it was suggested, were that she did not want to answer the necessary questions about her private life, since she had had two children by a political journalist, and had managed for several years to keep them secret from the public.

Harold Wilson reacted furiously to these allegations. He personally rang at least one political correspondent to deny it. The Prime Minister of the time, James Callaghan, also denied it. A few months later, Wilson showed two BBC journalists a letter from Robert Armstrong to Marcia Williams on 1 May 1974. 'Your positive vetting ought to be reviewed some time,' wrote Sir Robert. 'But there is no tearing hurry. It is less than five years since your last review.'   (Barrie Penrose and Roger Courtiour, *The Pencourt File*, London, Secker and Warburg, 1978, p. 324.)

The truth seemed to be that Mrs Williams, as she then was, had not been positively vetted since 1964 - a fact which she effectively admitted in a quotation in Chapman Pincher's book *Inside Story* - but that there was nothing at all sinister about that.

The point, for the purpose of this story, is that there were no published rumours to the effect that she had refused positive vetting until Joe Haines's book was serialised in the *Daily Mirror* in February 1977. In May 1974, when Armstrong wrote his note to Mrs Williams, and when Colin Wallace was constructing his Clockwork Orange notes, there was nothing published which even suggested that she had refused to be positively vetted. Where else could Colin have got this information except from the inner sanctum of the security services, which carried out the positive vetting, and who were the only people outside Marcia Williams's closest colleagues who would know about it?

The rumour that Marcia Williams had refused to be positively vetted did not start to circulate in the press until after Colin's notes had been written. Whoever gave him the information was starting a rumour, not commenting on it.

The next four 'notes' deal with the trade unions. The first states:

Purpose of visit by Soviet delegation – to establish links with the trade unions – see industrial unrest in 1973 and 1974.

The purpose of the visit *was* to meet British trade unions, as literally hundreds of such delegations did every year from all over the world. The notion that the visit of a Soviet delegation had any connection whatever with the industrial unrest of 1973 and 1974 was ludicrous. No Russian delegation since the death of Lenin (1924) had shown the slightest interest in striking trade unionists. Russian trade unions have no experience in industrial conflict – their members never engage in strikes. In Russia, the trade unions are tolerated on site precisely because they don't have any influence on management. Everything about the Russian delegation that winter suggests that they were playing the usual commercial diplomats' game of shaking hands and trying to find out a bit on the side about plant and machinery.

The next note says:

It is reliably reported that the Russians congratulated Jimmy Reid on forcing the Conservative Government to spend millions of pounds on a project on the Clyde where the water is too shallow to take huge tankers. Clearly Mr Gollan owes Mr Reid a reward much greater than that of having him on the national executive committee, or having won the affection of Mr Wedgwood Benn.

Jimmy Reid had been a shop steward in the Upper Clyde shipyard, where a long, bitter battle had been fought in 1971 against the Conservative government's plan to close the yard. Mr John Gollan was the General Secretary of the Communist Party, on whose national executive Jimmy Reid then sat. The fight for the Upper Clyde shipyard, which was partially successful in that the yard was not closed but sold to an American oil company, had been widely acclaimed throughout the Labour movement. The workers had been cheered at the 1971 Labour Party conference, whose chairman was Mr Tony Benn, a former Labour minister. The note's interpretation of this is so crudely biased as to place it well to the right of anything which was being said or even hinted at in the Conservative Party at the time.

One final note on this page on the unions says:

Communists strong in AUEW, T&GWU, NUM and TASS (formerly DATA).

There were communist officials in the AUEW (engineers' union) the draughtsmen's union (TASS) and the miners' union (NUM). But the T&GWU still operated the 'black circular' which barred all Communists from even the most minor office.

The conclusion of all this was noted on the top of page 124:

Civil unrest, political violence and industrial disputes engineered and controlled by the Soviet Union through Labour Party activists and Left-wing organisations.

This was a fantastic conclusion. The National Union of Mineworkers, for instance, which was embarking on a strike, was led by Joe Gormley, a right-winger. The miners' executive was heavily controlled by men of the Gormley stamp, on the far right of the Labour Party. Labour Party activists had no discernible influence on any of the large industrial disputes of 1973 or 1974, and left-wing organisations, including the Communist Party, were, even at this hey-day for the British left, microscopically small.

Nevertheless, the obsession that the Labour Party was dominated by the Russians continued in the notes and was taken to even more extravagant lengths.

On page 127, Colin jotted down:

KGB plot to leak radioactive waste near Polaris submarine bases – to cause
public concern in UK and support Labour's anti-nuclear stance – stop Trident.

The only 'proof' for this astonishing allegation was the reference in
the margin to '1 Directorate' and '3 Department', departments of the
KGB. The likelihood of the Russian government being involved in a
deliberate leak of radioactive material to support an anti-nuclear stance
was, to put it mildly, dim. The Russians had themselves embarked on a
prodigious programme of nuclear power, and had assured their people
that radioactivity was safely contained in them. It would have done their
own programme a profound disservice if international hostility to nuclear
power had been increased by a leak of waste anywhere in the world –
as they discovered to their cost in 1986 after a terrifying accident in
one of their own nuclear power stations caused profound international
dismay and threatened the whole nuclear industry. The story, then, from
whatever 'department' it emerged, that the Russians were plotting to leak
nuclear waste in Scotland was likely to have been another invention of the
fevered imagination which was supplying Colin Wallace with his 'material'
for Clockwork Orange.

Many years later, it was revealed that radioactive waste had indeed
been dumped in Holy Loch – by an American Polaris submarine. In a
Scottish TV documentary, *Scottish Eye*, broadcast on 14 January 1989,
Mr Jim Bush, who was captain of a Polaris submarine stationed in the
Holy Loch between 1961 and 1970, said that radioactive coolant from the
pressurised water reactors which drove his submarine had been discharged
in the Holy Loch. 'I think we should have done it in our country, and not
taken advantage of the Scots,' he said.

Very few people would have known this information at the time. Those
few in the security services who did know would have had good cause
to 'turn' the information and blame the Russians for the embarrassing
discharge.

The reference in the note to Trident led some journalists to doubt
the authenticity of the notes on the grounds that Trident was not publicly
acknowledged in 1974. This is not the case. The International Institute for
Strategic Studies Strategic Survey of 1973 refers to Trident (on p. 59) as a
'missile with a range of 6000 miles' and 'the US Navy's determination to
acquire it'. Brassey's *Defence Yearbook 1974* refers to Trident on pages
214, 216 and 280. 'The new system,' it declared, 'it is hoped will be
operational in 1978.'

The rest of page 127 dealt with allegations against the Labour Party.
These began with: 'Murder of Hugh Gaitskell to assist Wilson to power?'
to which was attached the note in the margin: 'Link disclosures made by

Oleg Adolfovich Lyalin: plans to infiltrate sabotage agents into UK to work inside trade unions.'

Hugh Gaitskell, leader of the Labour Party from 1956, died suddenly in January 1963 from a rare disease. The suggestion that he had been 'done away with' by the Russians who favoured a more left-wing Labour Party leader was widely disseminated among journalists in the middle and late 1970s. There was in the story a fatal flaw. The deputy leader of the Labour Party when Gaitskell died was George Brown, an even more right-wing, anti-communist politician than Gaitskell. Brown seldom missed an opportunity to express his detestation of everything Russian and everything communist. When Gaitskell died, Brown was the favourite for the succession. He was eventually beaten by Harold Wilson for a variety of reasons (Brown's drunkenness, his boorish attitudes to those with whom he didn't agree, Wilson's ability to say all things to all men), very few of which could have been foreseen by any external plotter. The most likely effect of secretly poisoning one right-wing Labour leader (as the rumours and Colin Wallace's notes suggested the Russians did to Gaitskell) was his replacement by another.

Wallace's informants had found one direct piece of evidence to link communist governments with the Labour Party.

Wilfred Owen – Czech intelligence agent and close confidant of Wilson.

Owen was discovered to have taken money from the Czech government in exchange for articles he had written for some of their government magazines. He was arrested, charged under the Official Secrets Act and acquitted in 1970. He resigned his seat soon afterwards. By no means was Owen a confidant of Wilson. He had never been in government. His career had been singularly undistinguished. It is extremely unlikely that he had even one conversation with Harold Wilson during the whole of the 1970s.

Other smears then came thick and fast:

Former KGB agent/prostitute's links with Labour MPs in London [no proof or detail added].

Michael Foot – a close friend of Tom Driberg who was associated with Guy Burgess.

Michael Foot was by now, to everyone's surprise, Secretary of State for Employment in Wilson's government. He had been all his adult life a close friend of Tom Driberg. Driberg never disguised his 'association' with Guy Burgess – he wrote his biography.

Stonehouse – shielded by Wilson for his protection??

The question marks were specially apposite here. In 1974, no one, least of all Harold Wilson, knew where John Stonehouse was. He had gone missing in mysterious circumstances in Miami. It was clear from articles in the press that Stonehouse had been engaged in spectacular frauds all over the world. Time and debts had caught up with him when he 'did his bunk'. He was eventually arrested in Australia, extradited to Britain, tried for fraud and (all under a Labour government) sent to prison for seven years.

There was still more to come on Wilson's fealty to the Soviets. Another note, the last one on page 127, declared:

> Information passed to Wilson by security authorities, *not* acted upon, action delayed – why? WILSON had refused to take action against the KGB officers clearly identified by security authorities.

Perhaps to remind himself that this was nothing new, and certainly nothing that had happened after Wilson became Prime Minister in 1974, Colin Wallace printed below the note the familiar name: RICHARD KONSTANTINOVICH VAYGAUSKAS.

The supposed connection between Vaygauskas and Lord Kagan, as we have seen, was 'spotted' before Vaygauskas was obliged to leave the country in the 'clear-out' of supposed spies in 1971. As we have also seen, far from taking no action, Harold Wilson took very prompt action and called in MI5. If 'action' had been 'delayed' as stated in Colin's note, it was the security forces themselves, not Harold Wilson, who were responsible.

Having established by these 'facts' that Harold Wilson was a Soviet agent, it was a short step to make him a covert agent of the IRA. The aim of the 'terrorists' (which on this occasion meant only the IRA) was, Colin's notes asserted, 'the establishment of an Irish Workers and Peasants Republic embracing all 36 countries'. He continued:

> This aim is supported, financially as well as by means of propaganda, from behind the Iron Curtain. Not only is Russia giving money to buy arms for the terrorists, but it is also providing expert help for the campaign.

Thus the Russians (who throughout the entire period of disorder in Northern Ireland showed a studied indifference towards the whole problem) became the *controllers* of the IRA. The Prime Minister was a Soviet agent. It followed that he sympathised with the IRA. The next notes record:

> 13.3.1972. Harold Wilson claims: IRA had a disciplined tightly-knit organisation and their writ did run to the extent that a truce could be honoured.

> 18.7.1972. Harold Wilson meets Martin McGuiness, Ivor Bell, Seamus Twomey, David O'Connell and Sean Macstiofain (all IRA leaders).

The meeting was authorised by Conservative ministers, who were also talking to the IRA.

The notes were not finished with Harold Wilson yet. On page 127, they record the facts about the *Claudia*, a boat which brought arms from Libya to Ireland for the use of the IRA. In the margin, opposite the names of some German directors, there is this instruction:

Link to Wilson's pro-Israeli stance – but beware of conflict with Soviet-Israeli attitudes.

Somehow, Wilson's extravagant support of Israel was to be *linked* to gun-running by states which were at war with Israel! It was as though the anti-Semitism of the author of the information had outweighed his anti-communism.

Page 128 opens with an extraordinary list of 'Labour policies which endanger Britain'. These were:

1). Defence Budget cuts.
2). Nuclear weapons.
3). South Africa.
4). Anti-Arab.
5). Anti-South Africa/Rhodesia.
6). Arab terrorism in Britain.
7). Increased strikes/union power.
8). Communist Party members in Government.
9). Freedom of Information Act and expiry of OSA [Official Secrets Act].
10). Withdrawal from Common Market.
11). Lack of financial confidence – less investment in Britain.
12). Why did Labour introduce Sexual Offences Bill?

The list makes no pretence at political objectivity. Many of the points derive from straightforward right-wing political propaganda against the Labour Party. The second more striking feature of the list, however, is its incoherence. Labour was anti-Arab – that was one 'danger to Britain'. Another, which apparently flowed from that, was 'Arab terrorism in Britain'. 'Communist Party members in government' (there were in fact none of these) is not a 'policy' at all – but a smear. The commitment to repeal Section Two of the Official Secrets Act commanded support across the political board. Finally, there is the curious question at the end: 'Why did Labour introduce Sexual Offences Bill?' This Bill became an Act in 1967. It did away with archaic laws banning homosexual acts between consenting adults in private. It was not introduced by Labour, but by a backbench MP as a Private Members' Bill. It won support from the Liberal Party and a substantial body of Tory MPs. It had no relevance whatever to any of Labour's policies and certainly did not feature in any controversy in the 1974 February general election campaign. Its inclusion on the list can only have had one purpose: political smear.

Who were the main 'targets' in the Labour Party, apart from Wilson? On page 130, there is a list of 'Labour politicians who are believed to be Communists and who hold positions of influence'. The list is: Benn, Mikardo, Heffer, Owen D, Hart, Driberg, Castle, Foot, Stonehouse.

All of these except Driberg, who was old, Mikardo, who was chairman of the Parliamentary Labour Party, and Stonehouse, who was missing, were ministers in the minority government.

Tony Benn, Eric Heffer, Michael Foot, Judith Hart, Barbara Castle and Tom Driberg were all left-wingers, but all uncompromising in their hostility to Russian communism. Owen D – David Owen, undoubtedly the most laughable name on the list – was on the extreme right of the Labour Party and left it seven years later for the much more right-wing Social Democratic Party. Stonehouse, when he was active, was very much on the right of the party. Only Mikardo of the bunch could be said to have any sympathy with the Eastern bloc.

Against this list is appended the note: 'Create/Expand rift Wilson/Rees.' (Merlyn Rees was Labour's very right-wing spokesman on Northern Ireland) and 'Role of Lever?' (Harold Lever, a right-wing financial minister in the Cabinet). Then, again, 'Despite assurances to the Commons that he would not speak to men of violence, Wilson, accompanied by Rees, met the IRA twice in 1972.'

These meetings, as we have seen before, were both well publicised, together with the reasons for them. They were approved by the Heath government.

Several other names of Labour MPs are mentioned, usually in long lists of those who gave support to the Campaign for Democracy in Ulster, the Anti-Internment League or the Troops Out movement. One glorious list of subversiveness on page 136 includes the names of Brian Walden, Bob Mellish, Reg Prentice and Roy Hattersley. All four were on the right of the party. Reg Prentice left the Labour Party soon afterwards and joined the Conservative Party. Brian Walden became a television interviewer and, later, a journalist who admired Margaret Thatcher. Bob Mellish defended Labour's right wing so staunchly against the left in his South London constituency that he supported right-wing 'rebel' independent Labour candidates against his own party. Ten years later, only Roy Hattersley of this dangerous quartet remained in the Labour Party, firmly on the 'hard right'.

A short essay in the notes on one Labour backbencher tells us some more about the way these notes were put together, and their purpose.

The most prominent activist in the above groups is Paul Rose, MP for Blackley in Manchester. Rose was appointed chairman of the Campaign for

Democracy in Ulster and has involved various other Left-wing Labour MPs in its activities. Rose is a lawyer who studied at Manchester University and was a key member of the University's Communist-controlled socialist society. He is a former contributor to the Communist youth newspaper and his wife was born in the Soviet bloc . . . He could become a source of embarrassment to the Party leadership because of his independent views on a number of matters eg: he supported Heath in the EEC split. He is also a member of the 'League for a Democratic Greece' or League for Democracy in Greece.

Most of his close associates are on the Left of the Party, and his role in the Party could be a key one in the event of a change in leadership. A potential (possible) Soviet agent, he appears to be well-liked by Wilson! His close links with Stan Orme at the Northern Ireland Office are important, and it may be significant that Orme was appointed to the Northern Ireland post by HW [Harold Wilson]. Thought to be pro-Israeli and strongly anti-South Africa . . . '

This long passage on a relatively obscure Labour backbencher dispels any lingering doubts that Colin Wallace's notes were all his own work. However well-informed Colin was, he could not have known from his own research, for instance, that Paul Rose had contributed to the Communist Party youth paper (as he had) or that his wife was born in the Soviet bloc (as she was). The passage reads exactly as if it was extracted from a secret service file. Its political tone, however, fits closely with the rest of the notes. Paul Rose *had* been a firebrand in his youth, but he was already moving sharply to the right. The idea that he was a 'possible Soviet agent' was ridiculous. The Campaign for Democracy in Ulster was not opposed to the partition of Ireland, still less for the 'establishment of an Irish Workers and Peasants Republic embracing all 36 Counties'. It asked no more than that the people of Northern Ireland should be properly represented in the voting system there and called for a return to the proportional representation which obtained when the Northern Ireland Parliament was first elected in 1921. Similarly, the League for a Democratic Greece asked only for a return to Parliamentary rule and an end to the fascist regime of the Greek colonels, which was not toppled until 1975. When Paul Rose was shown these notes in 1987 he became convinced that they originated in the intelligence services.

Paul Rose's 'close links' with Stan Orme (they were not very close, in fact) were part of the mythology of the Intelligence extremists who were outraged at the appointment of the known left-winger Orme as Minister of State at the Northern Ireland Office. The deep significance of the fact that Orme had been appointed by Harold Wilson must be judged against the fact that *all* ministers were, and always had been, appointed by the Prime Minister.

The final passage on the Labour Party makes the purpose of the notes quite plain. It speculates on what would happen to the Labour leadership 'if Wilson falls'.

> Callaghan could be a good choice because of his role as Police Federation representative, but he also has 'financial skeletons' relating to Welsh banking matters in his cupboard. Roy Jenkins is the unknown quantity but his 'liberal' policies at the Home Office have not helped his cause with the establishment – he is also very close to Wilson and could therefore be discredited with him.

'Discredited with him' – there is the central aim of the document in a nutshell. The aim of all the information on the Labour Party was to discredit the Wilson leadership and replace it with another, more acceptable to the reactionary minds which had supplied the information to Wallace in the first place.

This was extraordinary enough, but the notes become even more extraordinary when they turn away from the Labour government and apply their 'intelligence' to the opposition: the Conservative Party, the natural allies of reactionaries throughout the ages.

In the middle of the first page of notes, as we have seen, there is a reference to 'damage caused to Conservative Party by Heath, Pym and Maudling'. Though this theme gets much less space in the notes, it is an important ingredient in them. The references to Edward Heath crop up again and again, usually accompanied by a smear about homosexuality. On page 124, there is the curious note: 'Control over MPs – homosexual and other blackmail – Heath, St John Stevas, Van Straubenzee, Gilmore, Wilson – extra-marital relationship and Marcia Williams.' There were other references, too explicit to mention in a publication which could not defend them in a libel action, against these politicians.

Norman St John Stevas, a Roman Catholic and a moderate, was chairman of the Conservative backbench MPs Northern Ireland Committee. William Van Straubenzee was Minister of State for Northern Ireland in the Heath government from 1972 to 1974. Gilmore is probably a reference to Sir Ian Gilmour, also a member of Heath's government.

This ugly theme recurs again on page 130, with a brief reference in a list of 'factors' under the heading INDUSTRIAL UNREST: 'Homosexual link Heath/ Thorpe'. Jeremy Thorpe was the leader of the Liberal Party.

The notion that Edward Heath was a homosexual and was therefore in some risk of being blackmailed was fairly common in journalistic circles in the early 1970s. There was no evidence of any kind to support it, nor indeed was there anything at all to support any of the similar allegations against the others. The main base for the rumours was that Heath was unmarried and did not appear to have had any 'romantic attachment' to a woman. On this thin gruel, the rumours fed happily. All sorts of fantasies were circulated. I myself worked in those years for *Private Eye* (until October

1972) and for *Socialist Worker*. At both publications, especially the former, anonymous phone callers reported to me news of a 'new set of pictures of Heath and his Swedish boyfriends'. When the pictures were asked for, or the names of the callers demanded, the phone went dead. The regularity and frequency of these calls, however, all of them pretending to come from left-wing sources, left some of the muck sticking. If this was happening to me, who had never had any contacts in the intelligence services, what was circulating among journalists 'in the know', who had proved themselves receptive to the bigoted nonsense which was being churned out day by day to Colin Wallace and his colleagues in Information Policy?

The references to the Conservative leadership do not stop at a few sexual smears. A more serious matter, apparently, was the fact that Edward Heath, Prime Minister, was a Soviet agent.

The key sentence we have come across before, when dealing with Harold Wilson: 'It can be shown that both Wilson and Heath are under Soviet control through Dick Vasgaukas(?) and Lord Rothschild.'

Vaygauskas, as we have seen, referred to Wilson and his friend and benefactor, Lord Kagan. Lord (Victor) Rothschild was an altogether different character. At Cambridge in the 1930s he had been a close personal friend of Guy Burgess and Anthony Blunt, both of whom later became spies for Russia. He had been specially close to Blunt, as had the woman Rothschild later married, Tess Mayer, who also worked for MI5. He had owned the lease on the flat in Bentinck Street in London's West End where Blunt and Burgess had lived together during the war. Rothschild had many times been questioned about his role, and never succeeded in shaking off the suspicion that he was connected with the famous spy ring, whose base had been left-wing Cambridge undergraduates at Cambridge before the war. These allegations never interrupted his distinguished and versatile career, including many years at MI5.

In 1971, Edward Heath appointed Rothschild head of his newly-formed Central Policy Review Staff, or 'Think Tank'. This gave Rothschild a presence in government, but he was already influential enough to penetrate most of the ministries and the intelligence services. We shall come across him again later in this story. For the moment, the single reference to him in Wallace's notes shows that he was suspected by at least some people in Intelligence of being a Soviet agent. His appointment by Heath was excuse enough to suggest that the weakness of the Conservative leadership could be ascribed to the well-laid schemes of the KGB.

These smears – whether about Heath's sex life or about his connection with the Russians – were not written down with anything like the confidence which accompanied the smears on Wilson. There are only one or two references in all the notes. Nevertheless, Colin's *aim* as far as Heath was concerned was a very serious one. The first reference to this is an aside on page 130:

If both Liberals and Labour lost public confidence simultaneously would
the votes go to the Conservatives or just be lost by people not taking part
in the election? How would the situation alter under a different Conservative
leader?

This is plainly written in the period between the two 1974 elections,
during which the tone of the notes reflects a *strategy* for the next election.
The conclusion is quite clearly spelled out at the top of a section on page
135 headed POLITICAL APPRECIATIONS: GENERAL NOTES:

The results of the General Election indicates that unless there is a dramatic
change in the future of the Conservative Party it cannot win the next election
under Edward Heath's leadership. The key issue, therefore, is whether there
should be cosmetic treatment to help elect a weak government under Heath or
major surgery to bring about a change of leadership *before* the next election. If
Heath goes willingly before the next election, who would be his successor?

There then follows a long list of possible successors, which could
have been put together by anyone with a passing knowledge of politics.
William Whitelaw ('popular with senior members of the Party . . . would
attract the support of pro-Paisley Unionists'); Christopher Soames ('a
strong contender'); Enoch Powell ('has annoyed senior Tories by his
'vote Labour' call at the last election'); James Prior ('lacks experience
but well-liked'); Edward Du Cann ('possible financial skeletons in his
cupboard'); Nicholas Ridley ('too close to Powell'); John Biffen ('too
close to Ridley and Powell'); Lord Carrington ('strong candidate but not
enough to the Right').
The section concludes:

If Heath *loses* the next election and is forced to give up the leadership,
then the field is wide open and one of the 'new' faces may come to the fore
to depose the 'Old Brigade'. In that event, there will certainly be a marked
swing to the right.

This prophecy, brilliantly vindicated, could also have been devised
by anyone who studied the political scene. Indeed, most of the notes
on this page are no more than amateur psephology. What stands out
however is the extraordinary phrase from the first paragraph: 'The key
issue, therefore, is whether there should be cosmetic surgery to help elect
a weak government under Heath or major surgery to bring about a change
of leadership *before* the next election.'
For whom was that the 'key issue'? Obviously only for those on the
right and extreme right who wanted to get rid of Heath in the first place.
It was not 'the key issue' for the millions who voted Labour, Liberal,

Unionist or Nationalist; nor for the other millions who were quite satisfied with the leadership of the Tory Party. Secondly, what is meant by
the terms 'cosmetic surgery' and 'major surgery'? Who was to carry out
this surgery? The only intelligible interpretation of this passage is that
it was part of a plan by people with extreme right wing views who were
not sure whether to use their powers to try to change the Tory leadership in 1974, or after the next election.

The strategy outlined in the notes is quite straightforward: to cause
the greatest possible embarrassment to the Labour government and the
Heath leadership (and for that matter to the Liberal Party). The most
instructive section of the notes is a table neatly drawn up in Colin's
handwriting, entitled VULNERABILITIES.

The table speaks for itself. 'Financial' means that the politician is
involved in some City scandal, 'moral' means the same for sexual scandal,
and 'political' means that the politician can be shown to have some connection with Soviets or communists. Harold Wilson was the only one of eleven
top politicians who scored on all three counts.

VULNERABILITIES

	Financial	Moral	Political
Wilson	X	X	X D
Heath		X	X D
Thorpe	X	X	
Callaghan	X		
Paisley	X	X D	
Maudling	X	X	
Steel		X	
Slater	X		
Walker	X		
Foot			X
Benn			X
Short	X		

The political philosophy behind the Clockwork Orange notes was
summarised in an essay Colin wrote himself entitled: 'Ulster – A State
of Subversion'.

The essay starts with a quotation from Lenin, which harks back
to a letter written by Marx in 1867. Marx reflected that the eventual

'separation' of Ireland from Britain would come 'as a federation'. Colin at once saw the significance of that. 'It is remarkable,' he wrote, 'that some sixty years later during the present unrest both Loyalist and Republican groups have put forward federation as a possible solution.' Marx had suggested federation and Lenin had referred to it. It followed that Marx and Lenin were probably responsible for the federal suggestion of both Republicans and Loyalists in 1974. The fact that pretty well every historian who has ever studied the prospect of an independent Ireland has envisaged a federal solution was beside the point.

There is then a paragraph about communist propaganda on Northern Ireland, which contrasts the 'extreme over-simplification' by Moscow that the Irish issue can be fitted 'into the colonial mould' with the 'more balanced and factual' coverage of Rumania and Yugoslavia 'which have avoided attempts to make propaganda capital out of the Irish tension'.

From this rather sophisticated point, Colin leaps to a very unsophisticated conclusion: 'In the face of such propaganda, government information policy in Northern Ireland has been weak, ineffective, uncoordinated and defensive – like their security policies as a whole.' All this led to a loss of public confidence in Government, an increase in the 'violence of the mind' and a boost to the 'terrorist propaganda machine'.

The essay goes on:

> Given such a situation, it *must be clear to all reasonable people* [Colin's emphasis] that the present government's apparent lack of moral courage in dealing with the unrest is not simply the lack of resources or will, and that there must be more deep-rooted causes behind this sinister abdication of responsibility. In their worthy socialist thinking they see the solution as a red shamrock United Irish Workers Republic. Their answer, however, ignores Ulster's religious divisions and social conservation. Contemptible and risible as such blatant Marxist thinking is, their part in fomenting the present campaign of violence is considerable.

What was the reasoning that led to this conclusion – that there 'must be deep-rooted causes' for the government's position? It was circuitous. It started by showing that communists were fascinated by the Irish situation and made propaganda about it. It then asserted that the British government had been weak in its security policy in Ireland – and so concluded that the reason for that weakness was that the British government was controlled by the communists.

The 'evidence' for the Russian infiltration and control of the government is then set out in some detail: 'regular visits' by KGB agents to Ireland; the suggestion that a Russian embassy be opened in Dublin; the fact that a

Russian agent spoke at a meeting of a Connolly Youth Movement (which never pretended otherwise than it was controlled by the Communist Party); the visit to Dublin in 1972 of the Trotskyist Ernest Mandel, which we have come across already, and the links between leading Labour Party politicians (Foot, McNamara, Litterick, Maynard, Thorne, Lestor, etc.) and 'extra Parliamentary' groups like the Campaign for Democracy in Ulster and Troops Out.

The political conclusion of all this is unmistakable. If 'reason' is to be restored, the elected government must be defeated.

> Set against this background, there is an urgent need for a major re-thinking of the handling of the Northern Ireland situation, and that is most unlikely until the present government is defeated by public opinion. Terrorism must not end; it must be defeated and seen to be defeated. All previous IRA campaigns have ended with a ceasefire declaration being called by the terrorists. Psychologically this situation leaves the initiative with the terrorists and gives the community the impression that violence may ensue if and when the terrorists deem fit. Public confidence in the future cannot exist under any government allowing such a climate of uncertainty.

There was no room here for 'cosmetic surgery'; nor any policy outlined which could possibly be carried out as long as the Labour government stayed in office. The whole thrust of the Irish policy of successive British governments was called into question. Terrorism, it was suggested, had to be crushed so that it could never revive. The IRA and everything associated with it had to be obliterated. But it was being deliberately protected by the Labour government which was acting as the conscious agent of the KGB. No information was therefore of any use unless it damaged the government; unless it hastened the day when the Communist stooge at Number Ten Downing Street and his fellow-travelling ministers could be brought down.

It was the job of Information Policy to construct material, including completely false material, which could be used in the propaganda war against the government. Some of this material is preserved in two big black folders marked RESTRICTED which Colin compiled during his days at Lisburn. These folders were regularly shown to visiting journalists, especially American journalists. Many of the arms for the IRA came from America; Information Policy was therefore keen to spread round America the (quite unproven) notion that the IRA were working with the communists. Notes and sometimes forged articles were compiled and shown to visiting journalists as proof of the connection. The journalists were given to understand that these were documents and notes 'from the inside', gathered by secret intelligence sources; the documents could not be taken away by the journalists, though they were free to make notes on them and comment on them discreetly.

These 'documents' read very much like the Clockwork Orange political notes. One of them purported to be an election leaflet. Its headline was ULSTER IS BRITISH and its message, in equally big type, was VOTE LABOUR.

The document gave as its address 7 Carlisle Street, London Wl, the former address of the *Black Dwarf*, a revolutionary paper which had gone out of publication four years previously. The document's first sentence read:

> British capitalism has long exported its violence to its imperial possessions; it does so in full measure to its nearest vassal territory – the police state which it maintains in Northern Ireland. Irish workers and peasants have a revolutionary heritage, both of class struggle and of combat against British imperialism.

The tone is crudely Marxist. Its tone, style and meaning were entirely contradictory to anything which could have emerged from the Labour Party. But to many visiting journalists, the leaflet was 'clear proof' of the dreaded links between the Labour Party and the most violent hysteria of the IRA.

An even more preposterous example of Information Policy's secret forgeries was the pamphlet, *Economics: Master or Servant of Mankind*. This became a favourite of American journalists. The alleged authors of the document had their names printed on the cover. They were Denis Healey, Tony Benn and Stan Orme. In the bottom of the pamphlet, Colin wrote in his own handwriting, to assist the foreign journalists who were about to read the pamphlet.

1. (Denis Healey) 'Ex' Communist Party member.
2. (Tony Benn) Links with Czech Intelligence.
3. (Stanley Orme) Campaign for Democracy in Ulster.

The document was dated Autumn 1971. It pretended to be an internal paper in a series entitled 'The Labour Movement' and was sub-headed: *Imperialism – Crisis – Revolution*.

Once again the forgery would have been easy to detect by anyone who knew anything about the politics of the Labour Party. Denis Healey was a former Minister of Defence, who became Chancellor of the Exchequer (and stayed as such for six years) when Labour took office in March 1974. He was and had been for thirty years a supporter of the 'hard right' of the Labour Party. Though it was true that he had briefly joined the Young Communist League in the 1930s, he quickly shifted to the right and, after a gloriously revolutionary speech to the Labour Party conference in 1945, joined the International Department of the Labour Party, where he became a supporter of United States foreign policy. This he continued in office, from 1964 to 1970, earning the respect of the officer class. Like many others with the same sort of background, his membership of the Young Communist League for a brief period of his youth had no influence whatever on his subsequent political development, still less on his political position in 1974.

Denis Healey stood an enormous distance away from Tony Benn, who was rapidly becoming a spokesman for the socialist wing of the party, seeking to play down his role as a very moderate minister in the Labour government of the 1960s. Yet Tony Benn was still talking in ordinary Parliamentary language. There was not a trace of revolution in his speeches or his ideas. Similarly, Stan Orme, a much more reserved left-winger in the tradition of the Labour weekly paper *Tribune*, spoke in the accents of a conventional Parliamentary politician. In the Wilson government formed in the early days of March 1974, Denis Healey became Chancellor of the Exchequer, Tony Benn became Secretary of State for Trade and Industry, and Stan Orme became Minister of State at the Northern Ireland Office.

All three appointments greatly excited and infuriated the prejudices of the 'ultras' in the intelligence services. Healey would never be forgiven his communist past. Benn was increasingly a socialist menace. Above all, the appointment of Orme threatened the hegemony of the armed forces and their intelligence advisers in the place where previously they had felt least restricted: Northern Ireland. Thus an inflammatory pamphlet by three ministers urging its readers to violent revolution appealed hugely to the prejudices of the intelligence services. The fact that the three men could never have combined to write anything at all never bothered their detractors for a moment.

Foreign journalists visiting Lisburn barracks would be taken confidentially on one side by Colin Wallace or one of the other officers in Information Policy and shown the *Master or Servant* pamphlet, carefully conserved in Cellophane. He or she would read that three ministers in the Labour government had conspired only three years earlier to write, for instance, this:

> The essence of Marxist strategy, of revolutionary strategy of our time, is to combine the struggle for reforms with the struggle for revolution. This is the only way in which to build a revolutionary party capable of providing leadership to the masses and enabling them in revolutionary situations to make the transition of consciousness and in action from the struggle for reforms to the struggle for power and revolution.

There is no need to quote any further from the pamphlet to prove the point. The three authors were all, in fact, committed reformists. None of them could conceivably have written this passage. A single phone call to any one of them, a single inquiry to anyone who knew anything about contemporary Labour politics, would have revealed that the document was a forgery. But Colin Wallace and his colleagues in Information Policy showed it exclusively to the 'hick-men' from the more outlandish newspapers in the United States of America, to the malleable journalists supporting South American dictatorships and to any journalists anywhere who might be influenced (or whose readerships might be influenced) by the Roman Catholic church. If more was requested, the black files also included quotations from Stan Orme from the Labour Party conference in which he called for British withdrawal from Northern Ireland, long investigative pieces about the subsidy of the IRA by money from the United States, an essay on the New Left and several more assertions about the connection between the IRA and Moscow. Colin's own masterpiece, 'Ulster - A State of Subversion', also appeared in the files, as a summary of everything which went before. The whole collection had a single design: to convince the journalist concerned that the British Army could not properly fight the terrorists because at least one of its hands was tied behind its back by the British government and its 'revolutionary' ministers.

Some evidence of the effect of this propaganda at least in the United States of America came to light two years later. An article in the *Daily Telegraph* on 19 May 1976 by Nicholas Comfort, that paper's Washington correspondent, carried a headline CAMPAIGN IN U.S. TO SMEAR MPS. The article said:

> Persistent efforts have been made in recent months to discredit leading members of the three major British political parties by planting derogatory stories about them on news agencies in Washington. 'Shortly before Mr Heath lost the Conservative leadership last year someone presented us with an article on Mr Heath. This was quite derogatory on the lines of Mr Jeremy Thorpe,' said Dr Edward Von Rothkirk, senior editor of the large East Coast Trans-World News Agency.
>
> So far this year his agency and others have been offered similar material about some eleven MPs, a Conservative, two Liberals and eight Labour.

Dr Rothkirk went on to say that 'the really heavy approach' had come during 1975 and that his was not the only news agency which had been approached in this way. Complete strangers, he said, would ring the agency, offer them material and ask only for token payments. When two BBC journalists investigating the supply of this material asked Dr Rothkirk to send them copies of the original stories which were sent to him, Dr Rothkirk agreed to do so immediately. Some months later, he wrote to apologise for a 'screw-up'. He explained that the agency's sixth-floor storeroom had suffered a major burglary, after the burglar alarms had been disconnected. Following the burglary, there was a major fire 'which led to the destruction of nearly all the files stored there'. Dr Rothkirk also apologised, on behalf of the postal services, for the fact that some original material that was sent before the fire and the burglary had never arrived in Britain.

What were the ideas which inspired all this disinformation? They were, on any reckoning, unusual ideas, limited exclusively to the far right of the political spectrum. They were founded not on rational thought, but on the fear that the 'enemy' – red and foreign – was in our midst.

Some of the ideas could be traced back to a book by Major General Frank Kitson, who wrote *Low Intensity Operations* in 1969. The theme of the book was that the armed forces in the future would have to contend not so much with the enemy outside the country, but with the enemy within. Kitson argued that far too much military strategy was geared to fighting an enemy whom everyone could identify: the Russians, or the Chinese. The real threat, he suggested, came from subversives inside the country who were doing the communists' work for them.

In the hectic years of 1973 and 1974, the panic sown by the victory of the miners and the election of a Labour government threw up all kinds of extreme right-wing organisations whose leaders were unimpressed by traditional definitions of democracy. The Unison Committee for Action was formed in 1973 by G. K. Young, former deputy chief of MI6. In 1974, a founder of the Special Air Service, Colonel David Stirling, set up GB 75.

The ideas behind these organisations had long since influenced the intelligence services. Many years later, the proof of the extent of that influence in the mid-1970s came from two sources on different sides of the political fence. In 1987, Peter Wright, a senior officer in MI5, published his memoirs, *Spycatcher*. Wright's book from first to last testified to his extreme right-wing views. He freely acknowledged that some of his colleagues were convinced that Harold Wilson was a KGB agent, and even revealed that there was a group of MI5 officers, from which he modestly, but not very convincingly, excluded himself, who were plotting against Wilson when he was Prime Minister. There was in 1974, he disclosed, a conspiracy against the elected government inside the security services, which had been infected by very right-wing and racialist ideas.

Shortly before Wright's book was published, another former MI5 agent, Cathy Massiter, featured in a long and powerful television documentary in the *20/20 Vision* series. Cathy Massiter disclosed that she had been required to resign from MI5 when she complained about the amount of intelligence work which was inspired not by the demands of security but by extreme right-wing political ideas. In particular, she queried the obsession with tapping the telephones of officials of the Campaign for Nuclear Disarmament.

Cathy Massiter singled out 1974 as the year in which the mood in MI5 changed decisively: to a new devil-may-care offensive against 'subversives'. These two separate sources, entirely independent of one another, provided evidence that sections of MI5, which Colin believes was the source of the bulk of the Clockwork Orange information, were motivated by reactionary ideas, and directed their considerable powers against the elected government they were meant to be serving.

Nowhere was this right-wing influence more obvious than in Northern Ireland. All the splinters and factions were united in the belief that British troops must stay in Ireland. The view had been cogently set out in a paper written in 1971 for the Institute for the Study of Conflict, 'The Spreading Irish Conflict'.

The institute grew out of an organisation called Forum World Features, which had been funded by the Central Intelligence Agency. One of its most prolific authors, who also wrote part of the Irish paper, was Robert Moss, a right-wing journalist who was in 1974 completing a book on the coup in Chile in which an elected government had been overthrown by the armed forces, assisted by the CIA. In place of Parliamentary government, a military dictatorship had put itself in power.

Moss's part of the paper, called 'The Security of Ulster', did not offer any practical solution to the Irish problem. He was clearly not interested in the political problem. What concerned him was the awesome possibility that 'Britain will eventually decide to scuttle'. 'Solutions,' he concluded (though he did not favour any particular ones), 'must be found within the present constitutional framework.' And again: 'It will be possible to operate the social and political reforms that the Stormont government has introduced only if it is saved from foundering on the law and order issue.'

And again: 'The first condition for a settlement is that the IRA should be met with the necessary force.'

Moss did not seem at all interested in reforms, settlements or solutions: only in the first condition of any of them – the adoption of the toughest possible military line. He had unlimited faith in the British Army, which had conducted him round the Six Counties. 'The British Army,' he concluded, 'is the only force in the Province that can claim to be non-partisan.'

As the shift from MI6 to MI5 was taking place in Northern Ireland, the new Director-General of MI5, Michael Hanley, sent over a long-serving officer to 'take a look' at the situation. The officer was Peter Wright. In his book, *Spycatcher*, Wright recalls:

At first I thought Ireland might give me a new lease of life. I made a couple of trips. It reminded me a lot of Cyprus. A fierce, insoluble conflict, made worse by a vacillating British policy. At the time I first went, the Government were telling the world that the situation was getting better. I spent a fortnight reviewing the records of all explosions over a twelve-month period. I drew a graph and proved conclusively that the weight of explosive being detonated was a steeply ascending curve. So much for an improved security situation! But, as in Cyprus, the Army and the politicians simply refused to face reality.

Wright records that he put forward two plans. The first was to tap telephones in the Irish Republic, the second to plant booby-trapped detonators on suspected members of the IRA. The first idea proved unpopular with a government about to embark on talks with the Irish government; the second was turned down, to Wright's indignation, when, as he recalls, 'even the MI5 management took fright'. Wright lost interest and went back to Britain.

His reflections were an interesting indication of the predominating ideas among Intelligence officers in Northern Ireland at that time.

The old order, as laid down by Maurice Oldfield, was in disarray. The New Right was in the ascendancy. They were determined to do all in their power to smoke out and defeat the subversive forces whose agents were now government ministers. They would defend the British military presence in Ireland and do all in their power to countermand any effort by the new Labour government to appease the enemy.

Such people had watched in dismay while the Conservative government wrestled with a political solution to the problem of Northern Ireland. The Heath administration correctly identified the central political problem: Catholics were shut out of the political process. For them, the right to vote was a farce. Some forty per cent of the population – Catholics – could never vote in a government they wanted.

After the palpable failure of internment in 1971, the Heath government sought for a solution which would allow the Catholics some say in the government. They came up with a form of 'power-sharing' whereby certain offices in the government would be allotted to representatives of the Catholics. The proposal was, in effect, for a permanent coalition government which would always include several senior members who represented Catholics. The proposal split the Ulster Unionists. Protestant fundamentalists opposed it as the thin edge of the Papist wedge.

But the Unionist Prime Minister, Brian Faulkner, and other members of his Cabinet and of his party, were persuaded to attempt the experiment. At a conference at Sunningdale, Berkshire, in December 1973, the details were finally thrashed out. Without any elections being held, a power-sharing executive consisting mainly of ministers from the Official Unionists and the predominantly Catholic SDLP was established.

The solution did not commend itself to the ultras in Intelligence. They agreed with the Rev. Ian Paisley that it smacked of compromise and eventually of British troop withdrawal. Their fears had been stoked up by meetings between the Secretary of State for Northern Ireland, William Whitelaw, and the leaders of the Provisional IRA. These were followed, as we have seen, by meetings between Harold Wilson, leader of the British Labour Party, and the IRA.

Despite the grumbling on the right, however, the power-sharing executive took office. For a very short time, despite a horrific increase in assassinations, it looked as though it might succeed. What wrecked it was the February 1974 election, which gave the Northern Ireland people a chance to vote on the new experiment. The result was decisive: 422,000 people voted for candidates who opposed power-sharing; 246,000 for those who favoured it. The majority was bigger even than the majority of Protestants over Catholics.

The dam of resentment which had been building up in the Protestant populations in the Army and in Intelligence over the Sunningdale Agreement broke over the heads of the minority Labour administration which took office on 1 March. Any suggestion of retreat in Ireland served merely to confirm the worst fears of the ultras: that the Labour government was being controlled from Moscow by the IRA. Thus when the new Secretary of State for Northern Ireland, Merlyn Rees, announced that he was legalising the political arm of the IRA, Sinn Fein (as had been planned by the Tory Government), or when a Catholic was appointed commander of the forces in the Derry area (as had been planned by the Tory government), this was all proof that the government was 'selling out' its armed forces and preparing to 'scuttle'. Conservative newspapers, which previously had held their fire against the initiatives of the Heath government, now fulminated against those same initiatives as they were carried out by Labour.

During the extraordinary period of the 'interregnum' of 1974 - the period between the two elections of that year, in February and October – Colin Wallace and his colleagues in Information Policy were involved in a series of 'information offensives' which were designed to disorientate and disrupt the new Labour administration at Stormont and in London.

The issue which made the running in the early weeks was the release of internees. Internment without trial had been a disaster. It had fanned the fury of Irish people in the United States of America. It had even been denounced in the European Court of Human Rights. When they were converted to power-sharing, the Conservative government stopped internment and ordered the steady release of internees. Internees were released all through 1973 without anyone noticing. As soon as the Labour government was elected, however, a press campaign started about the release of internees. As early as 31 March, almost before the new ministers had got their feet under their tables, an article appeared in the *Sunday Times* (regarded at that time by the Army as a 'hostile' newspaper) about the number of released internees who had been 'drawn back into violent courses'.

This theme persisted all through the months of April, May, June and July. Colin Wallace recalls: 'Almost every briefing we put out about assassinations or bombings was accompanied by some reference to the release of internees. We would say something like: 'This was carried out by such-and-such a unit. The unit has been able to rebuild its strength since the release of its former leaders X and Y' – and then we would give the date of the release.'

This sort of propaganda infuriated Ministers. There was no clear evidence to refute it. No one save the intelligence services had the figures for the reinvolvement of internees in violence and even the intelligence figures were based on approximations and guesses. A classic example of the way the propaganda worked was in the Army's response to the release, early in July, of sixty-five internees, almost all of them on the Republican side. Rees himself had made it clear that he wanted the release to be 'discreet' and that there should be little or no publicity for it. But on 9 July, a select group of correspondents were personally invited to Lisburn for a press briefing. The journalists were told that the recent upsurge of violence could very largely be blamed on the rise in confidence in the IRA now that their ranks had been joined by a flow of internees, especially from the sixty-five just released. The following day the papers unanimously publicised 'Army Intelligence reports' that 'well over half' the released internees became reinvolved in violence almost at once.

This figure was also given to the politicians. Joe Haines, Press Secretary to the Prime Minister, was quoted in the *Sunday Times* three years later (3 March 1977) saying that 'figures given to the Cabinet' showed that 40 per cent of those released went back to violent activity. 'We felt that elements in the Army were working against us,' he said.

The *Sunday Times* article, written by David Blundy, concluded that the 'half' and '40 per cent' figures were pure fiction; and that the Army intelligence reports at the time deliberately inflated figures of reinvolvement. Blundy asked the Ministry of Defence for the real figures and was told that it all depended on what was meant by 'reinvolvement'. 'If you mean the number that went back to shooting and bombing, the percentage might be quite low,' a spokesman admitted. Yet that was exactly what Colin Wallace and his colleagues did mean in 1974 when they confidently told journalists of the reinvolvement of 'well over half'.

This repetition of completely false figures had a profound effect on the ministers' own confidence in their policies towards the Republican community. An interesting admission of this comes from the Secretary of State at the time, Merlyn Rees. Rees describes in his book, *Northern Ireland: A Personal Perspective*, the first Parliamentary debate on Northern Ireland after Labour took office. The debate was on 4 April and came at the climax of long and terrible weeks of assassinations and bombings, most of it inspired by the Protestant extremists, and responded to in kind by the IRA.

Rees confesses that he 'left it to Stan Orme', his beleaguered

Minister of State, who wound up the debate, to outline yet another government scheme about the internees. It was a scheme which specially commended itself to Stan Orme since it fused his socialist instincts with practical policy. Orme and Rees reckoned that one of the main reasons why so many released internees went back to violence was, as Rees put it, 'the lack of job opportunities'. They therefore decided to appeal to decent citizens in Northern Ireland to provide work for former internees. (M. Rees, *Northern Ireland, A Personal Perspective*, London, Methuen, 1985, p. 56.)

Stan Orme said, in the House of Commons: 'Perhaps the most important help that we could receive would be for courageous men and women in the hardline ghetto communities to come forward with offers of help in resettling detainees. We need that kind of help . . . ' (Stan Orme, *House of Commons Official Report*, 4 April 1974.)

Merlyn Rees reckoned that Stan Orme's appeal went down pretty well in the House of Commons, but it was ridiculed in almost all the press. Information Policy in Belfast was quick to capitalise on the fundamental absurdity of asking for special jobs for suspected terrorists, and the newspapers responded with satirical headlines such as RENT A TERRORIST. Rees wrote:

> We had slipped up in other ways too, for no sooner was the announcement made than it was leaked from Army headquarters in Lisburn that the staff there preferred a variant of the idea by which detainees would go through the resettlement scheme before being released. (Rees, *op. cit.*, p. 56.)

This 'alternative' was nothing of the kind. Rees pointed out: 'Once detainees knew they were going to be released they would not co-operate.' Indeed, the idea was preferred by the Army precisely because it was a non-starter. But at any rate the information offensive from Lisburn had the desired effect long before it was necessary to consider an alternative. As Merlyn Rees rather pathetically admitted:

> The plan had all gone too wrong, however, for us to proceed and as early as April 24 Stan reported that the proposal was 'unacceptable and unworkable'. Later in the year he tried again with a variant of the scheme but that too had to be abandoned because of practical difficulties. (Rees, *op. cit.*, p. 57.)

As so often in his memoirs of these months, the former Secretary of State was very ready to ascribe the collapse of his initiatives and his policies to their intrinsic weakness and not so ready to place the blame where it most fitted the facts: on the Army Information officers who were meant to be publicising the government's plans.

Another curious 'leak' which caused all kinds of difficulties to ministers was the strange story of SAS troops in Northern Ireland. On 19 March 1974, less than three weeks after Labour took office, Colin Wallace leaked a report to the highly-respected *Times* correspondent in Northern Ireland, Robert Fisk. Fisk checked the facts as far as he was able and *The Times'* front page of 19 March reported: SAS MEN SERVE IN ULSTER AS UNDERCOVER AGENTS.

Fisk reported that members of the SAS had been sent to Northern Ireland 'to serve as military undercover intelligence agents in Belfast and Londonderry'. He went on:

> In spite of the obvious political implications of the move, the decision to involve the SAS in the Ulster war was prepared at the highest ministerial level in London, although its presence here had been revealed only to a few selected senior officers.

The announcement caused a bit of a storm not least among the new government's own backbenchers who wanted to know whether it was true that the SAS were operating in Northern Ireland. The minister in charge, Secretary of Defence Roy Mason, was not able immediately to help. For although Robert Fisk had reported that the decision to send in the SAS had been taken 'at the highest ministerial level', the Minister of Defence knew nothing about it.

Mason made what inquiries he could. On 9 April 1974 three weeks after Robert Fisk's exclusive report in *The Times*, he told the House of Commons that there was absolutely no truth in the story. There were, he said, 'no SAS in Northern Ireland'.

The doubts persisted, however, well stoked by Information Policy. On 14 August, Robert Fisk returned to the subject with a report entitled: SAS TRAIN TROOPS FOR ULSTER. He reported that 'about 43' members of the SAS had been withdrawn from Northern Ireland after eight months' training there in surveillance, photography and patrolling. The decision to send them in had been taken, he said, by the Tory Cabinet the previous January, but the government had always been 'unwilling' to discuss their role. 'Even when *The Times* published details of their activities on March 19, the Army scarcely acknowledged them,'

Robert Fisk did not refer to Mason's categorical denial the previous April that the SAS were in Northern Ireland. No one asked how it was that SAS troops, sent in by a Tory Cabinet in January, were not known to a Labour Secretary of State in April. If they had asked the question, they might have considered another one: why did Army Information officers leak the presence of SAS troops in Northern Ireland in the first place? One answer might be that they knew perfectly well that Mason did not know the SAS were there; that he would publicly deny it and that he would look an incompetent fool when it was eventually revealed that the SAS, whose presence in Northern Ireland he had so vociferously denied, had been there all along.

Roy Mason, never the most radical or sensitive of the new Labour ministers, was at the centre of another early controversy in which Colin Wallace and his colleagues were involved.

On 24 April, Mason spoke to Staffordshire miners at Newcastle-under-Lyme. Most of the speech was standard Ministry of Defence rhetoric about the dangers of defence cuts. It sounded like a Ministry of Defence brief. Towards the end, the Secretary of State moved to Northern Ireland and made the not very controversial point that the people of that area should do more themselves to end the terror and rely less on British troops. To emphasise this argument, Mr Mason went on:

> Pressure is mounting on the mainland to pull out the troops. Equally, demands are being made to set a date for the withdrawal, thereby forcing the warring factions to get together and hammer out a solution.

There was nothing in the original draft of this speech which suggested that the minister had a view about these 'pressures'. He simply advanced the fact of the 'pressures' as an argument for the urgency of solving the Northern Ireland problem quickly, with more help from the people who lived there. The context in which the argument was put made it quite clear that he regarded the withdrawal of British troops with distaste.

Certainly there was nothing in Mr Mason's past to suggest that he had the slightest sympathy for the 'Troops Out' lobby. He was firmly placed on the traditional right wing of the Labour Party. He was not a Roman Catholic. He supported Labour Party policy one hundred per cent, and Labour Party policy was firmly *against* withdrawing British troops from Northern Ireland. Withdrawal had been proposed at the Labour Party conferences of 1971 and 1973 and heavily defeated. Merlyn Rees himself had made it plain in the House of Commons in the 4 April debate that the government's policy was to keep troops in Northern Ireland as long as they were needed.

Mr Mason was absolutely right to say that there were 'pressures' for withdrawal. In 1971, for instance, the *New Statesman*, then an influential journal of the Left, whose editor, Richard Crossman, was a former Labour Cabinet minister, had argued that a date should be set for withdrawing British troops from Northern Ireland. The argument had caught on in some sections of the left, though there were no more than a handful of Labour MPs who dared publicly to raise the issue. On the other hand, the (very rare) public opinion polls on the matter suggested a growing disillusionment about British involvement in Ireland.

Mason's speech was circulated in the ministry several hours before it was made and was quickly the subject of outrage among the 'ultras' in Intelligence and Information Policy, including Colin Wallace. Mild as Mason's words were, they seemed to provide the proof for all the wildest fears that the new Labour government, in due deference to their masters in the Kremlin or the Falls Road, were planning to 'scuttle'. To the intelligence services in Northern Ireland the speech *proved* that the traitors Mason, Wilson, Rees and Orme were preparing to lead the British Army into the worst (and far less glorious) defeat since Dunkirk.

They set to work among the more intelligent correspondents to 'draw their attention' to the apparently innocuous words in Mason's speech. One result on the day after Mason's speech was a huge headline in the *Guardian* by Simon Hoggart, one of the most perceptive journalists on that paper's political staff, who had first-hand experience in Northern Ireland. MASON LIGHTS A FUSE ON TROOP PULL-OUT was the headline. The article started: 'The Minister for Defence Mr Roy Mason hurled into Westminster the ticking time-bomb of a possible pull-out of British troops from Ulster.' Some effort was made to sustain this rather extravagant interpretation of the minister's words, which Simon Hoggart conceded were 'mild enough'. He highlighted the 'implication' which he suggested was 'quite clear' – 'if the Ulster people did not do more to help themselves, the pressure to pull the troops out could become overwhelming'.

That no such implication was ever intended was rapidly made clear by the Ministry.

The ministry Press Office had been under siege all the previous afternoon as correspondents from all kinds of papers were referred to the dangerous passage in Mr Mason's speech by Colin Wallace in Belfast and associates of Information Policy in Britain. The ministry press officers appeared to be surprised and shocked by the reaction, which they regarded as quite unjustified. When they found that their assurances were not enough, they resorted to the unusual device of putting out a statement to 'clarify' what the minister had said. On the first clarification, just an hour after he had made his speech, Mr Mason 'made it clear that he was merely reflecting the pressure on him for withdrawal, and registering a view which was presented to him'. He went on to make his own view clear: the troops must stay. 'As long as there is a job for the troops to do, then they must stay there.'

That sounded clear enough, but it did not satisfy the increasingly hysterical questioners. Half an hour after his first clarification, Mr Mason was panicked into another one.

The Secretary of State wishes to make it clear that the forces will stay in Northern Ireland as long as it is necessary. It is not, and will not be Her Majesty's Government's policy to set a date for withdrawing troops there, and there is no chance whatsoever that anyone would bomb the Army out of Northern Ireland, or their way to the conference table. The Government's policy is unchanged.

The Secretary of State had been bounced into line by his own information officers. It mattered not that the 'line' was one he had consistently held anyway. Nor did it matter particularly that his two 'clarifications' did not dissuade editors from headlining the non-existent change of line. What mattered was that the minister had been exposed, in the eyes of the people running his intelligence services and psychological warfare officers, as a potential traitor, and had been brought to heel for it.

The unfortunate Mason was never allowed to forget his 'withdrawal' speech. He never referred again to the pressures for withdrawal, though they continued to mount. He proved himself so loyal to his military officers that they eventually successfully backed him as Merlyn Rees's successor as Secretary of State for Northern Ireland. But he remained for ever, in their eyes, a closet withdrawer.

The same was true of the Secretary of State for Northern Ireland, Merlyn Rees. On taking office, Rees reiterated his faith in a British Northern Ireland and refused even to countenance whatever pressures there might be for British withdrawal from the Six Counties.

On 10 May, however, in conditions of great unrest in Northern Ireland, a letter was leaked to the press. Once more *The Times* was singled out for special favours. The letter had been written by Merlyn Rees on 19 March 1973, when he was Shadow Secretary of State for Northern Ireland. A woman had written to him from the Republic of Ireland saying she wanted the British out of the North. He replied patiently setting out his view that the British Army was not in occupation in Northern Ireland, that there was no economic or military advantage in its presence there and that the British Army's role in Ireland was not simply to satisfy the will of the British people. 'Frankly,' his letter ended, 'we have not the faintest desire to stay in Ireland and the quicker we are out the better.' If the sentence is quoted in isolation, away from paragraphs of earnest insistence that the troops must stay because it was their duty to prevent lawlessness and violence, it reads as though Merlyn Rees was for withdrawal of the troops. That interpretation, needless to say, was triumphantly paraded by the papers which used the letter, though none of them asked where it had come from.

The notion that the Labour leaders were secret supporters of a 'pull-out' from Northern Ireland was also used to split the consensus between the two major parties. On 2 June 1974, the day before a major debate on Northern Ireland, the *Observer* carried an article from the Parliamentary lobby which was headlined: TORIES FEAR THAT WILSON IS HEADING FOR A PULL-OUT. It predicted that 'Harold

Wilson's alleged personal inclination for pull-out would be the dominant preoccupation of Tory leaders in the two-day debate'.

Nothing in Harold Wilson's career had suggested a personal inclination for pull-out from Northern Ireland. Since taking office in 1974, he had on several occasions made clear that he stood unreservedly by his party's policy of keeping troops in Northern Ireland (a policy, which, incidentally, had been constitutionally laid down by the government of Ireland Act, 1948, when a Labour government was in office and when Harold Wilson, then twenty-eight, was President of the Board of Trade). Yet the 'prediction' in the *Observer* article became true. Francis Pym, the opposition spokesman on Northern Ireland, devoted a lot of his speech in the debate to rumours of a possible withdrawal. In the Labour Party, said Pym, there was an 'orchestration of the demand to bring our soldiers home'. The orchestration of the demand, however, came not from inside the Labour Party, where the Troops Out movement had negligible support, but in the Army and in Intelligence, especially in Lisburn.

Harold Wilson unwittingly played a major role in the next big offensive against his government by the information services of his own government in Northern Ireland. All through April, the violence in Northern Ireland, most of it started on the Protestant side, swelled. A grave constitutional crisis was not far away and it broke on the government in an unusual and unexpected form: a strike. The strike was called not to improve anyone's wages or conditions (such strikes are rarer in Northern Ireland than in Britain or in the Irish Republic) but in order to bring down the government. The Ulster Workers Council, a self-appointed group of shop stewards, Orange fanatics and extremist Unionist politicians, never for a moment disguised their political intentions. They intended to smash power-sharing, which was the official policy of the Conservative Party, the Labour Party, the Liberal Party, the Scottish and Welsh Nationalist Parties, and even of the Communist Party. Outside the ranks of Ian Paisley's Democratic Unionist Party there was hardly a political voice in all Europe which disapproved of the principle of power-sharing between Protestant and Catholic representatives in Northern Ireland. The Ulster Workers Council, however, believed (rightly) that they represented the majority of people in Northern Ireland; and they declared that they intended to stop all work in Northern Ireland until the power-sharing executive was dismantled.

This was a direct challenge to the British constitution and democratic government, upon which subjects Harold Wilson had so often intoned in the past, and which had brought him to high office. If the UWC strike even partially succeeded, the credibility of his administration and all other elected administrations would be called into question. If he could not defeat a gang of isolated sectarians in Northern Ireland, whom could he defeat?

The strike was called for Wednesday, 15 May. On Monday, 13 May, the Prime Minister rose in the House of Commons to make a statement about Northern Ireland. He did not mention the Protestant workers' strike. His statement was about something completely different.

The origin of his statement went back to 1969, when in the Divis Flats riot Protestant mobs in Belfast had attacked Catholic homes with familiar savagery. The police had joined in the fray with machine-guns on the side of the Protestants. Only the intervention of British troops prevented a pogrom which could well have ended in the enforced migration of a quarter of a million people.

One effect of 1969 was a rebirth of the comatose and almost entirely ineffective IRA, whose 'Provisional' section took up arms to defend the Catholic areas. Through the next three years, the leadership of the Provisionals reacted sharply to the criticism that they were not around to defend the Divis Flats when they were attacked in 1969. They felt it necessary to make plans in the event of any such attack in the future. Certainly they were convinced there was no point in relying on British troops as they had done in 1969. The troops considered themselves at war with the Provisional IRA and would, it was felt, be no more use in the event of a Protestant uprising than would the RUC or the (now disbanded) B Specials.

Accordingly, plans were made for resistance. In the event of a 1969-style attack from the Protestants, all armed Republicans would come together. Under cover of a 'scorched earth' campaign (burning cars, bombing lorries and so on) they would engineer the evacuation of the entire area under attack – perhaps 100,000 people – to the South. Part of this plan was first discussed in Long Kesh internment camp by the interned IRA leaders in 1971 and 1972.

Those plans were discovered by Intelligence officers and leaked to the press by Colin Wallace. The result was not dramatic, since a scheme to evacuate a population under attack was not specially unsympathetic. The *Daily Mirror's* Malcolm Nichol gave the plan rather short shrift in a report entitled: IRA RIVALS JOIN IN A 'DOOMSDAY' PLOT. The report made it clear that the 'Doomsday' plan was, crucially, a proposed *reaction* to a Protestant attack.

The same report appeared in other newspapers, without any sensational treatment. The word 'Doomsday', however, was universally used.

Two years later, in the week before the Ulster Workers Council strike was due to begin, the Army raided the homes of suspected IRA leaders. In one of them, documents and maps were found which referred, in rather more detail than previously, to the Doomsday plan. They were brought to Information Policy officers at Lisburn. Colin Wallace recalls it well.

'I remember being rather irritated because normally when something like this was found, we were asked for our opinion about what it meant. On this occasion, we were simply given the documents and told to prepare them for a press conference which would announce to the world that an IRA plan had been uncovered to blow up half of Belfast, including large areas occupied by ordinary people.

'I looked at the stuff and immediately recognised the Doomsday plan we had exposed two years earlier. I remember making it clear to our intelligence people that this was all old hat and that if we tried to turn what had been a *defensive* into an *offensive* plan, we could be made to look a bit foolish. The IRA had pretty good propaganda outlets too, and they were not amateurs. I warned about coming off second best in a rather silly propaganda offensive.

'I was told not to bother. It was made clear that this was not going to be an ordinary leak, or even an ordinary press conference. This wasn't going to be something which was presented to the world by the Army. I myself, for instance, wasn't going to be involved at all. A big press conference was going to be organised from Stormont. It would be a government initiative. And anyway the whole thing was going to be a back-up operation. The new Doomsday plot would be announced first in the British Parliament – by the Prime Minister.'

Colin also recalls that it was made clear that if the whole plan did backfire, it wouldn't matter too much since the man who would take the flak would be the Prime Minister. So Colin set to work to prepare those parts of the maps and documents which would reveal the IRA plan – and to take out anything in them which gave a clue to their defensive strategy.

On 13 May, Harold Wilson stunned the House of Commons with a 'dramatic revelation'.

In the last few days the Security Forces in Northern Ireland have come into possession of a number of documents . . .

These documents reveal a specific and calculated plan by the IRA by means of ruthless and indiscriminate violence to foment inter-sectarian hatred and a degree of chaos with the object of enabling the IRA to achieve a position in which it could proceed to occupy and control certain pre-designated and densely populated areas in the city of Belfast and its suburbs. The plan shows a deliberate intention to manipulate the emotions of large sections of the people by inflicting violence and hardship on them in the hope of creating a situation in which the IRA could present itself as the protector of the Catholic population.' (*House of Commons Official Report*, 13 May 1971.)

The IRA's intention, Wilson went on, 'would have been to carry out a scorched earth policy of burning the houses of ordinary people as it was compelled to withdraw . . . An apparent IRA operation,' the Prime Minister concluded, 'of potentially great danger has been brought to light.'

The documents proving all this would be published, he said, though only selectively.

The statement was greeted with a chorus of 'Hear Hears' around the House, especially from the Conservatives, who were delighted with the Prime Minister and said so. Edward Heath, leader of the Tory Party, and Captain Orr, spokesman for the Ulster Unionists, went out of their way to congratulate Wilson on his statement. In reply to Heath, Harold Wilson anticipated a possible objection:

> There will be an attempt to misrepresent this information – which is a genuine find by the security authorities – but I can assure the House that these documents are genuine and not even put forward by the IRA themselves for any other purpose except that which it had in mind to pursue. (*ibid.*)

That afternoon, at Stormont Castle, senior officers provided a press conference with the documents which had indeed come from a 'genuine find' by the security services. The documents were, however, as Wilson himself had warned, selective. They showed areas which would be occupied, buildings which would be burned and so on. They did not disclose the circumstances in which these plans would be put into effect.

The documents were confirmed the following day by an impeccable source – the Provisional IRA. They agreed at once that the documents were genuine; but said they were part of the plan drawn up in 1972 in the event of a Protestant attack on the Catholic areas such as the attempted pogrom in 1969. The IRA tried to persuade the more serious journalists in Belfast that the plan was old, the documents irrelevant and the importance given to it by the Prime Minister ridiculous.

They had some success at least with Robert Fisk of *The Times*. After reporting the statement of the IRA, Fisk added his own interpretation. 'There seems to be some evidence,' he wrote, 'that the plans were drawn up at least a year ago.' Fisk came at once to the crucial point:

> If, as Mr Wilson has said, they represented a campaign that was about to be put into action, then the Provisionals, who have always claimed to be non-sectarian, emerge as an organisation of awe-inspiring cynicism.
>   If the idea was to put such a campaign into action only in circumstances where an Armageddon situation already existed, then the IRA has only acted as many other extremist organisations have done in Northern Ireland. Loyalist groups have boasted in the past that they too have 'Doomsday' plans to be used if they thought Ulster was being pushed into a United Ireland. (14 May 1974.)

The line between a 'scorched earth campaign' *in defence* against sectarian attack and a similar plan as an *offensive* was absolutely crucial. But it was easily glossed over by withholding some documents and altering others. Even in the documents released, however, there is a clue which points to the defensive nature of the plans. The IRA's declaration accompanying the plans included the statement: 'In the emergency which has been forced upon us, the IRA has had no alternative but to employ its full resources to the defence of its people, in the face of the armed offensive against the Catholic working class.' (IRA declaration, *The Times*, 14 May 1974.)

If there had been no 'armed offensive against the Catholic working class', how could such a statement have been issued? And did not the sentence suggest that the plan and the declaration had been drawn up specifically to reply to such an armed offensive? If such was the case, as Colin Wallace insists it was, then the new documents had no significance whatever. They were merely proof that the Doomsday plan discovered in 1972 had been genuine (and had almost certainly been scrapped when the Official IRA, which was then still influential, had refused either to approve it or to pledge to take part in it).

Most journalists, however, were only too happy to take the Doomsday plot at face value, especially when it was so forcefully exposed in Parliament by the Prime Minister. If the documents had been tampered with, if the disclosures were not complete – why should anyone worry when they had so comprehensively convinced the Prime Minister?

People's political memories are notoriously short and no one at the time publicly recalled that Harold Wilson was peculiarly susceptible to 'plot stories' foisted on him by Intelligence. In 1966, he 'revealed' to the House of Commons the 'full story' of the communist plot which, he alleged, was responsible for the seamen's strike of that year. Without a moment's hesitation or embarrassment he told MPs about the meetings which had taken place in the homes of Communist Party members, in which the strike had been discussed. He knew of these meetings, of course, through buggings and telephone tappings by the security services. The meetings themselves were not remotely extraordinary. It would have been surprising if Communist Party officials had not met friends and fellow-travellers who were taking part in the seamen's strike. But the political conclusion to be drawn from such meetings – that the strike was all the fault of communists and would not have continued were it not for communist influence – was entirely fanciful. Indeed, the strike persisted long after Harold Wilson's exposé of the 'tightly-knit group of politically motivated men' who had caused it. The distorted information provided by the security services had been accepted by the Prime Minister together with the political conclusions which allegedly flowed from it. Exactly the same thing happened with the 'Doomsday plan'.

With the honourable exception of Robert Fisk, national newspapers and television reporters accepted the Wilson story hungrily. Huge headlines in the press the next day fulminated about the IRA plot to end civilisation as we know it. Only a few reporters mused, as Fisk did, on the likelihood of a small volunteer army of perhaps two hundred men and women putting a whole city to the sword.

The effect of the unanimous shock/horror approach to the plot was not only to antagonise the British public to the IRA. The IRA was already unimaginably unpopular – almost as unpopular as an enemy in time of war. The chief effect of the Doomsday plan publicity was to fix the minds of the public on planned atrocities by the IRA at just the time when Loyalist extremists were embarking on an act of sectarian rebellion against the British government. The day after Wilson's House of Commons statement, when the papers and television were full of the Doomsday plot, the newly-constituted Ulster Workers Council called its general strike throughout the Six Counties.

The strike was perhaps the most successful major industrial action in the history of the British Isles. It lasted barely two weeks. The one and only demand of the strikers, the end of power-sharing, was unconditionally conceded. By the time the House of Commons debated the new situation in Northern Ireland on 3 June (two and a half weeks after the strike began), the power-sharing Executive had collapsed. The Prime Minister of Northern Ireland, Brian Faulkner, had resigned and all his ministers with him. The entire constitutional reform, established with so much hope and effort at Sunningdale the previous autumn, had disintegrated. The British government remained in 'direct rule' over Northern Ireland, but the undisputed victor was the Orange supremacy.

The official view of this extraordinary episode was recounted some years later by the Secretary of State at the time, Merlyn Rees, in his book *Northern Ireland: A Personal Perspective*. 'We were in fact,' he wrote, 'beaten technically on all aspects of the strike.' (*Op. cit.*, p. 69.)

It was claimed by Rees, echoed by the Prime Minister and endorsed by the Conservative opposition and the Ulster Unionists that the strike in Northern Ireland had been so unanimous and so successful that no government could have withstood it. In particular, it was said, the problems of the supply of power became insurmountable. The Army could guarantee internal security, but they could not maintain the power supply. For that technical reason alone, the strike was bound to triumph.

There was, however, substantial evidence to suggest otherwise. The power stations – and there were not many of them – could easily have been kept running by a combination of Army technicians and, if necessary, technicians from the British CEGB flown in and protected by the Army. Even a moderate military campaign would have ensured that the power stations stayed open through the summer (and the summer was just starting: the UWC strike took place at the worst time of year for the strikers). There is also some evidence that at the start of the strike the Protestant people of Northern Ireland were split.

A vote in the Harland and Wolff shipyard, for instance, then as now entirely dominated by Protestants, turned (narrowly) against a general strike. The evidence was that if the government and the Army had set themselves, from the outset, resolutely to break the strike, they could have done so; and the Executive would have remained in office.

The Army was equivocal from the start. In his excellent account of the strike (which was detested by the government and the Army), *Point of No Return* (London, André Deutsch, 1975), Robert Fisk again and again drew attention to the Army's lack of purpose in breaking the strike.

> Military advisers at Lisburn had told some of the more senior Press Officers at Thiepval Barracks, Lisburn, that the Army was unhappy about the adoption of a strike-breaking role, and this view was passed on, in confidential conversations, to newspapermen covering the strike.   (p. 87.)

The 'unhappiness' spilled over into the Ministry of Defence. Fisk quoted the government's own Civil Service record for Saturday, 18 May:

> During the late evening, strong pressure had to be brought to bear on Ministry of Defence officials to hasten the arrangements for lifting troops to Northern Ireland.   (*ibid.*, pp. 87–8.)

As he drove around strike-bound Belfast, Fisk noticed again and again how the Protestant barricades were tolerated by the Army; and how troops refused to intervene to free the streets of the strikers' influence. 'When confrontations seemed almost inevitable, it was the Army who withdrew,' he concluded.   (*ibid.*, p. 93.)

Later he noticed a soldier and a member of the UVF (Ulster Volunteer Force – the most violently sectarian of all the Protestant extremist groups) side by side, pointing down the street with their rifles, 'UVF and Army together'.

> The loss of public confidence in the authorities during the second week of the strike had much to do with scenes such as this. It was the logical and inevitable result of a military and police policy that took no account of the political aims of the strike and which opted for expediency rather than confrontation on the streets . . . Would the UWC have sanctioned a war with the Army? It seems doubtful.   (*ibid.*, p. 156.)

Fisk records how the Prime Minister himself was shaken by this approach and changed his attitude to the strike. On the evening of Saturday, 25 May, he had made arrangements to broadcast to the nation on the serious emergency caused by the UWC strike. His mood, as he wrote the speech with the help of his adviser, Bernard Donoughue, was still defiant. He had a deep hatred of extreme Orangemen and was furious that the decisions of elected governments should be flouted. In the first draft of his speech, he referred to a 'rebellion against the Crown'; a rebellion, he went on to imply, which would be met with the firmest possible resolve by the government and its troops. This was the mood he had shown at a meeting at Chequers a day or two previously, in which he had reassured Brian Faulkner, the beleaguered Northern Ireland Prime Minister, that troops would be used on the ground and in the power stations to help break the strike. Fisk's account continues:

> But between twelve and two o'clock Wilson changed his mind about the statement. In those two hours, he took a sudden and final decision, sharply reversing the mood and content of his speech and abandoning the Executive to their fate. (*ibid.*, p. 197.)

All references to 'rebellion' were cut out. Robert Fisk had no doubt as to the cause of this volte-face:

> It was the Army's influence, the military expression of military influence, that caused Wilson to place a new interpretation upon his promise to the Executive of action against the UWC. . . (*ibid.*, p. 198.)

That conclusion was inescapable. If the Army and their ministry were reluctant to intervene against the strike, what hope had the government, armed with mere words, of victory! This was not the first time that the Army's refusal to intervene against rebellious Protestants in Northern Ireland had shaken a government. In 1913, as a Liberal government ordered its troops to intervene in the North of Ireland to break up illegal Protestant armies increasingly armed by illegal gun-runners, it was openly defied. Sixty-five Army officers stationed at Curragh wrote an open letter to the War Department demanding that they should not be ordered to take up arms against their countrymen and co-religionists in Belfast. The Liberal Secretary of State for War meekly complied with their demand. Though he was countermanded by the Prime Minister, Asquith, and sacked, the Curragh mutineers, as they were called, were not disciplined. Instead, the military operation was called off. The Protestant mutiny triumphed.

The historical comparison, however, ends at the show of defiance. In every other respect the performance of Harold Wilson, Merlyn Rees and their government over the Ulster Workers Council strike was immeasurably more abject and craven than was Asquith's and the Liberals' in 1913. In 1913, the Protestants of Northern Ireland could rely on vast and vocal support in Britain. Edward Carson and Andrew Bonar Law had spoken at enormous rallies under the slogan: 'Ulster Will Fight and Ulster Will Be Right'. 'There are things more powerful than Parliamentary majorities,' Bonar Law had told one huge meeting at Blenheim Palace. On behalf of the law-abiding Tory Party, he made it clear that he would break any law to uphold the right of Ulster Protestants to take up arms against their elected government.

No such circumstances obtained in 1974. There was very little support on the mainland for the striking Protestants. To most British people the Protestant extremists were indistinguishable from the IRA. The Conservative Party did not associate itself with the strike. On the contrary. Conservative politicians such as Heath, Whitelaw and Pym had set up the power-sharing which the strike aimed to smash. In 1913, the Curragh mutineers could expect overwhelming support from Conservatives, businessmen and landlords in Britain. The mutineers of 1974 could expect nothing of the kind.

The Ulster Workers Council triumph, however, was not entirely due to the British Army. The Army's attitude was one of hesitant abstention rather than open defiance. Organised defiance indeed came not so much from the Army, but from the increasingly powerful political forces inside MI5 and their colleagues in Army Intelligence and Information Policy.

Thirteen years after the strike, on 22 March 1987, the *Sunday Times* published a story on its front page entitled: 'MI5 "plotted" Ulster strikes'. Its author, Barrie Penrose, had been working for some weeks with Colin Wallace, and an article about Wallace and his background had led to a phone call from a James Miller, who described himself as a former MI5 agent.

Miller was an Englishman, born in 1932, who had married an Ulster Protestant and gone to live in Monkstown, County Antrim. He told Penrose he had been recruited by Army Intelligence in 1970 soon after the 'troubles' started. His job was to infiltrate extremist Protestant organisations, especially the UDA. He was quoted by Penrose as follows:

> I did a dangerous job over there for nearly five years and many UDA and IRA men went to prison as a result. But I could never understand why my case officers, Lt Col Brian X and George X, wanted the UDA to start a strike in the first place. But they specifically said I should get UDA men at grass-roots level to 'start pushing' for a strike. So I did.

Barrie Penrose went on to claim: 'Home Office officials working with MI5's legal adviser confirmed that Miller worked for the Northern Ireland security services.' He also reported that the Secretary of the D-Notices Committee, which vets newspapers for likely breaches of security, had asked the *Sunday Times* not to disclose Miller's whereabouts in Britain or the full identity of his case officers.

Miller's claims, according to Barrie Penrose, went even further:

> Miller said his MI5 case officers told him Harold Wilson was a suspected Soviet agent and steps were taken to force him out of Downing Street. Miller

said that in early 1974 his case officers instructed him to promote the idea within the UDA of mounting a general strike which would paralyse Northern Ireland.

None of these remarkable allegations was denied. Miller, who had told Penrose he was anxious to give his evidence to Merlyn Rees, the former Secretary of State, suddenly went quiet and did not continue with his allegations.

Colin Wallace recalls the great surge of confidence and enthusiasm when the Ulster Workers Council strike was won. 'Everyone seemed very pleased that the government had been forced to grovel,' he says. But military and civilian intelligence officers were worried that the staggering success of the strike had unified Protestant paramilitaries and provided them with a power base which could prove dangerous. 'We'd created a potential monster,' Colin says, 'and MI5 now felt that the extremist Protestants must be kept in check.'

In June 1974, as the dust settled after the strike, the security services hit out at the Protestants. They raided Orange Halls throughout the Province and found several arms caches. In the caretaker's house next to the West Belfast Orange Hall, for instance, they found fourteen pistols, eighteen rifles and shotguns, four home-made mortars, six smoke grenades and five thousand rounds of ammunition. Seven Orange Halls were raided, almost all of them leading to substantial arms finds.

MI5 set out to establish that the Orange extremists had been infiltrated by communists and left-wing revolutionaries. At Lisburn, Information Policy forged a leaflet entitled 'Workers Unite', illustrated with a photograph of a Kalashnikov rifle and followed by a few choice words calling on the Ulster people to free themselves from capitalist tyranny. The final slogan was appropriate: FREE THE PEOPLE.

This forgery convinced the correspondent in Belfast of the *Daily Telegraph*, 'the paper you can trust'. Kenneth Clarke wrote in the issue of 15 June 1974:

> The Orange Hall searches also yielded some evidence to support a feeling among the security forces that an unlikely alliance is being forged between Protestant and Catholic working-class groups. One poster, depicting a hand clutching a Russian-made rifle states: 'Protestant and Catholic working people have the same common enemy: the Imperialist ruling class. Every blow struck against the capitalist state machine is a blow for a free and independent Ulster. Workers Unite.'

As the summer of 1974 wore on, two projects in particular caused Colin Wallace to reflect on what he was being asked to do. Both involved Northern Ireland politicians: John Hume, the prominent young Social and Democratic Labour Party leader from Derry; and Ian Paisley, the tub-thumping leader of the Protestant Democratic Unionist Party. The two men were on opposite sides of the political fence, but both were seen as enemies by the 'ultras' in Intelligence. Their chief crime was support for the Labour government. John Hume was a social democrat and a natural Labour Party supporter. Paisley's role was more complicated. He and his followers in the newly-formed Democratic Unionist Party were conservatives of the most extreme kind. But their party was not the poodle of the British Conservative Party as the old Unionist Party in the North of Ireland had traditionally been. The Democratic Unionists were renegades, prepared to vote for anyone who, in their view, might help their extremist cause. In 1974, in particular, when the Labour government was in a minority, Paisley and his colleagues were not averse to some tacit support for the Labour government.

This breach of loyalty to the Tories by the more extreme Ulster Protestant politicians infuriated the reactionaries in Intelligence. Colin Wallace was asked by the MI5 officer with whom he worked on Clockwork Orange, whom he knew by the pseudonym 'John Shaw', to produce an analysis of the likely consequences of the assassination of Ian Paisley. Several different situations in which this assassination might be planned were outlined, including a souped-up feud between rival Protestant factions quarrelling over the proceeds of Shankhill shebeens or blackmailing each other over a homosexual vice ring. As part of this exercise Colin received a forged bank account, in Paisley's name, indicating substantial purchases of shares in two companies in Canada. Colin kept a copy of this forgery. It was published in the *Sunday Times* in 1987, and featured in a debate on the Thames Television programme, *This Week*. In the programme the Rev. Paisley denounced the forgery. He said it fitted precisely with all sorts of leaks and innuendoes which were made against him in 1974.

Colin also recalls (though he cannot find it in his papers) a forged bank account in the name of John Hume, which showed him receiving substantial sums from dubious charities in North America. John Hume, too, was obliged to deny allegations based on this wholly false document.

The forged bank account was a device which had been used elsewhere in equally mysterious circumstances. In July 1974, newspapers of all kinds (including *Socialist Worker*, where I was editor) and some MPs received copies of a bank account in Switzerland in the name of Edward Short, who was then Deputy Leader of the Labour Party. The account showed him having received several thousand pounds from a mysterious source. Mr Short had been named during the financial scandal involving the corrupt Yorkshire architect John Poulson. Poulson's web of corruption had spread to the north-east, where his chief henchman was T. Dan Smith, the Labour leader of Newcastle City Council. In the Poulson bankruptcy hearings, Short, who represented a Newcastle constituency, was shown to have received £250 from T. Dan Smith for assisting one of his projects. To journalists who had probed the Poulson affair, as I had done, Short's 'Swiss bank account' seemed genuine. Ted Short angrily denounced it, but the smear was left all over him until a police report many months later confirmed that the bank account did not exist, and the document was a forgery. No one has ever found out who the forgers were, or brought them to justice.

The use of public documents to smear Labour politicians was not new. A year earlier, in 1973, another document was circulated with the assistance of a clerk at Scotland Yard. This looked like an official letter to the Director of Public Prosecutions from the police recommending prosecution of eight named Labour MPs for their corrupt activities over the Poulson scandal. The eight names were highly credible to those versed in the Poulson story. The document (though not the names) got wide publicity in press and television.

In the summer of 1974, the Scotland Yard clerk who had helped to forge the document was exposed. No one (except *Socialist Worker*) took the story up. The man retired from Scotland Yard and eventually became a councillor in Sussex. He was not prosecuted, nor did anyone ever reveal whether (as seems likely) he had close connections with (and was protected by) MI5.

Such were the documents which were circulating in that extraordinary period. Their object was to discredit any politicians who supported the minority Labour government, especially in Ireland.

The chief victims of the smear campaign in Northern Ireland were the Secretary of State, Merlyn Rees, and his Minister of State, Stan Orme.

Throughout his first few months in office Rees was plagued by leaks. These leaks were especially destructive of any initiative he took to lower the tension between the British government and the Catholic community. Through the early summer of 1974, for instance, he worked to set up an 'auxiliary police force' in Catholic areas. Citizens would be recruited as special constables on an unpaid, voluntary basis, and would have police powers. The auxiliary police force was designed to restore some semblance of respect for law and order in those areas where the Royal Ulster Constabulary was regarded, with every justification, as a sectarian force, defending only Protestant laws and Protestant order. The plans were to be announced at a special press conference in late July. Its success depended on catching the parties by surprise. If the case for the new police force could be put as persuasively as possible before the Royal Ulster Constabulary or the Protestant 'loony right' was able to get into the television studios, they would get a head start.

Imagine Rees's consternation, therefore, when the full plans were laid out on 23 July, on the morning before his proposed Press conference, in *The Times* under a big heading: 'Government Considers Volunteer Community Police Force for Hard-line Areas in N. Ireland'. The whole initiative was spiked. The auxiliary force never emerged. Merlyn Rees admitted to me several years later: 'Oh, there's no doubt the leak torpedoed the plan.' (*Daily Mirror*, 9 April 1987.) But no one ever found out where the leak came from – until Colin Wallace confirmed that the source was Information Policy.

Merlyn Rees himself is the best witness to the way in which his conduct of the Northern Ireland Office was constantly sabotaged by the Army Information Service. In the middle of the Ulster Workers Council strike, for instance, he decided on a secret visit by aeroplane to the Prime Minister who was holidaying in the Scilly Islands. He wrote in his book, *Northern Ireland: A Personal Perspective*:

> I felt it important for my journey not to be publicised and asked Frank King [Commander-in-Chief of Northern Ireland forces] to accompany me in my helicopter as far as Aldergrove so that it would look at the [Stormont] Castle as if I was going back with him to Lisburn. However, when I arrived at Culdrose (Cornwall), after a nostalgic flight over the valleys of South Wales where I was nurtured, it was to find that my trip had already been announced on BBC News. Was the leak from prying eyes at the Castle or from Aldergrove? Or was it from other sources? (*Op. cit.*, p. 81.)

The leaks about rows within the Army during the strike, wrote Rees,

> came from Lisburn, from those in the Army Information Service with press contacts, and not from the Army staff who knew the facts. At a Cabinet meeting in London a few days after the strike ended, Denis Healey for one was very angry at the leaks and their source. As a former Secretary of State [for Defence] he knew what he was talking about. (*ibid.*, p. 84.)

It was to try to stop these leaks and restore some semblance of responsibility and loyalty to the government in the Army Information Service that Michael Cudlipp, a former Fleet Street journalist, was appointed to take charge of Northern Ireland information services on 25 July (two days after the leak to *The Times* about the auxiliary police). But Cudlipp could do little to stop it.

In October 1975, writing in the Irish paper *Hibernia*, Robert Fisk reflected on the previous two or three years of information policy and news management. He concluded:

> Rees's men have found that far from smothering the Army's dissatisfaction, they have only driven it underground. Instead of the Press officer's unhappy briefing they now have to cope with the embarrassing leak. They have to face the reality that there are a number of fairly senior soldiers who want to destroy

Merlyn Rees's political integrity. These soldiers want Mr Rees to go . . . this
must be the first time in history that British Army officers, however few in
number, have distrusted a British Minister more than have the IRA.

By early September 1974, almost all the information which came to
Colin Wallace concentrated not on terrorists, but on politicians. A lot of
the information, which was uncheckable, was gossip about the personal
lives and sex habits of prominent politicians. Wallace's instructions were
to circulate as far as possible rumours about the alleged homosexual
inclinations of Northern Ireland ministers and politicians. He noticed,
to his surprise, that the politicians he was being asked to smear were
not only, nor even mostly, in the Labour Party. Edward Heath, leader
of the Conservative Party, was high on this list. So was William Van
Straubenzee, Heath's Minister of State in Northern Ireland until March
1974. The telltale ticks in the column 'moral' on his Clockwork Orange
'Vulnerabilities' table meant that the 'ticked' politicians could expect to
be rung up by the most unlikely journalists with the most unlikely charges.
In other cases, the rumours were simply floated, without being put to the
minister. It was just 'made known for future reference' that so-and-so
had done such-and-such and was therefore not to be trusted, a target for
possible blackmail.

These instructions, which rose to a crescendo as Parliament was
prorogued in September and another election called for October 1974,
caused Colin Wallace to take stock of his position.

Throughout that turbulent year, the situation in Northern Ireland had
steadily deteriorated. Colin noticed that in 1974, as in every other year,
there were more assassinations of Catholics by Protestants than vice versa,
and for the first time began to worry about the close connections between
the intelligence services and the extremist Protestant organisations. He
learnt for the first time in September, for instance, that the explosives
used to kill nineteen people in the indiscriminate bombing of a main
Dublin street during the UWC strike might have been supplied by British
Intelligence. He suspected too that some personal assassinations carried
out by the UDA or the UVF had been inspired by British Intelligence.
He was concerned in case the huge increase in assassinations in November
had been planned to coincide with the secret ceasefire talks between the
government and the paramilitaries of both sides.

The killings had penetrated the officers' mess at Lisburn. Bernard
Calladine, a close friend of Colin's, was called away from the bar where
he and Colin were drinking to deal with an unexploded bomb. He never
returned. A keen young explosives officer David Stewardson arrived in
Northern Ireland. Colin met him and his young wife at Lisburn. He
escorted them round the barracks and reassured the wife that her husband
was safe in his new job. The wife flew back home. The next morning,

Stewardson went out to handle a mysterious package dumped outside a church hall. Colin followed him to take photographs. As his car climbed the hill to the hall, Colin heard the bomb go off. When he got there, the young officer had been blown to pieces.

'I wondered about how badly we were doing,' Colin says now. 'We didn't seem to be getting anywhere. I'd come into this business to fight terrorism, but terrorism was on the increase and, in some respects, we seemed to be helping it along. My own friends and colleagues were being killed. We should have been concentrating all our efforts on sniffing out the terrorists and making life difficult for them. But we weren't. We were told more and more about these politicians, what they felt about communism, what shares they'd got in Canada, even what they did in bed. The situation was getting very serious by the middle of 1974 and I felt I'd had enough. I was genuinely anxious to get back to the basic business of fighting terrorism and I decided that Clockwork Orange didn't have much to do with that any more.

'One afternoon early in October I saw "John Shaw" from MI5. I sat having a quiet drink with him at the White Gables Hotel, near Hillsborough. At one stage, I told him I didn't want to go any further with Clockwork Orange without political clearance. He seemed surprised and suggested that I already had clearance. But I made it clear I wanted some proof that the whole programme had been seen and approved by a minister.

'Of course I was pretty certain that "Shaw" couldn't get ministerial clearance for Clockwork Orange. I was pretty sure that no minister had a clue that Clockwork Orange even existed. But I knew I couldn't go on doing it, and I wanted to get on with other things.'

'John Shaw', Colin recalls, appeared to be sympathetic. He agreed to put Colin's proposal to his superiors. On 16 October, Colin was summoned to Stormont Castle and offered a job in the government's information office. He turned it down. He wanted to be with the Army, of the Army. Indeed his main reason for wanting to stop working on Clockwork Orange was that it was too political. At the end of October, he handed back to 'John Shaw' the voluminous files of information he had compiled under the code-name Clockwork Orange. He kept only his own handwritten notes.

He never saw 'Shaw' again. In some relief he went back to his more formal duties in the information office. He did not know how seriously his refusal over Clockwork Orange would affect his future. Indeed, he had little time to reflect on it. For before a few days had passed he was writing a memorandum to complain about an even more serious matter. It concerned a Belfast boys' home with a fine old Irish name: Kincora.

CHAPTER THREE

Kincora

Divided and warped societies like Northern Ireland breed more than their fair share of divided and warped personalities. A peculiar example of that is William McGrath, the central character in the Kincora Boys' Home scandal. McGrath was a typical product of the fanaticism which has sustained the Protestant supremacy in the North of Ireland ever since it was planted there in the sixteenth century. He had little or no natural ability, save a certain slick gift of the gab, and a pedantic acquaintance with obscure religious texts. In the 1950s and early 1960s he was full-time secretary of the Christian Fellowship Centre and Emancipation Crusade, which was based at Faith House, Finaghy, South Belfast. There he would preside over meetings of young men, whom he recruited by speaking at Orange Lodges and Missions throughout Northern Ireland. The young men were attracted by the extremism of his views, and especially by the mystique and the secrecy with which McGrath built up his political organisation. His followers made up for their small numbers by the extreme levels of dedication which McGrath always demanded of them (though never of himself).

Politics in Northern Ireland in the 1950s were deceptively becalmed. The 'Protestant state for a Protestant people' which had been proclaimed in 1922 appeared to be working without too much fuss. The minority (Catholic) population, though they hated the state, did not express their hatred in violence. The IRA campaign of 1956 to 1961 was a disaster. The Protestant power complex, which was founded on the Orange Lodges, was getting older and more complacent. Nothing, it seemed, could loosen their grip.

William McGrath challenged this complacency. In his sermons, which were illustrated by slides of Roman Catholics carrying out weird and fanatical activities, he denounced the traditional notion that the Protestant case rested on a separate state in the North, which was bound to Britain. McGrath insisted that Protestant power must have an Irish dimension. He was not afraid or ashamed to describe himself as Irish. He argued that the 'British statelet' was a distortion of Protestant theory. All Ireland, he insisted, should be Protestant, and one day would be.

He backed up this view with the theory that the 'lost tribes of Israel' had come to settle in the British Isles, and that the 'chosen people' therefore had been in Ireland long before the Catholics. The Protestants were not 'planted', he argued, but had been there all along, as part of a plan laid down by the Almighty. To the meetings of young men in his home in the 1950s and 1960s, McGrath would introduce members of the British Israelite Society from England and Scotland – people with views even more bizarre than his own. The difference was that while the British Israelites held their views in the privacy of their homes without upsetting or bothering anyone else, McGrath's ideas, among introspective superstitions of Northern Ireland politics, struck a chord.

McGrath denounced the pussyfooting of the Ulster Unionist Party and the Protestant churches on the Roman Catholic question. The only answer, he claimed, was to smash the Catholic Church and all its manifestations. Catholic schools should, in his view, be abolished. He emphatically rejected the idea that Catholics were entitled to civil and religious liberty. If Protestants were the Sons of God, Catholics were the Sons of Satan, and had to be treated as such. It was, in his view, nothing but collaboration with the forces of evil to allow Catholics to worship anywhere in Ireland; and the continual collaboration with Catholics was sapping the lifeblood of the Protestant religion and its state in Northern Ireland. Those who agreed with him should bind themselves together in a tightly-knit conspiratorial group committed to pushing the Protestants towards their true heritage. Any means towards that end were justified.

McGrath preached a text from Oliver Cromwell: 'Trust in God and Keep Your Powder Dry'. His admiration for Cromwell began and ended with the Protector's 'final solution' to the Catholic problem. He did not agree with Cromwell's views about kings and queens. He believed the monarch of the British Isles was the symbol through which God should finally rule over the whole earth, and he supported Queen Victoria's statement (often inscribed on Orange banners) that the Bible was 'the secret of England's greatness'. He thought that the Protestant message should be carried to the people 'with a Bible in one hand and a gun in the other'.

His ambition was to form a secret society which would have the nerve and the weapons to seize power in the Armageddon which he was sure was coming. In 1965, the embryo of such an organisation was formed by a Church of Ireland minister. It called itself 'The Cell'. McGrath and his gang joined up at once, but McGrath was appalled when he heard the chairman say out loud, in public, that the Catholic Church was Christian. There was only one remedy for that kind of revisionism. McGrath decided that a new organisation should be formed of which there would be only one (unchosen) leader: himself. Thus in the autumn of 1966 he formed TARA, a name taken not from any British connection but from the seat of ancient Irish kings.

Despite, or because of, these views and the fanatical way in which they were applied in practice, McGrath's influence on the Orange Order increased sharply in the late 1960s. It was true – though not for the reasons McGrath gave – that the old Protestant Order was losing its relevance and its bite. The Orange Order was run by elderly men who had stopped thinking many years earlier. McGrath could fashion a good phrase. He wrote, and published, his own Irish hymn book. He specialised in sermons, and Acts of Dedication which were read out at Orange ceremonies. A measure of his influence was that in 1966 his Acts of Dedication was read out at two of the main Belfast Orange Lodges at their Boyne Anniversary Service, the main Orange service of the year. His ideas, with their challenge to the old Order, appealed to many intelligent young Protestants, who joined him.

A young man from the Shankhill, Roy Garland, first heard McGrath speak in a mission hall in Belfast in 1955, and was immediately converted. Garland stayed with McGrath for sixteen years. He became second-in-command of TARA. In three remarkable articles in the *Irish Times* many years later (13, 14 and 15 April 1982) he described the monthly meetings of TARA, which he called to order before the grand appearance of the Commanding Officer, William McGrath. He revealed the discussions about links with South Africa, the right-wing International Council of Churches and extremist Protestant sects, notably in Holland. He exposed the military organisation of TARA, founded on 'sergeants', platoons, and a steady supply of weapons. 'For the most part,' he explained, 'the objective was to be prepared and wait for the appropriate moment when, if the right political leadership existed, TARA could be offered to the security services to work alongside them.'

TARA was taken very seriously by the rising extremist Protestant politicians of the time. In 1966, for instance, the Rev. Ian Paisley, who was also protesting about the complacency of the Orange old guard, organised a demonstration to protest against the celebrations of the fiftieth anniversary of the Easter Rising in Dublin. He asked McGrath to provide the banners for the demonstration, and McGrath readily agreed. The banners proclaimed his own peculiar beliefs: 'FOR GOD AND IRELAND' and (most curiously) 'BY RIGHT OF CALVARY IRELAND BELONGS TO CHRIST'. The banners were a great success, and Paisley moved closer to McGrath. In September 1966, McGrath and Garland went to see Paisley at his church. In his most conspiratorial tones, McGrath warned the politician that he was being linked with the paramilitary Ulster Volunteer Force. He duly produced a number of posters and leaflets dissociating Paisley from the UVF, which TARA posted up and distributed around East Belfast.

When the 'troubles' burst on Belfast in August 1969, McGrath and Paisley joined forces once more to lobby the Prime Minister (James Chichester Clark) for the formation of an official 'People's Militia', a new Protestant army, financed by government. When the Prime Minister demurred, Paisley went ahead with his own plans for a militia and asked various colleagues to enlist men. The most enthusiastic response came from William McGrath.

In these hectic days, McGrath's fanaticism attracted more and more people. TARA met as a paramilitary organisation though it used a respectable name – the Orange Order Discussion Group – for its regular meetings in an Orange Hall. In the summer of 1970, McGrath achieved his ambition of forming a new Irish Orange Lodge. It was based on his view that Protestants could only win if they insisted on their Irishness. On 28 June 1970, Ireland's Heritage Orange Lodge was formed. The Grand Master of the Orange Order, the Rev. John Bryans, who was also a British Israelite, and the future Grand Master of the Orange Order and Member of Parliament, the Rev. Martin Smyth, helped to inaugurate the lodge. A hymn – 'Let me carry your cross for Ireland, Lord' – was chosen from McGrath's own hymn book. Roy Garland pointed out some years later: 'The song had been written by Thomas Ashe, an IRA hunger striker who died in a Dublin jail in 1917.'

Contradiction was the theme of William McGrath's life and works. He supported the British connection, but he wanted a united Ireland. He was against violence, but his members stockpiled weapons. He exposed secret Catholic conspiracies by means of a most secretive conspiracy. Money, he had told the youthful Roy Garland, was an insult to the Lord, and he persuaded Garland, rather against his will, to build up his family bleaching business so that the Lord's work (and McGrath's personal expenses) could be paid for.

McGrath himself left his full-time job at Faith House, Finaghy. For a time he tried to run a business in furniture and carpets. Garland lent him money for this as well. When he mentioned to McGrath, much later on, that he would like to be repaid, McGrath flew into a temper accusing him of consorting with the anti-Christ. Garland was eventually obliged to sue – successfully – for £1,300. Money was always a problem for William McGrath, and it was usually solved for him by one or other of his disciples.

McGrath's attitudes to sex were contradictory as well: rigid in principle, flexible in practice. The principle was plain. In the TARA declaration of 12 April 1973, he wrote: 'Every home, office, factory should be bright and shining, showing the world that Protestantism stands for, at least, cleanliness and order and industrious living.' As for practice, Roy Garland gave a graphic description of his first meeting with McGrath at Faith House, on a dark cold November evening:

> He said that his fellowship at Faith House was following the ancient Celtic tradition of a kind of monastic set-up. Most of the men at Faith House had

outside jobs and pooled their wages to be used for the salvation of Ireland. One problem was that men tended to leave after being married.

At one point in the discussion he touched my leg and asked me what this meant to me. I was shocked and replied that it meant nothing. He touched me again and I responded similarly. Possibly realising my shock he stated that I must never permit anyone to touch me . . . He went on to talk about the very high standards which were required of young people in relation to sex.

While he condemned homosexual relationships, he told me that a balanced individual must have a close relationship with a member of his own sex. He said that David and Jonathan, Jesus and John the beloved disciple had close friendships which had a physical side to them. He quoted the verse of a hymn: 'Touched by a loving hand, wakened by kindness, chords that were broken will vibrate once more.'   (*Irish Times*, 15 April 1982.)

McGrath went on talking to Garland about sex during the entire period that the two men knew each other. Though he failed to seduce his lieutenant, he never stopped trying. Garland's refusal to co-operate, McGrath explained, was due to an 'emotional block'.

Roy Garland later discovered that McGrath tried the same line, often with more success, with almost every other young recruit to TARA. 'I felt he was using sex to brainwash them with his political ideas,' wrote Garland. The truth, more probably, was the other way round.

TARA's members continued to occupy high places in Protestant politics. By the early 1970s, its administration officer was deputy editor of the *Protestant Telegraph*. Its second-in-command (who replaced Roy Garland) held high office in the Ulster Unionist United Council.

McGrath's business affairs, however, were a disaster. His carpets and furniture business collapsed and in 1971 he found himself without regular income. In the late autumn of that year, he got a job in a boys' home in the Newtownards Road, East Belfast. The home was called Kincora. It is hard to discover when it got that name, or how. Like TARA, Kincora is a name associated with the old Irish kings, and is part of the folklore which McGrath and TARA peddled.

TARA had close contacts in the Northern Ireland Eastern Health and Social Services Board under which Kincora had been set up thirteen years earlier, in 1958. The man in charge of the Kincora home, Joseph Mains, shared McGrath's ideas, though he was not active in TARA. His deputy, Raymond Semple, was politically active in a junior capacity in the Orange movement. McGrath himself had worked occasional shifts, and once during the holidays, at another home in Belfast where he propagated his peculiar ideas about politics and sex.

McGrath's job at Kincora was categorised with the friendly name 'housefather'. He had to supervise the boys, especially at night, wake them in the morning, prepare their breakfasts and look after their general welfare. Kincora catered for boys in the care of Belfast City Council between the ages of fifteen and eighteen. Its aim was to 'tide boys over' in the awkward period between childhood and adulthood. All the boys came from broken homes, or where housing conditions were so bad that they could not live at home. Kincora's purpose was to establish a friendly and relaxed atmosphere – less strict than in the homes for younger children but with the security of an ordered existence. Corporal punishment was strictly banned. An assistant director of the Social Services Board summed up the attitude in the home like this: 'Discipline and control must be achieved through personal relationships by way of example.'

Joseph Mains was appointed director of the home when it was set up. He had worked in children's homes and his chief qualification was a first aid certificate from the St John Ambulance.

Raymond Semple went to Kincora as Mains's assistant in 1962. He left for a short break in 1964, but was approached by Mains to come and help him again in 1966, and agreed. Semple had no qualifications or training, nor any experience in the care of young people. He got in solely on the recommendation of Joseph Mains, who specially sought him out.

One reason for Mains's enthusiasm for Semple is that both men regularly had sex with the boys in their charge. No doubt Joseph Mains felt that his activities in this field might be safer if his assistant, and the only other adult permanently on the premises, was indulging himself as well.

The partnership between the two men was described much later by one of the boys in the home, 'John Brunson'. (All names have been changed, for obvious reasons.) Brunson's parents had separated when he was seven. His father and mother were too poor to keep their five children, who spent all their youth in Belfast homes. John Brunson went to Kincora when he was seventeen. Many years later he told the police:

> About a fortnight after I was in, Joe Mains called me into his bedroom and asked me to give him a wank. I said 'No' and he said 'Come on, I was told you do that kind of thing'. I wanked Mains and he felt all round my balls. As I wasn't at school or working I used to do jobs about the hostel and nearly every afternoon when Mr Mains and I were on our own, Mains would wank me in his bedroom and I would wank him.
>
> I always objected but he would threaten to stop my pocket money or put me to bed early.

Before long, Mr Semple was in on the act. Brunson's story went on:

> About four weeks after I started wanking Mains, Raymond Semple spoke to me one day when I was vacuuming the bedroom and said that I was to give him a wank because if I could do it for Joe Mains I could do it for him. After that, I think it was a toss up who would get me first. After a while Semple started to

take me to his bedroom and put Vaseline on his cock and ride me. When he put his cock in it hurt me at first but as the weeks went by it got easier . . . All this would occur in Semple's bedroom and it happened nearly every day or night.

John Brunson was not homosexual. He married in 1976, and never had sex with a man after his experiences in the care of the Eastern Health and Social Services Board.

Much the same sort of thing happened to 'Patrick Hill', who was in care when he was ten years old, and went to Kincora when he was fifteen. He too was assaulted by Mains and by Semple, though he managed to keep them at a greater distance than had Alan Brunson. It seems that almost every boy in care was either propositioned for sex by Mains and Semple, or was obliged (or wanted) to engage in it. In 1966, Patrick Hill and three other boys at Kincora constructed a letter to the Belfast Welfare Department at 16 College Street. They complained about the way they were constantly propositioned, fondled and assaulted. They posted the letter at the corner of North Road opposite the hostel. They never heard a word about it – and nor did anyone else.

'Harry Docherty' was abandoned by his mother when he was two weeks old and was brought up in Belfast homes and foster homes. He went to Kincora in 1960 when he was fourteen years old:

> I cannot remember how long I had been at the hostel when Joe Mains started inviting me into his bedroom. Initially I thought he did it for company and I felt quite privileged. This normally happened late at night after most of the other boys had gone to bed. I don't exactly know when it first occurred but one occasion when I was in his bedroom, Joe Mains asked me to masturbate him. I refused at first but he said if I didn't do as he asked he would get me sent to Borstal. At that time I had quite a bad temper and had tantrums. When I had those tantrums he used to threaten to get me sent to Borstal. So when he threatened me with it if I didn't masturbate him I believed him. I didn't enjoy masturbating him, but I was frightened to go to Borstal.

The pressure on Harry Docherty increased. Joe Mains took the boy to bed and buggered him about once a week for three years. There were some advantages for the boy:

> When Joe Mains was having a relationship with me, he would give me extra privileges. He would take me out with him, he taught me to drive. I wasn't the only boy who was treated like this . . .

Harry Docherty kept in touch with Joe Mains after he left Kincora.

> I have a certain amount of resentment towards Joe Mains for what he did to me, but I have kept in touch with him because when you are an

orphan you have no one other than the people who run the homes you have lived in.

Another reason may have been that Docherty himself, who was homosexual, used, on his return there, to pester the boys at Kincora for sex. One boy complained – to Joe Mains, who was not in a strong position to do much about it.

In 1967, the regime of Mains and Semple was suddenly threatened. 'David Smith' was sent to Kincora just after leaving school, aged fifteen. He was irritated by Mains's habit of 'touching up' the boys as they walked past him in the passage. One evening he was washing when Mains came into the room and stood behind him. Suddenly he slipped his hand into the bottom half of the boy's pyjamas and grabbed his penis. Smith forcefully pulled the hand away and told the director to 'fuck off'. Mains responded to this very apt advice by sending Smith to bed early and making him scrub floors for a week. After a similar incident at a holiday camp in Portrush, David Smith and another inmate of Kincora went down to the Welfare officers in Belfast and reported Mains's behaviour. When they came back, Mains behaved very strangely:

> He asked where we had been. He started shouting at us and told me to bend over a table in his office. He had a length of wooden rod in his hand and he intended to hit me. I told him he wouldn't be hitting me because I had reported him to the Welfare and they were coming up to see him. When I told him this his nerves went and he started giving Harry and me cigarettes.

There was nothing much to worry about, however. Robert Moore, who was employed by the Belfast Child Care Services, recalled many years later that he went to Kincora after David Smith had complained. Joe Mains explained that he was very concerned about the children's personal hygiene and often pulled their underpants out by the elastic to see if they were clean inside.

'Taking into account Mr Mains's previous good record over a number of years,' Mr Moore explained, 'and the fact that it wasn't unknown for boys to make malicious complaints about residential staff, I informed Mr Mason (the director) that there was nothing to substantiate the allegations.'

Mr Mason was the City Welfare Officer. He accepted the report and passed it on to the city solicitor and town clerk. The crisis at Kincora was over. Things could go on as before, and they did. The evidence suggests that very few boys who went into Kincora – and there were often only one or two boys staying there – were left alone by Mains or Semple or both.

This was the staff which the Protestant evangelist and idealist, William McGrath, joined in late 1971. After a few weeks he joined in the spirit of

Kincora with a verve and enthusiasm which even Mr Mains or Mr Semple had not been able to muster.

Mains and Semple had at least established some kind of relationship with the boys they assaulted. They talked to them, took them out in cars, taught them and helped them so that in many cases the assaulted boys came back to renew the acquaintanceship.

McGrath's attitude was quite different. He helped himself to the boys in his care, often without even speaking to them. There was a silence and an insatiability about the way he went about his business which scared the boys into sullen co-operation.

His most consistent habit – testified to by at least half a dozen of the boys – was to masturbate them as he woke them up. The best reaction to this was that of 'John Flaherty' who went to Kincora in 1972, when he was fifteen.

> When I was about 3–4 weeks in the hostel McGrath was wakening us up as he usually did when I felt a hand under the bedclothes. I felt the hand rub my inner thigh and the hand gradually moving up and rubbing my privates. I jumped up and saw McGrath. I told him never to do that again. I told him I would kill him if he ever did that again.

That approach worked. Nothing of the kind happened again to John Flaherty for the five years he spent at Kincora.

'William Moggs' was of a milder disposition and more easily intimidated than John Flaherty. He kept himself very much to himself when he arrived at the hostel in 1973. One night he was alone in the hostel with McGrath when the housefather beckoned him into the toilet and locked the door.

> He didn't speak but opened the button on the waistband of my trousers and then opened the zip. I didn't open my mouth because I was afraid. He then pulled my trousers and underpants down to my ankles. Mr McGrath opened his own trousers and pulled them and his underpants down to his ankles. Mr McGrath then told me to put my hands down and hold onto the toilet seat. He then took hold of me round the tummy underneath my clothes . . . I felt his cock entering my arse. It was very painful and I screamed out.
>
> I didn't tell any of the others what had happened because I was too scared in case they would say anything.

After retailing several other incidents in which McGrath had, in a similar, silent way assumed that Moggs was available for his gratification – on one occasion even insisting that Moggs 'suck him off' – Moggs concluded: 'I didn't know I was doing wrong at the time, but I didn't like it. I was frightened by Mr McGrath that's why I did it. I never told anybody what happened . . . '

'Eddie Masters', 'David Cumberland', 'Clinton Ferguson' and 'Clive

Ramsay' all confirmed later that they had been sexually abused by McGrath in the same way – all in the first three years.

Perhaps the most dreadful story of all was told by 'Ronald Johnson'. He was in Kincora about six months. During all this time he was systematically abused and raped by McGrath, always against his will. Almost every time he was reduced to tears of pain and humiliation. At last came the day when his foster parents were due to take him away.

I was in my bedroom packing my clothes when Mr McGrath came into the room. It was sometime in the afternoon. He said I heard you're leaving and I said yes I am. Mr McGrath said one more time before you go. I said no and he said if you don't do it this time I'm going to tell your foster parents what you're like. I asked him what he meant and he said, I'll tell them about the other times. I was a bit scared. Mr McGrath told me to take down my trousers and get onto the bed. I pulled my trousers down to my ankles and got onto the bed, I was lying face down. Mr McGrath pulled my trousers right off. He got up onto the bed on his knees and took his cock out. He told me to open my legs and he got on top of me. He put his hands on my bum and put cream inside my bum. He did this with his finger. He pulled the cheeks of my bum open with his hands and put his cock up me. He moved up and down for about ten minutes. He pulled his cock out and got up of [sic] the bed and fixed himself. He told me not to say anything to anybody and my foster parents about what happened in the hostel. He then left the room. I then started to cry and went to the bathroom. There was blood on my backside and legs and my backside was very sore. I then went back to my room and finished packing. I left Kincora Hostel the next day and I haven't seen Mr McGrath since.

William Moggs and Ronald Johnson, like most of the other boys at Kincora who were abused by McGrath, were too scared to tell anyone. One or two others told Mr Mains, who naturally could do nothing to help them. McGrath knew perfectly well that Mains and Semple were in no position to moralise, let along breathe a word to the authorities. Occasionally, though, a boy would rebel. One such was Clive Ramsay, who went to Kincora in 1973, when he was sixteen.

I had been in the hostel about two or three weeks when one night there was only Mr McGrath and my brother and me in the hostel. He came to the kitchen where I was standing and grabbed me by the balls from behind. I was scared and didn't know what to do. I told him to go but he didn't . . . He was laughing when he done it.

The next morning I went and told Mr Mains what happened and he said to forget about it and he would see about it. Later that day I went to my sister's and told my Mother and Father. My Mother said she would take it to court.

'Mrs Janet Ramsay' didn't take it to court but she did take it to the welfare authorities. The day after her son reported McGrath to her, she and her husband 'George' went to the Shankhill Road office of the Belfast Welfare Department and reported everything they had heard to 'a tall woman with glasses'. The woman told the Ramsays not to go to the police and assured them that she would raise the matter with her superior. She said there would be a committee meeting to see what should be done about it. A few days later (less than a week) the Ramsays got a letter from the office agreeing that both their sons could be moved from Kincora. They were satisfied and let the matter rest. Mr Ramsay recalled many years later that Clive made allegations against McGrath twice – 'but owing to my son being a little backward I did not believe him the first time'.

What happened to the complaint in the Welfare Department of Belfast Corporation? Sharon McClean was the social worker who took it up. She had notes of what the Ramsays had told her and she telephoned Joseph Mains. Mains at once denied that anything of the kind could have happened. Miss McClean seemed to be satisfied. She made a report to her superior, Ronald Orr, the senior social worker in her area. Mr Orr recalled the many difficulties his department had had with the Ramsay family and the terrible housing conditions in which the family lived. He explained later:

> My view of the Ramsay family and their problems centred round their hoome circumstances rather than the location of the boys. I assumed that Mrs Ramsay had made the allegations in an attempt to undermine the credibility of the home and was attempting to provoke a change in decision concerning the boys' future care.
>
> With the low level of credence I attached to Mrs Ramsay's report and the expectation that the officer in charge of Kincora could be relied on, I did not require any further investigation once assurances that no sexual interference was occurring had been given.

Four years later, in 1971, Mrs Margaret Robinson, a senior Welfare officer in Belfast, received a letter from a former inmate at Kincora. The letter detailed the assaults that he and others had experienced at the hands of Joe Mains. Mrs Robinson was amazed. To her, and to many female social workers in Belfast, Mr Mains was what she later called 'a ladies' man'. He was, she said, 'very attractive'. As a result, although the boy's letter of complaint was very clear and very detailed and very descriptive, she 'just couldn't believe it'. She spoke to Mr Mains, who told her there was no truth in the allegations. 'I had complete trust in him,' she declared.

Thus *three times* in the years 1967 to 1973 there were complaints of assaults and abuse against adolescent boys in the care of the Belfast City Welfare Department. On each occasion, the department officials believed the abusers, not the abused – and nothing was done. That does not include the letter which Patrick Hill and his mates sent off in 1966 – to no effect whatever.

If the Belfast Corporation, from town clerk downwards, could not believe the allegations from the boys, some policemen could. In 1972, when McGrath was well established at the hostel, Detective Constable Cullen, a former drug squad officer who had been in the Belfast police for twenty-seven years, got information from a witness, a former inmate at Kincora, whom he named as 'B'. DC Cullen initiated his own inquiry and took evidence from B and some of his friends. The results were devastating as far as McGrath was concerned. They exposed not only his assaults on the boys in his care, but the political chicanery and cant which accompanied them. One moment he would be lecturing the boys on the need for Protestant purity, the next, without a word, he would be stripping and raping them in the toilet.

DC Cullen wrote up his report and sent it to his superior officer. Many years later he produced his notes to show that he had sent his report to Assistant Chief Constable William Meharg. Mr Meharg denied ever receiving the file. One barrister concluded that the file may have got 'lost in the internal post' at the headquarters of the Royal Ulster Constabulary. Whatever the likelihood of this, and whatever confidence it inspired in the RUC, the Cullen/Meharg affair was unquestionable proof that at least one police officer, and probably many more, knew exactly what was going on at Kincora Boys' Home, but that no action was taken about it.

Another person with some suspicions of McGrath was Valerie Shaw, a full-time missionary in the Free Presbyterian Church in Belfast between 1971 and 1975. Miss Shaw first heard from a South Belfast minister that William McGrath was a practising homosexual and was working in a boys' home. She then had a meeting with Roy Garland, who gave her copies of the love letters he had had from McGrath. These were quite specific, if clumsy, in their attempt at seduction. Miss Shaw was horrified. She says she went at once – on 29 October 1973 – to see the head of her church, the Rev. Ian Paisley. Mr Paisley was already a powerful politician in the North of Ireland and undisputed leader of its largest party, the Democratic Unionist Party. Paisley read the material and asked Miss Shaw if she would be prepared to go to the Church Session with her allegations. She agreed at once and pressed for action. None came. A few days later, Valerie Shaw got a handbill announcing that McGrath was due to speak at John Knox Memorial Free Presbyterian Church on 4 November. Once again she contacted the Rev. Paisley and asked him to intervene. This time, he rebuked her for hounding McGrath. 'Sister, judge not that ye shall not be judged,' he quoted. 'Thank God that *you* are not a pervert.'

In spite of this uncharacteristic show of tolerance, however, Paisley promptly banned McGrath from speaking in his churches. He did not, however, take the matter further.

Paisley's attitude did not at all satisfy Miss Shaw who continued in 1973 and 1974 to lobby politicians and top people of every kind with her protest about McGrath. She said later she had complained to no less than eight different important people about the Kincora housefather.

Through friends she knew she contacted a senior officer in the Belfast police, Superintendent Graham. In March 1974 he came to her home and she poured out her story to him, showing him the McGrath letters and exposing his career. The superintendent listened. He promised to put a watch on McGrath's home and on the hostel and see whether there was any sex traffic between the two. Miss Shaw heard no more from Superintendent Graham. He retired soon afterwards. When she met him at a function several years later, he gave her the impression he was aggrieved that the information which she had given him, which he had passed on to other officers, had not been acted on.

Among the other senior politicians whom Valerie Shaw approached was the Rev. Martin Smyth, Grand Master of the Orange Order, who had presided over the formation of McGrath's 'Irish' Orange Lodge only two years previously. The Rev. Smyth later insisted, as did Mr Paisley, that although Miss Shaw had mentioned William McGrath's homosexuality, she had not mentioned the boys' home. Miss Shaw has always maintained that the whole point of going to Mr Paisley and Mr Smyth with her complaints was to ensure that something would be done about McGrath's job at the boys' home.

This was confirmed by Roy Garland. He insisted that he tried to tell everyone he knew in authority about McGrath and the boys' home. He said he saw Mr Paisley about it in January 1974, and Mr Smyth about the same time. He says he told the police and the Health and Social Services Board in late 1973 and 1974. None of these people or organisations, he says, were prepared to take any action.

Thus by early 1974, it can be asserted with absolute certainty that a wide variety of people in authority in Northern Ireland had definite information about McGrath's bizarre behaviour and sexual inclinations. Three times, the Health and Social Services Board had been informed. Twice (at the least) through Detective Cullen and Superintendent Graham, the Royal Ulster Constabulary had heard that all was not well at Kincora, and had initiated inquiries. Roy Garland knew and tried to interest almost anyone who would listen to him. The Rev. Ian Paisley and the Rev. Martin Smyth knew that William McGrath, at the least, wrote weird and salacious letters to his colleagues. A whole host of people in TARA, many of whom had climbed outside the secret society and up the ladder of Unionist politics, Clifford Smith, for instance, and Frank Millar, Junior, who married McGrath's daughter (the Rev. Paisley presiding) before he became Press Officer for the Official Unionist Party – such people knew what Roy Garland knew, that McGrath was a very strange character indeed, and perhaps the last person in the city to be trusted with the care of disturbed young men in adolescence.

The only people who knew nothing about any of this were the public. For *twenty years* during which the inmates of Kincora were (in the choice words of a Unionist MP who acted as barrister for two of them) 'systematically sodomised', not a single word on the Kincora Home appeared in the newspapers or on television in the North or South of Ireland, or in Britain.

Another influential person in the North of Ireland who in the early 1970s knew perfectly well what was going on at Kincora was Colin Wallace, Senior Information Officer at Lisburn barracks.

Colin had studied TARA in the course of his inquiry into extremist Protestant organisations. He referred to TARA as one of the splinters of such organisations when he lectured to British troops all over Europe about the origins of the conflict in Northern Ireland. He knew that TARA was an ultra-right, secretive sect which had close associations with extremist Protestant leaders.

When he returned from the tribunal into the 'Bloody Sunday' killings in Derry in the summer of 1972, however, he discovered something more. He got a phone call from a woman who seemed very agitated and asked him for a meeting. He met her in a café near the Arts Theatre in Belfast. She was, as Colin remembers, 'a cheery woman in her late thirties'. She didn't say what her job was or give her name, but she was clearly a Welfare worker of some kind.

She said that she had been in charge of a youngster who had alleged that he had been assaulted by William McGrath. She said the matter had been referred to the police, but the police didn't seem to be doing anything about it. She had been given Colin's name by a clergyman who had met him at a parachute display, and she wondered if the Army could do anything to persuade the police to take action. She thought the matter important not just because of the one youngster, but because others in the home might be at risk.

Colin took the story back to Intelligence at Lisburn. He reminded the Intelligence officers that McGrath was well-known as the commander of TARA and was very high up in the Orange Order and in extremist Protestant politics. The Intelligence officer agreed to look further into the allegation, but came back in a day or two with the news that it was already being dealt with.

Colin heard nothing more about it until early in 1973, when Information Policy was approached by Army Intelligence and asked if they could arrange for publication of a press exposé about TARA. Colin has kept the document which was provided by Intelligence to Information Policy, headed 'Some "off the cuff" information on TARA for the Press'. The document is initialled as being received by the head of Information Policy at the time, Lieutenant Colonel Adrian Peck. It is also initialled by Peter Broderick, head of the Army press desk, and by Colin, who had the specific job of placing the material in the press. In full, it read as follows:

> TARA first came to notice in the late sixties when the group issued a statement to the press claiming to be 'the hard core of Protestant resistance', and it is thought that the organisation was set up as a counter to the civil disturbance associated with the NICRA [Northern Ireland Civil Rights Association] marches.
>
> The name TARA is derived from the place where the ancient high kings of Ireland were crowned and is, therefore, an unusual choice of title for a Loyalist paramilitary group.
>
> Operating from its HQ at Clifton Street Orange Hall, Belfast, as 'The Orange Discussion Group', TARA was organised initially into platoons of 20 or so men and run on military lines not unlike the old Ulster Special Constabulary ('B' Specials). Membership is drawn almost exclusively from the Orange Order and each platoon has a Sgt/QM (Quartermaster) and IO (Intelligence Officer). Contributions: 50p per month – half to a central fund – half at ptn [platoon] level. Ptns are able to draw on the central fund if the opportunity to buy stores arises. Training includes radio, weapons and guerrilla tactics.
>
> *The OC* is William McGRATH. He is a known homosexual who has conned many people into membership by threatening them with revealing homosexual activities which he himself initiated. He is a prominent figure in Unionist Party politics and in the Orange Order.
>
> McGRATH uses a non-existent evangelical mission as a front for his homosexual activities and also runs a home for children on the (236) Upper Newtownards Road, Belfast (Tel: B'fast 657838). Also at *** Newtownards Road (B'fast [no. blocked out]).
>
> The *TARA 2 i/c* is Roy GARLAND, he said he resigned, a close personal friend of McGRATH and his former employer.
>
> *McGRATH's 'ADC'* is Clifford SMITH who lives with McGRATH, and the group's *'Admin Officer'* is David BROWN from Bangor Co Down. BROWN is Deputy Editor of Rev PAISLEY's 'Protestant Telegraph'.
>
> Other people closely associated with McGRATH and aware of his activities are Thomas PASSMORE, Rev PAISLEY, Rev Martin SMITH [sic], James MOLYNEAUX and Sir Knox CUNNINGHAM QC MP.

Using this information, Colin constructed his own briefing paper for the press, which he distributed to several selected journalists. These included David Blundy of the *Sunday Times*, Jim Campbell of the Protestant *Sunday News*, David McKittrick of the *Irish Times* and Kevin Dowling of the *Sunday Mirror*. All these journalists recalled this some years later.

David Blundy wrote in the *Sunday Times* of 13 March 1977:

> At an Army briefing at which the *Sunday Times* reporter was present attempts were made to link Paisley with the Protestant paramilitary group called TARA, a small, obscure and ineffective group as Ulster paramilitary organisations go. The *Sunday Times* has a copy of an Army intelligence summary on TARA which contains accurate details about its organisation.

David McKittrick wrote in the *Irish Times* on 21 March 1981:

Once for example I asked him (Wallace) what he knew about a small loyalist group – TARA. My notes, which I still have, show that he gave me the name, address and telephone number of its commanding officer and the names of four other prominent members (including two who are now in senior positions in a Unionist political party).

Jim Campbell wrote in the *Sunday World* on 31 January 1982:

The man who circulated this document and later gave verbal briefings to myself and other journalists was a British civil servant ostensibly working for the Ministry of Defence as a press officer at Lisburn – Colin Wallace.

The *Irish Times* of 12 March 1982 reported:

Mr Kevin Dowling a reporter with the *Daily Mail*, told the *Irish Times* earlier this week that in August 1973 Colin Wallace informed him that William McGrath was a known homosexual and an officer in the Loyalist paramilitary group TARA, which he called a 'bizarre homosexual army . . . '

Mr Kevin Dowling, who in fact was working for the *Sunday Mirror*, confirmed this to me in 1987 and 1988. He told me that he had submitted an article based on Colin's briefing to the *Sunday Mirror*, for which he worked in 1973 as the Northern Ireland correspondent. He sent the article to his editor, Derek Jameson, and argued fiercely for its publication, saying that it had come from a most reputable source in Army Information. Jameson refused to publish it.

So did every other editor in Britain and in Ireland. One of the most scandalous and salacious stories of modern times was presented to the press with the necessary names, telephone numbers and addresses. The press unanimously, quality and popular, serious and gutter, turned it down. To this day Colin has never understood how the biggest (true) story he ever leaked never got into a single newspaper.

The following year (1974), the Kincora issue was raised again in different circumstances. The Clockwork Orange programme had started out with the purpose of isolating and exposing sectarian assassins. Colin's early work for Clockwork Orange drew his attention to the Red Hand Commandoes, an extreme Protestant group whose members were trained to kill Catholics, and whose leader was a brutal assassin called John McKeague. McKeague was known as a homosexual and the information which Colin collected about him brought him back in a circle to William McGrath and TARA. McGrath and McKeague had been close friends and shared political and sexual inclinations, until they had fallen out and split. While Colin was preparing this line of information for Clockwork Orange,

Army Intelligence approached him and asked him to have another go at exposing TARA in the press. He became puzzled and a little frustrated by the conflicting instructions: from MI5 and Clockwork Orange to keep all this sexual gossip secret; from Army Intelligence to try to get the same gossip published.

The conflict grew during the year (1974), but after he broke with Clockwork Orange at the end of September, Colin made an attempt to resolve it, and to bring the Kincora business to a head.

He could not understand why, when so much was known to Intelligence and to the police about McGrath and where he worked, no action was taken over it. He suspected that the same political motives which inspired so much of the information he was getting under the heading of Clockwork Orange might be obstructing action on the scandal at Kincora.

His suspicions were well founded. TARA often intervened in such a way as to upset the unity of Protestant extremists. More than once, for instance, it issued a 'proclamation' calling on Protestants not to resort to violence – usually at times when violence was being advocated by most Protestant leaders. Such proclamations often upset the other paramilitary organisations, and helped to create an atmosphere of disarray where none in fact existed. Colin wondered whether the gang which centred on Kincora was being 'held in place' to assist with such secret intelligence initiatives. If so, if the boys at Kincora were being sacrificed to the machinations of Intelligence, the process had gone too far. As with Clockwork Orange, the time had come to call a halt.

On 8 November 1974, Colin wrote a memorandum. He is not clear today (because he only has a copy) for whom the memo was intended, but it would certainly have gone to his superior officer Jeremy Railton, Head of Information Policy, and almost certainly also to Army Intelligence and the Army's RUC Liaison Officer at Police Headquarters in Belfast.

The memo was headed: ' "TARA" – Reports Regarding Criminal Offences Associated With the Homosexual Community in Belfast'.

To the memo were attached three documents, none of which Colin managed to keep: an RUC paper on TARA (Reference A); a forensic report on the murder in 1973 of a ten-year-old boy called Brian McDermott (Reference B); and the Army's earlier request for a press briefing on TARA.

1. Reference A adds nothing of real significance to what we already know of the background to 'TARA'. Furthermore, it contains a number of inaccuracies and there are various items of important information missing from it. It is difficult to say whether these flaws are the result of poor intelligence or whether they are disinformation provided for our consumption.

2. If we are to interest the press in this matter with a view to exposing

what has been taking place and thereby stopping further assaults on the youngsters in these hostels, then I would strongly advise that we make use of our own background information and exclude the rather contentious and, indeed, politically suspect material contained in the above. As you know I did try to develop press interest in this matter last year but without any success. I also feel that it is difficult to justify our involvement in what is purely a police and political matter because, in my opinion, 'TARA' is no longer of any security interest.

3. In theory, 'TARA' was basically a credible concept from a Loyalist paramilitary point of view, but it never progressed beyond the planning stage. Such a body could, no doubt, have made good use of the Orange Order's normal selection and 'vetting' system for screening potential recruits, and it would have had ready-made facilities for clandestine training by making use of the Orange Halls throughout the Province. The idea failed for a number of reasons, mainly because of WILLIAM McGRATH's rather strange political views which are more akin to Irish Nationalism or Republicanism than Unionism, and the fact that other organisations which appeared to be more in keeping with the needs of the Loyalist community at that time sprang up during the period.

4. Reference A deals with McGRATH's background in considerable detail but it is inaccurate in a number of respects. The Kincora hostel in Newtownards Road where he works was opened in 1959 under the control and administration of Belfast Corporation Welfare Department. He does not, as the paper claims, 'run the hostel' – he is employed as a 'housefather'. The Warden of Kincora is JOSEPH MAINS and the Deputy Warden is RAYMOND SEMPLE. MAINS was appointed in 1959 and SEMPLE in 1964. Both men are known homosexuals. Indeed, various allegations of homosexual assaults on inmates of the hostel were investigated by senior Welfare Department staff in 1967 but no action was taken against anyone (see notes of a report by Mr H. Mason at flag 'N').

5. It is untrue to say that allegations of assaults on the inmates of Kincora 'began shortly after his appointment'. As I have pointed out in para 4 above, allegations were made as early as 1967 and there is also evidence that assaults may have taken place as early as 1959, soon after MAINS was appointed.

6. Reference A claims that McGRATH 'is a known homosexual' but it avoids any mention of his links with various other key figures in the local homosexual community, other than to insinuate that a number of well-known political personalities with whom he came into contact were also homosexuals. For example, in para 6 of reference A, it is claimed that McGRATH left his previous employment 'as a result of a lovers' quarrel' with his employer, whereas our information would tend to indicate that he left following a row over an outstanding debt. His former employer, ROY GARLAND, is well known in Unionist Party circles (see also CLIFFORD SMITH) and was for sometime 2 i/c of 'TARA'. Admittedly, some of the personal correspondence between the two men during this period cannot be regarded as normal between employer and employee (see flag 'M'). Whatever the real reason for the row between GARLAND and McGRATH, there is certainly considerable animosity between them at present, and GARLAND has been actively engaged in trying to

have McGRATH removed from his post at Kincora. GARLAND's own version of events (see flag 'O') is, of course, very enlightening, but I would suggest that it should be treated with caution until it can be substantiated because of the antagonism between them. It would also appear that many of the RUC source reports on this matter after 1971 originated from GARLAND.

7. McGRATH was himself the subject of an internal investigation by the Belfast Corporation Welfare Department in 1972/73, following allegations of more homosexual assaults on the inmates of Kincora. One of our own sources confirmed in 1972 that a number of complaints has been received about his behaviour and that, although the complaints had been passed to senior welfare staff and to the RUC no action had been taken against him. This would appear to be confirmed, to some extent, by Mr ORR (see flag 'R') in 1973. There were, of course, similar allegations relating to other hostels during this period (see Bawnmore, Westwinds, Burnside etc.) and this conflicts with reference A's assertion that the allegations were confined to Kincora.

8. It should be remembered that the 1967 Sexual Offences Act does *NOT* apply to Northern Ireland and homosexual intercourse between adults or with minors is a criminal offence. The apparent lack of interest, therefore, by the Welfare Authorities and the RUC is quite remarkable. Furthermore, the claim made by .... (see flag 'Q') that key individuals in the Welfare Department were themselves homosexuals and thus, not only appointed homosexuals to such posts but also covered up the offences that took place and protected the offenders, requires very serious examination. In particular, I view her allegations about ...... with great concern because it illustrates the political difficulties we are likely to face if we become involved.

9. Reference R which deals with the circumstances surrounding the murder of BRIAN McDERMOTT last year puts forward the theory that the killing had both sexual and witchcraft overtones. The only link that can be identified between the murder and the homosexual community is via JOHN McKEAGUE. McKEAGUE's own statements (see flag 'S') raise more questions than they answer. Certainly, his boast that he will not be prosecuted because 'he knows too much about some people' merits serious investigation, but I suspect that he will no [sic] be prepared to talk until he is released. [McKeague had been arrested and detained in 1973.] It is also rather remarkable that no charges have be [sic] preferred against him, at least during the past 3–4 years. Our own investigations of instances of alleged witchcraft or other satanic rites in the Province would tend to dismiss the RUC's theory that BRIAN McDERMOTT's murder could be part of these activities. In the past, 'Black Magic' practices etc have been mainly confined to groups operating from Republican areas, with the possible exception of three cases in Co Antrim. I think, however, that from a press point of view, we would be very foolish to give any credence to such claims without the most convincing evidence. The forensic reports on the McDERMOTT murder (see flag 'T') would tend to indicate that someone tried to dispose of the body by cutting it into pieces and burning them. It would also appear that when this failed, the pieces were dumped in the river. The insinuation made in the document regarding the boy's

disappearance and the proximity of the Rev PAISLEY's church is dangerous nonsense.

10. Reference A claims that a number of key personalities in the political arena 'are aware of' the Kincora situation and, in particular, of McGRATH's background. It does not, however, explain the extent of their awareness nor of each individual's involvement with McGRATH. In summary, it would appear that the document is claiming that:-

(a) Senior members of the Grand Orange Lodge are aware of the situation because of the discussions and correspondence relating to McGRATH within the Orange Order (see flag 'C'). It is further alleged that THOMAS PASSMORE and the Rev MARTIN SMYTH have blocked any action against McGRATH.

(b) The Rev PAISLEY is aware of the situation but has failed to take any action because of possible blackmail pressure owing to his connection with McGRATH, DAVID BROWN and JOHN McKEAGUE. On the face of it, the statements made by VALERIE SHAW and TOM McNEILLY (see flag 'F') would tend to support only part of such a claim. There are also a number of inconsistencies: McGRATH would appear to be strongly anti-communist and anti-U.V.F. and this conflicts with the document's views on links with TOMMY HERRON, ERNIE 'DUKE' ELLIOTT, 'The Ulster Citizens Army' etc.

(c) Various public and political figures who hold positions of power and who are also homosexual protect each other from prosecution. The claims of a prostitution ring involving juveniles and centred on Bangor is not really substantiated, other than by GARLAND's own personal account. It would be interesting to check, however, the number of charges brought against people involved in homosexual activities in the greater Belfast area in the last 5 years. I also think that the RUC report on drug abuse in this connection merits close examination because this is a natural area of fund raising for terrorists. There is, of course, the obvious problem of security with the possible blackmailing of civil servants, politicians etc.

Conclusions and recommendations

I am far from happy with the quality of the information available on this matter, and I am even more unhappy because of the, as yet unexplained, failure of the RUC or the NIO [Northern Ireland Office] to take on this task.

I find it very difficult to accept that the RUC consistently failed to take action on such serious allegations unless they had specifically received some form of policy direction. Such direction could only have come from a very high political or police level. If that is the case then we should be even more wary about getting involved.

On the other hand, if the allegations are true then we should do everything possible to ensure that the situation is not allowed to continue. The youngsters in these hostels almost certainly come from problem families, and it is clear that no one will fight their case unless we do. Those responsible for the murder of BRIAN McDERMOTT must be brought to trial before another child is killed, and if it can be proved that there is a connection with this homosexual group, then the RUC must be forced to take action irrespective of who is involved.

I would recommend therefore that:-

    (a) We make one final attempt to get the RUC to investigate the matter or at least discuss the matter with RUC.

    (b) We obtain very clear and unambiguous authority from London to proceed with a press disclosure.

    (c) We approach a responsible journalist whom we are confident will make a thorough investigation of the matter and not simply write a sensational type story purely on the information he is given.

    (d) We continue to look for additional information on this matter to ensure that we are not just being used as part of some political disinformation scheme.

Various attempts throughout the years have been made to cast doubts on this document. The *Irish Times*, which published the document in full on 25 June 1985, eleven years after it was dated, submitted the four pages to forensic scientists together with other material which was written in Lisburn barracks in 1974. The tests were inconclusive because the memorandum had been photocopied. However, other checks on the document by the *Irish Times*, including the reference to the RUC background report on TARA and other documents referred to in the memo, indicated that the document was genuine.

The suggestion that the document has been forged, which was later repeated in an official report, is entirely groundless. The chief argument for its authenticity is that it fits closely with the press briefing documents which are confirmed by journalists who received them. Clearly, Colin Wallace knew about McGrath and TARA as early as 1973. In that context, the 1974 memorandum is wholly credible.

The section on the murder of Brian McDermott is probably, as the memo suggests, not strictly relevant to the Kincora scandal. McDermott's murder may well have been a one-off crime by a sexual sadist not necessarily connected to the Kincora gang. Certainly there is no direct evidence to point to Kincora, and the issue is mentioned only because of the suspicion of a connection with John McKeague.

The section on witchcraft throws some interesting light into the activities of Information Policy at the time. Colin's memo is anxious to cast some doubt on the suggestion in the RUC reports that there may have been some connection between the Protestant extremists operating at Kincora and the outbreak of witchcraft and demonology which had fascinated the media in Northern Ireland for several months in 1974, and terrified whole sections of both communities.

Colin's scepticism on this point was well founded. He himself, as he wryly admits, was instrumental in setting off the witchcraft hysteria. Information Policy, with the generous help of one or two selected serving officers, had set up 'magic circles' in derelict houses in the Republican areas. Colin bought bundles of black candles for the purpose. Out in the country the Army's own 'covens' were even more realistic. Colin and his colleagues managed to get hold of some genuine chicken blood and feathers. They made crosses which they hung upside down on bushes leading to the 'satanic sites'. He still has his notebook in which he has meticulously drawn up instructions on how to construct witches' circles. He read several learned books on the subject and became an expert on the order of satanic service.

The results were devastating. The popular press, delighted at some diversion from the 'troubles', fell headlong for the witchcraft allegations. The *Sunday World* in Dublin published a whole supplement on witchcraft ceremonies in an old castle near Newry, all of which had been instigated by Colin Wallace and his merry witches. The effect of the publicity on the population was instant. A naturally religious and superstitious people became very easily frightened by the prospect of their children being seduced by the new craze for satanism. Children were ordered home early and forbidden from areas where the 'witches' pranced at night. These areas were carefully selected by the Army so that they could be kept clear. The witchcraft craze proved the most effective method yet discovered by the British Army for clearing an area of human beings. Observation posts in these areas were trouble-free.

The other purpose of this imaginative exercise was to smear the paramilitary organisations, especially on the Republican side, with a bit of anti-Christ. This too proved very effective.

Naturally, therefore, when Colin read in a police report that there might be some connection between Kincora and the new outbreak of witchcraft, he was keen to play down the idea, without of course revealing the reasons for his scepticism. Hence his tongue-in-cheek reference in his memorandum to the fact that witchcraft was more common among Republicans, and was therefore unlikely to be connected to TARA. He knew this, because that was the thrust of his own witchcraft experiments.

But the more serious and remarkable part of the memorandum is the conclusion: namely that the police must investigate Kincora and take action; and, if not, that the Army must approach a 'responsible journalist' and blow the scandal to the public.

Neither of these things happened *for six years*.

One man in authority in 1974 who can't be blamed for that is Colin Wallace. In spite of his recent promotion, his days in Northern Ireland were numbered. Within six weeks of his issuing his Kincora document, he was banished from the Province.

CHAPTER FOUR

Kaymar

On 30 October 1974, about a fortnight after Colin's conversation with 'John Shaw' of MI5 that he wanted no further part in Clockwork Orange and the 'disorientation' of ministers and Labour politicians, he had a three-hour meeting with one of the most prominent and meticulous journalists operating in Northern Ireland, David McKittrick of the *Irish Times*. McKittrick had a strange story to tell. The previous day, he said, he had been telephoned by Andy Tyrie, the 'commander' of the Ulster Defence Association, the main Protestant paramilitary organisation. Tyrie had given the name of 'George Horn' as the leader of a shadowy organisation called the Ulster Citizens Army. Tyrie alleged that the UCA had circulated inflammatory leaflets against UDA leaders. This sort of allegation between the UDA and one of its many splinter organisations was not in itself remotely interesting, but the sting in Tyrie's information to McKittrick was that 'George Horn' was a former serviceman in the British Army, and that the information about his connection with the Ulster Citizens Army had come from a former junior Information officer for the Army at Lisburn. In other words, Tyrie suggested, the Ulster Citizens Army may well have been a front organisation created by British Army black propaganda.

Colin doubted this, but to make sure, and in McKittrick's presence, he telephoned a colleague who was in charge of Intelligence on Loyalist paramilitary groups. He reported no record of anyone of the name 'George Horn'. Colin and McKittrick then discussed at some length the past history of the Ulster Citizens Army.

The Citizens Army had its roots in the catastrophic splits which had been developing in the main paramilitary Protestant organisation, the Ulster Defence Association (UDA). These splits had been widening all through 1972. They are very well documented in *Political Murder in Northern Ireland* by Martin Dillon and Denis Lehane (London, Penguin, 1973). They were due in part to personal and geographical rivalries and to the protection rackets which were increasingly sustaining the Protestant gangs. The splits were often articulated in political language. The influence of socialistic ideas which were gaining ground throughout the world at that time were beginning, in words at least, to have some influence even in the UDA.

In October 1972, the Ulster Citizens Army had its first mention in the media, when a manifesto was issued in its name. It referred to the UCA as 'more socialist orientated and class conscious' than the UDA. The main thrust of the manifesto was to attack the British Army for its policy towards Protestant rioters. The Army had roughly broken up some of these riots in East Belfast a few days earlier and the manifesto furiously denounced this 'brutality'.

In November 1972, three influential members of the UDA – Tommy Herron, Ernie 'Duke' Elliott and Dave Fogel, a former British soldier who had been court-martialled and who ever since had been one of the UDA's full-time officers – met at Girton Lodge Hotel in East Belfast and drafted a 'charter' for a reformed UDA, which was couched in leftish language. The UDA took the new organisation very seriously. On 7 December 1972, six weeks after the UCA manifesto was published, Elliott, perhaps the most blatantly socialistic of all the paramilitary Protestant leaders, was kidnapped and assassinated. His body was found in a box in the back of a Mini Traveller. No one was ever charged for his murder.

Soon after Elliott was assassinated, a second suspected founder member of the UCA, David Fogel, fled to England, where he gave a press conference denouncing the official Protestant paramilitary organisations, especially the UDA and the UVF, for carrying out assassinations and running extortion rackets (*The Times*, 28 January 1973). On 14 September 1973, Tommy Herron himself was kidnapped in the Newtownards Road, not far from the UDA headquarters. His dead body was found near Lisburn two days later. He had been shot through the head.

The fury of the UDA and the UVF against their new opposition knew no bounds. In a statement on 5 October 1973, the ultra-right UVF warned that they would 'take action from time to time' against the UCA, and accused it of being a 'Communist organisation closely linked to the IRA'. Any other supporters of the UCA cannot have been assisted by a statement from the Official IRA in Dublin confirming that contact had been made with 'the Protestant community' in an effort to lower sectarian tension (*Belfast Telegraph*, 5 October 1973). However, there was enough spirit left in the UCA to issue yet another statement of defiance, announcing that if the British troops persisted in their policies of attacking Protestant extremists, then 'hostilities' would have to be opened against them.

From time to time in the next few months, there were references to the UCA in the newspapers, but its influence never recovered from the assassinations of 1973. What is certain is that everyone concerned – the UDA, the Army and the media – were agreed that the UCA was a genuine, if loose, organisation which purported to represent a new strand of thought among Protestant paramilitaries. Of course, Information Policy and especially Hugh Mooney of the Information Research Department were keen to drive a wedge into the split. An Information Policy document of early 1974, stated: 'After the assassination of Herron, a decision was taken by IP to conduct a low-level campaign to highlight intimidation, extortion and assassination within the Loyalist extremist ranks using the UCA title as a cover.'

Thus the dwindling resources of a nearly-defunct organisation were to some extent boosted by unwanted Army black propaganda, but no one, least of all Lieutenant Colonel Jeremy Railton, Head of Information Policy, who wrote the document, doubted that the Ulster Citizens Army had genuinely existed and had certainly not been formed by the British Army.

Most of this Colin Wallace and David McKittrick recalled that October afternoon. The two men parted on their usual familiar terms. McKittrick had already visited a man called Ron (not George) Horn, an Englishman and a former bandmaster in the British Army, who had vehemently and convincingly denied any association with the Ulster Citizens Army or indeed any political organisation. McKittrick had also rung one alleged source of the information, a former junior Army Information officer, Keith Hamilton, who, then as now, was working for the *Evening Echo* in Southampton. Hamilton too denied any knowledge of passing any information about the UCA to the UDA or anyone else; indeed, he said he had never heard of the UCA.

Any 'story' that might have emerged from Andy Tyrie's 'leak' to David McKittrick had not, it seemed, materialised. For the moment, nothing was published.

At Lisburn, however, Colin Wallace got a note from Captain 'Adam Williams', the Intelligence officer he had asked about Horn and the UCA.

The note, a copy of which Colin has kept, read as follows:

George Horn (music teacher)
Formerly 26 Dublin Road; now Stiles Farm Housing Estate,
Antrim.
Bde [Brigade] Staff Ulster Citizens Army.
So is wife.
Claims Tyrie killed Herron and Harding-Smith walked off
with the money. Signs letters J. Moore.'

Captain Williams worked for Army Intelligence and was in charge of the 'Protestant extremist' desk.

On 30 October, when Colin rang him with the inquiry about Horn, Williams had not been able to find any information about anyone of that name. Now, on the 31st, he suddenly had a lot of information.

The note with its reference to 'music teacher' caused Colin some anxiety. He knew Ron Horn, who had been a bandmaster in the Royal Irish Rangers at Ballymena. He had heard recently that Horn had married Joan Fletcher who lived in Randalstown and had gone to the same church and grown up in the same circle as Colin had. She was a devout churchwoman and, like Colin, was an officer in the Randalstown Boys' Brigade. For a few years when Colin had lived in Ballymena, he had visited Joan's house and gone out with her.

As he became absorbed in his heavy workload at Lisburn he gradually lost contact with Randalstown and the church community, and saw less of Joan. By October 1974, he had not seen her for several months. 'We didn't fall out or anything like that,' he says. 'I was just too busy to keep up the contact. When Mike Taylor told me she'd got married to Ron Horn, I was delighted.' Mike Taylor confirms that he told Colin about the marriage and Colin's reaction.

Colin knew that Ron and Joan Horn were not even remotely political, and had no association with paramilitary groups of any description.

As soon as he read Williams' note, Colin went to see his colleague Mike Taylor, whose little girl went to the school where Joan Horn taught. The two men anxiously discussed the extraordinary suggestion, which appeared to originate in the UDA, but which was also confirmed by their own Intelligence colleagues, that Ron and Joan Horn were active in the UCA, and were being named as activists to the press. They felt that the Horns were in some danger. Both men went at once to see Colonel Peter Goss, then Head of Army Intelligence at Lisburn. Mike Taylor remembers strongly recommending to Goss that the Horns should be warned of the smear that was so mysteriously circulating about them. 'We told the Colonel in no uncertain terms that everything we knew about the Horns contradicted the information which we'd got from his department.' (Interview with author, 9 December 1987.)

The Colonel was unimpressed and gave Colin and Mike Taylor strict instructions to do nothing more about the matter, and certainly not to contact the Horns.

On 8 November, Colin circulated his memorandum about Kincora, which insisted that the Royal Ulster Constabulary get to the root of the allegations about child abuse at the home.

On 16 November, eighteen days after he first received (and checked) the information, David McKittrick published a story in the authoritative *Irish Times*, under the curious heading: ACCUSED UDA SEES BRITISH ARMY HAND. The article started:

> The UDA has named an English ex-serviceman and accused him of the authorship of pamphlets holding the organisation responsible for the present campaign of sectarian assassinations and other crimes.

In a statement issued yesterday the organisation also accused British military intelligence of either hiring the man or giving him false information to use against the UDA and the UVF.

McKittrick's article did not name Mr or Mrs Horn. It quoted 'British Army sources' (Colin Wallace) as saying that 'no real trace of the UCA had ever been found'. The tone of his article, however, was very much to substantiate the rumour about Horn which, on McKittrick's own admission, he had received nearly three weeks previously and had been denied by Horn and by Hamilton, the former Information officer, the alleged source of the information. Neither Horn's denial nor Hamilton's were published in McKittrick's article.

In spite of its thin base, however, the rumour grew rapidly. On 4 December 1974 Robert Fisk of *The Times* reported the story without any substantial addition. On 5 December, the *Daily Telegraph* reporters Christopher Bramwell and Gerard Kemp took the story a stage further. They had been to see Ron Horn, who by now was very disturbed at the inquiries into his alleged and entirely non-existent political activities. He told Kemp and Bramwell that another man (presumably McKittrick) had visited him recently and asked him about a meeting he was alleged to have had with a former British Army Information officer in a pub called the Pig and Chicken. Horn cheerfully volunteered the information that he could not have been in the Pig and Chicken, since he was teetotal and on principle never went into a pub.

The resourceful *Telegraph* men, however, went straight down to the Pig and Chicken where, they reported: 'One of the bar staff gave us an extremely accurate description of the man we had just left.' (*Daily Telegraph*, 5 December 1974.)

The next day, 6 December, Derek Brown, correspondent for the *Guardian* in Northern Ireland, was able to take the 'story' one stage further. Suddenly, the finger of suspicion was pointed not to the unlikely bandmaster of Antrim, but to Colin Wallace.

It emerged yesterday that he [Ron Horn] was married about six months ago to a local woman, formerly a friend of a senior civilian employee in the Army intelligence department at Lisburn. This man is closely concerned with collecting information on obscure organisations like the Citizens Army.

The 'senior civilian employee' was of course Colin Wallace. He was bound even further into the plot in a *Daily Telegraph* article the following day (7 December) which adds to the Wallace/Joan Horn association the juicy fact: 'the couple [the Horns] said that the intelligence man was upset by their marriage'.

There the matter rested. It was buried so deep in so few newspapers that it can, at the time, have had little impact on the public mind. But this was the origin of the smear that Colin Wallace, out of unrequited love for Joan Fletcher/Horn and bitterness at her marriage to the bandmaster, had deliberately leaked his name to the extreme Protestant paramilitary UDA as the leader of the Ulster Citizens Army.

What likelihood is there that Colin Wallace did any such thing?

In the first place, as we have seen, his relationship with Joan Fletcher was certainly not intimate. Secondly, no one ever suggested at the time that the leak to Andy Tyrie about Ron Horn came from Colin. The former Information officer named by Tyrie as his source was Keith Hamilton (who himself promptly denied it). Tyrie has always said that the man who passed him the information was an Englishman, which Colin isn't.

Thirdly, as Colin says: 'I knew perfectly well that Ron Horn had nothing whatsoever to do with politics, and absolutely nothing to do with organisations such as the UCA.

'I also knew that the UDA too knew that. It was so blatantly obvious. If I had wanted for whatever reason to plant suspicion against a likely UCA leader, I would never have chosen Ron Horn, since no one in the UDA would have been convinced for a moment that he was the leader of anything remotely political, let alone paramilitary. Moreover, it would have been plain stupidity for me to have had anything to do with such a smear because it would only have drawn attention to my psyops activities when the whole point of what I was doing was to keep in the background, anonymous.'

Fourthly, if it had been Colin's plan to smear Horn, he would have reacted positively when McKittrick first mentioned Horn's name. In fact, on McKittrick's own account, Colin immediately dismissed any notion that Horn was connected with the UCA, and described the idea as 'very fishy'. He then contacted Army Intelligence who at that stage had never heard anything of Horn. In all the discussion with McKittrick, as the journalist himself records, Colin never gave the slightest indication that he credited the rumour about Horn.

However, the rumour clearly originated somewhere. Some Englishman definitely did give the name Horn to Andy Tyrie, who passed it on to McKittrick, a journalist known for his special contacts in the Protestant political world.

Where could the name have come from?

A clue to the answer to that question comes from the story of what happened after McKittrick had left Colin's office. The note to Colin from Military Intelligence clearly states that a man called Horn was a member of the Brigade Staff of the UCA. This information had not been readily available to the same officer when Colin first asked him about it on the scrambler telephone when McKittrick was present, but had only emerged later.

Then there is the strange reaction of the Colonel in charge of Army Intelligence when approached by Mike Taylor and Colin Wallace, and asked permission to warn Horn of the smears against him. He ordered no action.

A prime candidate therefore for the original smear must be Intelligence, probably MI5. The only conceivable reason for passing such information to the UDA and thence to the press was the connection between Horn and Wallace, through Joan Horn. Since Ron Horn had no political allegiance whatever, his name can only have been of interest to anyone because of Colin's former association (slight though it was) with Horn's wife. In other words, the information could well have been planted on the UDA in the first place precisely because it would, in the end, publicly rebound on Colin Wallace, as it did.

Anyone seeking to smear Colin Wallace at that time was faced with a difficult task. Colin, as we have seen, lived in Lisburn garrison. His entire life was devoted to the Army. When he left the barracks he was engaged almost exclusively in military duties or associated functions, which he was organising such as parachuting, adventure training, or guest nights.

With the exception of his small group of friends in Randalstown and Ballymena, with which he had lost contact, Colin had no association with any civilian circle. Moreover, from June of 1974, he had been seeing more and more of Eileen Streather, who had come to Army Headquarters as a secretary earlier in the year. Eileen, who came from the English Midlands, had become a keen member of Colin's parachute club.

The esteem with which Colin was held in Army circles at that period is well illustrated by the comments made by his superiors in his Annual Confidential Report that year. The 'assessment of his performance' was described as 'outstanding'. Under the heading of 'Special Factor' is written 'his total dedication and sheer professionalism' and under 'Professional Knowledge' is 'he teaches the rest of us'.

Colin's report concluded with these comments:

'One of the most effective contributions of any to the standing and reputation of the Army in these troubles.'

'He wishes to stay in Northern Ireland. He is irreplaceable.'

'For knowledge, loyalty, professionalism, Mr Wallace is in a class of his own.'

Whatever the source of the UCA smear, however, and however slight the connection, it had been publicised (effectively only in one sentence each in the *Guardian* and the *Telegraph*). And it stuck firmly to Colin's reputation.

Already, in spite of his confirmed promotion, Colin had a curious feeling that something strange was happening to him. In mid-November (he can't remember the exact date) David McDine, Head of the Army Information Department at Lisburn, came into Colin's office with a curious story. He had, he said, been returning the previous evening from an Army function with the Chief of Staff, Brigadier Len Garrett. Garrett had asked, out of the blue: 'How do you think you could get on without Colin Wallace?' McDine had replied that he would find life very difficult, and had been puzzled by the question. Colin was also puzzled, confused and annoyed.

The puzzlement continued with another intervention from David McDine in December, 1974. McDine told Colin he was wanted for interview by the Ministry of Defence Information Department in London. No reason was given for the interview.

Colin duly travelled to Whitehall on Christmas Eve and was shown into the office of Tony Chinneck, Assistant Chief Public Relations Officer at the Ministry of Defence. Chinneck told him bluntly that he was being moved out of Northern Ireland because his 'life was in danger'. Colin protested that his life was certainly not in danger; that he was one of the safest people in Northern Ireland since he lived inside the heavily guarded Lisburn barracks. He also pointed out that he had been promoted to do a specific job in September; that he was uniquely qualified to do that job because of his Northern Ireland background; and that he wanted to get on with it. Chinneck was adamant. No reason was given. Colin was instructed to choose between two posts of equivalent rank working for Army Information at either Preston (North-West District) or Taunton (South-West District). In some dismay he left to spend Christmas with Eileen and her parents in England, and a short skiing holiday in Austria.

On holiday, he mused over the strange events of recent weeks. Ever since his conversation with 'John Shaw' and his refusal any longer to take part in black propaganda against his own ministers, life had become more and more difficult. First, there had been the Horn affair which for the first time had brought him personally into the public eye as an Intelligence officer. Then there had been the curious warning from McDine; then the totally unexpected and unexplained posting out of his native Northern Ireland where he wanted to work, and where his local knowledge and expertise had been commended on all sides as irreplaceable.

He reflected on the furious feuds which had broken out at Lisburn ever since the appointment by the Prime Minister Harold Wilson of Michael Cudlipp as Chief Government Information Officer in Northern Ireland. Colin knew that Cudlipp had been appointed by Wilson and by Merlyn Rees, the Secretary of State for Northern Ireland, because both politicians suspected the growth of anti-government influences in the official government information services. The feud which most affected

Colin was for the control of psychological warfare, or black propaganda. Colin's confirmation as Senior Information Officer in September, with a false job description, was a clear sign that 'psyops' in Northern Ireland was to remain firmly under the control of the Ministry of Defence. Colin felt, however, that after his refusal to do any more for Clockwork Orange and his testy memorandum about TARA and the boys' home in Belfast, a powerful effort was being made by MI5 to take charge of psyops and to push him to one side in the process.

When he returned to Northern Ireland on Monday, 27 January 1975, he voiced some of these fears to the General Officer Commanding Northern Ireland, Sir Frank King, and to the Chief of Staff, Brigadier Garrett. Neither man could do anything to help him, though Sir Frank expressed surprise and disappointment at Colin's posting and tried unsuccessfully to get it changed. Colin had no alternative but to accept his posting, and he opted for Preston.

Before he left, however, there was a piece of unfinished business. For several weeks Colin had been engaged in a counter-offensive against a series of leaks and public attacks on Information Policy. His aim, and that of his superiors, was to deflect public attention from the official 'psychological operations' or 'black propaganda' carried out by his unit. In December Colin had written the script for a 'study day' in which representatives of the Army, the Ulster Defence Regiment and the Royal Ulster Constabulary would be 'briefed' on what went on in Information Policy. The purpose of the briefing was to pretend that Information Policy was entirely concerned with 'white propaganda': that is the circulation and collection of legitimate and true information to counter the propaganda of the terrorists. Colin's imaginative script provided 'scenarios' for press officers and Information Policy officers in which white propaganda was disseminated in make-believe situations corresponding to what went on day by day in Northern Ireland. It was sufficiently 'secretive' and 'confidential' to catch the imagination and interest of the audience, and at the same time (its main purpose) to distract attention from the really secret and confidential aspect of Information Policy: black propaganda, the circulation and collection of *false* information, forged documents, and so on.

The briefing was on Friday, 31 January. Colin, though he had written much of the script, did not take part. He was due to leave Northern Ireland the following week. On the eve of the briefing, 30 January, he was the guest of honour at a huge farewell party attended by almost every leading journalist in Northern Ireland (and a considerable number from the South). A cartoon by the celebrated Northern Ireland cartoonist Rowel Friers was commissioned by the journalists, depicting Colin as they knew him best – in mid-air, attached to a parachute, talking to three telephones at once, wearing rugby boots and carrying a squash racket. The Army paid for the party; but the press were not satisfied. They hosted yet another farewell party for Colin the following Monday (3 February) at the Royal Avenue Hotel, in which Colin was presented with a wooden carved eagle, with a plaque inscribed 'From the Belfast Press Active Service Unit'. Ian Sanderson, Head of News of the ITV station Ulster Television, could not make the party. He wrote a warm letter to Colin to apologise.

Dear Colin,

Just a brief note to express my sincere regrets, both at not being able to join in your farewell 'thrash' tonight, and at the fact that you're heading for pastures green.

I have a commitment that can't be cancelled, and while I'd hoped to be able to join the party late on, I've been told it will be wrapping up around 10.00 pm which, unfortunately, is too early for me.

My regret at your departure is somewhat tempered by the knowledge that you'll be installing yourself in a beautiful part of the world . . . and also that, perhaps more than anyone I know in your end of the business, you deserve the break!

I can say no more than that, from a professional point of view, I've come to regard you as an incredibly fine operator and a superbly reliable contact; and from the personal standpoint, it's been a pleasure and a privilege . . .

May good luck go with you.
All very best wishes,
Ian

One journalist who didn't attend either party was Robert Fisk of *The Times*, who was covering a story in Dublin. Fisk was constructing a long article about black propaganda and the British Army, and had talked to Colin about it. Colin had assured the journalist (wrongly) that the Army were not engaged in black propaganda. The clearest proof of that, he said, was the 'briefing' on 31 January. Colin told Fisk he would be happy to let him see on the usual 'unattributable' terms, a copy of the script he had written for the briefing.

On the morning he was due to leave Northern Ireland (4 February) Colin drove with his luggage to the docks where an Army logistic ship was waiting. As he drove, he was followed by a Hillman Hunter with four men inside. His anxiety slackened a little when the car followed him into the docks, which were closely restricted to the British military. However, as he returned to Lisburn, he noticed the car was still following him. He shook the car off in Lisburn and drove out to the cottage near Hillsborough where Bob Fisk lived.

Fisk was not at home. Colin could not show him the document (as he usually did) so he popped the envelope with his script through the letter box. He was surprised, since the cottage is in an isolated country road, to see a yellow Post Office van parked outside, and a man sitting inside it.

He returned to barracks at Lisburn, packed up his remaining things, and that night sadly left the barracks where he had worked so enthusiastically for six years. He took the ferry to Liverpool and never again returned to Northern Ireland for the British Army.

Four days later, on Saturday, 8 February, Robert Fisk published a remarkable story:

> Three CID officers who called at my home outside Belfast on Wednesday morning said that 'Restricted' papers ('Restricted' is the lowest security classification) had been found on my doormat the previous day and late on Thursday night an official from the British Embassy in Dublin came to my hotel in the City and, without telling the Irish Foreign Minister in Dublin that he was making such an approach to a British citizen on Irish soil, said that if I did not hand over 'papers belonging to Her Majesty's Government' I would be committing an offence.
>
> On Wednesday morning there was a knock at the front door of the cottage and three men in civilian clothes identified themselves as RUC officers. The first introduced himself as Detective Inspector Cairns from the CID at Castlereagh police station, one of the largest police barracks in Belfast and headquarters of the Special Branch. And the second officer said he worked there too.
>
> The third man apparently came from CID at Lisburn.
>
> Inspector Cairns said he had come to inquire about a document and held up a brown paper envelope containing a large number of foolscap sheets. He said the woman who cleaned the cottage had found them lying on the doormat the previous day, when I had been in London, and that she had passed them on to the RUC because she saw 'restricted' printed on the top and the letters IRA inside.

Fisk was asked if he had ever seen classified documents before and he said yes, he had, and had indeed published articles arising from them. He was not shown the documents which had landed on his doormat and had so mysteriously been 'passed on' by his cleaning lady. He assured the officers he knew nothing about them.

After his long article in *The Times*, which was followed up in the *Sunday Times* (9 February), he heard no more about it.

Colin Wallace, however, did. On the day after he arrived at Preston, as he was finding his way around the officers' mess, he was told there were two police officers to see him. They turned out to be Inspector Cairns of the Royal Ulster Constabulary (the same officer who, the same morning, had questioned Robert Fisk at Hillsborough) and a Special Branch detective superintendent from the Lancashire Police. They asked about Colin's job, about when he had last met Robert Fisk and what information he had passed to him. Colin refused to answer any questions, indicating that he needed clearance to do so. But he did allow the officers to inspect his personal belongings.

After the officers left, Colin, who by now was becoming more and more convinced that he was being framed, went down to a public telephone at Bamber Bridge and rang 'John Shaw', the MI5 officer at the Northern Ireland Office. He asked what information he could give the RUC. Shaw told him not to give the RUC any information about psyops activities against Loyalist paramilitaries and to deal only with bland operations against the IRA.

The following day, 6 February, Colin went as instructed to the headquarters of the Army's United Kingdom Land Forces at Salisbury to meet the officers in charge of Information there. He had hardly got into the HQ when he was told to return at once to Preston, on the instructions of the Ministry of Defence. He had been suspended from duty. He returned disconsolately to Preston.

A week later Inspector Cairns arrived again, with a CID officer from Lisburn. During a desultory interview in which Colin told the police something of the activities of Information Policy (but nothing politically sensitive), Inspector Cairns revealed that the results of his investigation would be going not to Belfast but to London. He also said, Colin recalls, 'I don't know much of what this is all about, but it would seem to me you are being stabbed in the back by your own people'.

On the same day, Colin got notice of his official suspension on full pay because of his alleged mishandling of official documents.

It was a lonely and depressing time for him. The other officers in the mcss had been instructed by their Colonel not to discuss the appointment of Colin Wallace. He had nothing to do and he knew no one. 'I just sat in my room and went for walks,' he recalls. It wasn't until the end of April that Inspector Cairns rang up with the good news that the Director of Public Prosecutions was not going to prosecute for the leaking of the briefing document to Fisk.

Colin's relief was short-lived. On 18 May, he got a letter from the Ministry of Defence listing charges of 'breaches of discipline amounting to serious misconduct'. These were that he had 'retained' a document which he should have given up when he left Northern Ireland, and had passed it on 'to a person not authorised to have access to it'.

Colin's reaction to this charge was one of mixed horror and outrage. For three years at least he had had access to the most secret and confidential information. 'In order to do his job,' his boss Peter Broderick wrote, 'he had constant and free access to information of high classification and extreme sensitivity.' Broderick also wrote: 'Wallace's primary job was to win friends among the Press and to gain their total confidence as a reliable source of information.' (Report to Civil Service Appeal Board, October 1975.) Indeed, in his Annual Confidential Report written only a few months earlier, one of his superior officers had written: 'Mr Wallace's main aim is to feed stories to the press and to influence their writing. He does this better than anyone I have ever met.'   (Annual Confidential Report.) In other words, the whole point of his job was to pass confidential information to journalists, and to do it in ways which the official press officers could not do. His entire working life had been spent showing journalists documents, some true, some false, with the intention of spreading information which was thought to be useful to the British Army and the Ministry of Defence. His new job at Army Headquarters in Lisburn had been created precisely for that purpose.

This is what he had done in the case of the briefing paper and Robert Fisk. The paper itself was a smokescreen. It gave out interesting information whose central aim was to deflect an able journalist from tracking down and exposing the black propaganda operations of 'psyops'. The document was marked 'Restricted' – the lowest possible classification. When Colin Wallace dropped it through Fisk's letter box, he was only doing what his superiors required of him, what he had always done, and what he was employed to do.

Though his suspicions were now growing, he still believed that there had been some dreadful breakdown in communications between different factions of the military and security authorities, and that the matter would eventually be cleared up.

He opted, because of the complicated nature of his job, to make oral representations in his defence. On 30 May 1975, he went to London and put his case to John Groves, Chief Press Officer at the Ministry of Defence and R. T. Fairbairn, a senior officer in the ministry's civilian management department. The two civil servants sat silently while Colin put his case at some length and then sent him back to Preston. He kicked his heels there for another month. On 25 June, he got a fateful letter from W. Geraghty, Deputy Under-Secretary of State at the Ministry of Defence.

Dear Sir,

I regret that I have to inform you that the first two charges against you – namely the unauthorised retention of a classified document and the improper passing of it to a person not authorised to have access to it have been held to be proved.

A most serious view is taken of these breaches of trust by an officer in the position which you held. It has accordingly been decided that you should be dismissed from your employment in the Civil Service.

After reminding him of his right to appeal, Mr Geraghty's letter concluded:

Meanwhile you will be suspended without pay from the 1st July 1975.

Someone at the ministry had made a mistake, a mistake so unlikely that it could have been deliberate. There were in the envelope two copies of the dismissal letter. The first was the top copy. The second was the circulation copy, which included at its head the list of people who also received the letter. These included the Permanent Secretary to the Secretary of State (Mr Roy Mason), the Private Secretary to the Permanent Under-Secretary, the Military Assistant to the Chief of the General Staff, the Deputy Under-Secretary of State for the Army, the Director of Army Security, Chief Public Relations Officer at the Ministry, Mr J. P. Waterfield of the Northern Ireland Office, and two assistant under-secretaries in civilian management.

This list was of senior officers in the Army and in the Civil Service, whose seniority not only reflected Colin's high standing in the ministry but also the sensitivity with which Whitehall regarded the matter. But there was another name on the list of a man who was not a normal civil servant, nor an Army officer, and whose immediate interest in Colin's dismissal was remarkable. This was the name 'Mr B. Sheldon'.

Mr Sheldon is a solicitor. His name does not appear, however, in any solicitors year book or even in the Civil Service book. He was, and still is, the Chief Legal Adviser to MI5. Under normal circumstances, Colin's 'offence' would have been entirely internal to the Ministry of Defence. Ministry of Defence security officers would, of course, have been informed of it. If, however, as everyone at the Ministry of Defence and in government has consistently claimed ever since, Colin's work in Northern Ireland had nothing to do with Intelligence, why was so influential an officer of MI5 informed of his dismissal?

As Colin read the letter he reflected ruefully that his life and career were shattered. He had sold his family's house in Ireland to come to a job in England which had turned into nothing. In less than a year since his promotion at an astonishingly young age to an equivalent of the rank of lieutenant colonel he was suddenly a nobody in a 'foreign' town, with no prospects of a job or even a house to live in. The only bright spot on the horizon was Eileen Streather, who had been moved from Belfast to London. A few weeks before he was sacked, Colin and Eileen were engaged to be married.

They were married on 8 August and honeymooned in Barbados. When they returned at the beginning of September, Colin went back to Preston to prepare his appeal. The hearing was in front of a Civil Service Board chaired by Sir Leslie Williams, a former Civil Service Union General Secretary. Colin appeared with Cliff Crook, Assistant Secretary of the Institute for Professional Civil Servants, who had agreed to pay for and present his case; and Peter Broderick, his former boss in Northern Ireland, who made a strong statement in his defence, stressing in particular that Colin had been given the false job description, now being used by the Ministry of Defence in support of their case against him, because Colin's real job specification for his work in 'psyops' was classified as secret.

The three representatives of the Ministry of Defence were to have been John Groves, Chief Press Officer, R. T. Fairbairn from civilian management, and Lieutenant Colonel Jeremy Railton who had been Head of Information Policy when Colin was thrown out of Northern Ireland.

Groves and Fairbairn, of course, had only a passing knowledge of the background to the case. The key witness for the ministry was to have been Railton. Colin was looking forward to cross-examining Railton about the nature of his work in Information Policy, and about Railton's express agreement that the contents of his script for the study day on Information Policy should deflect the press from the real activities of the unit.

He never got the chance. The tribunal opened with the announcement that Colonel Railton had missed his plane from Belfast and was therefore unable to attend. The tribunal consisted in the main of Colin and his colleagues putting his case, but without anyone who could be questioned about the real work of Information Policy.

The result was announced a fortnight later, on 31 October. It was by way of a draw. The official letter to Colin from the tribunal accepted the ministry's complaint that Colin had passed a restricted document to a journalist without specific permission of his superiors. They brushed aside Colin's assertions that such documents were always being leaked as part of official Information Policy disinformation activities and that his secret job obliged him constantly to leak material of this kind. On the other hand, the tribunal accepted the statements of Cliff Crook and Peter Broderick that Colin's service had been outstanding. The letter ended:

> We conclude that there is justification for the Department's decision that Mr Wallace's services cannot be retained. However, having regard to his previous good record of service, if Mr Wallace wishes to offer his resignation, we recommend that the Department should accept this as an alternative to dismissal.

The effect of this decision for Colin was that he was out of a job anyway, though he got an extra six months' pay, and his future references would not be overtly smudged by a previous dismissal. It was on the whole a grim picture.

As he accepted his lot, sent in his resignation to the Army he loved, and moved into a rented house with Eileen in Blackheath, South London, Colin's main reaction was one of anger. 'I knew that just about everyone in authority was quite clear that I had been stitched up, but none of them except Peter Broderick came forward to help. I was just chucked out and

I was now pretty sure the only reason was that I had refused to continue with their political dirty tricks and that they had to find some means of discrediting me in case I blew the whole story to Fleet Street.'

Despite his anger he decided to seek remedies against the authorities from within the system.

On 27 November 1975, he consulted a local solicitor in Blackheath, Graham Dodd. He told Dodd his story and asked if there was any way he could continue to challenge what had happened. Graham Dodd recalls the consultations with Wallace very clearly. Twelve years later he told *Channel Four News*:

Colin Wallace said he was involved in dirty tricks against politicians in Northern Ireland and he also said this had started to move over onto the mainland against mainland politicians – and in particular he mentioned Harold Wilson.

Eleven years later, a mighty political row blew up over the allegation by a former MI5 officer, Peter Wright, that there had been an Intelligence plot against the elected Prime Minister, Harold Wilson. It is worth recalling that Colin Wallace's statement, in confidence, to the Blackheath solicitor in November 1975 was the first time ever any such allegation had been put on the record.

It went further. Mr Dodd was impressed with Colin Wallace and made several attempts to help him. First, he suggested a visit to the local MP, Roland Moyle, who was coincidentally a junior minister in the Northern Ireland Office. Colin and his solicitor went to see Moyle in his constituency. They saw him twice and Colin spelt out his complaint at length. Colin felt, he said, that he had been pushed out of his job, at which he excelled, for refusing to rubbish Roland Moyle's colleagues in the Labour government.

Mr Moyle listened carefully and took a lot of notes. When I spoke to him twelve years later, he could still remember the interviews and the main thrust of what was said there: 'He was telling me about some dirty tricks operation designed to blacken the names of Northern Ireland politicians.' (*Daily Mirror*, 9 April 1987.)

What did Mr Moyle do about these very serious allegations? 'I can't remember, I'm afraid,' he told me. 'I have destroyed my notes.'

A still more succinct answer to the question can be found in the bill which Graham Dodd eventually submitted to Colin Wallace. It includes an item: 'Arranging appointment with you and attending with you on interview with your Member of Parliament. Correspondence further on the matter when no satisfaction could be obtained.'

Mr Moyle did nothing at all. After an undistinguished spell in government, he eventually lost his seat and left politics to become Deputy Chairman of the Police Complaints Authority.

Graham Dodd then suggested engaging a barrister to advise on whether or not there was any legal remedy against any of the authorities who had dealt with Colin. They consulted Mr Dennis Cowley QC. Mr Cowley did not favour an aggressive approach. 'After a tentative meeting in the Ministry of Defence,' wrote Graham Dodd to Colin, 'Mr Cowley has ascertained that he would in fact be able to obtain a meeting with someone in sufficient authority to make decisions.'

That Mr Cowley could aspire to such heights was not all that surprising, since, unknown to Colin or Dodd, he was retained as counsel to the Ministry of Defence. In spite of these valuable contacts, however, Cowley was unable to persuade anyone in the ministry to take any further action on Colin's behalf.

A final, rather desperate attempt was made to take a case for constructive dismissal to an industrial tribunal. Colin had been told by a Ministry of Defence official that if he submitted any information to the tribunal which was confidential he could be prosecuted under the Official Secrets Act. Colin wrote, therefore, to the Department of Employment and got a reply from Mr D.A.J. Lord, an official there.

Mr Lord's letter which, curiously, had no reference, explained:

> Where the dismissal was necessary to safeguard national security, an industrial tribunal must dismiss the complaint. A certificate signed on or behalf of a Minister of the Crown will be conclusive evidence that the individual was dismissed to safeguard national security.

Colin took this as assurance that any application from him to a tribunal would be met with an immediate retort that his dismissal was necessary to safeguard national security.

His attempts to get some remedy from the law with the help of Mr Dodd went on for two and a half years. It was not until February 1978 that Graham Dodd finally submitted a (very reasonable) bill for £172, including £100 for the influential Mr Cowley QC.

In the meantime, Colin spent a lot of his time hunting for jobs. During the second half of 1975 and almost all of 1976, he wrote off dozens of applications for all sorts of jobs for which he was supremely well qualified. He was, often, successful at the first fence. For instance, he passed a board interview for a job as a press officer to the BBC. The BBC took up references from the Ministry of Defence, and wrote to Colin saying he had not got the job. He travelled with Eileen to Harwell for an interview for a job as a police officer in the Atomic Energy Authority Constabulary. He passed the medical and all the tests, and was appointed, subject to vetting. The AEA took up his references with the Ministry of

Defence, and wrote saying he had not got the job. He even applied for a job as Principal Information Officer at the Royal Ulster Constabulary, and went over to Belfast for an interview. Shortly afterwards, a London policeman came to his door and told him he had been successful, and that he was carrying out 'routine checks' on people who were going to work in responsible positions in Northern Ireland. The interview went well, and soon afterwards references were taken up with the Ministry of Defence. The RUC wrote to Colin saying he had not got the job. Joseph Lucas Defence Systems at Lightwater near Guildford liked Colin so much that they jumped the gun. He was offered a job as a sales adviser, subject to vetting. Before the vetting could take place, however, the company wrote to him asking him to start work. Then references were taken up with the Ministry of Defence and Colin got another letter apologising that 'due to unforeseen circumstances the offer of employment has been withdrawn'.

At last he had better luck. Arun District Council, West Sussex, advertised for an Information and Liaison Officer. He travelled to Littlehampton for an interview and to his enormous relief was told on the spot, before any references were taken up, that he had got the job. He and Eileen moved to Arundel in November 1976, and bought a modern detached two-storey house with a garden on the outskirts of the town. At last, after two years in rented properties without a steady job, the couple could settle down. A year or two later they were joined by Fred, a vast and voluble Old English Sheepdog to whom they both became devoted.

Throughout all this time Colin had continued to campaign in an attempt to expose and reverse the injustice which he felt had been done to him by the Ministry of Defence and the intelligence services. To this end, he had made a habit of lunching in the Silver Cross and the Sherlock Holmes, two pubs round Trafalgar Square favoured by the huge Ministry of Defence Information Department. One or two of his former colleagues still hailed him there and engaged him in conversation.

Some time in late July 1976, three months before he moved to Arundel, Colin had a conversation with one former colleague who asked if Colin had received a message from Airey Neave MP. Colin said he hadn't, but the Information officer told him that Mr Neave had been anxious to get in contact.

Airey Neave was then Conservative opposition spokesman on Northern Ireland and on the security services. He had escaped from Colditz prison during the war and had taken part in the fight against the Nazis by the Yugoslav Partisans and in the prosecution of Nazi leaders at Nuremberg. He was a barrister and had been Tory MP for Abingdon since 1953. Throughout his political life he had maintained his wartime connections with the security services. He was a tough right-wing politician. It was

Neave who persuaded Margaret Thatcher to stand for the Tory right against Edward Heath for the Conservative leadership in 1975 – a contest which she surprisingly won. The campaign rallied the growing forces of the hard right in the Conservative Party and Margaret Thatcher's victory was heartily applauded by the ultras in and around Intelligence.

Colin was delighted to hear that so influential a politician wanted to meet him, and wrote at once to Airey Neave making himself available. Neave replied, and the two men met in early August. Colin happily supplied the MP with much of the information he had gleaned during his compilation of the material for Clockwork Orange. He concentrated on the alleged international Communist links which supposedly bound the IRA to organisations like the Palestinians' Black September and to Libya's Colonal Gadaffi. Neave was delighted with the information.

A few days later, the MP made a speech to Young Conservatives in Brighton in which he 'tried out' the Wallace material. 'Communist agitators,' he said, were 'sowing seeds of despair and encouraging withdrawal of the Army. They know such action would lead to civil war in Ireland and delight in the Soviet Union.'

The *Daily Telegraph*, which reported the speech on 7 August, commented: 'The allegation of Communist involvement in Northern Ireland is a new theme for Mr Neave, who has long criticised the government's handling of the situation there.'

It was indeed a new theme and Mr Neave was hungry for more information to sustain it. He met Colin Wallace at least twice more that August and wrote to him on 31 August:

Dear Mr Wallace,

I enjoyed our talk last week, but I fear it was shorter than intended. I would like you to ring me on Thursday or Friday morning. I read your material with great interest and wonder if it could be updated to form the basis of a speech on September 10.

What had attracted Airey Neave's attention was Colin Wallace's summary of his Clockwork Orange material, entitled 'Ulster – A State of Subversion'.

Colin worked enthusiastically on the 'updating' of the material and Neave obliged with a speech at Seaton Delaval, Northumberland:

Both wings of the IRA, but especially the Officials, have increasingly Marxist aims. The first is the creation of a socialist republic in Ireland for which Cuba is the model. They also work to end the links between the UK and Northern Ireland and the overthrow of the Irish Government in Dublin. (*Belfast Telegraph*, 11 September 1976.)

He concluded that the real enemy was 'subversive organisations' linked with each other all over the world, and especially to the IRA.

All this not over-sophisticated analysis had come from Colin Wallace and the Neave speech reads like exactly what it was: an 'update' of 'Ulster – A State of Subversion'. Colin went on meeting Airey Neave that autumn, and had evening drinks at the Turf Club with one of Neave's assistants whose name was Grattan de Courcey-Wheeler.

Neave suggested that Colin should write an article for the *Daily Telegraph*, which was edited by Neave's friend William Deedes, later Lord Deedes. Colin obliged at once. The article 'Ulster's Two Basic Needs', which was based on the Clockwork Orange document 'The Red Hand in Ulster', was published on 26 October. One conclusion from the article commended itself to the new Thatcherite Conservative leadership: 'British governments have failed badly in this respect but it now appears that the present Conservative leadership is prepared to give the problem the time it requires to solve it.'

The article was by-lined 'a soldier who served in Northern Ireland for eight years'. Colin still has the letter from William Deedes personally thanking him for it, not to mention the statement of payment for the article: £70.

That £70 was the only tangible advantage which Colin got from his brief association with Airey Neave. He had hoped through the association to raise once more his treatment at the hands of the Ministry of Defence. Airey Neave listened sympathetically to his story, but did nothing to help.

Looking back on this curious episode, which contrasts rather oddly with Mrs Thatcher's later insistence that Colin Wallace's allegations had not a shred of evidence to support them, Colin believes that the ultras in Intelligence were using him to disseminate their rather colourful propaganda on Ireland. 'I suppose I was useful to them because I was no longer working officially for the government, and was what they would call "totally deniable" if anything went wrong. I am sure now that I was deliberately put in touch with Airey Neave so that the stuff which had been fed to me through Clockwork Orange would see the light of day without involving an active Intelligence officer.'

By the time the *Telegraph* article was published, Colin had started work for Arun District Council. The appointment was published in the *UK Press Gazette*, and read there by an old friend of Colin's from Belfast days – David Blundy, a journalist on the *Sunday Times* Insight team. Blundy's father lived not far away in Bognor, and David rang Colin at work one day to suggest a meeting. The two men met several times in 1976 and 1977, and David Blundy often visited the Wallaces' house.

Shortly after their first meeting, Blundy talked to a former paratrooper who claimed that he and some of his colleagues had blown up a weighbridge and carried out other explosions in Co. Armagh as part of psychological operations against the IRA. Colin confirmed that he had known about this, and helped Blundy with a full-page article, published on 13 March 1977. The article was headlined THE ARMY'S SECRET WAR IN NORTHERN IRELAND:

> Over a period of five years the British Army in Ulster has taken part in what can only be described as 'dirty tricks', sometimes aimed at politicians and Ministers as well as its natural enemy, the IRA, according to our sources.

The chief of these sources was Colin Wallace and Blundy's article went over much of the information already retailed here. The undermining by Intelligence and Army Information officials of Merlyn Rees's policy on internees, for instance, was spelled out in some detail.

No one in MI5 or in Information Policy in Northern Ireland could fail to detect the hand of their former colleague Colin Wallace in the Blundy article, which started on the front page and covered a whole page. Here Wallace was, for the first time in print, leaking his 'Army Intelligence summary' on Kincora and the 'dirty tricks' which had been used to sabotage the policies of Merlyn Rees. Up to now, Colin Wallace had been watched suspiciously, but he had kept his protest very much within the bounds of the Civil Service machinery, the law and the ministry. Now he was going 'out of bounds' and 'fraternising' with his former friends and associates in a 'hostile' paper – the *Sunday Times*.

The next person to stir Colin into action was Harold Wilson, the former Prime Minister. Those who take the fashionable view that allegations of a plot against Harold Wilson while he was Prime Minister started with the former MI5 officer Peter Wright in the late 1980s should recall that the main source for the plot was more contemporary and more reliable: Harold Wilson himself. Within weeks of his shock resignation as Prime Minister in 1976, Wilson called two BBC journalists, Barrie Penrose and Roger Courtiour, to his London home and gave them a very full account of the plot against him.

> 'I am not certain that for the last eight months when I was Prime Minister I knew what was happening fully in security,' he said with obvious annoyance. He really could not rule out the possibility that individuals working inside MI5, and even MI6, had contributed to the 'smears' which, he complained, had frequently appeared in the Press and elsewhere while he had been at No 10.
>
> He told the reporters that some people in the security services were 'very right wing'. 'They would naturally be brought up to believe,' he said, 'that socialist leaders were another form of Communist. They are blinkered; the sort of people who would have spread the stories of No 10 and the Communist cell'.' (Barrie Penrose and Roger Courtiour, *The Pencourt File*, London, Secker and Warburg, 1978, p. 9).

Wilson went on to tell the journalists that he had raised the matter with the head of MI6 and the head of MI5; that both had promised to do something about it, but had done nothing.

These extraordinary conversations, which were tape-recorded and backed up by Wilson's political secretary Marcia Williams (later Lady Falkender), were eventually published in the book *The Pencourt File* in 1978. The book was woefully marred by the authors' style and their insistence throughout that the main characters in the story were themselves. Anyone who doubts, however, that Harold Wilson was saying these things, and meaning them, need look no further than the Royal Commission on the Press, which Wilson had set up when Prime Minister (and appointed to it his own Press Secretary, himself an outstanding journalist: Joe Haines).

Wilson had personally raised the activities of MI5 with his successor, James Callaghan. When Callaghan refused to set up the top-level inquiry Wilson demanded, Wilson was furious. He decided, rather oddly, to use his evidence to the Royal Commission on the Press to publicise his own fears about what had happened to him and his staff while he was in the highest office in the land. He describes in vivid terms (as does Joe Haines, in his book about the period) the constant barrage of inquiries from the media about his and his colleagues' personal, financial and political leanings. Many of the allegations were strikingly similar to what Colin Wallace wrote in his Clockwork Orange notes. During his evidence he referred to burglaries and break-ins which had taken place with incessant regularity on his own premises and those of his staff. In April 1977, he added a postscript, as follows:

The record needs to be brought up to date in respect of the following incidents:

1). Seven burglaries of the homes of members of my staff took place in the three months before I announced my resignation of the Premiership. Two of these might have been common crime, as they involved household effects and valuables.

2). Within the week of the announcement of my forthcoming series of interviews with Mr David Frost on Yorkshire TV the contracts section of YTV was burgled and papers examined. This fact was publicly announced by Mr Frost in a broadcast interview in October 1976, and although the Press carried extensive coverage of the interviews, I did not see in any of the national newspapers a report of the break-in.

3). Since that time my political secretary has had two burglaries from her home while she was absent, though on each occasion a television set was stolen, nothing else of value was taken and papers were rifled through.

4). Shortly before Easter 1977, a break-in took place in my study at my home in Buckinghamshire. Nothing of value was taken. The haul consisted of certain personal letters, bank statements and the typescript

of·a book by a former colonial judge about his dealings with agencies of
the South African government, and of what he discovered in the course
of those dealings.   (*The Times*, 4 May 1977).

There was other evidence that Harold Wilson strongly believed in
an MI5 plot against him.

In his book *Inside Story*, published in 1978, the *Daily Express* journalist
Chapman Pincher, whose links with Intelligence agents were so close that
it was often difficult to tell him apart from them, wrote:

> A most eminent Oxford professor wrote to me to describe what had happened
> over a literary lunch he had attended in Leeds in January 1977. 'I happened
> to sit next to Sir Harold . . . He told me that MI5 had spied on him when he
> was Prime Minister, plotted against him, tried to secure his downfall. I was
> embarrassed by this conversation. Finally I said: 'But isn't MI5 under the Prime
> Minister?'
>   He replied: 'Oh, yes, on paper, but that didn't make any difference.'   (Chapman Pincher, *Inside Story*, London, Sidgwick & Jackson, 1978, p. 15.)

In the summer of 1977, Pincher revealed in a *Daily Express* scoop
that 10 Downing Street had been 'bugged' during Harold Wilson's
premiership. In the House of Commons the opposition leader, Margaret
Thatcher, demanded a full inquiry. The Prime Minister James Callaghan
dithered, and did not initiate an inquiry until August.

Colin Wallace read the reports of the Parliamentary row and promptly
wrote to Harold Wilson, assuring him that his fears that he was being
discredited by MI5 were amply justified, and that he, Colin, had been part
of the plot. Marcia Williams, Wilson's secretary, wrote back on 5 August,
politely thanking Colin for his letter and asking him to set out his points
in greater detail. This he did. Unfortunately he did not keep a copy of
this long letter and when, ten years later, he asked Lady Falkender (as
Marcia Williams had become) for a copy, she replied that the letter had
been stored away in Wilson's papers.

Colin recalls that in the letter he dealt at length with the way in
which he and Information Policy had disseminated information hostile
to the government and its ministers. He gave tasty examples from the
Clockwork Orange material, and asked for an interview in which he could
put the full story. Colin was still at this stage anxious to proceed through
'the proper channels'. He believed that since Harold Wilson had been
Prime Minister during Clockwork Orange, he had every right to know
what was going on, and to be told so by a government information officer
working closely with MI5.

Strangely, however, he never got a reply, and the interview never
materialised. In May 1980, Harold Wilson was admitted to hospital with
a serious stomach illness. He underwent a long and painful operation. He

never recovered his former strength or fighting spirit, and never again publicly repeated his deep suspicions of the security services and MI5.

Colin was greatly disillusioned by Wilson's failure to reply. If the man who was at the centre of the Intelligence intrigues was not prepared even to hear him out, where else could he turn? Why indeed should he bother to persist with his campaign?

By late 1977, Colin was utterly engrossed in his new job. Arun District Council was an awkward amalgam of five former local author-ities, and there were endless problems in the reorganisation. Colin's job as 'Information and Liaison Officer' was not just to answer press inquiries and organise Council publicity. He was also in charge of all emergencies, and had to write the detailed 'emergency plan' for the district. In particular, he wrote an emergency plan in the event of an oil spillage off the south coast which would spread oil many miles up the tidal River Arun. He ran the office of the Council Chairman, a former prison governor called Arthur Coomes.

The Council officers at Arun could not believe their luck with their new information officer. Colin threw himself into his new duties with all the enthusiasm and single-mindedness which had so impressed his fellow officers in Northern Ireland. His versatility, his cheerfulness and his organising skills were quite outstanding for a relatively lowly officer in a sleepy rural council. He was universally popular and respected.

As at Lisburn, Colin was quite careless with the time he gave to his job. He was always the one who volunteered for the extra duty, or the extra committee meeting. He left home early in the morning and often did not return before ten at night. 'After the difficulty I'd had finding a job and the fear of being unable to settle down, I think I worked much harder than I needed to, just to make sure I didn't let down those who employed me,' he says. 'I certainly didn't want to make any great fuss about my dismissal from the Army. It still rankled, and I still felt bitter towards the intelligence services and the promoters of Clockwork Orange. If any journalist – like David Blundy – came to see me, I would be happy to help them as I had in the past, but I didn't want to get any publicity myself. I was nervous of any public association with a campaign against the Ministry of Defence, and I didn't want to embarrass my employers who were a very Conservative authority, at a time when it looked as though we would soon have a Conservative government. After Wilson didn't reply to me, I really felt it was better to leave things where they were. I wasn't in the mood to take any more initiatives about the past. I'd got a new life and I was happy with it.'

A curious incident towards the end of 1978, however, showed that some interest was still being taken in him by his former tormentors. Colin got a telephone call from a Detective Sergeant Bingham of Littlehampton CID who asked him to come down to the police station.

On arrival there, he was introduced to a warrant officer from the Army Special Investigation Branch in Northern Ireland. The investigator asked Colin if he owned a Browning automatic pistol. Colin said yes, he had bought one in Northern Ireland for personal protection and left it, together with a revolver and a shotgun, in the armoury at Lisburn when he departed in 1975. He had renewed the firearms certificate for the weapons at Arundel police station on 28 October 1977. He produced the certificate which he kept in his wallet. He said he had bought the Browning at a registered firearms dealer in Belfast. As with every firearm bought in Northern Ireland, the pistol had been tested at the RUC ballistics department and its details recorded there. He had an endorsement from the RUC Chief Constable granting special permission to carry the pistol for his personal protection.

None of this impressed the Army investigator who told the astonished Colin that the pistol belonged to the Army and had been stolen some ten years earlier in Aden. When Colin protested that he had never been to Aden, and that there must be a long string of documents proving his legal entitlement to a weapon which anyway he had left in Northern Ireland, the investigator replied that the firearms dealer had gone out of business and all his records were missing; that the RUC Firearms Department had lost Colin Wallace's file and there were therefore no documents to prove Colin's legal ownership of a weapon which had been stolen from the Army.

As he absorbed what was being said to him, Colin suddenly became frightened. Illegal possession of a firearm is a very serious offence. If he was even charged with such a thing, his job would be threatened. All his past in the Army, including his shadowy dismissal, would become public knowledge in an area and at a time when his public image was important to his job. Suddenly he remembered in relief that he had paid for the pistol with a cheque. He rushed home, found his bank statement with the reference to the firearms dealer, and returned to the police station with it. He also remembered that he had not, himself, collected the weapon after he had paid for it, but that Mike Taylor, his Information Service colleague, had picked it up at the same time as he too had bought a pistol there. He gave the investigator the bank statement and the investigator left.

Several weeks went by, as Colin fretted. Finally, in some desperation, he persuaded a journalist friend to make inquiries of the Army and the police about the curious allegations about the pistol. The inquiries worked wonders. Immediately Colin got another phone call from Sergeant Bingham at Littlehampton to say that the matter of the pistol had been satisfactorily concluded and that no further action would be taken. Later Colin heard from Mike Taylor that the special investigator had travelled to Germany to check with Taylor that he had indeed picked up the pistol as Colin said he had.

Colin reflected ruefully on what might have happened if he had not paid the dealer by cheque, and if he had not had a witness to its collection. There would, apparently, have been no evidence that he had legitimately bought a stolen weapon; or that he was authorised to carry a weapon at all.

His relief that he had been able to prove his legal ownership of the pistol then turned into suspicion as to how it was that inquiries came to be made about it. The investigator had explained that a check had been made of the serial numbers of the weapons at the Lisburn armoury, and the Browning emerged from it as a stolen weapon. But why had no such check been made in the three and a half years since Colin had left Northern Ireland? Colin recalled checks being made at the armoury every week, if not every day. Finally, there was the extraordinary business of the 'lost' RUC firearms file. Colin was certain that his file could not possibly have been lost by accident. The uneasy feeling that he was constantly being watched, and was permanently vulnerable to wild and fantastic allegations from people with access to secret information lingered with him.

The pistol episode convinced Colin that he should devote himself exclusively to his job. At the start of 1979, he was confronted with additional duties. Arun Council entered a team for that year's *It's A Knockout* competition. This popular BBC programme involved teams from different areas in the United Kingdom competing in races usually in exotic costumes and against ludicrous backgrounds. Councils, especially in areas which attracted tourists, took the competition very seriously. The publicity was said to be invaluable. For a new Council like Arun (whose name was constantly being confused with that of a Scottish island) it was felt that considerable effort should be put into picking a competent team and doing well in the competition.

A BBC production team visited Arun and met up with Colin Wallace and other Council officials. They approved Arun as a suitable entrant. The Council team did very well in the early months of 1979 and eventually won through to the final which was held in Charnock Richard, Lancashire. So well did Arun compete there that they were chosen to represent Britain in the final of the European Jeux Sans Frontières, an international *It's A Knockout* competition at Ascona, on the Swiss-Italian border.

Colin did not go to Italy with the team though he had been involved in the administration of Arun's effort in the early months of that year.

In the summer of 1979 there occurred another of those strange events which arose out of nothing to haunt him.

As with the pistol episode, the story started with a phone call to him at his office. A woman said she represented an advertising agency called

Kaymar Studios. The studios needed, she said, pictures of a man in a GQ parachute which they were marketing. She said the firm had been given Colin's name by a Ministry of Defence official as someone who had often used a GQ parachute while in the Army in Northern Ireland. She said that their contacts at the Ministry of Defence had suggested that Colin still had such a parachute.

Colin assumed at once that this information came from a former colleague since very few people would know that he owned a parachute of that particular type, and had kept it. The caller asked if he would be prepared to put on his parachute for some photographs which would greatly assist them with their promotion. She said they wanted to make artists' impressions from the photographs, and asked if Colin would oblige them by posing in his parachute kit both as a civilian and with military insignia. She said she understood that Colin had been attached to the SAS, and specifically asked if he would wear the New Zealand SAS insignia for one set of photographs. Colin knew that there had been teething problems with the first model of the GQ parachute and that the manufacturers were keen to boost its image. He also knew that one of the sales advisers for the GQ parachute was a former SAS corporal. Colin had bought a GQ because it was British-made while the more popular parachutes of the time were American. He did not doubt the authenticity of the call, and was therefore quite happy to do what he could to help.

The woman at Kaymar Studios asked if he knew a local photographer who could do the work and Colin at once mentioned James Clevett, a professional photographer from Littlehampton, who did a lot of work for the Council. He agreed to arrange for the pictures to be taken by James Clevett. The caller asked, finally, if he could ensure that they were in colour and black and white; and that some of them should show him in military uniform.

Colin dressed up accordingly, donned his parachute, and the pictures were taken at Ford airfield. Colin rang Kaymar at the south-west London telephone number he had been given, which was answered. He said that the pictures had been taken and asked to whom and in what form they should be sent. The answer was that the firm wanted large blow-up pictures from all angles. Colin agreed to see if this work could be done, and discussed it with Jimmy Clevett. They found a firm which could do the blow-ups and Colin rang again to confirm that the work could be done. This time, the telephone number was unobtainable. Directory Enquiries said there was no Kaymar Studios and that the number which Colin had given did not exist.

That was, for the moment, the end of the matter. Jimmy Clevett remembers the incident very clearly and was as mystified by Kaymar Studios as Colin was. Neither he nor Colin was ever able to find out who made the original phone call. Jimmy Clevett never got paid for his work, which remained for the time being in negatives. Once again, Colin was unsettled by the suspicion that he was being surreptitiously harassed by people who were connected with his military past. He could not begin to understand why anyone should want a local photographer to have pictures of him in uniform and in a parachute, but he marvelled at the apparent effort which had been put in by the phantom advertising agency.

There was little time to brood, however, before Arun Council was informed of a new triumph. In the New Year of 1980, they were told that the efforts of the *It's A Knockout* team in Italy the previous summer had so impressed the judges that Arun had been selected as the hosts for the Jeux Sans Frontières European finals the following July. Suddenly what had been a bit of a laugh had become for the Council a most serious matter. The finals were an international event which would involve organising accommodation for six teams from all parts of Europe, interpreters, a site for the games themselves, publicity and advertising on a vast scale. The delight of the Arun councillors at what they saw as an unexpected boost to the fortunes of the area was enhanced by the knowledge that they had in their midst a man who was more than capable of handling the administration for this grand event. Colin Wallace was asked if he would take complete charge, and he agreed at once to do so. The rest of the administration team were Jane Lewis, Colin's assistant; Ned Wayne, the Council's tourism officer and Tony Baker, a Council engineer.

So absorbed was Colin in his new work that he didn't even notice an event in Northern Ireland which was to take up much of his time and effort in the decade which was starting. On 24 January 1980, the Dublin paper, the *Irish Independent*, published a front-page article which, at long last, exposed the TARA child abuses at Kincora. The abuses had gone on apace ever since Colin had left, rising to a crescendo in 1977, 1978 and 1979. They were stopped not by the authorities but by the press. Although the impact shook the whole political structure of Ireland, it was hardly noticed in the weeks that followed the *Independent*'s scoop. Police inquiries, of course, started at once – Joe Mains and Raymond Semple admitted their offences as soon as they were interviewed. Only the 'bright white' William McGrath tried to lie his way out. He vigorously denied he was a homosexual, until a police surgeon did tests which proved beyond all doubt that he was. He vigorously denied the multiple masturbations and rapes on boys in the Home, until confronted with statements from sixteen boys, all of them corroborated by forensic evidence which showed the living room, the toilets and most of the bedrooms of the Home to be covered all over with the remnants of semen – mainly McGrath's semen.

None of this emerged of course in the early months of 1980. Quick charges stopped all further press investigation for the moment. But the cat was out of the bag at last. Some time sooner or later there would be a court case and ugly questions asked: in particular, why was the raping of boys in care allowed to continue for so long when so many people knew about it? If a cover-up was to be prepared, it would obviously affect anyone who claimed to have known about Kincora in the 1970s, and didn't mind talking about it. One such person was Colin Wallace, who was quite oblivious of all these developments as he and his team bent their brains to the international *It's A Knockout* contest.

An enormous administrative task opened out in front of them. Not only had the arrangements to be made for the visiting teams, but a huge arena had to be built on the chosen site, near the Avisford Park Hotel, about 3 miles from Arundel. The Council, to make matters worse, decided that a festival would be thrown in the days before the competition on an adjacent site. This festival which came to be known as Summer Magic involved horse-jumping, stock car racing, parachuting, clowns, hot-air balloons and stall-holders from all over the county selling their wares. The team for Arun had to be picked and trained – needless to say at the Parachute Regiment's Assault Course at Aldershot. Somehow, all of this had to be accomplished while the normal duties of the Liaison and Information Officer did not go away. Sponsoring organisations also had to be found, and one of these, Wadham Stringer, who run a chain of car sales showrooms, obligingly agreed to provide the organisers with a set of Austin Princess cars gaudily decorated in Union Jacks and the slogan ARUN: THE GREAT BRITISH TEAM. The first of these cars was delivered in March, and allocated to Colin.

In March, also, the BBC hosted a grand function in London to introduce the press to the six European television companies who were sponsoring their teams in the Jeux Sans Frontières finals. Colin travelled with the Arun organiser to London for the Press conference. On the same evening, he went to the Washington Hotel, Curzon Street, for another appointment.

David McKittrick, the Northern Ireland correspondent of the *Irish Times*, had phoned Colin in his office a few days previously. He said he wanted to come to England to talk about the implications of a recent book by Colonel Robin Eveleigh, a former officer in the British Army in Northern Ireland. Colin agreed, as always, and McKittrick booked him in at the Washington Hotel, where he himself was staying. The two men talked late into the night and McKittrick returned to Northern Ireland. A few days later, he phoned Colin again and said that he wanted to come back to England to clarify some of the matters they had discussed. Colin agreed once more, in spite of his heavy programme. McKittrick flew over in early April and Colin met him at Littlehampton station, driving his new Wadham Stringer Jeux Sans Frontières car. He drove the journalist to the Avisford Park Hotel. Once again they talked for several hours that evening and the following morning.

The result of the conversations was a series of three articles in the *Irish Times* published on 22, 23 and 24 April 1980.

The most striking of the three articles was the third, entitled SETTING SPY AGAINST SPY. The article starts tamely, but halfway through, it published the first ever suggestion from an Intelligence source that there had been an MI5 campaign against the elected Prime Minister, Harold Wilson.

Intelligence sources have now said that MI5 personnel in Northern Ireland were working against Wilson. MI5 objected both to Wilson being Prime Minister and to his government's Northern Ireland policy. They regarded him as being soft on the Provisional IRA . . .

'It would be an exaggeration to say that 5 (MI5) saw Wilson as coming to power on the back of a Communist revolution,' said a high-placed source. 'But the exaggeration is only slight.'

The 'high-placed source' was Colin Wallace, who was also the 'intelligence sources' for the first paragraph. The same source was behind the detail in the rest of the article – the story (for the first time) of how Wilson was tricked into telling the House of Commons of the Doomsday plot; of how Merlyn Rees was deceived as to the number of recalcitrant former internees. 'A former intelligence officer' (Colin Wallace again) was quoted as saying: 'Rees was a very genuine and fair-minded bloke, and he wanted more intelligence traces on people before he would intern them. So we made up the information.' There followed a very detailed account of how false information about potential internees was circulated round the various agencies, thus increasing the 'traces' and official mentions of 'terrorists'.

The article ended on a high note.

In the end Wilson and Rees realised something of the intelligence campaign to undermine them and a reorganisation of intelligence took place. But there is evidence that in other periods too parts of the intelligence machine have worked against the political masters they are supposed to serve. The irony of intelligence is that they themselves can show such expertise at the thing they are allegedly guarding against – subversion.

The possibility that sections of MI5 had been plotting against Wilson had, as we have seen, some currency before these articles. Wilson himself had been the main source, and had tried to interest journalists in the idea. Penrose, Courtiour and Pincher had all in their different ways given some space to the allegations, but in general they had not been taken too seriously. Although Margaret Thatcher, leader of the Conservative Party, had asked for a full inquiry, the inquiry which was eventually ordered, in a half-hearted fashion, by the Prime Minister James Callaghan had not even investigated the possibility that MI5 were campaigning against Wilson. It was concerned only with the bugging of No. 10 Downing Street, and found no evidence of this.

Until McKittrick's articles, there had not been a single word of corroboration of the 'dirty tricks' against Wilson from a source inside the Intelligence services themselves. Colin had kept his allegations very much to himself – to a private circle round him which consisted of a solicitor, a barrister and a few close friends. McKittrick's articles for the first time identified a definite source with contacts in Intelligence as exposing a campaign against Harold Wilson. Though McKittrick of course did not in any way identify the source, and indeed pretended that several 'senior intelligence sources' had disclosed information to him, it cannot have been difficult for MI5 in Northern Ireland to trace the mischief-maker. It cannot have been difficult to discover that McKittrick and Colin had stayed a night in the Washington Hotel, Curzon Street in early March and that McKittrick had travelled to Littlehampton in early April. The troublesome Wallace was 'leaking' again; and this time he was touching on the most sensitive of all sensitive subjects in the Intelligence world: the 'dirty tricks' against Wilson.

Colin had a moment's doubt and anxiety when David McKittrick sent him the articles. 'They weren't bad articles,' he says, 'but he did seem to have used an awful lot from me. I was faintly worried that I might be traced, but I thought on the whole that I had kept myself so much to myself and so much time had gone by that there was nothing much to worry about. Clockwork Orange and the Wilson plot seemed a very long way from Arundel Castle and *It's A Knockout*.

'Looking back on that time, I felt that I'd been through a nightmare just after I was sacked in 1975 and in the months of unemployment afterwards. Now I was in harness, rebuilding my life, and every month the nightmare seemed to get further and further away.'

Three months later the nightmare returned in a guise more horrible than he or any of his colleagues could possibly have imagined.

CHAPTER FIVE

It's A Knockout

Through the spring and early summer of 1980 Colin was absorbed in the preparations for the *It's A Knockout* European finals. He and his colleagues were often away from Arun. In early June, they travelled in Colin's presentation Austin Princess, plastered with *It's A Knockout* stickers, to Charnock Richard in Lancashire for the British finals of the competition; in late June they were off again to Freibourg, Switzerland, for one of the European heats. The climax in Arundel was the summer Magic Festival which started on 19 July, and the great event itself on the 23rd. The specially built arenas in the grounds of the Avisford Park Hotel were packed with thousands of people. Although the Arun team made a terrible mess of the competition, the week was hailed everywhere in the district as an unqualified success.

Arun Council officials knew where the credit belonged for the triumph. On 28 July the Chairman of the Council wrote praising Colin and his colleagues for the way they had organised the show, and quoted the two celebrities from the BBC as saying that the staging of the event, the hospitality and organisation were the finest they had met during the sixteen years' life of the show.

The preparations for the event had brought Colin close to his assistant Jane Lewis. Jane had joined Arun Council in the same year as Colin – 1976 – as a Tourist Information Officer. In 1978, she applied for a job in Colin's department as his assistant. From the outset they enjoyed each other's company. Jane's boyfriend, a Brighton antiques dealer called Jonathan Lewis, whom she married in the summer of 1979, became friendly with Colin and Eileen, and the quartet often went out together. Jonathan engaged in a long and fruitless quest to beat Colin at squash, and Eileen often played (equally fruitlessly) with Jane. Until the climax of the *It's A Knockout* competition, Colin and Jane were friendly workmates. The huge amount of work in June and July brought them together for eight to ten hours a day. They also travelled together on the two trips out of Arun and stayed in hotels in Charnock Richard and in Switzerland.

At Charnock Richard, they moved closer to each other. On the last evening they were there Jane came to his room in the hotel, and the couple talked long into the night. In Switzerland a few weeks later, the same thing happened. Perhaps the best description of what was going on was given by Jane in a formal statement to the police a few weeks later: 'An association had developed between us which had stopped short of adultery but had involved kissing, cuddling, etc and going on three occasions for a walk in the country.'

She also said: 'He has told me on several occasions that he loved me.'

Colin does not dispute that he was 'extremely fond' of Jane, and that in June and July of 1980 the relationship had gone some way beyond mere friendship. He remembers with special pleasure two long walks during the competition, both of which had started with Jane in tears over a row with her husband. Colin's affection for Jane blended with admiration for her as an administrator. 'She worked all the hours that God gave; she was brilliant. She organised the competition more than any of us.'

Colin organised two dinner parties at the Avisford Park Hotel to thank the workers and organisers of the festival and the competition. The first dinner, on Monday 4 August, was for the site staff hosted by the Council engineer, Tony Baker. Colin was in the Avisford Park Hotel that night. He played squash in a hotel court with Jonathan Lewis. He and Jonathan were having a drink after their game when Tony Baker and the other guests came in. Shortly afterwards Jane Lewis arrived. She and Jonathan left for a dinner at the Old Timbers restaurant near Chichester. It was the first anniversary of their wedding.

Unknown to Jane, she was to have dinner out the following night as well. The second dinner which Colin organised was in her honour, as chief administrator of the competition. A great deal of effort was devoted to keeping this party as a secret surprise for Jane. All thirteen guests – Colin and Eileen, Jonathan, Tony Baker and his wife, Council treasury officer Bernard Taylor and his wife, tourism officer Ned Wayne and his wife, the divisional police chief Bill Taylor and his wife, and the hotel owner Tony Fynn and his wife – all had strict orders to keep quiet about it.

The surprise was spiced with a joke. Jane had had all sorts of trouble with stall-holders during the festival. Colin and Jonathan conspired to pretend that the stall-holders had called a meeting at the Avisford Park Hotel for the evening of 5 August to protest against the Council's arrangements at the festival. Colin insisted that he could not be there to answer the protests, and that Jane must do so. She was appalled at the idea, but had no option but to agree. The plot was, therefore, to get Jane to arrive at the Avisford Park keyed up for an awkward meeting with angry stall-holders, only to find a banquet laid on in her honour.

One problem was how to stop Jane eating anything before the time when the guests had been invited (8.00 p.m.). Eileen persuaded Jane to play squash after work at the Leisure Centre at Bognor Regis, some five miles from the hotel.

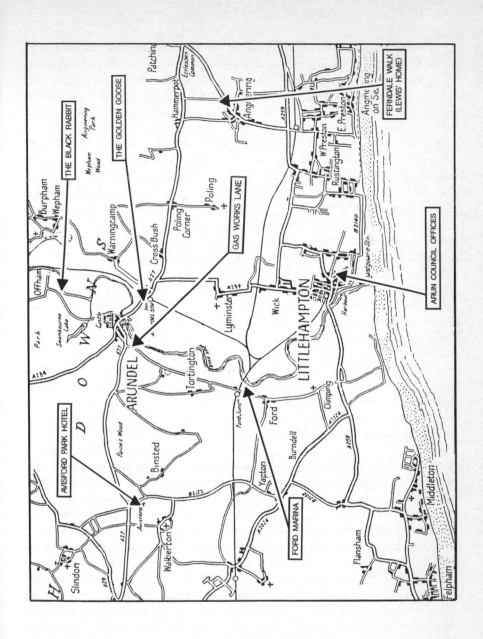

Everyone who knew about it joined enthusiastically in the deception. Colin kept Jane hard at work until 6 p.m., and she rushed off to Bognor for squash. After the game, she put on her working clothes once again and hot-footed it, full of apprehension, to the Avisford Park Hotel. The plan worked perfectly. All the guests were there before her – except Eileen, who followed, grinning, soon afterwards, and Jonathan. The guests waited, drinking merrily, until about half past nine. Although Jonathan still had not arrived, they sat down to dinner. Jane ordered a meal for her husband, but he still did not appear. After the first course was served, Colin said he was feeling ill and could not properly eat his meal. He said he must go home and get some Kaolin and Morphine to settle his stomach. He returned about forty minutes later, in time for coffee.

The only blight on a cheerful evening was that Jonathan still had not turned up. Jane was increasingly worried, and occasionally left the table to ring home and Jonathan's warehouse. There was no reply from either place. The meal broke up just after midnight. By this time Jane was seriously concerned. After a hurried conversation with the Wallaces, she, Colin and Eileen all headed for the Lewis's house in separate cars – Colin in the Austin Princess still, Eileen in her Datsun and Jane in her Renault.

When they arrived at the semi-detached house in Ferndale Walk in Angmering where Jonathan and Jane lived, Jonathan was still not at home. Jane, now in some panic, rang her close friends, Jill Belt, a social worker at a school for autistic children, and John and Joy Muggeridge, who also lived in Angmering. Though it was after one o'clock in the morning, the Muggeridges and Jill Belt came round at once, and the six friends sat anxiously discussing what could have happened to Jonathan. Colin said that Jonathan had phoned in the afternoon to say he would be a little late for the surprise party. John Muggeridge said he had taken Jonathan into Brighton and had been with him all morning. Jane noticed that he had been home in the afternoon to change his clothes. No one offered any information about Jonathan's movements for the evening and night. What could have gone wrong? Most of the discussion centred around Jonathan's work, and his business associates. Jane startled the company by saying that Jonathan had warned her recently that something grim might happen to him. She rang some of her husband's antique dealer colleagues. She rang the estranged wife of Peter Semus, a Brighton antique dealer, who told her that Jonathan and Semus may well have been dining that night with 'some American businessmen'. She rang local hospitals and the police, who sent a motorcycle patrolman at about four in the morning.

John and Joy Muggeridge drove off to Jonathan's warehouse and shop in Brighton, but could not see his car. On the way back they made a detour to pass by the house of Jennifer Gwatkins, a graphic designer and a former girlfriend of Jonathan. His car wasn't there either.

At dawn, there was still no information. Jane knocked up the next door neighbour, who confirmed that Jonathan had left home in his orange Volvo estate the previous evening at about 6.30. That was the latest anyone could trace Jonathan's movements.

The group which had been at Ferndale Walk on and off throughout the night broke up. Colin went home to walk Fred, the dog, and to prepare his *It's A Knockout* car for its return to its dealers that day. Eileen came home at eight o'clock and went to work at nine. Jill Belt and John Muggeridge searched car parks as far as Gatwick for Jon's distinctive Volvo estate – without success.

Wednesday dragged on and still no news. In the evening, Colonel Lewis, Jonathan's father, who lived in Worthing, went with Jane to Littlehampton police station where they spoke at length to police officers about Jonathan's disappearance. Once again, Jane stressed Jonathan's grim prophecy that something awful might happen to him, and his suspicion of some of his colleagues.

Jane and her friends began to lose hope, though no one said so. They clung to the chance that Jonathan, who had been suffering from severe headaches, might have lost his memory.

Thursday's local papers carried the story of the disappearance, which brought nothing but an offensive hoax telephone call. On Thursday at about mid-day Colin went to Angmering with the newspapers, and for the first time since the dinner party found himself alone with Jane. He raised with her the possibility that they might disclose to the police the facts of their relationship. Jane thought not, for the time being, and Colin dropped the matter. On Friday morning, Mr 'Joe' Pescott, the superintendent of the Council swimming baths at Arundel, was idly reading the local paper report of Jonathan's disappearance. Something seemed familiar about the registration number of the missing man's car. Mr Pescott walked out into the swimming pool car park and studied the registration of an orange Volvo estate which had been parked there since the previous Tuesday night. It fitted the report, and he phoned the police. They did not have far to come. Arundel police station is immediately across the road, and the Volvo had been in full view of the police station front windows.

Superintendent Bill Taylor, one of the guests at Jane's surprise party, rang Colin not long afterwards and said he was sorry he had not heard about the disappearance since he'd been away on two days' holiday. He announced, however, that the Volvo had been found. Colin drove to Angmering, picked up Jane and went straight to the swimming pool car park. On the way, Jane asked him anxiously: 'Has this got anything to do with you?' Colin assured her it had not. When they got to the car park, the Volvo had gone. Joe Pescott told them the police had taken it. As they left Arundel again, Jane told Colin she thought they should now go to see Superintendent Taylor and tell him about their relationship.

At Littlehampton police station, Mr Taylor heard them sympathetically. He was interrupted by a phone call. He listened gravely, and beckoned Colin outside. The news was grim. Jonathan's dead body had been found in the river near Ford Marina, between two and three miles downstream from Arundel. The two men went back into the room and broke the news to Jane.

She reacted calmly, as though she had been expecting the worst. Almost at once, her parents-in-law, Colonel and Mrs Lewis, arrived at the police station. They had been told the bad news by telephone. Colonel Lewis agreed to go to Worthing mortuary to identify the body. He got there shortly before 5 p.m., and made a formal statement identifying the dead body as that of his son, and stating that the young man was in good health, and had last seen his parents at their Worthing home at teatime the previous Saturday.

Meanwhile, Colin drove Jane and Mrs Lewis back to the house at Angmering, where the closest friends of the family started sadly to assemble: John and Joy Muggeridge; Jill Belt, Eileen, and an Arundel antique dealer called Spencer Swaffer. Jane went for a short walk with Swaffer during which she confided in him about her relationship with Colin. Then, overcome by shock, she went to bed. A doctor came and gave her a sedative. Most of the friends were still gathered downstairs waiting for some news of the autopsy which was being performed on Jonathan's body that night by the Home Office pathologist, Dr Ian West. At about 7 p.m., Spencer Swaffer rang the police station at Littlehampton. They told him that the autopsy was over; that Jonathan had drowned and that there were no suspicious circumstances.

The news was soon made official. That Friday evening (8 August), a press release was issued by the Sussex Police. It was printed the following day (Saturday 9th) in the local evening paper, the Portsmouth *Evening News*. After a six-paragraph report that the body had been found, the article ended: 'Police have ruled out foul play.'

If there was no foul play, of course, there was no need for any detailed inquiry into the death. An inquest was announced for the following Tuesday. Only two statements were taken by the police that day, Friday, after visits to Littlehampton police station by John Muggeridge, Jonathan's closest friend, and Colonel Lewis, the dead man's father. John Muggeridge said that Jonathan and Jane were 'exceptionally happily married'. He said he knew that Jonathan 'went out' with another girl, Jennifer Gwatkins, before he was married (while he was living with Jane). His statement went on:

I know that Jonathan was at one time in partnership with a man called Peter Semus, and that soon after the partnership was finished a few months ago, there were problems. Jonathan told me that Peter Semus had been off-hand with him, and was sometimes a bit sharp with him. As far as I know, Jonathan did not have enemies in the business and did not socialise with other Brighton dealers. (All the quotations from witnesses, unless otherwise stated, are taken from the statements made to the police and deposed for the trial.)

John Muggeridge went on to say that Jonathan had been specially fond of the Arundel area and was accustomed to walk with his dog along the river to the north of the town towards the Black Rabbit pub. He was an occasional drinker, and frequented a number of pubs including the Golden Goose near Arundel station.

On the day Jonathan disappeared, 5 August, he and John Muggeridge had travelled in the latter's car to an antique restorers' shop at Washington, near Horsham. They had spent two hours there and Muggeridge had dropped Jonathan off near their Brighton shops at 2.30.

The business relationship with Peter Semus took up most of the second statement made that day – by Colonel Lewis. He also went to Littlehampton police station where he spoke to Sergeant Don Kent.

In 1977 or thereabouts, Jonathan and Peter Semus floated another company Semus/Lewis Containers Ltd solely for export. This company dealt mainly to America but there have been exports to Israel.

Earlier this year the partnership between Semus and Jonathan was disbanded, as a result of falling off trade and a desire to detach ourselves from Peter Semus in formal business association.

Since then Semus has used the ground floor of the premises and Jonathan Lewis Antiques the first floor. Shortly afterwards, Jonathan found a letter by chance in the premises at North Street, Portslade, in which Semus had written some derogatory comments. Jonathan spoke to Semus about the letter, with the result that Semus stated he was looking after his own interests. I know from Jonathan's point of view there was acrimony after that towards Semus.

Colonel Lewis said that Jonathan was right-handed, tall, strong and a good swimmer. He said he could take care of himself and was frightened of no one, but not a violent man, indeed a gentle one.

Towards the end of the statement there was another reference to Peter Semus.

I have been concerned about £3,000 which is outstanding to us in America as a result of our last transaction with Peter Semus. Semus has to pay us.

After making this statement, Colonel Lewis went to his dead son's house at Angmering. He later explained to the police what happened there. 'In the house was my wife, Colin Wallace and his wife. I said to Colin Wallace in the presence of my wife that the police had an open mind as to what had happened, but appeared to favour the theory that

Jonathan had fallen into the river by accident and drowned. I told Wallace
that when Jonathan was found his fly was unzipped which indicated he had
been spending a penny.'

All that Saturday, nothing more sinister was suspected. The police
were reassured by the post-mortem that there had been no foul play on
Jonathan Lewis. They had issued a press release to that effect, and the
two statements they had taken at Littlehampton, from John Muggeridge
and from Colonel Lewis, suggested that their diagnosis – no foul play –
was probably right. Jonathan and Jane, it seemed, were happily married.
Any problems with a former business partner were, except for a relatively
small matter of £3,000, all in the past. The police inquiries continued under
the supervision of Superintendent Bill Taylor, Colin's friend and guest at
the dinner the previous Tuesday at the Avisford Park Hotel. Mr Taylor
was a uniformed officer, who was conducting an investigation not into a
crime but to assist the coroner at the inquest, which it was hoped would
be held the following Tuesday.

Something happened later that Saturday which shattered this calm
and changed the whole nature of the investigation.

Some time that Saturday, Jane Lewis went to Littlehampton police
station. Her long statement was dated the next day - Sunday 10 August.
She had been there the previous Wednesday with her father-in-law, and
had told police officers all about her husband's warnings of the business
associates who, they suspected, were likely to do him harm. On this
occasion, however, none of these things were mentioned. 'Certainly my
husband never appeared to have any financial worries,' she said. 'He never
complained of being worried, or frightened of anyone he met in connection
with business.' This seemed sharply to contradict not just with what she
had told police four days earlier but with what her father-in-law had said
the previous day, when he knew that Jonathan was dead. Without any
further reference to her late husband's business affairs, Jane went on to
talk almost exclusively about Colin Wallace.

> The first occasion was when I returned from Switzerland . . . Upon my
> return home Jonathan was dressed up ready to go to the Chichester theatre. I
> was later than he expected and he said: 'If you've been sleeping with Colin, I
> will divorce you'.
>
> The second occasion that Jonathan asked me if I was having an affair
> with Colin Wallace was on the evening of Monday 4th August when we were
> leaving Avisford Park at about 8.25 in Jonathan's car to go to the Old Timbers
> Restaurant to have a dinner to celebrate our anniversary.
>
> Jonathan said: 'Are you having an affair with Colin?'
>
> I said: 'Of course not.'
>
> I hadn't told Jonathan the truth about my relationship with Colin Wallace.
> Although we had worked together for about eighteen months since mid-June
> 1980 when we went to Lancashire, an association had developed between us

which had stopped short of adultery but had involved kissing, cuddling etc and going on three occasions for a walk in the country. There was no question of Jonathan being obsessed by the thought of our association.

Statements made to the police often read a little awkwardly. This is because they are put together as a result of question and answer. The initiative stays with the police, the questioner.

It is, for instance, most unlikely that Jane Lewis would have volunteered the sentence: 'There was no question of Jonathan being obsessed by the thought of our association.' Rather, the police would have asked the question: 'Was he obsessed with the thought of your association?' to which Jane would have replied in the negative.

Jane went on to describe Colin's attitude to her as 'one of resignation to the extent of our relationship which was a casual affair'. She described his demeanour at the dinner party in her honour as 'cheerful'. She recalled that he had left the meal for 'about 25 minutes' because he was feeling unwell. 'I remember he had spoken earlier about his being ill at the weekend,' she concluded.

This interview – which was conducted by a senior officer from the CID, Detective Chief Inspector Gordon Harrison, was entirely different from the interviews of Mr Muggeridge and Colonel Lewis the previous day; and from the various interviews conducted by junior uniformed officers of people who had seen Jonathan the day he went missing. The questioning directed itself almost exclusively to Colin Wallace and concentrated on the relationship between Jane and Colin Wallace. Sussex Police of course already knew of this relationship. They had been told about it two days earlier by Jane and Colin themselves. DCI Harrison's questions did not extend the police knowledge of that relationship. Wherever the questions suggested that there had been some serious row between Jonathan and Jane over Colin Wallace, the answer was firmly 'No'. However, it was plain already that Sunday morning that the police inquiry was shifting from the uniformed police to the CID; from a routine inquest inquiry to a murder hunt. It was also plain that the chief suspect was Colin Wallace.

Colin did not see Jane that Sunday. He had hardly seen her since they had been together when they heard of Jonathan's death. That Sunday evening, as Eileen was preparing dinner, the front door bell rang. On the doorstep were two plain-clothes police officers, DCI Harrison and Sergeant Kent. They asked Colin if he would come to the police station to answer questions about Jonathan's death. They said they were taking statements for the inquest. Colin agreed at once, and told Eileen to hold up the meal as he wouldn't be away very long.

In the car on the way to Littlehampton, Colin recalls: 'The conversation of the police officers was obviously being carried out for my benefit. They talked about the amount of information you could get from a corpse. They weren't referring to this particular case, but it was obvious to me that they were trying to unsettle me. I could remember these techniques from my days in Northern Ireland.

'They asked me about my Army background, but didn't say anything about Jonathan until we were in the police station. They then started to question me about when I'd last seen Jonathan.'

Colin replied with the story he had given ever since the previous Tuesday evening. He said he had played squash with Jonathan on the Monday. Jonathan had rung him at the office at about 4.30 on the Tuesday afternoon to say he might be a little late for the celebration dinner. Colin made a short two-paragraph statement repeating this story.

The police officers then said that they had reason to believe that Jonathan's death was not accidental. They produced Jonathan's diary for the day he'd gone missing which contained the entry: 'Colin, 6.30.'

There was an easy and quick explanation for the entry. Colin had arranged to play squash with Jonathan that day – at 6.30; just as he had done the previous day. But the arrangement had been cancelled when both men realised they could not fit the game in before the celebration dinner.

Mr Harrison and Sergeant Kent, however, were not satisfied. They insisted they were not getting the true story. They told Colin that a *Knockout* car similar to the one he was driving was seen near the swimming pool car park in Arundel on Tuesday, 5 August. Was it his car? Was he driving it? Did he meet Jonathan that evening? Would he tell the truth?

Gloomily, Colin asked: 'Can I tell Jane first?' When the officers prevaricated, he agreed to tell them the truth.

He then made a statement entirely different from his first statement. His second statement said:

> Jon Lewis rang me at about 4.15 last Tuesday, 5th August. He asked me if he could meet me briefly before the dinner – at 6.30 by the swimming pool car park at Arundel. He gave no indication why. I agreed, and met him at about 6.30 pm. We went home in my car. We had a drink at my home and he said he had reason to believe Jane and I were having an affair – was it true? I said it wasn't strictly true, but a relationship had developed, and I explained the background to It's A Knockout. We talked until about a quarter past seven, when I had a phone call from Mrs Ryder. He said he wouldn't discuss the matter with Jane. I didn't tell you the truth straight away, because I believed I was the last person to see him alive. He seemed calm and took the whole thing as if it wasn't a problem.

Colin went on to say that he had driven Jonathan back to Arundel, and dropped him in the centre of the town at about 7.20. The change in his story was devastating for Colin. On its own, of course, if the new story was true, it was harmless. But Colin was not only contradicting his first statement to the police that night. He was contradicting what he had said to everyone else: even to his own wife and to the wife of his dead friend. While Jane and all Jonathan's friends fretted about his absence during and after the dinner on 5 August, Colin moved among them without telling them that he had seen Jonathan on the very evening that he had disappeared.

Not surprisingly, DCI Harrison and Sergeant Kent were not satisfied with Colin's lame explanation for this crucial change of evidence. They asked him repeatedly why he had deceived so many people and harboured such important information about his friend.

Colin's explanation was the same then as it has always been. He said that he had not wanted anyone except Jane to know about the meeting with Jonathan, and the embarrassing conversation the two men had had together. He thought that Jonathan should be the first to disclose the meeting – and Jonathan had expressly said that he did not want to, and did not intend to. The circumstances Colin faced that evening of 5 August were, he said, extremely awkward for him.

'I had intended to tell Jane after the celebration dinner,' he says. 'I thought at first that Jonathan would just walk in late. When I went back for medicine, I took a run down to the swimming pool car park. When I saw his car was still there, I felt a sense of relief. I thought he was doing a deal with someone and would soon turn up. During the dinner it seemed pointless to say I had had a confidential meeting with him. The purpose of the meeting would come out (or I would have to lie about it) in front of all those people. And, I repeat, I expected him to come in late. So I kept quiet, and stuck to the story that I had not met him all that day.

'I meant to tell Jane about it in confidence while driving her home after the dinner. But Eileen insisted on coming too, so we all had to drive back in separate cars.

'When we got to Angmering, we were all in a crowd. I didn't want the embarrassment of what he'd said to me to come out with all the others around.

'The more time went on, the more I was stuck with the original story. I couldn't see any way out of it. When I heard that foul play was not suspected, I was relieved. It suddenly didn't matter any more whether I'd seen him or not. So I wasn't worried when the police took me off for questioning, and simply told them the same story.

'When they said they thought he might have been murdered, I suddenly realised I couldn't any longer keep the truth from them. My meeting with him might help them in their search for his killers. So I told the truth.

'It's easy to see in hindsight how wrong I'd been to tell a false story at the beginning, and how much damage it did to me. But at the time it didn't seem like that. Even after I'd changed my story, I didn't think it would damage me. I simply assumed that the police would get on with their investigations and sort the whole horrible business out.'

This somewhat tortuous explanation cut no ice with Detective Chief Inspector Harrison nor with Sergeant Kent. After some tough questioning, they asked if they could inspect Colin's clothing, and he agreed. They then locked him up in a cell, without charge. Eileen found out that he was being held in custody when two officers came to the house and took away two suits, shirts and two pairs of shoes. The following day (Monday, 11 August) DCI Harrison and some policemen came to the house, questioned Eileen closely and took tests for blood. They also carried out forensic tests on the furniture and carpets, and, rather strangely, took samples from the water tanks in the roof.

The next morning (12 August) Eileen contacted James Morgan-Harris, from a solicitors' practice in Chichester. Morgan-Harris, a large square bear of a man who takes no nonsense from anyone, appeared in Colin's cell the next day, Tuesday, 12 August, and talked to him for a while. He then told DCI Harrison he was taking his client home. The Chief Inspector protested that they were carrying out a second post-mortem on Jonathan's body, and might want to ask Colin some more questions when it was finished. James Morgan-Harris boomed that he would sit and wait until the police were ready, would accompany his client during questions, and would then take him home.

At about 5 p.m., DCI Harrison started another interview. Colin stuck closely to his new story – his meeting with Jonathan at 6.30, their going home, the short embarrassed conversation about Jane; and the return to Arundel, dropping Jonathan off by the bridge in town at about 7.20. 'During the time Jon was in my house, he did not suffer any injury,' said Colin. He was asked about the lining of the boot of the *Knockout* car he was driving but he said he knew nothing about it 'unless it went into the dustbins at the Council offices along with the other rubbish' when he had cleaned the car out before its return on 6 August. When Jonathan left him, Colin said, 'I am fairly certain he was carrying his jacket.'

The interview ended. Colin went home, and the next day he was back in his office at the Council. The police, however, were now certain that they had a suspect for the murder of Jonathan Lewis. In every murder inquiry in the British system of criminal justice there comes a stage when the general investigation to find out facts about the murder turns into a hunt of a suspect. In the Jonathan Lewis case that stage was reached between Saturday evening (9 August) and the second interview with Colin (12 August).

At 3.10 p.m. that Tuesday Dr West, the Home Office pathologist, who had travelled from London for the second time in four days, started another post-mortem examination. It was – and is – not clear why it was thought necessary to recap on Dr West's initial autopsy, which had led the police to conclude that there had been no foul play. Something happened on the Saturday evening before Colin was interviewed on the Sunday – something which is still unclear – which shifted the police approach from accident to murder. Dr West was carrying out a second autopsy in circumstances in which, he was told by police officers, there were good grounds to conclude that Jonathan had been murdered. In his second autopsy, which took less than two hours, he found injuries which he had not found the previous Friday – injuries which he thought were sustained during life.

This new information enabled the police to start a full- scale murder inquiry. On Wednesday 13th, a police caravan was set up on the bridge over the Arun in the middle of Arundel. It was illustrated by a huge picture of Jonathan Lewis and the caption: MURDER: HAVE YOU SEEN THIS MAN? People were asked through press and television to come forward with any relevant information about Jonathan on the afternoon and evening and night of 5 August.

The coverage of the case in the press took a new turn. What had been announced as a death without suspicion or foul play suddenly became a mysterious murder. On Monday the 11th, the local edition of the Portsmouth *Evening News* carried the first appeal to the public for information. 'Police,' said the report, 'are puzzled by his [Jonathan's] death because he apparently had no financial or marital problems.' The paper quoted Colin Wallace saying that Jonathan was 'in great form' when he had played squash with him on the day before he died. The newspaper was apparently unaware that Colin was brooding in a cell in Littlehampton police station. By the Tuesday, 12 August, the case had made the front-page headline: NEW PLEA OVER DEALER'S DEATH. The report revealed that a search for Jonathan's corduroy jacket and a large bunch of keys he always carried with him had proved fruitless. 'At the same time,' it stated, 'it was revealed that Mr Lewis had suffered a head injury on the night of his death.'

On Wednesday, 13 August, the doubts had vanished. POLICE WORK ON MURDER THEORY screamed the Portsmouth *Evening News* front-page headline. 'At this stage,' said Detective Chief Superintendent Charles Johnstone, head of Sussex CID, 'we cannot definitely say it was murder, but we are also not satisfied it was not.' The next day (Thursday, 14 August) Mr Johnstone was much more definite:

'We are treating this as a murder inquiry,' he said.

The newspaper report revealed a 'mystery drive' which Jonathan had taken in an Austin Princess before meeting his death. It called on the public for more information about an *It's A Knockout* white Austin Princess and its movements on 5 August. It specially asked for information about a black boot-lining for the Princess, which had gone missing. As Colin read these reports he realised that the inquiry was concerned almost exclusively with checking his story, with a single suspect in mind: himself.

In fact, however, there was evidence of another suspect who had seen Jonathan Lewis alive after Colin said he dropped him off in Arundel. For a day or two after the caravan was set up on the bridge, a young woman went past it without absorbing its message. When she finally read the police message, and looked at the picture of Jonathan, she realised that she had seen him – in the pub where she worked. Amanda Metcalfe worked at the Golden Goose, a hotel and pub next to Arundel station. She rang the police at Littlehampton and said she had something to tell them about the man in the picture on the bridge.

On 21 August, Sergeant Snelling and a junior officer went to the Golden Goose to interview Miss Metcalfe. In forty minutes he took a statement fifteen lines long.

I am a single woman and I live at the above address. I am a Riding Instructress but I do a lot of work at the Golden Goose Hotel which is owned by my parents. Part of this work involves serving behind the bar. I have been shown a photograph of Jonathan Lewis and I am able to say that this man has been a fairly regular visitor to the bar. He was normally accompanied by a dark-haired girl with a fringe, aged about in her twenties. They were evening visitors. The last time I saw Jonathan Lewis was during the evening about two weeks ago when he came into the bar with another man. I think the time was some time after 7.00 p.m. because between 6.00 p.m. and 7.00 p.m. I am on my own in the bar and when I saw him I was with another bar man. It was still daylight. I am unable to recall at what time they left or what they were drinking. I am unable to describe the man he was with except that he was slightly older than Lewis. I do not think that this man was a regular in the bar. It might have been Tuesday, 5th August because I believe it was on the same day that Vince, a new bar man, started which was 5th August, 1980.

This was sensational. At last, after nine days of the murder inquiry, a witness had come forward of her own free will with information that Jonathan Lewis was alive, and with another man, after seven o'clock on the day he died. Apart from Colin's statement that he had dropped his friend off in the middle of Arundel at about 7.20, there had been until this dramatic statement no other witness who had seen Jonathan alive on the evening of 5 August. Miss Metcalfe, moreover, could point to independent witnesses to back up her impression that the night she saw Jonathan was 5 August. She clearly had a good memory and would make a good witness.

It was, surely, a matter of time before the police set in motion a huge investigation into Amanda Metcalfe's statement. Here was their first independent witness. Here was a place where Jonathan may have been seen – a place where plenty of other people may have been present. In such circumstances, in any ordinary murder inquiry, senior police would have been back in a flash to re-interview Miss Metcalfe, to corner the regulars in the pub to see who else was there on Tuesday, 5 August, to round up and speak to the other staff: in short to leave no stone unturned in the hunt for the strange man who may well have been drinking with Jonathan the night he was killed.

None of these things happened. After that brief forty minutes interview, no further effort of any kind was made to discover the identity of the man in the Golden Goose. No one re-interviewed Miss Metcalfe. Nine years later, Amanda Metcalfe recalls her surprise at the lack of interest shown by the police officers who interviewed her. 'I started to describe the man with Lewis,' she said, 'but they kept telling me not to say anything unless I was absolutely certain. I tried to tell them what Lewis was wearing, but they told me again to be absolutely sure before I put anything in a statement. So I just stuck to the bare bones of what I saw – and I never saw them again.' (Interview with author, 9 April 1989.)

For this quite astonishing lapse on the part of the Sussex Police, there is only one explanation. The time for general inquiry was over. The police now had their suspect. Any information which fitted the suspect was relevant, and demanded the most thorough investigation. Any information which did not fit the suspect was of no interest whatever. However crucial it might appear, it could be consigned, as Amanda Metcalfe's evidence was, to the prosecution's dustbin: 'additional evidence, not to be called'.

The whole inquiry focused on Colin Wallace. On 20 August, rather oddly, the local papers carried pictures of police frogmen searching the tributaries of Swanbourne Lake, whose water, unlike that of the River Arun, which is tidal and salty, was fresh.

On 23 August, Colin was pulled in for another round of questions from DCI Harrison and Sergeant Kent.

He was asked again to account for his movements on 5 August, and he told exactly the same story he had told ten days previously. This time, however, there was a sharp new twist to the police questions. Mr Harrison told Colin that they had found traces of blood in the boot of his *It's A Knockout* car – blood which could have come from Jonathan Lewis.

Colin knew now that he was likely to be charged with the murder of his friend, but he was powerless to do anything about it. He went quietly on with his job. Eileen's birthday was on 19 September, and the couple had booked to eat out at a Greek restaurant in Bognor. Just after supper on the 18th, however, Mr Harrison and a colleague were at the door. Colin was taken once more to Littlehampton police station. On the next morning he appeared in front of Arundel Magistrates charged with the murder of Jonathan Lewis. He was remanded in Lewes Prison.

He stayed there until 5 December 1980. He was formally committed for trial on 1 December and applied for bail. When the Arundel Magistrates refused bail, James Morgan-Harris went straight to a judge in chambers, who granted it. Bail in a murder case is very rare; Colin heard in prison that his was only the third case in all history where a man charged with murder had been bailed. The surety was remarkably low: £4,000. It was met by the Duke of Norfolk (£1,000), the Mayor of Littlehampton, and former Governor of Dartmoor, Strangeways and Brixton Prisons (£1,000), the Chairman of Arun District Council, a retired Wing Commander in RAF Intelligence (£1,000) and the solicitor to Arun Council (£1,000). So Colin was home for Christmas, suspended on full pay from his job and able to give his whole mind and effort to preparing his defence.

In the meanwhile, James Morgan-Harris had briefed Michael Kennedy QC who took an interest in the case beyond the call of duty. Colin was particularly impressed by the way the barrister set out to inform himself about the terrain, tramping up and down the Arun with an Ordnance Survey map. Kennedy's junior was Simon Coltart. The leading prosecution barrister was Dan Hollis QC, who the previous year had defended one of the men charged (and convicted) of the murder in the Midlands of the newspaper boy Carl Bridgewater. Hollis's junior was Mr David Blair. The trial was started at Lewes Crown Court on 3 March 1981. The judge was Mr Justice Kilner Brown.

Above left: John Wallace, Colin's father.

Above right: Colin, aged twenty-four, as a cadet officer with the Royal Ulster Rifles.

Below: Colin with his mother Jean.

Colin leading a detachment of Royal Ulster Rifles cadets on Remembrance Day, 1967.

Amongst the top brass, 1969. Colin, aged twenty-six, now a captain with the Irish Guards cadet detachment, sits flanked by the Northern Ireland Prime Minister, Terence (now Lord) O'Neill and Field Marshal Earl Alexander of Tunis. Also in the picture are the Regimental Lieutenant-Colonel of the Irish Guards, Colonel Tony Aylmer, and General Sir John Anderson, Commandant of the Imperial Defence College.

Above left: Colin with the New Zealand Ranger Squadron of the SAS in training at Waiouru on North Island, New Zealand, 1971.

Above right: Colin with Lieutenant-General Sir Ian Harris, General Officer Commanding Northern Ireland, on adventure training in the Mourne mountains.

Below: Colin (*right*) with members of the Guards Independent Company, The Parachute Regiment.

Colin with Edward Heath, Prime Minister, and William (now Lord) Whitelaw,
Secretary of State for Northern Ireland, during a visit to troops in Londonderry,
November 1972.

Colin with Harold Wilson at a press conference at RAF Aldergrove,
15 November 1971.

Colin inspects a selection of terrorist weapons at the Royal Ulster Constabulary Data Recording Centre. This photograph was produced by the Sussex police in court in 1980 without identifying its origin, as evidence of Colin's 'obsession' with weapons, to prevent him from being granted bail.

Colin disguised as a clergyman – during a raid on Belfast Airport to test security there.

Above left: Colin examines a captured IRA Thompson sub-machine gun with Keith Hamilton, a fellow Army information officer.

Above right: William McGrath.

Below: Joan Horn (*front row, second from left*). It was alleged that Colin had set up her ex-Army husband as a target for Loyalist paramilitaries because of their relationship before her marriage.

Army Headquarters at Lisburn, Northern Ireland, as it looked in 1971. Colin worked there from 1968 to 1975.

Colin's office in Army Headquarters. Major Tony Staughton, Colin's first boss (*standing left*) and (*sitting next to Colin*) Lieutenant-Colonel Warren Sillitoe.

Cartoon presented to Colin by the Northern Ireland press at his farewell party in 1975.

Army Information Services staff at Tony Staughton's farewell party in 1973.

Jonathan Lewis, the man Colin is alleged to have killed.

Sussex police appeal, August 1980, showing the very distinctive *It's A Knockout* car.

DID YOU SEE THIS MAN
IN ARUNDEL
BETWEEN 6·15ᴘᴍ - 11·30ᴘᴍ
ON TUESDAY
5ᵀᴴ AUGUST 1980
OR THIS CAR

DID YOU SEE A CAR LIKE THIS
IN ARUNDEL ON THE EVENING
OF TUESDAY 5 AUGUST

Jane Lewis, the victim's wife.

The River Arun, near where Jonathan Lewis's body was found on 8 August 1980.

The staged picture of Colin in his parachute gear produced during his trial. Colin posed for this picture in 1979 at the request of the mysterious Kaymar Studios, who disappeared and subsequently could not be traced.

It's A Knockout organisers: Colin (*right*), Jane (*centre*) and Eddie Waring, one of the presenters (*left*).

Colin's friend, the former Army Special Military Intelligence Officer, Fred Holroyd.

Colin after his release in 1986.

CHAPTER SIX

The Man in the Golden Goose

Mr Hollis's opening speech at the trial told a story of premeditated murder. He alleged that Colin Wallace had planned for several weeks to get rid of Jonathan Lewis, because he was in love with his wife. He had deliberately 'set up' the dinner at the Avisford Park Hotel as a decoy and an alibi; had secretly arranged to meet Jonathan on the evening before the dinner; had arranged for his wife and Jane to play squash; had taken his friend home and knocked him out. He had then, Mr Hollis's story went on, bundled Jonathan's body into the boot of his car which he had reversed up to his garage. With the unconscious body in the boot, he had driven to the Avisford Park Hotel, cheerfully greeted his guests, and sat down to dinner with them. At about 10.30, feigning illness, he left the company, drove his distinctive *It's A Knockout* car to the bank of the Arun down a track called Gasworks Lane, hauled Jonathan, still unconscious, out of the boot, and threw him into the river by the sluice gate. He had then returned to the dinner party, as though nothing had happened, and had pretended to Jane, to Eileen and to others that he had not met Jonathan that day.

The evidence for this macabre story started from the unchallenged facts that Colin wasn't seen by anyone between arriving home at about 6 p.m. and arriving at the Avisford Park Hotel at about 8 p.m.; and that all the witnesses at the celebration dinner, and some of the people who were serving the dinner, agreed (as Colin did) that he left in the middle of the dinner, returning after about three-quarters of an hour. Thus the theory was that the murder was committed between six and eight o'clock, and the body disposed of in the second period.

The evidence for what happened in these two periods was as follows.

The Forensic Evidence

In the first post-mortem on Jonathan's body carried out on Friday, 8 August, the day it was found, Dr Ian West found a number of injuries which he assumed had been caused after the body had entered the water. He and everyone else were in no doubt then and ever since that Jonathan died from drowning. It was only when he was prompted by the Sussex Police to carry out a second autopsy the following Tuesday that Dr West found injuries which he believed had been caused to Jonathan in a fight before he died.

The largest of the injuries was:

a deep band of bruising extending from the lowest vertebrae in the neck across the back of the right shoulder with some bruising extending to the left of the midline. There was bruising over the spines of the mid-thoracic vertebrae and over the base of the lumbar spine. (All the quotations from witnesses, unless otherwise stated, are taken from statements made to the police and deposed for the trial, or from what remains of the official transcript.)

There was another set of injuries to the right arm and a 'small bruise at the base of the left nostril'.

The defence commissioned Keith Mant, Professor of Forensic Science at Guy's Hospital, and on 19 August, he and Dr West carried out a third post-mortem on Jonathan's body. Professor Mant discovered further injuries to the knuckles of Jonathan's right hand.

Dr West's conclusions after this third post-mortem were as follows:

The injury to the base of the skull could have been caused by an upward blow directed against the base of the nose. The injury to the region in front of the left ear could have been caused by a blow from a hard surface, and would be consistent with an injury produced by a kick. The laceration on the right forehead has been accompanied by swelling and could have been caused by a direct blow.

The injuries to the right arm could have been caused by gripping. The bruising of the deceased's right hand is consistent with the deceased striking a hard surface with his clenched fist.

As Professor Mant put it: 'The deceased was engaged in a fracas.'

He had been attacked, and fought back. He had been either lying on or dragged across rough ground while he was alive. At some stage he had been gripped by the right arm, either in the fight, or afterwards when he was being dragged along.

Both pathologists concluded that Jonathan had been knocked unconscious by the blow to the base of the nose. Dr West told the court at trial:

This is a very unusual injury. The nose has been used as a piledriver. If sudden pressure is applied to the cartilage of the nose, the bone plate to which it is attached is forced upwards, fracturing the skull. It would appear to be an injury caused by some cushioned but firm surface such as the heel of a hand applied in an upward direction. It would be quite difficult to produce this injury with a clenched fist. It could be done with the edge of the hand but that would be a difficult blow to produce.

How many people were involved in the fight? This question wasn't discussed in detail at the trial. Professor Mant did not give evidence, since he was engaged in another important trial in Birmingham. Mant had written in an earlier report: 'It is possible that the assault on the deceased was committed by two persons; one of whom held the deceased's right arm while the other delivered the damaging blows.'

Dr West said in court that the blows to the neck, marks on the arm and the knockout blow could have been caused by one assailant.

When did Jonathan die? This was one of the most important unanswered questions. The long time that the body had spent in the water made it difficult to tell the time of death with any accuracy. Dr West opined that the evidence was consistent with Jonathan dying on the night of 5/6 August. Professor Mant, however, could conclude: 'The drowning took place within a relatively short time of the assault.' This was supported by another forensic expert, Mr P. Morrison, lecturer in forensic toxicology at Guy's Hospital, who made a statement for the defence. After studying the police reports of the amount of alcohol found in Jonathan's blood and urine, he concluded: 'Death occurred less than one and a half hours after the ingestion of the alcohol.'

Mr Morrison did not appear at the trial for reasons which are not clear. Had he and Professor Mant given evidence they would have done some damage to the prosecution case. For if the death occurred soon after the assault or within one and a half hours of having the gin and tonic with Colin, then Jonathan must have died long before 10.30, when the prosecution said Colin dumped him in the river. Dr West was not questioned on these points and the police forensic scientist who carried out the blood and urine tests, Dr William Wilson, was not called – again for reasons which are not clear. So the court never had an accurate assessment from anyone about the time of death.

Did Jonathan bleed after his assault? This question, too, was not definitively answered at the trial. Dr West was quite certain that the blow to the base of the nose would not have bled. There was, he said, only one injury which might have bled: this was a cut above the right eye which had swelled up and which if inflicted during life would have 'bled profusely'. Dr West was careful to say that the cut might have been caused after death, when the dead body collided with the propeller of the boat which retrieved it – evidence for which was given by the boatman and the boys who recovered the body.

The position about the bleeding was therefore this. Either Jonathan would have spurted blood all over the area where he was attacked, and over the person who was attacking him. Or he did not bleed at all.

On the Monday, 11 August, three days after Jonathan's body was found, while Colin was held at Littlehampton police station DC James Small, a scenes-of-crime officer from Hove went to Colin's home with the latest equipment for blood testing. He said in evidence:

> I carried out an examination of the house – of all rooms with the exception of the three bedrooms on the first floor, searching for traces of blood using the KM screening test. I only obtained one positive reaction for blood throughout my examination. This was on the tiling of the wall behind the toilet bowl in the first floor bathroom.

For a short time before the trial the prosecution flirted with the notion that Jonathan may have gone to the lavatory to urinate and that Colin attacked him while he started to do so. This would have explained the unzipped fly, which, according to one forensic scientist, was unlikely to have come undone in the water; and the spot of blood in the upstairs toilet.

The theory did not last long. The 'minute spot', as he described it, which DC Small had found behind the upstairs lavatory was, as he and other blood specialists admitted in court, not necessarily blood at all. So vague was the test that the 'minute spot' could have been animal blood (from Fred, the dog, for instance) or shoe polish, or fruit juice or almost anything. Moreover, there are two lavatories in the Wallace home. Guests naturally use the one downstairs. DC Small went on to say that he had taken a wide variety of fibres, samples from the water tanks and pieces of carpet throughout the house. He had submitted all of these for forensic examination. None showed the slightest sign of blood; or of a struggle.

This was awkward for the prosecution. For if the cut above Jonathan's right eye had been inflicted in life it would, according to Dr West, have 'bled profusely'. The presence of blood from such an injury would be almost impossible to obliterate even by the most scientific methods. Yet there was none in the house – or on Colin's clothes.

It was possible for the police to conclude that the cut had been inflicted by the propeller – long after death. That conclusion however would have done a great deal of damage to the next part of the evidence.

*

As we have seen, DCI Harrison informed Colin on 23 August 1980 that traces of blood were found in the boot of the *Knockout* car he drove. These traces became a central point at issue in the trial, and engaged the attention of both barristers, the judge and two blood experts in long and complicated analysis.

Colin had returned his *It's A Knockout* Austin Princess car to the Aldershot branch of the car dealers, Wadham Stringer, on 6 August. On the evening of August 9 (the day the local press announced that there were no suspicious circumstances in Jonathan's death) police collected the car and took it away for examination. It was inspected first by DC Small who used the same KM blood test which he had applied so unsuccessfully to the Wallace home. DC Small got positive reaction for blood in two places in the boot of the car: above the offside wheel arch and on the outside lip of the lower edge of the boot. The spots of blood were in DC Small's own word 'minute'. He drove the car the next day to the Metropolitan Police Forensic Laboratory in Lambeth, London, where it was tested by Leslie Silverman, the laboratory's scientific officer. Mr Silverman concluded:

> There were many small spots of blood on the offside rear roof and side of the interior (of the boot). Spots and stains of human blood were present on and around the offside and nearside rear light covers. Smears of human blood were found around the lower edge of the petrol pipe cover, and in the spare wheel well. There was a single discrete light spot of human blood on the nearside rear wheel arch. On the offside rear wheel arch and panel above it were three small heavy downward runs of human blood. Several areas of splashed human blood were present on the inside luggage compartment lid. On removal of the petrol pipe cover two small grimy pools of dried human blood were found.
>
> There was a small discrete dirty stain of human blood on the outside surface of the rear of the vehicle to the upper left of the offside rear light.

This sounded like a tremendous amount of blood in the boot. When Mr Silverman started to examine the spots and splashes, however, he found that the majority were so small or so old that they could not be typed. Mr Silverman had at his disposal some of the most sophisticated blood testing equipment in Europe. There were, he told the court, eleven separate tests which could be done on the blood. The most effective way of narrowing down the possible source of blood was to carry out more than one type of test and combine the findings.

In his first report, which he submitted on 16 September, however, Mr Silverman had to admit that sixteen out of the twenty spots of blood could not be typed at all. He did not give any reasons, though he agreed with Michael Kennedy, Colin's counsel, that the blood could have been too old. Jonathan Lewis, it is important to remember, had died only eight days before Mr Silverman made his first tests. It was therefore unlikely that any blood which came from him was too old to be typed.

In that first report, Mr Silverman 'typed' four of the twenty blood areas; numbers 1, 7, 14 and 17. Only one of those could be 'typed' by the old O/A 'group' test. Number 7 proved to be Group O, which was Jonathan Lewis's group and that of 46 per cent of the population. Three blood traces, numbers 7, 14 and 17, responded to the 'M' test. So Number 7 was Group O and M+, a grouping which included Jonathan Lewis and 37 per cent of the population. Numbers 14 and 17 were just M+, as were Jonathan Lewis and 79 per cent of the population.

The prosecution's theory – that Jonathan Lewis had been bleeding profusely from a cut to his right eye while he was lying unconscious in the boot of Colin's car – was hardly vindicated by the shadowy conclusions of Mr Silverman's tests. In that first report, none of the bloodstains in the boot could be convincingly narrowed down to Jonathan Lewis. The most that could be said was that one of the twenty blood spots was narrowed down to a group of people which included Jonathan Lewis and 37 per cent of the population. That was poor evidence on its own. But the most unsatisfactory aspect of Mr Silverman's report from the prosecution's point of view was that there was so much blood in the boot of the new car which could not be typed. It looked remarkably as if there had been another source of blood in that boot – a source which might have nothing to do with Jonathan Lewis or Colin Wallace. Yet try as they could – and statements were taken from everyone whom the prosecution could find who had driven or ridden in the car – they could not find anyone who had bled into its boot.

Then on 26 February 1981, a week before the trial, came different news. Mr Silverman had altered his view on one of his tests, known as the 'AK' enzyme analysis. In a new report he revealed that in his opinion 'Area 10' of the blood (which he had in his initial statement described as 'unsuccessful'), had faintly responded to the AK test. It was, he said, not AK 1, so it was either AK 2 or AK 2-1. Jonathan Lewis's blood was AK 2-1, a rare group. Only about 8 per cent of the population were AK 2-1. At last, from this second investigation, there appeared to be some hard evidence to connect the spots of blood in the boot with that of Jonathan Lewis.

There was, however, an immediate problem. Most of Area 10 of blood was under the cover of the petrol pipe which intruded into the boot. The cover was riveted into the floor of the boot and the area under the pipe was inaccessible until the forensic laboratory staff took the cover off. The question then for Mr Silverman was: how could the blood have got under the cover? He was asked this repeatedly by Mr Kennedy. He agreed that it could not have been washed under there, nor could it have trickled there. There was, he also agreed, 'no scientific explanation' as to how the blood had got there except of course that it had been there before the cover had been put on. This was admitted by Mr Silverman in cross-examination.

Q. So all you found for Area 10 was consistent with the stain having been there before the cover was put on: indeed, if you like, even before the loom was put in? It is consistent with that, is it not?

A. That is a possibility, yes.

Q. It is the most apparently acceptable possibility, is it not, in view of the way you found it and what it looked like? Is that not right?

A. Yes, it is.

Nevertheless, the blood was there: it was a very rare group which could include Jonathan Lewis and a small section of the population. It prompted Mr Silverman to tell the court jury that if Area 10, and the very rare blood group there was taken into account with the other areas, it narrowed the field to a very small number of people: 'If you include areas 1, 7 and 10, with that combination of groups, it occurs in approximately 1.6 per cent of the population, or one in 63.'

This was startling. But was it fair? The cross-examination of Mr Silverman by Mr Kennedy was one of those rare instances where the process of question and answer in court produced something very different from what was said at the outset.

Mr Kennedy established first of all that Area 10 of the blood was absolutely crucial. Without Area 10, most of which was under the petrol pipe cover, the prosecution could say nothing about the blood in the boot save that it was consistent with that of Jonathan and a large percentage of the population. It was Area 10, and Area 10 alone, which suggested that the blood might be Jonathan's, since the AK 2-1 reaction was so rare.

But was it AK 2-1? In a series of careful questions and answers, Mr Silverman explained that he had not been able to prove that the reaction was AK 2-1 – just that it was a reaction in the '2' range. There were therefore two possibilities. It could have been AK 2 or it could have been AK 2-1.

The difference between the tests which separated the two was very complicated. Mr Kennedy, Mr Silverman and the judge did their best to make them sound simple. Basically, the '2' reaction showed up on the results of the tests as a single band. If the grouping was AK 2-1, a further band appeared in the test results. Only one band had appeared in the tests on Area 10. How, then, did Mr Silverman conclude that the grouping might have been AK 2-1?

Mr Kennedy persuaded Mr Silverman to read an extract from a book on the typing of bloodstains by his witness's boss, the Head of Biology at the Metropolitan Police Laboratory – a Mr Culliford. This passage suggested that all bloodstains were subject to a deterioration in enzymes. The AK test was a test of enzymes, and was therefore often affected by this deterioration. The passage in Mr Culliford's book stated that the '2' band is more sensitive to deterioration than the '1' band. Thus, if Mr Silverman had only found the '2' band, it was a fair deduction that there had never been a '1' band. If there had been, it would have lasted longer than the '2' band.

Mr Silverman disagreed with his boss. He did not know, he said, 'of any biochemical reason' why the '2' should deteriorate faster than the '1'. He still insisted that there may have been a '1' band alongside the '2' band, but that the '1' band had deteriorated so that it no longer existed. This supposition, he said, led him to conclude that the blood grouping of Area 10 might be AK 2 (which he had seen in the test) or AK 2-1 (which he had not seen). The matter was vital. AK 2-1 was rare enough, but AK 2 was very rare indeed: only one in 500 of the British population has blood of that type, though the proportions are higher among Asians and Africans.

Mr Culliford's book suggested that the '2' would vanish before the '1'. That was one guide, not accepted by Mr Silverman. It was not until after he had been cross-examined, however, and was being asked questions once more by the prosecution that Mr Silverman was able to produce another guide. The court was poring over the diagrams of the results of Mr Silverman's tests, at the end of which he said:

> It must be a 2 or a 2-1, but I cannot see any way of assuming one or other of these two.
>
> *Q.* As being more likely?
>
> *A.* As being more likely.
>
> *Q.* Finally on that, have you got any indication of what you actually saw. You mentioned a photograph, I think?
>
> *A.* I did have some photographs here of the original plate.

Mr Silverman fished in his briefcase and handed some photographs to the court. Mr Hollis's questions about the photograph did not go very far, but when Mr Kennedy got up, the story shifted dramatically.

Mr Kennedy asked Mr Silverman to explain what would appear on the diagram if a fresh sample of AK 2-1 blood was being tested.

> *Q.* You would expect to find, would you not, in the uppermost position a strong line?
>
> *A.* Yes.
>
> *Q.* Below it, in the second position down, a line almost as strong – is that right?
>
> *A.* Yes; similar intensity.
>
> *Q.* And below it a very much weaker one?
>
> *A.* Well, as you can see from the photograph, somewhat weaker.

Q. Moving over to your 2 result, in the outermost or top position, a stronger reaction diagrammatically than anything we have looked at so far – is that correct?

A. Yes, it is. It is not necessarily stronger than the others. It is stronger than the next one, obviously, but the actual intensity, as I have said, depends on the amount of enzyme present.

Q. It may be so, but diagrammatically, there it is. You are trying to help us. The sample 2 reaction on the right-hand side of your diagram is much stronger at the top than the one next to it, is it not?

A. Yes.

Q. So there is a real difference between the top and the middle one for a 2 as compared to the top and the middle one for a 2-1.

A. There is more difference, yes.

Q. If you go to your photograph and look at the actual result of the 10, you have got that faint line in the top position have you not, and nothing below?

A. That is correct.

Q. If you scale them all up – do you see my point – and make the top one in the photograph even darker – do you follow?

A. Yes.

Q. It would follow it could not be any stronger below; the most you could hope for would be a much weaker line below as you turned the whole thing up?

A. Yes.

Q. That is a picture of a 2 reaction; very strong at the top, much weaker below.

A. Yes.

Q. All right?

A. 2 may fade like that eventually.

Q. That is it, is it – it looks more like a faint 2 rather than a faint 2-1 reaction, does it not?

A. It does look like a faint 2 reaction, as you say, but I still could not say anything about what is not there. It is just not possible.

It does look like a faint 2 reaction. In that simple sentence, Mr Silverman weakened his evidence for the prosecution: namely that Area 10 could be AK 2-1 blood, and therefore pointed to Jonathan Lewis. Confronted with his own photographs, which were not even shown to the court in his evidence-in-chief or in cross-examination, he was obliged to admit that the band which appeared on the diagram after his test suggested a reaction which was '2' and not '2-1'. The 2 reaction was proved by a strong line at the top and a weaker one at the bottom; the 2-1 by a strong line at the top and a line of equal strength underneath it. Therefore, if the top line is on its own, and if the bottom line has deteriorated so that it no longer exists, it is far more likely, scientifically, that the reaction was 2, not 2-1. Mr Silverman's proviso was not very convincing. 'I still could not say anything about what is not there,' he said, suggesting of course that there might have been another line underneath the one at the top, indicating a 2-1. But although Mr Silverman couldn't say anything about something which was not there, he could certainly say something about the fact that it wasn't there. The fact that it wasn't there suggested that it had been fainter than the one above it, which was there. If the blood had been 2-1, the bottom line would not have been fainter, but, in Mr Silverman's words, 'of similar intensity', and therefore not more or less likely to deteriorate than the top one.

The AK 2-1 theory had been destroyed, not by independent tests carried out for the defence – the defence could carry out no tests: there was no blood left for that from any of the samples – but by the prosecution's own expert witness and his photographs. 'It looks like a faint 2 reaction' was the conclusion, and it knocked right out of court the close association with the blood in the boot and Jonathan Lewis. AK 2 was not Jonathan's group, and the other groups which did fit Jonathan's blood also fitted a large proportion of the population. If there was in that spot under the petrol pipe cover some AK 2 blood, it was incontrovertible proof that someone else had bled into the boot: a possibility which the prosecution from first to last vigorously contested.

Though they could not prove satisfactorily that Jonathan Lewis's blood was in the boot, the prosecution sought to establish that Colin had gone to great lengths to clean out the boot of the car. In their first appeals to the public after taking possession of the car, the police had asked for any information about a black rubber lining, which was not in the boot when they took possession of the car. What could be more suspicious than a missing boot lining, when the allegation was that a bleeding man had been dumped in the boot, and left in it for at least three hours?

During their first inquiries, the police found evidence to suggest that Colin may have got rid of the boot mat the morning after Jonathan went missing. Colin himself had given them the idea in his question and answer with Detective Chief Inspector Harrison on 12 August:

Q. I am convinced that the lining of the boot is missing. Have you any idea where it is?

A. No, unless it went into the dustbin at the Council offices with the other rubbish from the boot.

It didn't take the police long to get down to the Council offices to ask questions about the rubbish bins, and what Colin might have emptied into them. They found three witnesses who remembered a man coming into the Council car park very early in the morning of 6 August, the day after Jonathan Lewis went missing. He had come, he told them, to clear out his *It's A Knockout* car which had to be returned that day. The three witnesses were all cleaners.

John Barnes said he remembered the man, who was Colin, taking a cardboard box, with something like a car jack sticking from it, out of the boot. Maisie Blight, a cleaner, saw the man wiping the boot with a cloth. Vera Tombs said, in her first statement (20 August 1980):

> I noticed there were some items in the bin which I didn't expect to be there. Normally there was just waste paper in the bins, but on this occasion I was slightly surprised to see this different rubbish. However, I did not notice what it was. I just put my rubbish on top of it.

This evidence changed at the trial. The Portsmouth *Evening News* of 10 March 1981 reported:

> One of the office cleaners, Mrs Vera Tombs, said the car was already there when she arrived about 5.45 am. She had looked in the council rubbish bins afterwards and there was a dark object like a jacket or a coat inside.

This incident at the Council offices, looked, on the face of it, odd. What was Colin doing so early in the morning after Jonathan's death clearing out his boot, in which, the prosecution alleged, the unconscious and bleeding body of his friend had spent so much of the previous evening? Colin's answer from the witness box was very simple. He did have to clear out the boot, which was full of polystyrene plastic cups and other paraphernalia from *It's A Knockout*. He was there very early in the morning dressed up in his suit because he had come straight from Jane's house where he had spent the night. All this was supported by other prosecution witnesses. Ned Wayne, Council tourism officer, confirmed that Colin reminded him at the celebration dinner that they had to deliver the car the following day; and that he and Colin had delivered it to Mr Galliford of Wadham Stringer, another prosecution witness, at Aldershot. Ned Wayne told the court he remembered meeting Colin at about 9.30 on the morning of 6 August, and he had said he was delivering the car that morning.

If there was nothing specially suspicious about cleaning out his car in full view of the cleaning staff in the bay reserved for him in the Council car park, what had happened to the missing boot mat? That it was missing was not in doubt. Ned Wayne, for one, who had inspected the car before it went back to Aldershot, noticed there was no boot mat, as there had been in the other *Knockout* Princess which he had driven.

Police sought high and low for the mat, and for anyone who had seen a boot mat in Colin's car. The best witness they could find was Patricia Ifould, a Council employee, who had travelled once or twice in Colin's car. In her first statement (15 August), she said:

When asked by police officers whether there had been a mat in the boot,
I could not remember. However, at 11.55 am on Friday 15th August I went
with a police officer to Arundel where I was shown an identical car to the
one Mr Wallace was using, both with and without a mat in the boot. I am
now fairly certain that there was a mat in the boot when I loaded it on the
18th July.

Patricia Ifould stuck to this not altogether overpowering evidence at
the trial. So, however, did John Ford, an employee of Wadham Stringer
who had looked in the boot of one of the *Knockout* cars (he couldn't
remember which) at the end of July. He said: 'I cannot recall seeing a
boot mat in the vehicle, but I am sure if there had not been one I would
have noticed it.'

Others were more certain. Philip Thorpe, who ran a promotions
company, and who borrowed Colin's car in July, said: 'I believe there
was no boot mat or carpet in the boot.'

His partner, John Wells, said: 'I remember the boot was all white, and
although I am not a hundred per cent certain I do not believe there was
a floor mat in the boot at the time.'

David Manton was an electrician who installed radios in the *It's A
Knockout* cars, on 10 June. He said: 'To the best of my recollection
one vehicle was fitted with a carpet lining mat and the other wasn't.'

Mrs Noelle Evans, wife of an Arun councillor, looked into the boot
of Colin's car as early as 9 June: 'I thought it looked tinny for a new
car,' she said. 'And I got the impression there was no boot mat in the
vehicle.'

No one could be sure they had seen the boot mat for which the
police had hunted so desperately after Jonathan's disappearance. The
overwhelming impression from the police's own evidence was that for
whatever reason (and we shall come to a very good reason in due course)
Colin's *It's A Knockout* car never had a boot mat.

The image still persisted of Colin vigorously wiping out his boot with a
cloth on the morning after his friend had vanished. He did not deny it. Was
he wiping away at the bloodstains? A good answer to that came from Mr
Silverman, the prosecution's blood specialist. Mr Kennedy asked him:

Q. In respect of none of these blood samples did you find anything – is this
right? – which looked like blood that had been washed or wiped over, that is
in the whole 20 of them – washed first?

A. That is correct.

Q. None washed, correct?

A. Yes.

Q. Nor wiped, correct?

A. Correct, yes.

Q. The spots did not appear to have been diluted, correct? Did not appear to have been the subject of washing, swabbing or anything like that?

A. That is correct.

Even before the defence brought its evidence, it was difficult to argue that there was any of Jonathan Lewis's blood in the car, or that Colin behaved at all suspiciously in cleaning it out, or that there was ever a boot lining for him to throw away. The evidence from the car was no stronger than the evidence from the house: there was little or none of it.

The police case was that Colin had rushed away from the hotel and driven straight to Gasworks Lane, near the Ford Roundabout. They said he had reversed his highly conspicuous car down the narrow, one-carriageway lane which was a very popular walking route, especially on fine summer evenings, as on 5 August. He had then carried the body to the sluice gate and tipped it into the river. High tide that evening was about 8.45 p.m. Low tide was about 3 a.m. At 10.30, therefore, the tide would have been two-thirds of the way up the bank.

It was a curious place to choose for the disposal of a body. The sluice gate is overlooked by a row of houses on the other side of the river, and another row on the same side. The much-used footpath runs past the sluice gate, which is also overlooked by the bridge over the Arun, part of the Arundel bypass. It is one of the most exposed parts of the river. If anyone, even at dusk, drove a white Austin Princess covered with Union Jacks down that track, and then single-handedly took a body from the boot and tipped it into the Arun, it would be a miracle if no one saw him.

No one saw Colin do this, however. No one saw his car in that position. Moreover, there was evidence from the river bank near the sluice gate which cast considerable doubt on the prosecution story.

On 6 August 1980, the day after Jonathan went missing, Miss Phyllis Pointer, was taking her usual walk by the riverside when she found Jonathan's watch just off the towpath by the sluice gate. The strap was broken. It was still ticking, and the time read 9.40. She handed it in to the police the next day, though it wasn't definitely identified as Jonathan's until 13 August, when it was shown to his father.

Did the condition of the watch disclose any information about what had happened to Jonathan? On 21 August, police took a statement from Michael Sergeant, a Worthing watchmaker who had sold the watch to Jonathan's mother (she gave it to him as a birthday present). Mr Sergeant said:

> The glass had been scratched with light and heavy scratches going in all directions which in my opinion had been caused by a swivelling movement

on rough ground. The strap was wrenched at the six o'clock position with considerable force. The bezel had been hit also with considerable force, and there were three or more dents at the eight o'clock position. To clarify the wrenching movement, I would describe the wrench as being down the arm towards the hand.

Mr Sergeant's evidence at the trial was 'that the damage to the watch could be consistent with an inert body having been dragged along the ground by somebody pulling it under the armpits with the watch catching onto something'. (Portsmouth *Evening News*, 10 March 1981.)

Mr Kennedy thought there was a considerable difference between this interpretation and the statement Mr Sergeant had given to the police the previous August which had suggested, at least, a violent encounter. Mr Sergeant was obliged to read out his earlier statement to the court, and was greeted by Mr Kennedy with a curt: 'No further questions.'

Two days after the watch was identified, police found another crucial piece of evidence. Constable John Fielding told the court that he was searching the area around the sluice gate when he saw a large bunch of keys in the long grass two feet off the footpath. The keys were quickly identified as the bunch which Jonathan carried with him, often in his hand rather than in his pocket.

The keys and the watch which were found within a few yards of each other inevitably suggested that the sluice gate area was the scene of an attack on Jonathan Lewis. Yet the police story which was eventually told to the jury at Lewes suggested no such thing. Instead the jury were asked to believe that Colin had tipped an unconscious Jonathan into the river after reversing his car down the track, and lugging the body to the river's edge.

Conceivably, the watch might have come off in such an operation, though the damage to it suggested a fight. But the keys could not be explained in the same way. If Colin or anyone else had tipped Jonathan's inert body into the water at the sluice gate, why would he have drawn attention to the spot by throwing the keys into some long grass beside a well-used footpath and a watch in the other direction? This was a question which more than once was asked of the prosecution. There was no credible reply.

Had Colin tipped the body into the river by the sluice gate? Had anyone disposed of the body there? The prosecution produced Police Diver James Cannon, who had been searching the River Arun near the sluice gate on 14 August, the day after the watch was found. 'On the south side of the sluice,' he said, 'I noticed there were marks on these blocks – they were just a few feet from the top of the grass bank that surmounts the concrete blocks. There were no marks leading up to these marks, and there were no marks continuing down the bank away from them.'

The marks had been photographed and the prosecution case was that they had been caused by a body sliding down the bank and into the river.

This argument didn't impress Mr Kennedy, or the judge. On 11 March the Portsmouth *Evening News* reported:

> Under cross-examination by Mr M. Kennedy for the defence PC Cannon agreed that there were many explanations for how the scuff marks could have been made. He agreed with Mr Justice Kilner Brown that if this had been the place where a body had been dragged to the river's edge and dumped into the water, he would have expected to see more marks on the bank.

The marks, PC Cannon agreed, would have been more likely to have been caused by someone walking down the bank into the river, or climbing up out of it.

Walking into the river at that spot would be dangerous and unlikely. But there was one witness who suggested that someone might have been walking in the river at the sluice gate later on the fatal night.

Douglas Hart, a steel fixer from Arundel, gave a statement to police on 14 August 1980, the day that PC Cannon found the scuff marks on the river bank facing.

> My hobby is night bass fishing. On Tuesday 5th August 1980, I left home at between midnight and 00.30 on Wednesday morning. I cycled to the new bridge where I normally stop and look into the water for signs of fish.
>
> This time I stopped and rode up onto the pavement, I looked over the bridge facing away from Arundel town centre when I saw what appeared to be a torch light. The light was stationary on the river bed immediately in front of the sluice gate, which comes out by the 'slipe' near the old gas works. As I looked, I saw the figure of a person walking past the light. I could not make out what the person was doing as it was so dark. It struck me as being unusual for anyone to be fishing there, or being down on the water's edge.

The tide at midnight was much lower than it had been at 10.30 when Colin Wallace is supposed to have heaved Jonathan's body into the river.

Douglas Hart gave evidence at the trial. He told the same story. No one knew what to make of it. Whoever it was on the river bed was not Colin Wallace. He was still at the Avisford Park Hotel, as plenty of witnesses testified.

One other prosecution witness had something to say about the place where Jonathan's body went into the Arun. Andre Buller, a boatman at Arundel, had hired out boats on the Arun since 1936. On the day they found Jonathan Lewis's body the police took a statement from him about the movement of the tides on this, the second fastest-flowing tidal river in Britain.

Mr Buller confirmed that high tide in Arundel was at 8.45 p.m. on 5 August. The water rose to a height of 4.9 metres, about 15 feet, and moved at a current speed of two knots. Mr Buller had fished many bodies out of the river, and had wide experience of the way in which bodies moved in the water. He said:

> In my opinion any body that entered the river at its junction with Queen Street [in the centre of Arundel] . . . would travel very slowly in the movement of the river, and would not reach the Ford area in three days.

Mr Buller's experience suggested that Jonathan Lewis's body was put in the water much further downstream. There are plenty of places further down the river where there is access to the river by road and track – all of them more remote than Gasworks Lane.

The prosecution evidence from the river and its bank seemed to favour Colin rather than damage him. Not only was there no evidence that he had tipped the body into the river at the sluice gate, there was a great deal of evidence, most of it brought by the prosecution, to suggest that such an act was most unlikely.

The Car Sightings

The cars for the *It's A Knockout* Jeux Sans Frontières were donated by the car dealers, Wadham Stringer. The decoration and delivery of the cars for the competition was organised by the firm's Worthing manager, Richard Harper, who gave evidence. Mr Harper said that the first decorated car, a white Princess, XOR 777V, was supplied for the use of the competition organisers on 16 March. That car was first used by Colin until May when a second white Princess – HPC 182V – was handed over to the Council. This second car was driven by Colin until 6 August, when he returned it, and the original car was taken over by the Council's tourism officer, Ned Wayne.

Two more white Princesses – WPF 450S and WPA 659S – and ten champagne-coloured ones were delivered a few days before the competition started in mid-July.

In all, fourteen Princesses were donated, four of them white, ten champagne, and all marked with Union Jacks and the slogans: THE GREAT BRITISH TEAM and ARUN: IT'S A KNOCKOUT.

The cars were distributed round the competing countries' teams, their doctors, the referees and the BBC. They were returned immediately after the competition, and sent back to Wadham Stringer. Mr Harper told the court that the cars were stripped of their *It's A Knockout* insignia as soon as they were returned. He said he had the keys for all except three of the cars by 31 July. All the champagne cars and one of the white cars were by that time stripped of their *It's A Knockout* livery. There were therefore, on 5 August, three white Princesses still marked with the distinctive slogans and flags. Colin had one, HPC 182V. The other two were parked outside the Avisford Park Hotel. On 24 July, WPA 659S – which had been allocated to one of the BBC producers, Tony Williams – broke down near the hotel. The throttle cable was broken. Richard Harper collected it and by pulling out the choke had been able to drift slowly into the car park. He said 'the car was immobile'. It was taken back to Worthing on 9 August.

The third car, WPF 450S, said Mr Harper, had been returned to Avisford Park on 31 July. It was not driven back to Wadham Stringer in Worthing until 6 August. The keys to the car had been handed by Mr Stathan, the BBC wardrobe master, to the receptionist at the Avisford Park Hotel the day he returned it, 31 July.

Mr Harper was asked what happened to the keys of this third car after that. In his first statement, only five days after Jonathan Lewis's body was found, he said: 'I believe it was on Monday, 4th August that I called at Avisford Park when I collected the keys for this car from reception.'

Eileen King, the hotel receptionist, said that she was on duty on that day in the afternoon when 'a man who I recognised as being from Wadham Stringers called at reception. He asked for a set of keys which had been left for him by Mr Stathan, and I handed him the keys in a sealed envelope.'

Mr Harper went on to say that he left the car outside the hotel and kept the keys. He couldn't remember what he did with the keys in between that time and the afternoon of 6 August, when he finally drove it away.

Thus a white Austin *It's A Knockout* Princess in good running order was outside the Avisford Park Hotel between Monday, 4 August and Wednesday, 6 August. There was no evidence from anyone that they had driven this car in that time.

A flood of witnesses responded to the police call to anyone who had seen an *It's A Knockout* car on 5 August, the day Jonathan Lewis went missing.

A large number of witnesses were called by the prosecution and testified to seeing an *It's A Knockout* car between 5.50 in the afternoon of 5 August and 8.00 in the evening. The first of these was George Godden, who saw Colin Wallace driving his car along the Ford Road towards Arundel at 5.50. No one ever disputed that this was Colin going home from the Council offices at Littlehampton, as he says he did. The last two witnesses, Mr

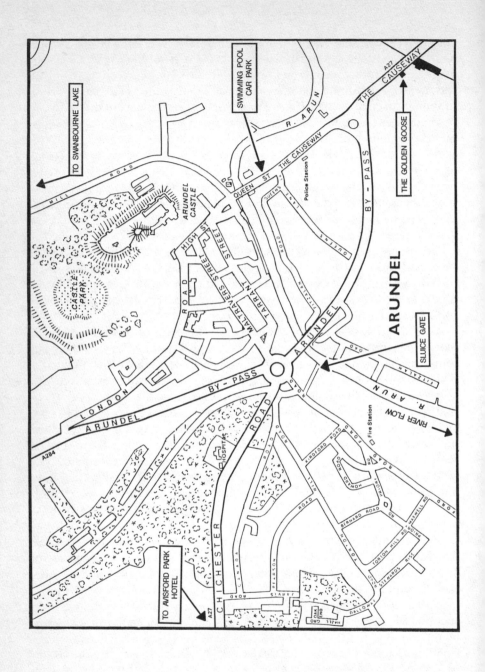

and Mrs (Roger and Jane) Towle saw an *It's A Knockout* car travelling west on the A27 near the Avisford Park Hotel 'between 7.40 and 7.45' (Jane) and '7.40' (Roger). No one disputed that this was Colin on his way to the celebration dinner. The time fitted neatly with the evidence of dinner guests who saw Colin in the hotel shortly before eight.

There were then twelve sightings recorded for the prosecution by the following witnesses:

At 'about 6 p.m.' Mrs Kathryn Vagg, who was in a coach on its way from London to Bognor, saw an *It's A Knockout* car at the Climping crossing on the road between Littlehampton and Bognor, travelling east. This car was heading in the opposite direction from the car seen by George Godden.

At about 6.30 p.m. John Taylor, supervisor of the swimming pool at Arundel, drove Pat Pescott, who worked at the swimming pool, home. They both said they saw an *It's A Knockout* car parked outside the police station opposite the swimming pool car park. One man was getting out of the car. No one disputed that this was Colin who had come to meet Jonathan as arranged.

At 6.25 (a time she could remember because she was catching a bus at 6.30) Mrs Dorothy Gregory saw a car parked on the eastern side of the bridge at Arundel, facing against the traffic. The prosecution said that this was Colin who for some reason had stopped on his way to the Lewis rendezvous. Colin said he hadn't stopped there.

Also at 6.25, Mrs Beatrice Budd left her home in Arundel to get fish and chips in the shop beyond the bridge. She came out of the shop and set off down Queen Street towards the station. Coming towards her was an *It's A Knockout* car. This could easily have been Colin on his way to pick up Jonathan at the swimming pool car park. His recollection puts him there a little later. Mrs Budd recalled that the *It's A Knockout* car had the letters WP in its registration. Colin's registration was HPC 182V. The other roadworthy *It's A Knockout* car was registered WPF 450S.

Between 6.30 and 7.00, Robert Brake, Colin's next-door neighbour, said he came home from work and saw an *It's A Knockout* car in the drive outside Colin's house. His sister Mrs Celia Phillips, however, who was visiting him that day, was less vague about the time. She said he had promised to be home 'about six': 'He came back a little later than he had stated. I would say about forty minutes – which would mean he arrived home at approximately 6.40,' said Mrs Phillips. Once again, this matches Colin's story that he was home, either with Jonathan or shortly before he picked him up, at that time.

'Between 6.40 and 6.45' Mrs Elizabeth Henton left her home in Arundel to take her little boy to the circus. She was pretty certain about the time because the circus started at seven and she got there in time for the start. She went onto the Arundel bypass and had to wait at the eastern roundabout for traffic. She saw a white car with a Union Jack on it and red, white and blue stripes on the side. It had 'It's A Knockout' and 'Jeux Sans Frontières' written on it. 'This vehicle travelled onto the roundabout from the Crossbush end,' she said.

Mrs Henton's evidence seemed to contradict the story which Colin told about his movements. Within five minutes of his car being seen outside his house, an *It's A Knockout* car was seen at the eastern roundabout, at least five minutes' drive away, heading onto the roundabout from the opposite direction. Mrs Henton recalled that the car had 'It's A Knockout' written on it. Colin's car, alone of the three which were on the road at the time, had had the 'It's A Knockout' sticker removed the previous Sunday from front and back windows. The other two cars still had the stickers on them.

At about 7 p.m., Mrs Rita Mills was walking by the New Bridge. She saw an *It's A Knockout car* coming towards them over the New Bridge. 'I couldn't be certain but I believe that the vehicle contained two people,' she said.

This could have been Colin bringing Jonaaaaaaathan back to his house. Mrs Mills could not be sure of the time, and it could have been a bit earlier. Colin insisted that he had not taken Jonathan back via the New Bridge, but had gone straight through Arundel and had joined the roundabout on the edge of the town. Once again, Mrs Mills remembered seeing the inscription 'It's A Knockout' which had been taken off Colin's car. She had good reason to remember this, since she recalled in her statement only eight days afterwards that she was surprised that the competition was still being advertised when it had finished.

Some time between 6.00 and 6.45, John Duffield, barman at the popular Black Rabbit pub on the other side of Arundel looked up from the bar to see, parked outside the pub, an *It's A Knockout* car. 'I can remember it,' he said twelve days afterwards, 'because I was surprised the vehicle was still being used so long after the competition had ended . . . During the competition a number of people came to the Black Rabbit for drinks and meals. I can remember looking in the bar for any of them when I saw the car, but there was nobody in the bar that I knew was involved with *It's A Knockout*. I do know Colin Wallace, an organiser, by sight and name and he was not in the bar that evening.

'The bar faces outwards and from behind the bar you can see the driveway in front of the inn and part of the car park. I started behind the bar that evening at 6 pm when the bar opened and was behind the bar for my first session until 6.45. I can't remember the exact time I saw the car but it was definitely during my first session.'

Mr Duffield was absolutely certain that this happened on 5 August, because that evening he went on a water-skiing holiday.

It is at least eight minutes' run from Colin's house to the Black Rabbit. It is hard to see how Colin could have picked up Jonathan at about 6.30

(Pescott, Taylor and Budd), returned to his home by 6.40 (Brake) and somehow got to the Black Rabbit before Mr Duffield finished his first session at 6.45.

Between 7.15 and 7.20, Leslie Holdsworth was driving with Norman Gaskin to Chichester from Littlehampton. He left Littlehampton at 7.10 and drove along the A259 west towards Bognor. As he approached the junction with the Ford Road which leads to Arundel, he saw an *It's A Knockout* car stationary in the Ford Road waiting to turn left into their road, towards Littlehampton.

The prosecution suggested that this car was driven by Colin who had left his home (where his car had been seen half an hour earlier) to carry out 'a reconnaissance' of likely places where he could dump Jonathan's body in the river. The problem, as the defence pointed out, was that the car seen by Messrs Holdsworth and Gaskin had driven past all the remote areas of access to the Arun and, if it had turned left as the two witnesses said it was doing, would have met the river in the centre of Littlehampton which in high summer on a fine evening was swarming with people.

At 7.20 p.m. (less than five minutes after Messrs Holdsworth and Gaskin saw the car near Littlehampton, driving from Arundel) Mrs Celia Phillips saw Colin's car parked outside his house. Mrs Phillips, as we have seen, was the sister of Colin's next-door neighbour, Robert Brake. She had visited him that evening, hoping that he would return by six. He had come back late, at about 6.40, and testified that he had seen Colin's car outside his house at that time. Mrs Phillips spent twenty minutes with her brother and then took her leave.

'At approximately 7 p.m.,' she said in her last statement, five days after the event, 'I got up to leave. We walked out to my car a few minutes later, and stood in the road talking for a while as we said goodbye to each other. It was at this time that I saw the white Austin Princess with the red and blue on the side. I knew that this car was something to do with the Arun *It's A Knockout* contest. I am positive that it was 7.20 p.m.'

Finally at 8 p.m. or shortly afterwards Peter Ayling and his girlfriend Angela Smith were driving north along the Ford Road towards Arundel. They came up behind an *It's A Knockout* car travelling slowly in the same direction. 'I eventually overtook the car just before the roundabout at the New Bridge,' said Mr Ayling.

Ten minutes earlier the car had been seen travelling in the opposite direction – towards the Avisford Park Hotel, where at least four witnesses saw Colin in the bar at almost exactly the same time Mr Ayling said he saw a *Knockout* car on the Ford Road.

These witnesses, the prosecution argued, all saw Colin's car, driven by Colin. It was, by any measure, an extraordinary hour and a half for that car. It was seen at ten to six near Littlehampton travelling towards Arundel, which was at least ten minutes away (Godden). Ten minutes later it was seen at exactly the same spot travelling in the opposite direction (Vagg). Thirty minutes later it was parked outside Arundel police station (Pescott, Taylor). Ten minutes after that (6.40) it was outside Colin's house (Brake). Five minutes later it approached the eastern roundabout from the opposite direction to Arundel (Henton). At some time during all this, it was parked outside the Black Rabbit pub (Duffield). Half an hour later (7.15), it was back near Littlehampton at almost the same spot as it was seen at 5.50, although once again it was heading in the opposite direction (Holdsworth and Gaskin). At the same time it was seen once more parked outside Colin's house (Phillips). It was going towards the Avisford Park at 7.40 (Mr and Mrs Towle), and going away from it at Arundel roundabout ten minutes later (Ayling). During this amazing journey, none of the witnesses, except the first, identified Colin as the driver.

The overall picture that evening was that more than one *Knockout* car was travelling about in the area. That picture becomes clearer from further sightings of *Knockout* cars in the morning of 5 August.

Three witnesses came forward with evidence that they had seen an *It's A Knockout* car in the Arundel area that morning. Jennifer Homer, a journalist, saw an *It's A Knockout* car at 10.10 a.m. parked on the road to the Black Rabbit near a local beauty spot, Swanbourne Lake. The car seemed to be empty, she said. At 12.45, Mary Tubb was passed by an *It's A Knockout* car heading north towards Arundel on the other side of the town. She didn't notice the driver. Most curiously of all, Councillor John Hinchcliffe, a barrister who was legal adviser to the *News of the World* newspaper (and who knew Colin), was driving past Swanbourne Lake towards the Black Rabbit. In front of him was an *It's A Knockout* car. 'There was one person in the car. I believe it was a girl,' he said. The time was about 1.45 p.m.

Could any of these cars have been Colin's? It was unlikely. Colin was working that morning. He spent most of it at the Arun Leisure Centre at Bognor Regis, attending a function with the Chairman of the Council. The Council were entertaining a party of German school children. The children and their hosts ate lunch at the Leisure Centre. Colin was at the Leisure Centre, surrounded by people, from about 10.00 that morning until after lunch. His car was parked in the car park there.

Three more witnesses cast still further doubt that only one *Knockout* car was on the road that day. They saw an *It's A Knockout* car later on the fatal evening. The evidence of these three witnesses provided nothing but embarrassment to the prosecution, who called them.

Robin Arnold, a store manager from Rustington, made a statement to the police on 13 August and another one four days later on the 17th. He told them he had met his girlfriend, Vivian, at her house at Fitzalan Road, Arundel, at about 7 p.m. on 5 August. Some time later, he drove her to the Black Rabbit for a drink. On the way there, he saw an *It's A Knockout* car parked on the Black Rabbit side of the bridge by Swanbourne Lake. 'It was on the left side of the road, on the lake side of the bridge. I cannot say which way it was facing. I did not see anyone in the vehicle,' he said.

The couple stayed at the pub for about half an hour. Vivian felt ill, so Mr Arnold ran her back to Arundel. He didn't see anything on the way back. After dropping his girlfriend, he returned to the Black Rabbit where he met his twin brother Roger, a drug store manager in Bognor, and Roger's friend Mark Robinson, a car salesman. The three men left the pub after about an hour. On the way into Arundel, said Robin, he saw an *It's A Knockout* car on the other side of the bridge – the Arundel side – again parked on the lake side of the road.

On 17 August (four days after his first statement) Robin Arnold was seen again by the police. He was able to fix the time of his first sighting of the car at about 8.45 p.m.

His twin, Roger, corroborated all this. He had picked up Mark Robinson in Littlehampton at about 8.30, and drove straight to the Black Rabbit, which took him about fifteen minutes. He didn't see anything on the way to the pub, but when he and Mr Robinson came back from the pub at about 9.45, he noticed 'a white Austin Princess with red and white and blue markings on the side. It was parked on the west side of the bridge by Swanbourne Lake on the right hand side of the road facing towards Arundel.' He reckoned he was home at Rustington at 10 o'clock, and was able to remember the date very clearly since, on his arrival home, his mother told him that the burglar alarm had gone off at his Bognor store. The store had been broken into, and Mr Arnold had to go to the police. All this was checked by the police. There was no doubt that it happened on 5 August.

Had there been any doubt about this it was laid to rest by Mr Mark Robinson, who confirmed everything the Arnold twins had said. On 13 August he told police: 'We left the pub at about 9.45 and on driving over the bridge by Swanbourne Lake I saw a white car parked on the right hand side of the road. I did not notice any markings on it, but Roger remarked on it being a Princess. We then had a short conversation criticising the make of car in general.'

Mr Robinson said he met a friend in a Littlehampton restaurant by 10 p.m.

All these three witnesses were fielded by the prosecution. Colin Wallace could not possibly have driven the *It's A Knockout* car which they saw. In the company of a large number of witnesses, including the divisional commander of the Sussex Constabulary, he was attending a dinner at the Avisford Park Hotel.

Mr Hollis, prosecuting counsel, tried to make the best of a bad job. He pointed out that in his statement to the police on 23 August, Colin had admitted to leaving the hotel when he felt ill, and driving to the Black Rabbit in a search for Jonathan. No doubt, argued Mr Hollis, Colin had stopped off at Swanbourne Lake, ten minutes' drive from the hotel, perhaps to survey the possibility of dumping the body there. While he was on such a reconnaissance, his car was spotted by the Arnolds and Mr Robinson.

There was a problem with this theory. Robin Arnold had said that he had first seen the car on the way to the pub with his girlfriend at 8.45. The time checked with the story of the other two witnesses. It could also have been checked with the girlfriend, Vivian Troyne, who for some reason was not asked to make a statement.

At 8.45, without any doubt whatever, Colin Wallace was at the Avisford Park Hotel. All the guests – there were twelve of them – testified that they waited at least until 9.15 before going in to dine. During all that period Colin Wallace was with the company. The car which Robin Arnold saw at a quarter to nine at Swanbourne Lake could not have been taken there by Colin Wallace.

What about the second sighting, at 9.45, at the latest? Mr Hollis strove to prove that this car was driven by Colin after he had left the dinner. In a dialogue with the judge, he argued that the evidence of the people at the dinner was that Colin had left in time to get to Swanbourne Lake by a quarter to ten.

> My Lord, we have got the evidence of Mrs Taylor who says the main course started at 9.40, the witnesses who say, broadly speaking, if they noticed at all, that it was – Mrs Fynn says that the main course had just been served, which she puts at 9.45 to 9.50, then the estimate of the time that he was away. My Lord, we could say 9.40.

Even if 9.40 was a fair time to estimate Colin's leaving the dinner, it was still a rush for him to be at Swanbourne Lake, park the car and get out of sight before the Arnolds and Mr Robinson saw it at 9.45.

But all the guests except Mrs Taylor put Colin's departure from the hotel much later. They had waited at least until 9.15, according to some witnesses, and as late as 9.30, according to others, before starting their meal. There was a soup course, and a main course. Colin did not leave until after the main course had been served.

It is true that Mrs Bernard Taylor had said in her very first statement that the main course was served at 9.40 and that she had remembered the time because she had checked it on someone else's watch. (Mrs Fynn, incidentally, had not estimated a time in her first statement, and was only persuaded to do so by an insistent Mr Hollis.)

This was contradicted by evidence of a most precise nature from the waitress in charge of serving the meal, Mrs Eileen Whiting. She had good cause to remember the meal, since it was so long delayed. When she spoke to police on 14 August, only nine days after the event, she was quite specific.

> The party sat down at 9.30 pm. The starter was served at 9.40 or just after. Most of the guests had soup, which was served at 9.50. Mrs Lewis didn't have soup. The gentleman next to her, who I now know to be Mr Wallace, didn't have soup either. I served Mr Wallace with a fish course. I can't remember what he said to me, but he struck me as being very polite and jolly.
>
> During the time that the main course was being consumed, Mrs Lewis again went to the telephone, returned, and Mr Wallace then got up and left the room. I noticed that he was away for some time and that he had eaten barely half of it. The main course was served at approximately 10.20 pm. Mr Wallace left approximately five minutes after the main course was served. This would have been at about 10.25 pm.

Mrs Nancy Chadwick, the other waitress, was not quite so precise about the times. She said (on 14 August): 'The party took their places for dinner at approximately 9.30 pm. It was not until about 10 pm that the main course was finally served.'

Michael Gibaux, head waiter at the Avisford Park, said (on 14 August): 'In fact, I believe that it was after 10 pm before the main course was served.'

James Parker, deputy manager of the Avisford Park Hotel, told police (on 14 August):

> The main course was held back as well. And a few people left the table for various reasons. I called Mrs Wayne away to see to her baby who was being looked after in the office. Mr Wayne went to see what his wife was up to and Mr Baker went to the toilet. After they all returned, one of the waitresses went to see Mr Fynn to ask if the main course could be served. He said yes, and the main course was served between 9.50 and 10.10. The serving was finished near 10.30.

Everyone connected with the serving of the dinner agreed that the main course had not been served at 9.40 (when Mrs Taylor checked on someone else's watch) but much later than that – at least half an hour later. Indeed the probability is that in checking on someone else's watch, Mrs Taylor had misread the time by an hour: and that the main course was not fully served until 10.40.

Final evidence of the lateness of the meal was provided by all the guests and staff, who confirmed that the party did not rise from the table until just after midnight. If the main course had been served at 9.40, they would have finished a great deal earlier.

There was, in short, no credible evidence 'capable of corroborating' Arnold and Robinson as Mr Hollis claimed. He had the statements from the waitresses. His selection of one unlikely statement to counter all the other specific timings of the staff did not present an accurate picture of what happened. The plain fact is, as Mrs Whiting and Jane Lewis testified, that Colin Wallace did not leave the hotel until long after the Arnold twins and Mark Robinson, in two separate sightings, saw the mysterious *It's A Knockout* car in the gloaming, parked either side of the bridge by Swanbourne Lake.

Several people made statements to the police about car sightings on 5 August which conflicted so sharply with the prosecution case that they did not call them at the trial. Some were called by the defence.

James Mackay said he saw an *It's A Knockout* car on the A27 near the Avisford Park Hotel travelling towards Arundel. The time was about 6.30, give or take ten minutes. The car was driven by a male driver with dark hair and wearing a blue jacket. Colin had very little hair indeed, and what little he had was greying. At 6.30, three other witnesses (and the prosecution) had him picking up Jonathan at the swimming pool car park. Mr Mackay made his first statement on 13 August. In February 1981, shortly before the trial, police visited him again and suggested he had got the date wrong. He resisted this, pointing out that he and his wife, only a week after the event, had worked out that they saw the car on 5 August. Mr Mackay was equally firm when he gave evidence for the defence.

Mrs Muriel Ward was cycling down Priory Road towards Ford Road on the outskirts of Arundel. When she reached the junction of Ford Road, she saw an *It's A Knockout* car travelling away from Arundel on the Ford Road. It was certainly between 6.30 and 6.45, she said, because she arrived on her cycle at Littlehampton at 7.30. The man driving the car had a brown jacket on; 'I think he was wearing glasses,' she added. Mrs Ward was a highly credible witness who was sure of her story. The car she saw hardly fitted Colin's car, which was outside his home at 6.40. Colin doesn't have a brown jacket and he doesn't wear glasses. He was meant to be killing Jonathan at that time, so the prosecution didn't call Mrs Ward. She spoke up firmly for the defence, and was not shaken.

Lynn Phillips, a schoolgirl, said she was walking over the main bridge in Arundel at 6.45 when she was passed by an *It's A Knockout* car driving into the town. She could not say anything about the driver, but Colin and the defence believed this to be his car, driven by him after picking up Jonathan. The defence called Lynn Phillips to reinforce their story that Colin had driven through the town after picking up his friend, and not back via the western roundabout and the New Bridge, where an *It's A Knockout* car had been seen.

David Bull, a printer who lived at Arundel, said he went for a drink at the Bridge Hotel at about 8.30 on 5 August. An *It's A Knockout* car was parked outside in the forecourt. Mr Bull wasn't absolutely sure of the time – it could have been up to half an hour later, he said. Colin Wallace, either at 8.30 or at 9.00, was in the Avisford Park.

Mr Bull's story got even stranger. He said that he went back to his printing works late that night. As he walked back from work at five past one in the morning, he saw an *It's A Knockout* car parked facing the wall outside the ladies toilet opposite the Swan Hotel. The car, he said, was unoccupied.

At five past one in the morning of 6 August, Colin Wallace, together with five other people, was at Jane Lewis's house at Angmering, and his car was parked outside.

Mr Bull's statement, like Lynn Phillips', was taken by the police, but not originally submitted in the prosecution bundle. What he had to say was relegated to the bunch of 'statements not tendered' where it was discovered by a diligent defence.

Michael Hoath, who was not called by the prosecution, said he was towing a boat down the Ford Road from Arundel as 'it was approaching dusk'. Just south of the level crossing at Ford junction he passed an *It's A Knockout* car travelling north towards Arundel.

According to the Meteorological Office, sunset on 5 August was at 8.41. Dusk could be up to an hour or even an hour and a half after that – all of which time Colin was in the hotel. Mr Hoath's testimony may have had rather more significance than appeared at first sight. The boatman, Andre Buller, as we have seen, said that the body of Jonathan Lewis was unlikely to have floated down as far as the Ford Marina if it had been dropped in at Arundel. He reckoned it would have to have been dumped much further south. There are several places near where Mr Hoath saw the *Knockout* car 'in the dusk' where there is easy access by road to isolated spots on the River Arun. However, Mr Hoath was never called.

When all the evidence about the cars is taken into account, there is only one permissible conclusion. It is that throughout the day, evening and night of Tuesday, 5 August, more than one *Knockout* car was being driven about in the vicinity of Arundel. Some of the sightings confirm Colin's movements, as he outlined them to the police. Some do not confirm those movements. But a large number of sightings were of a car or cars which cannot have been Colin's. Three witnesses in the morning and as many as eight witnesses in the evening and night saw *Knockout* cars which could not have been driven by Colin Wallace. Another car seemed to be dogging his path, but also seems on more than one occasion to have been in places where he could not have been.

Was such a car a phantom or could it have been WPF 450S, which was roadworthy and was left at the Avisford Park on the 4th, and not picked up till the 6th? One important witness may have helped answer that question.

Superintendent Bill Taylor told the court he had been a detective for twenty-seven years and had developed a habit of paying attention to detail. When he arrived for the dinner party at the Avisford Park Hotel, he said:

> When my wife and I arrived at the hotel, I did see two Austin Princess motor cars parked in the forecourt near the hotel entrance.
>
> We arrived at the hotel at 7.55 and were met at the door by Mrs Fynn. Whilst we were speaking to her, Mrs T. Baker walked into the hotel and said her husband had gone to park the car. When her husband came into the hotel we were still waiting for him in the foyer with Mrs Fynn. After a very short conversation Mrs Fynn told us to go through to the bar where the other guests were. The four of us went into the bar. In this bar was Mr Ned Wayne and his wife and one other person whom I believe was Colin Wallace. I remember Mr Baker speaking to Mr Wallace at the bar and asking him what he would like to drink. I asked Mr Wallace how he was, and he said he was fine but he had had a stomach upset during the last few days.

This was corroborated by Mrs Miranda Taylor, another of the guests:

> We arrived at about 7.55 pm. When we arrived the following people were already there, Supt Taylor and his wife, Tony Baker and his wife, Tony Fynn, Ned and Honor [Wayne] and Colin Wallace. I know they were all there because my husband introduced them to me when I arrived.

This did not prove that Colin got to the hotel before Bill Taylor, as the superintendent himself suggests. One other guest, Tony Baker, suggested (though he was far from certain) that Colin arrived after the policeman.

If the superintendent was right, however, if he arrived after Colin, the fact that he noticed two *Knockout* cars parked at the hotel is extraordinary. One of the cars, WPA 659S, had a broken cable and was immobile. That was certainly there. If Colin arrived before Taylor, and parked his car, as he remembers, alongside another one, that made two. Yet there was a third car. If the senior police officer with an eye for detail was right, that he arrived after Colin Wallace and that there were only two *Knockout* cars parked outside, one of the three, the elusive WPF 450S, had gone missing.

The Motive

Central to the prosecution case was that Colin had a motive to kill Jonathan. He was in love with Jane, and felt that the only barrier to a permanent relationship with her was her husband. In his opening speech Mr Hollis drew a picture of a man increasingly frustrated that his advances to Jane were being repelled. There was, Mr Hollis admitted, no sexual intercourse in the relationship. 'The normally cheerful PR man would become quiet and withdrawn' he said. After the *It's A Knockout* competition, he said, 'she pulled herself together and started behaving to him normally, as she had done before. What was the effect on Colin Wallace? Did he feel frustration that he couldn't have her because she was married?'

Only one witness gave evidence for the prosecution on this relationship – Jane Lewis. She went into the witness box on the fourth day of the trial, and was there for most of the day. She stuck to the story she had told police from the moment she started making detailed statements to them on 10 August, the day after her husband's body had been found. In these statements, as we have seen, Jane admitted to 'an association' with Colin which 'stopped short of adultery but had involved kissing, cuddling etc and going on three occasions for a walk in the country'. In court Jane expanded a little on this, admitting that she had felt guilty that she had been leading Colin on to expect a deeper relationship, when in fact she did not want one. She was asked about Colin's reaction to this, and she repeated that Colin's 'attitude was one of resignation'. There was nothing in her evidence which gave the slightest hint that Colin felt angry or resentful or even jealous towards Jonathan. Equally, though she went through her conversations with Jonathan about a possible relationship with Colin, which she had denied, she repeated that Jonathan was not in the least 'obsessed' with this, as the prosecution suggested.

Jane Lewis was an impressive witness. She spoke up clearly and truthfully. There was also no doubt in Colin's mind (nor in the mind of anyone else who heard her) that she believed Colin Wallace had killed her husband. She repeated the charge which she made to him as they drove to Arundel when Jonathan's car was first found there: 'Has this got anything to do with you?' and Colin's instant denial. Her suspicions against her former boss had started then, and grown.

Michael Kennedy cross-examined her gently. He reminded her in a series of delicate questions that the liaisons between her and Colin in hotels in Switzerland and Lancashire during the *It's A Knockout* competition had taken place in Colin's room, to which she had chosen to go. She agreed that she had initiated many of these meetings, and that Colin had in no way been importunate. Nor had he made any advances to her after Jonathan's death.

The police had interviewed all Colin's colleagues at the Council. None of them were able to say anything about the relationship between Colin and Jane. Most of them had no idea that there was anything between them. Jane's evidence did not seem to contradict Colin's assertion, in his description of his last meeting with Jonathan, that the short-lived 'affair' (if it was worthy of that description) was rapidly coming to an end. When Michael Kennedy asked her if the affair, 'rather like the affairs of *Knockout*, was in the process of being wound up', she agreed at once.

The best summary of the evidence on this question came from the judge, in his summing up. 'The evidence all indicates that the tension had largely gone out of the situation in so far as those two were concerned.'

Colin's Interviews

By far the most powerful part of the prosecution's case was their account of Colin's interviews with the police after the murder – and his lies not only to the police but also to his wife and his closest friends about his last meeting with Jonathan. We have seen how he kept back from the dinner guests that he had met Jonathan earlier in the evening; how he failed to tell any of the people at Jane's house that he had seen Jonathan; how he kept up his subterfuge after the car was found and during his and Jane's awkward admission of their relationship to the police chief, Bill Taylor. On 10 August he made a false statement to the police, sticking to his story that he had not met Jonathan the night he died.

Detective Chief Inspector Harrison gave the court a dramatic account of the change in the story which followed. He said that he told Colin that the police had a witness who had seen the *It's A Knockout* car by the swimming pool car park on the evening of Jonathan's death – and that the police also had Jonathan's diary which had an entry 'Colin, 6.30'. He said he had told Wallace: 'This is not a game of squash with me serving up the questions and you hitting back the answers. Your whole attitude is defensive and untruthful.'

Mr Harrison continued: 'Wallace then rested his chin on his right hand and sat in silence for two minutes.' Harrison drew up his chair and told him: 'Now tell us the truth.' Colin had then asked: 'Can I tell Jane first?' When the detective said they would think about it, Colin told the quite different story of his meeting with Jonathan at 6.30; the phone call arranging the meeting; the conversation about the affair; and dropping Jonathan off in the centre of Arundel some time before 7.30.

Under cross-examination Mr Harrison agreed that since that time Colin's story had been absolutely consistent, and that there were several witnesses, including the next door neighbours, who went some way to corroborate it. But the damage done by the change in statements was irreversible. If all the other evidence for the prosecution was hopelessly jumbled, the one fact which came out clearly was that Colin, for no obvious reason, had lied about meeting Jonathan on the night he died, and that lie cast grave doubt on the truth of his account of that meeting.

In evidence for the defence Colin repeated what he has always said. He was, he argued, trapped by the awkward circumstances of the occasion. He had not wanted to talk about the meeting with Jonathan in public, especially in front of his wife. He had wanted to tell Jane about it in private, but had no chance to do so that evening, because of the way the three of them – Colin, Eileen and Jane – had travelled in separate cars back to Angmering. As soon as he had lied, he was stuck with his lie. He did not think it mattered very much as long as he was expecting Jonathan to turn up. Even after the body was found, he felt the truth about their meeting was unimportant – and he was sustained in that by the news that foul play was not suspected.

When he went to the police station on the Sunday night, he reminded the court, he had assumed that Jonathan had died by accident, since that had been the official view of the police, reported in the newspapers. He still felt it was better not to disclose the embarrassing meeting with Jonathan. But when the police told him they thought Jonathan had been murdered, he realised that the whole scene had shifted. Now it was vital for the police to know exactly what Jonathan's movements had been. Now he had to tell the truth. His question to the police: 'Can I tell Jane first?' is some proof that his central worry – that Jane would be upset by the conversation the two men had had – was uppermost in his mind.

This explanation gives some reason why Colin should not have told the truth at once, but it did little to endear him to the court. It was not so much his false statements to the police which did him damage: it was his deceit of the woman who had lost her husband; his failure to disclose to her friends who were rushing round the county talking to garages, car park attendants and antique dealers in the search for Jonathan that he had seen him as late as 7.20 on the night he died. Colin's naturally secretive nature, developed no doubt by all those years of covert operations, had opted for the safety of secrecy in an embarrassing situation – with devastating results.

Amanda Metcalfe

The fact that a man had told lies about his movements in the first few days after the disappearance of his friend did not make him a killer. The prosecution could not expect Colin to be convicted simply because he had told a false story before he knew that Jonathan had been murdered. As the prosecution case drew to a close, its contradictory and insubstantial nature irritated even the judge. The worst moment for the prosecution came when they called Amanda Metcalfe, the barmaid in the Golden Goose pub.

We have seen how Amanda Metcalfe first came to the notice of the police. She told police there that she had seen a man who looked like Jonathan Lewis in her pub some time after seven o'clock on, she thought, 5 August. The police reaction to this vital witness, who was certainly the only person, apart from Colin, who told them they had seen Jonathan after seven o'clock on the night he died, was to do nothing. A few days later (21 August), Sergeant Snelling made his way up to the Golden Goose and took a statement from Amanda, in which she confirmed in a few lines that she saw Jonathan Lewis 'after 7 pm'. The day 'might have been Tuesday 5th August because I believe it was on the same day that Vince, a new bar man, started which was 5 August 1980'.

Amanda Metcalfe's statement was shoved aside as 'untendered evidence'. An uncommitted solicitor, playing by the book, might never have noticed it. But Colin's team insisted on seeing all the untendered statements. When they saw what Amanda Metcalfe had said they could hardly believe it. Private detectives were sent to interview her. The defence urged the prosecution to call her as a witness. The prosecution were in a dilemma. Amanda Metcalfe had been interviewed by the police. She did have something crucial to say. Not to call her would look odd. To call her, as they did, obliged them to discredit their own witness.

In the witness box, Amanda Metcalfe stuck closely to the detailed statement she had given to the defence, on 9 January, five months after the event, and two months before the trial. In full, it read like this:

> I work and live at the Golden Goose Hotel which is owned by my parents. I have been living and working here since November 19th 1979.
>
> During the course of my work in the hotel bar, there is only one bar, I have noticed a man and woman visit these premises on several occasions for drinks. They have always kept themselves to themselves and I was not aware who they were. The gentleman always came in with the same woman, a dark-haired girl with a fringe. Although I am not good at estimating ages of people I would say the gentleman was about 25 to 28 years, and the girl slightly younger. The gentleman was about 5' 10" tall, slim to medium build, with mousey brown hair. He was usually dressed in a casual/conservative manner and from my recollections may have worn a cardigan sometimes. I have never seen him get out of a car and I have no idea of what make of car he owns. Their visits to these premises were mainly mid-evening and I have never seen him here

during lunchtimes when I have been working and previously never without the girl.

On Tuesday, 5th August, 1980 I worked in the bar from 6.00 pm until 7.00 pm and after that time I stayed on to assist possibly because there was a new member of staff starting i.e. 'Vince' who still works here, I do not know his surname. I know positively that it was not between 6.00 pm and 7.00 pm but after that time I noticed the gentleman referred to earlier in my statement was sitting in the bar. I particularly noticed him because firstly he was not accompanied by the girl instead he was with another man and secondly he was dressed up a little more trendy in a light coloured jacket, creamy beige colour, brown tie, dark coloured socks, may have been chocolate brown. I have an impression that his trousers were light also but I could not swear to it. He looked smarter than his normal casual wear seen by me previously. At the time I noticed him I was engaged in carrying some crockery or glasses on a tray through the bar which necessitated me walking towards him. When I was about 6–7 yards from him he turned and looked in my direction and I recognised him. He was sitting in a chair opposite the bar with his legs crossed and stretched out full length in front of him. He didn't look particularly happy from his expression although at no time did he speak to me. The other man accompanying the gentleman I now know was Mr Lewis appeared to be a little older with hair that was brushed back over his head. I do not recall seeing a parting. He was not balding as far as I can recall. I did not see him standing so I cannot give any estimation of height. I really cannot give any other further information concerning this man as I did not have cause to speak to him for any reason. I had not previously seen this man on these premises and I do not recall seeing him since.

The reason I am fairly certain about the time is due to the fact that I was not behind the bar when Mr Lewis and the other man came in, in fact, I am not aware whether they came into the premises together or separately and further at no time did I serve them with any drinks.

I have seen a very unclear photograph of Mr Wallace in the newspaper but I could not identify him from that.

The reason I am certain that the gentleman I have referred to as Mr Lewis is Mr Lewis is due to the fact that I saw Mr Lewis's photograph displayed by the Police in Arundel on a Police caravan. I reported my observations to the Police.

I should add that I did not see either Mr Lewis or the other man leave the Hotel on the 5th August, 1980 and I am not aware of any vehicle they may have had.

The first part of the statement contains a very accurate description of Jonathan and Jane Lewis (he was 29, she 27); he was 5' 10½", slim to medium build, with dark brown hair. He often wore a sweater and rarely dressed formally. He and Jane did visit the Golden Goose on a number of occasions – though not frequently.

The next part of the statement confirms Miss Metcalfe's certainty that the day she saw Jonathan in the pub was the day he died, and that the time she saw him was after 7 p.m. Both matters were corroborated by the fact that 'Vince' was a new barman, had started work at 7, and that it was after Vince had started work that she had seen the man she described.

A crucial part of the statement deals in the most extraordinary detail with Jonathan Lewis's clothes. Her description exactly corresponded with what Jonathan was wearing on 5 August. Jane Lewis in her evidence had described Jonathan's beige corduroy suit, which he had changed into for the celebration that evening. He rarely wore a suit. Miss Metcalfe's description of the shoes, tie, and even the socks was absolutely accurate.

All this she stuck to closely and convincingly. If the police had bothered to make detailed inquiries when they first got the statement, this matter could have been settled once and for all. Jonathan Lewis could not have visited the Golden Goose on any day after 5 August – he was dead. Could Amanda Metcalfe have seen him on any other day before that? On Monday, 4 August, Jane Lewis testified, she and Jonathan went out to dinner to celebrate their first wedding anniversary. Jonathan played squash with Colin that night at the Avisford Park. Jane collected him there at about 7.30 and the couple drove off to the Old Timbers restaurant near Chichester, in the other direction from the Golden Goose. Jonathan Lewis, therefore, certainly did not go to the Golden Goose on the Monday.

It would have been an easy matter to have closed up several other days into the preceding week, but no inquiries were made. Apart from a brief reference in Colonel Lewis's statement to the fact that Jonathan and Jane had had tea with them on the Saturday, Jonathan's movements in the evenings of the previous days were not covered in the evidence. Much later, Eileen Wallace recalled, when noting down the events of the night Jonathan went missing: 'After the dinner, finally, all departed; JEL, JCW and EW went to JEL's home in close convoy. JLL (Jonathan) not there, but brief case gone, suit cleaning labels on bed.'

The cleaning labels on the bed suggested that the suit had just come from the cleaners, and could not therefore have been worn in the days before the 5th, and certainly not during the weekend of the 2nd and 3rd.

If there had been another day in the week before the 5th when Jonathan's movements could have led him to the Golden Goose, the police and the prosecution would have discovered it, and used it in their examination in chief of Amanda Metcalfe. No such suggestion was made. The whole Metcalfe affair was from first to last nothing but an intense embarrassment to Mr Hollis and his team.

Mysteries

The prosecution case was founded on the notion of a happily-married couple without a serious worry in the world. Very little of the stories and facts which emerged from the statements of Jonathan's friends and relations immediately after he went missing came out at the trial. Colonel Lewis, for instance, said little or nothing about his son's business involvement with Peter Semus, the Brighton antique dealer from whom they had broken away early in 1980. John Muggeridge gave evidence, and indicated his surprise that Jonathan had preferred in the days before his death to ride around in Muggeridge's car, rather than his own. But he said very little of what he had originally imparted to the police about Jonathan's breach with Semus. The expected £3,000 from America hardly featured at all in the information provided by prosecution witnesses. Mrs Semus, who had said on the night Jonathan went missing that he might be with some Americans, did not give evidence. Only when Jane gave evidence was there a reminder of her anxiety on the night Jonathan went missing. Mr Kennedy asked her:

Q. 'You told Colin Wallace early on after Jon failed to turn up that he had said that if anything happened to him you should look out for a particular person.

A. Yes, it's true. It was a person he had had disagreements with in the past.

The court agreed to refer to this man as Mr Y – and Jane wrote his name down for the judge and the jury.

Jane told the court that she originally suspected the antiques trade of having something to do with her husband's death, but she later switched her suspicions to Colin Wallace.

Nor were there any disclosures about any affairs Jonathan may have had with other women while he knew Jane. Peter Semus had said in his statement to the police that the relationship between Jane and Jon had been 'independent and easy-going'. 'I am aware,' he said, 'that he did have a relationship with a neighbour who has now moved away. Jon told me that the woman had confessed her indiscretion to her husband.'

There was, tactfully perhaps, no reference to this when Peter Semus gave evidence at Lewes Crown Court. Nor did John or Joy Muggeridge refer in their evidence to the relationship between Jonathan and Jenny Gwatkins, whose home they had driven past anxiously on the night Jonathan had gone missing.

There was however a little batch of evidence which hinted at a different life which Jonathan may have been living in the few days before he was killed.

There had been some surprise among Jonathan's friends that his car had been found in the swimming pool car park. None of them could remember him parking there before. Spencer Swaffer, the Arundel antiques dealer, was quoted in the *West Sussex Gazette* immediately after the murder, saying: 'He came into Arundel quite a lot in the evenings to look in the window of antique shops – but he never, ever parked at the swimming pool.'

The car park superintendent, however, told a different story. He said that he had problems with people who used the car park without going to the swimming pool, which was against the rules. He said that several times he had had to remonstrate with the owner of an orange Volvo estate EWV 202V – Jonathan's car. 'Normally the vehicle was parked only for about 30 minutes,' said Mr Pescott, 'and usually it is always in the same position . . . After parking his vehicle each time he would usually walk through the twitten and disappear from view.'

The 'twitten' runs between the swimming pool and two pubs on Queen Street, the White Hart and the General Abercrombie.

Mrs Jean Bradbeer worked in the General Abercrombie. She remembered coming to work on 3 August and parking in the car park. At about 6.35, she said, she saw the Volvo parked. 'There were two people sitting in the front of the car,' she said. 'A man and a woman. The woman had dark hair.'

The police took this statement from Mrs Bradbeer. The prosecution were not keen to use it at the trial. Mrs Bradbeer was relegated to 'untendered evidence' where she was discovered by the defence. Mrs Bradbeer came to the court and told her story. Who that woman in the car was and what Jonathan was doing parking regularly for half an hour in the car park and leaving it through the twitten was never investigated. Once again, the notion that there was something secret in his life, and that he was doing things and meeting people that neither his friends nor his close business associates knew about was kept quiet throughout the trial.

No Case to Answer?

For seven days from 3 March to 12 March, the prosecution paraded some fifty witnesses, at which point Mr Kennedy rose and asked the judge to end the case there and then. The prosecution evidence, he said, was so contradictory and unconvincing that there was a serious risk that Colin could be found guilty on mere suspicion. The case, he argued, should not go to the jury.

Defence barristers often make such submissions before opening their case. Usually they are short and formal. In this case, however, Mr Kennedy's submission was taken very seriously indeed. The jury were sent out for the best part of two days – Friday, 13 March and Monday the 16th – while the barristers and the judge argued about what should be done. Mr Justice Kilner Brown said at the outset that he was extremely sympathetic to Mr Kennedy's submission, and he allowed it to be fully deployed.

Mr Kennedy argued that there was not enough evidence to convict his client; and that what evidence there was was contradicted by other evidence which had been brought to court by the prosecution. His central point was that the prosecution had come to court with the suggestion that Jonathan Lewis's blood had been found in Colin Wallace's car boot. This suggestion hinged on the single area of blood, Area 10.

This central plank of the prosecution platform Mr Kennedy submitted, had been smashed. Asked to show his photograph, Mr Silverman had agreed that it 'looked like a faint 2 reaction' – not Lewis's group at all.

'One cannot get away from his answer, then, that blood in the boot must have come from somebody other than the deceased and all of it could have come from somebody other than the deceased,' argued Mr Kennedy. The real significance of Mr Silverman's switch was that it opened out the possibility that someone else had bled into the boot.

The judge was highly sympathetic to Mr Kennedy's submission on the blood. He attacked Mr Silverman and the impact of his change of evidence on the prosecution case. He told Mr Hollis:

At the end of it all the situation is such that quite frankly I think the scientists have got themselves in a mess. It is intolerable, in my view, if they really stop to think, as Mr Silverman should have stopped to think. If he was going to give that final answer to Mr Kennedy, which he did, he had no business to have said the things in chief and misled the Director and misled you. It is characteristic, I regret to say, particularly of these blood scientists.

In another passage he said:

This is why I am somewhat cynical and sarcastic when the scientists get carried away with their own scientific endeavour . . . My impression of it was, and one gets impressions quite apart from the actual words, that in effect Mr Silverman was resiling [going back on what he said at first].

What could be done about it? The judge started by suggesting that Area 10 of the blood might be left out of the evidence altogether, but Mr Hollis was very worried about that:

If Your Lordship is inviting me to leave out Area 10 – if Area 10 has gone – I am arguing against my own case at this time – I am not at all sure that one can safely leave the blood in at all . . .

He explained why with a simple question, which echoed precisely what Mr Kennedy had said:

> Is it safe to say that any of the blood in the boot came from the deceased man, if there was blood there coming from someone else?

And again, later (remarkably):

> [If Area 10 is left out] I cannot commit myself to the boot. There is no direct evidence that the body did go in the boot.'

Eventually, the argument was boiled down to a wrangle about what was actually said by Silverman. The shorthand writer was called. From Silverman's answers the prosecution suggested that he had left the issue of Area 10 open because he had said he was still 'not sure' it was a 2 reaction. Mr Kennedy insisted that he had gone back on his original suggestion, as indeed he had. Mr Kennedy denounced the suggestion that the blood 'might have been' AK 2-1 as nothing but a 'speculative suggestion'. But somehow, Mr Hollis managed to persuade the judge that Mr Silverman had not quite done a U-turn on his evidence, and the dubious Area 10 was allowed to stay.

Mr Kennedy was even more forceful on the car sightings. Without much difficulty he showed that the car sightings did not correspond to the movements of any one car, let alone his client's car. He pointed out that there was another *Knockout* car available in the area on 5 August, and that no evidence had been brought to describe its whereabouts on that day. He showed that if even the most certain and reliable car sightings were accepted, his client could not have been in different places at the same time. He could not have been at both ends of the Arundel roundabout going in different directions at the same time and he certainly could not be in the Avisford Park Hotel feeling sick during the first course of the meal, and parking at Swanbourne Lake at the same time. Mr Hollis tried to make some sense from some of the car sightings but the judge cut him short.

Finally, Mr Kennedy raised the question of Amanda Metcalfe. 'There is no basis,' he argued, 'for putting her into the category of witnesses who do not necessarily give a reliable account.' By all the tests that were available to the court, Amanda Metcalfe's account *was* reliable. She had accurately described Lewis's clothes on the evening she died. She had given good reasons for remembering the date and the time. If the time was wrong, if Lewis had been there earlier in the evening, there was no time left for Colin to have killed him. If the time was right, then Amanda Metcalfe was the last known person to see Jonathan Lewis before he died, and she saw him in the company of someone else who had never been interviewed and never even been hunted by the police.

Mr Hollis was so embarrassed by his witness that he said nothing about her. The judge said little about her. But the judge did direct a sharp jibe at the prosecution: 'I never am very impressed and never have been with the fact that the prosecution call 50 witnesses and half of them are at sixes and sevens. Then they call another one [Metcalfe] who is not only at sixes and sevens but does not even start.'

Mr Kennedy urged him to stop the case. 'There is a real risk,' he said prophetically, 'of a wrong conviction . . . All the prosecution are left with in this case is a man who is having an affair with the deceased's wife at one end of it, and a man who told lies about his last seeing the deceased at the other end.'

The judge was sympathetic. In the end, however, he preferred the 'old-fashioned view' that the jury should decide the matter, however contradictory the evidence. He interrupted Mr Kennedy in full flow, to tell him that his points were all very good and he could have 'a field day' with the jury.

The judge then went on, off his own bat, to consider another issue. Was there any evidence of murder, or should the proper charge be manslaughter?

This question had not been asked by Mr Kennedy or Colin Wallace. In private, Kennedy had told his client that 'the worst thing which could happen to us is that we get lumbered with manslaughter, and the murder charge is taken away.' Throughout his submissions, Mr Kennedy at no stage asked the judge to consider manslaughter, not murder. His case was that Colin had not attacked Jonathan at all. He had not murdered him and he had not killed him. The prosecution evidence had not established that he had done either. The judge, however, ruminated to himself as to whether the prosecution had proved any intention to murder, as they had set out to do. He concluded that there was no evidence of any *intent* to kill. If Colin had attacked Jonathan, he might not have intended to kill him. The judge then supposed that Colin had dumped Jonathan into the river thinking him to be dead, when he wasn't. In such circumstances, he would not have been guilty of murder. By dumping the body in the river he would not *knowingly* be killing. On these suppositions, entirely unasked for by the defence and entirely unsupported by any evidence, the judge decided that he would direct the jury to find Colin not guilty of murder: but he would allow the case for manslaughter to proceed.

There were several features of this bizarre decision which could not effectively be commented on by either barrister.

Mr Hollis made no complaint at all. Perhaps he thought himself fortunate to be proceeding with his case. Mr Kennedy could not comment, except to continue to press the judge to stop the case, in which he was unsuccessful.

But if there was no evidence to convict his client of murder, where was the evidence for manslaughter? One of the strongest planks in the prosecution platform was that Colin was in love with Jane, and killed her husband because of his love. That was stronger evidence in favour of murder than of manslaughter. If he killed from passion, was that not killing with intent, planning to do it? The weakness of the prosecution evidence – the back-tracking on Area 10 of the blood, the contradictory car sightings, the evidence of Amanda Metcalfe: all these weak elements in the prosecution case were part of the argument that Colin killed Jonathan in any way. None of them had any bearing on intent to kill. Finally, there was the absurd notion that a trained soldier such as Colin – a man who had the very highest qualifications in adventure training and first aid – would have assumed his unconscious victim was dead when he wasn't. Without checking for a moment whether he was dead or not after hitting him under the nose, he allegedly assumed he was dead, bundled him unconscious into the boot and later dumped him, still alive, into the Arun. There was evidence for that scenario, the judge surmised, but there was no evidence of intent.

This astonishing conclusion can only be explained as a compromise. The judge was clearly irritated by the prosecution and said so many times (though the jury was absent throughout). His indignation was expressed in terms rarely heard from the bench. He described the entire case as 'a mess' and 'wished' the prosecution had been 'properly sorted out'. On the other hand, inspired perhaps by his old-fashioned principles, he was reluctant to end the whole matter himself. He preferred the case to go, as manslaughter, to the jury.

The effect of the decision was twofold. The first was that the prosecution now had to start to tell a completely different story from the one with which Mr Hollis opened the case. Gone was the 'plan', and the 'passion' and the 'evil intent' with which Colin was meant to have organised the entire events of 5 August. Gone were the plots, thickly laid all over Sussex, to provide himself with an alibi at the Avisford Park Hotel. In the place of the evil genius was the reckless hooligan, striking out at his friend in the middle of an argument which he did not foresee. There was no way of course with which the prosecution could change its evidence – it had all been given. The same evidence which was meant to prove the plan to kill Jonathan Lewis was now presented to prove the lack of a plan to kill him.

The second effect was more subtle. The removal of the murder charge left everyone with the impression that Colin had 'got away' with something. He was 'lucky' to have convinced the judge, no doubt on a difficult point of law, that he was not guilty of murder. Manslaughter was a much less serious offence. It did not carry with it a mandatory life sentence. There was a feeling throughout the court that Colin could hardly complain (after being found not guilty of murder) if he went down on a manslaughter charge.

The Defence Case

The defence case took only two days – 17 and 18 March. Most of the first day was taken up by Colin himself, who was in the box for four and a half hours. At the start of his evidence, Mr Kennedy referred him to a curious feature of the reporting of the case. From Day 2, pictures had started to appear in the press of Colin in his parachute and his SAS insignia. The defence strategy up to that time was not to mention Colin's military background. This had been agreed and accepted by the prosecution as irrelevant to the case. As soon as the SAS pictures began to be published, however, the defence were obliged to change tack.

The photographs, it will be remembered, had been taken by James Clevett, the Littlehampton photographer, at the request of the mysterious Kaymar Studios in South London who had contacted Colin a full year before Jonathan went missing. Naturally, Mr Clevett was keen to capitalise on his unexpected treasure. Before long the newspapers – both local and national – were happily publishing striking pictures of Colin in a New Zealand SAS beret. The connection was obvious. Someone with experience in the SAS was likely to know how to knock someone out with a specialist hand blow.

The court never heard how the photographs were made available. Colin was questioned, however, about his role in the SAS. He said he had been on attachment from the Irish Guards in Hong Kong to the New Zealand SAS squadron in 1971. He had spent two months there in tactical training. At no time, he said, had he been trained in unarmed combat.

The curious story of the SAS photographs was not the only time during the trial that reference was made to Colin's background. In the pub one lunchtime, Colin and his solicitor had a conversation with James Nicholson, then chief crime correspondent for the newly-launched *Daily Star*. Nicholson had been a reporter in Northern Ireland in the 1970s and had worked with Colin there. He said that the police had been briefing journalists who were reporting the trial on the details of Colin's activities in Northern Ireland. James Nicholson confirmed to me (interview, 8 April 1989) that 'as far as I can remember' the police were telling all the journalists about Colin's background in psychological operations. 'Of course, Ken Clarke [of the *Telegraph*] and I knew this anyway,' he said. But not everyone did. One witness at the trial, who asked not to be identified in this book, has told me that he was approached by journalists who told him that Colin had 'done this before, you know' in Northern Ireland. The fabrication about the bandmaster Ron Horn and Colin's alleged naming of him as a breakaway Protestant extremist was circulating among journalists, observers and even witnesses throughout the trial. There was also a strange incident in which James Morgan-Harris and

Brian Knowles, his assistant solicitor, saw a juryman being interviewed by a journalist who was covering the trial. They complained to the juror, and later to the Home Secretary – but no action was taken when the police said they couldn't identify the juror.

In Colin's long cross-examination, he answered interminable questions about his interviews with the police and his early failure to disclose his meeting with Jonathan on 5 August. Patiently, coolly, he repeated his case: that he had not wanted to disclose the confidential and embarrassing subject of the conversation he had had with Jonathan without first talking to Jane in private; and that there had been no opportunity for such a talk. Mr Hollis tried hard to prove that Colin had lied because he was involved in Jonathan's killing, but Colin stuck firmly to his story.

He was questioned closely about a discrepancy. In his statement to the police when he first told the truth, Colin told them that while Jonathan was in his house on the evening he disappeared, the phone had rung (see p. 142). The caller was a Mrs Ryder who was trying to arrange a squash match with Eileen. Colin put the time of the call at about 7.15. Mrs Ryder, who gave evidence for the prosecution, agreed she made the call but timed it at eight o'clock or shortly before eight. She was quite sure about the time, she said, since she had looked at the clock on the wall.

The prosecution suggested that Colin had deliberately got the time wrong because he was killing Jonathan at the earlier time. This was faintly absurd, since Colin would hardly have given a false time, knowing that Mrs Ryder could contradict it. Moreover, Mrs Ryder cannot have been exactly right since so many witnesses saw Colin at the Avisford Park Hotel at the earliest at 7.55, at the latest at 8.05. Even if the latest time of his arrival was right, he would have had to have left home well before eight o'clock.

Almost all the rest of the defence case was crammed into one day: Wednesday, 18 March: the four car sightings' witnesses mentioned earlier; the witnesses who remembered his car had no boot mat; Mrs Bradbeer, from the General Abercrombie; and two supporting witnesses from the Golden Goose. These were Michael Priest, the barman who confirmed that Vincent Vaughan started work at the Golden Goose on 5 August, and Vaughan himself. Eileen Wallace spoke briefly about her husband's movements after the celebration dinner (when he was not on his own for a single moment all night) and a character witness, Philip Owens, secretary and solicitor of Arun District Council, who spoke warmly on Colin's behalf.

The only substantial addition to the trial made by the defence was on the crucial subject of the blood in the boot. One night during the previous Christmas holiday, James Morgan-Harris had woken up at about three in the morning, and set to puzzling, as was his custom, on the Wallace case. The blood in the boot was an infernal nuisance, and, in his view, did his client much undeserved damage. Yet the prosecution had interviewed almost everyone who had ever used the car, and no one recalled a single instance when they or anyone else could have bled into the boot.

Morgan-Harris turned over in his mind once again the distribution of the blood spots: some under the wheel, but not on the wheel; one under a petrol pipe cover, but not on the petrol pipe; some under wiring, but not on the wire itself. A thought came to him quite suddenly – such a simple thought that he wondered why it had not yet occurred to the prosecution. Could the bleeding have taken place while the car was being made: before the spare wheel went in, before the pipe cover or the wiring was fitted? The next day he put in a call to the British Leyland plant at Cowley, Oxford, where the Austin Princess was manufactured. He was delighted to discover that the company kept detailed records of what happened to each model, and could from the chassis number of each car identify the assembly line and the workers on it.

Brian Knowles, James's assistant, went at once to Cowley. It was the first of several visits, in which the accident books for the relevant assembly lines were closely investigated. The lawyers were able to identify the exact day when HPC 182V was made, 6 June 1979. The accident record books showed that three men working on the assembly line had reported injuries on that day, all of which had resulted in bleeding.

All three men gave evidence at Lewes Crown Court. Brian Weaver reported that on 6 June 1979 he had suffered 'a deep cut' to his right thumb. 'I shook the loose blood off, and called the chargehand and asked for a relief . . . '

Robin Shrewsbury said he had suffered a cut to his right index finger. 'The cut bled but I finished the job on the car before reporting to the nurse . . . As far as I can remember I was at this time working on rectification work to the car body before the trim was fitted. This work would have involved examining the boot of an assembled car to ensure that light fittings, boot strap and boot lock etc. are fitted.'

Mahboob Alam was part of the same gang. 'During the time that I have been at work,' he said, 'I cut myself slightly on the finger with a screw.'

Dr Geoffrey Barnes, British Leyland's doctor at Cowley, confirmed that all three men had been cut, and that he had taken samples of blood from Shrewsbury and Weaver. Mahboob Alam was tested separately at Guy's Hospital.

The defence blood specialist, Ian Bradbrook from Guy's Hospital forensic unit, told the court that three of the five blood spots which were typed could have been Mr Shrewsbury's; and another three Mr Alam's. Mr Weaver's blood did not fit any of the five typed spots, though Mr Bradbrook recalled that there were fifteen spots of blood which had been too small (or too old) to be typed. As for the controversial Area 10 – the spot under the petrol pipe cover which the prosecution's expert Mr Silverman had reckoned, could be the rare group AK 2-1 (though he later said it looked like an AK 2), Mr Mahboob Alam revealed in the court that his blood group was AK 2-1. Even if, as seems unlikely after his cross-examination, Mr Silverman was right about Area 10 and AK 2-1, here was a worker on the car who had bled into the boot at an early stage of its manufacture, and whose blood was in that rare group.

The effect of these five witnesses was to inflict deadly damage on the prosecution evidence of blood in the boot. Here was evidence of blood in the boot in circumstances which explained the fact that the blood was not fresh, and that there was very little of it. It had been hard for the prosecution to suggest that all or any of the blood was distributed in the boot in such a way that it could have come only a few days earlier from a bleeding body. Now there was an explanation both for the different groupings of the blood and for its random distribution.

The barristers started their closing speeches on the morning of 19 March. Mr Kennedy stuck closely to what he had said to the judge in the absence of the jury after the prosecution case had finished. He said there really wasn't a case to answer. The blood in the boot had been explained – it had nothing to do with Jonathan Lewis. The car sightings were not evidence for the prosecution at all – if anything they proved that one or even two cars not driven by his client were circulating around Arundel that day. Colin's *Knockout* car almost certainly never had a boot mat perhaps because so many people had bled into the boot that the mat wasn't fitted pending a special cleaning which never took place. The marks on the river bank did not indicate that a body had been thrown in at the sluice gate. There was absolutely no forensic evidence which could convict Colin Wallace.

Mr Hollis's closing speech was notable for its incompatibility with his opening speech. Three weeks earlier he had told the jury of a foul plot to murder Jonathan Lewis by his wife's desperate lover. The celebration dinner, Mr Hollis had suggested, had been part of that plot. Now he was saying something completely different, that Colin had killed Jonathan without intending to in a fight which flared up after an argument. Mr Hollis stuck firmly to his theory that Jonathan had been knocked out at Colin's home, put in the boot, kept there during the dinner, and tipped into the river after dark over the sluice gate. The watch and keys, therefore, must also have been dumped by Colin, perhaps in a desperate attempt to simulate a fight on the river bank.

Naturally Mr Hollis devoted most of his speech to an attack on Colin Wallace's behaviour after the disappearance. Strangely, his case seemed stronger after the defence had given their evidence than it had done beforehand, but the bias of the evidence and the closing speeches still seemed to favour the defendant. Mr Justice Kilner Brown started his summing up on the evening of the 19th.

The summing up started with a simple statement, absolutely true. 'Here there is no direct evidence from any witness that the accused was responsible for the crime against him. The evidence is all circumstantial.'

That need not necessarily favour the defendant, warned the judge. Circumstantial evidence can be the strongest type of evidence, and it certainly was strong in this case. But there was no direct evidence from anyone that Colin had done the crime – no forensic evidence which tied Colin to the killing, no witness to the dumping in the river, nothing.

Most powerful of all the forensic evidence was the blood in the boot of Colin's car. By the time he started his summing up Mr Justice Kilner Brown seemed to have got over his early testiness with the blood specialist Silverman.

If that blood area 10 had been 2, Mr Silverman said that would exclude it from being Lewis, the dead man's blood. But at the end of it all, agreeing with Mr Kennedy that if you looked at the photographs and these scientists did all their weird tests and mumbo jumbo and whatever, that at the end of it all you could see that the only visible trace was 2.

Ah, said the Defence, if it is 2, then that excludes it being Lewis's blood. 'Yes,' said Mr Silverman, 'if it is 2 but the enzymes fade. I came to the conclusion that there had been both indications of 2-1 and 2 and if the indications of 2-1 had faded, you cannot come to the conclusion on something that is not there.'

From this the judge concluded:

And it fits and is consistent with, if you take the ultimate real key grouping, say the prosecution, not only with the deceased but with a very small minority of the population, 1.6 per cent.

This emotive statistic was referred to again, right at the end of the summing-up.

All that it is possible to say is it could be and it is of a particular type in one area limited to a very small proportion of the population, which rules out the likelihood of it being open to a number of other possible sources.

This was not the evidence. Mr Silverman had *not* come to the conclusion that there had been 'indications of 2-1'. There were no indications of 2-1. The blood could only have been 2-1 if the enzymes on the '1' band had faded. Mr Silverman had said in evidence, and Mr Bradbrook had agreed with him that, if anything, the enzymes in the 2 element were more likely to fade earlier than the 1 element. There was *no evidence whatsoever* to suggest either that the enzymes in the 1 had faded or that they could or might have faded. It was a distortion of the evidence to refer to '1.6 per cent of the population', or the 'very small minority' which could have produced the blood in the boot. The probability on the evidence from the prosecution's own experts was that the blood on Area 10 was not Lewis's at all. If it was not Lewis's, then someone else had bled into the boot.

So wrong was the judge on this point that Mr Kennedy felt bound to intervene. He wrote down a much fairer summary of the evidence and submitted it to the judge. The judge, very fairly, agreed to read it out.

> The effect of Mr Silverman's evidence ought to be summarised in this fashion, that the test on Area 10 now looks like the faded AK 2 reaction and if that is what it was, it could not be Lewis. I thought I had said that yesterday, but Mr Kennedy may be correct that I had not.

He had not said it – he had said the opposite. But now he had corrected his mistake, right at the end of his summing-up. He ended with the words: 'Anything else, Mr Kennedy?' 'Thank you, no, My Lord' was the reply.

Mr Kennedy did not correct another mistake made by the judge on the blood, just a few sentences before he finished. Dealing with the evidence that British Leyland workers had bled into the boot, he said:

> If the existence of Area 10 under the cover showed some enzyme activity, but fading so far as 2-1 is concerned and you can only keep an enzyme activity, as Mr Bradbrook agreed, for a matter of some months, what the prosecution invite you to say is that any blood put there in June 1979 really is neither here nor there because you have got one area which shows some enzyme activity.

Mr Bradbrook, however, had said nothing of the kind. When he was asked if the enzyme activity of any blood which had been in the boot since 1979 would not have lasted until August 1980 he replied: 'I cannot agree with that statement.' Later, he said: 'There is no scientific means, to my knowledge, of ageing a stain and it is possible that after that period of time AK activity would be present.' Asked by the judge what was the longest time he had ever known enzymes last in a bloodstain he said he had done no experiments on that matter. It was therefore quite the opposite of what the expert said to suggest, as the judge did, that the stain in Area 10 could not have been caused by bleeding when the car was being manufactured. No evidence was produced on that matter.

When the case came to the Court of Appeal [Lord Justice Ackner presiding] on 12 February 1982, the court agreed at once with Mr Kennedy's submission that the judge had erred twice on the crucial question of the blood. He had wrongly summed up the evidence – first by suggesting that there were indications that Area 10 was AK 2-1; and secondly by ruling out the possibility that the blood may have come from British Leyland workers. The first point, said the Appeal Court, was covered by the correction which Mr Kennedy had persuaded the judge to make. The second point was not raised by Mr Kennedy when he could have raised it, and was therefore not a new point in the appeal.

After dealing with the blood, Mr Justice Kilner Brown turned to the evidence about the cars. His attitude to the car sightings was very similar to what it had been when he had dealt with the submission that there was no case to answer. Then he had suggested that the evidence about the cars was so contradictory that it might be better 'to leave it out altogether'. This he did not do, but he passed over the evidence about the *Knockout* cars with a flippancy for which he apologised.

> Without wishing to appear unduly flippant, you may have got the impression that there were *It's A Knockout* cars all over the place at different times . . . They seem according to the evidence, to have been popping up all over the place at different times . . . A *Knockout* car is correctly, you may think, seen to be parked outside the swimming pool car park at about half past six, because that is the defendant's own case, but then there is another one at almost the same time down by the junction below Ford Prison on the way to Worthing . . . It sounds almost as if we were dealing with unidentified flying objects. But there they were.

There they were indeed, but what to make of them? The judge advised the jury to make little, or nothing of them. Dealing with the conflict with the evidence of the Arnold brothers who saw a *Knockout* car parked on different sides of the bridge near Swanbourne Lake at 8.45 and again at 9.45, at both of which times (absolutely certainly the first time) Colin was in the Avisford Park Hotel, the judge said:

> It is a bit difficult, you may think, to fit all this in; . . . you have to ask yourselves how can that account, on the timings, some of which you may think are fairly sure, even fit with the Arnold brothers – yet again if it cannot fit . . . well does that not point to another car? Back again we go, two cars immobilised in the car park.

The judge was most anxious that the jury should not even try to explain the different car sightings. 'The more you go into detail in a case like this,' he warned them, 'the more you are bound to find, you may think, inconsistencies.' The best way to deal with these inconsistencies, he suggested, was to leave them on one side. If they didn't fit, they could best be forgotten.

The same approach inspired the judge in his handling of the crucial evidence of the prosecution witness, Amanda Metcalfe. He made no effort to explain her evidence to the jury: to find out how and why it had been given or to test it against the facts which could be proved or disproved. There was no way, he admitted, very fairly, that Amanda Metcalfe's evidence could be consistent with the guilt of Colin Wallace. If her evidence was correct – if she had seen Jonathan in the Golden Goose with another man after 7 p.m. on 5 August – then there was no way that Colin could have knocked out Jonathan as the prosecution said he had.

> It is absolutely vital, members of the jury, that you should concentrate upon this. I would go so far as to advise you that you must rule out the accuracy of Miss Metcalfe's evidence before you can reach any safe conclusion that this man knocked out the deceased, as the prosecution say he did, stuffed him in the boot and dumped him in the river.

Mr Justice Kilner Brown did not attempt, as some judges do when they come across witnesses who are difficult to reconcile with any general thesis, to blackguard Miss Metcalfe or to suggest that she had been silly and got the date wrong. But he did urge the jury to consider a simple question:

> Does the other evidence so convince us that we are driven to the conclusion that we have to put Miss Metcalfe's evidence on one side and we have got to say she must be wrong, she must have made a mistake?

This was a curious thing for the judge to say. There were other more specific and scientific tests which could have been carried out on Miss Metcalfe's evidence. Could she have got the date wrong? For instance could Jonathan have gone to the pub with a man on any other day round 5 August? He wasn't there on the Monday. So what other day could she have seen him? Again, could she have seen someone else and mistaken him for Jonathan? She could describe in the most impressive detail what Jonathan was wearing that night – a suit he did not normally wear. These were tests to see whether Miss Metcalfe was telling the truth. They were not suggested to the jury by the judge. Instead, he asked: are you so convinced by the other evidence that you can just dismiss Amanda Metcalfe in the same way as you dismiss any of the car sightings which don't 'fit'? Thus the jury were faced not with specific evidence and specific ways to test that evidence, but with a pre-conceived notion of what happened which, if they found it convincing, could simply discount any evidence which contradicted it.

On what was that notion based? It was based on the fact that Colin had had an 'affair' with Jane, and that Jonathan had come to know of it. The judge accepted that 'all the evidence' pointed to a waning in the relationship between Jane and Colin but suggested that because Jonathan had got to know about it, and because he raised it with Colin, the stage was set for a violent conflict.

By far the most powerful point for the prosecution, to which the judge devoted well over half the summing-up, was the fact that Colin lied to everyone about his meeting Jonathan on 5 August. He lied (as the judge reminded the jury three times) to Jane when she was at her most distraught. He lied to his own wife, to his other friends and to the police. And it was only when he was confronted with the certainty that the police knew that he had met Jonathan that night that he finally changed his tune.

The judge summed up on this last question as follows:

> Then, finally, once it is brought home to him, say the Crown, that he had got to face up to the fact that it is going to be said by the police and would be said by almost everybody involved in this case that he met him on Tuesday evening at about half past six, he then said 'yes'.

It is true that Colin knew when he went to Littlehampton police station on that first Sunday evening (10 August) that a *Knockout* car had been seen near the swimming pool car park at about six o'clock. He did not know any more than that. There was no suggestion that anyone had seen him with Jonathan that night. He could easily have continued his lie and his bluff. He had, as we have seen, a perfect explanation for the entry in Jonathan's diary – the two men had agreed to play squash that night and had only cancelled when they realised they could not fit in a game before the dinner.

It was absurd to suggest that 'almost everybody involved in the case' would say the two men had met that night, or would have any evidence of it. There was, moreover, a much more powerful reason why Colin should decide to tell the truth that Sunday evening. This was the entirely new revelation that Jonathan had been murdered. Only the previous evening the Portsmouth *Evening News* had carried the information that the police had ruled out foul play. Now, suddenly, there was a murder inquiry. That was why, Colin said, he decided to retract his lie, and tell the truth. From that moment on, moreover, much as the judge dwelt on the detail of the interviews, almost everything he said was corroborated by independent witnesses.

'Let us try and see the main points,' the judge urged the jury as he came to the end of his summing-up. 'Let us try and disentangle from all this quantity of detail certain salient features. Let us remember that the prosecution have to prove their case. Let us remember that lies may not necessarily indicate a cover-up.' There then followed this remarkable passage:

> In the end, I venture to suggest to you that each one of you will have to ask yourselves, what did you think of him when he stood in the witness box? If he told you the truth, of course acquit him. If he may have told the truth, if he has raised doubts about it, of course acquit him. But if you think that pattern of lies, of cover-up, of deliberate evasion of the truth starting right from the denial of any meeting at 6.30 persisted in until it is broken down by the police saying: 'Look at that diary' – cover-up, say the prosecution. Never a word if the story was true, to Jane throughout those agonising hours the early hours of Wednesday morning. Would he ever have disclosed the meeting until the police confronted him with the diary entry? If that pattern of deliberate withholding the truth has continued throughout those interviews, throughout those statements, and continued there in the witness box so that there has been an attempt to hoodwink you, then, however painful it may be for a man of such excellent character and such good service to the community, if you are driven to the conclusion from which there is no escape that his demeanour there in the witness box was too smooth by half, that he could not really answer the questions, that he was too composed, that is where you come in, members of the jury, because the prosecution say he was in this man's company at 6.30 until sometime after seven. There is only one car with blood in the boot, and that car is the one that this man drove.

It was a grandiloquent, if slightly incoherent, peroration. It had purported to bring the jury's attention to the 'main points' and the 'salient features' of the case, but it had done nothing of the kind. It had instead conjured up for them an image of a liar and a cheat. It had provided only one explanation for Colin's refusal to tell anyone about his highly confidential and embarrassing meeting with Jonathan; there were others, every bit as convincing as the one the judge gave. And the picture of a witness 'too smooth by half' can only be compared to any equally lurid description which the judge might have applied if the witness had been 'rough' or 'flustered' or 'embarrassed' or 'incoherent'. Many of the 'main points' and the 'salient features' of the case – the only witness to say she'd seen Jonathan on the night he died, for instance, the numerous cars which were seen that night but which Colin could not have driven, or, for that matter, the police diver who said the marks on the concrete by the sluice gate were not those caused by a body falling (a 'salient feature' which the judge did not even mention) – all these had been cast aside for an impression of a perjurer and hoodwinker, 'too smooth by half'.

Colin and Eileen knew as soon as they had heard the judge that the chances of acquittal were slim. They both resent the judge's gratuitous attack on Colin. But neither of them makes the familiar mistake of blaming the judge's summing-up or the conduct of the lawyers in the case for what happened. Colin, indeed, has always been full of praise for Michael Kennedy, who worked hard for him; and his appreciation of the work done by his solicitor knows no bounds. Nor does he feel at all bitter against the prosecution lawyers. Despite his absurd coda, the judge himself dealt fairly with the bulk of the evidence.

The real weakness in the trial was that the jury were left with one scenario, and one only. It is true that this scenario had changed since it was first outlined by Mr Hollis. But always the jury were faced with one story, and asked what fitted it and what didn't.

There was no other motive for the killing, no one else who might have killed Jonathan. This theme of the *only possible* alternative cropped up again and again throughout the judge's summing-up, and, even in retrospect, seems particularly persuasive:

> There is no evidence, is there, that the deceased man was involved in any matrimonial misconduct nor that he had any enemies who would be minded to use violence on him? . . . We have heard of a mysterious man who was named for your private consideration. You have heard him and seen him. You may think that part of the case has disappeared.

Then again, on the next page:

> The only person who really on the evidence as a whole might get involved in violence as far as the evidence goes, says Mr Hollis, is the defendant himself.

On the next page still, the judge says:

> A word of warning here, members of the jury. It is not right to say 'Well it could not have been anyone else. Therefore it must be him.' That is jumping to conclusions. I am sure you follow that. But you are entitled to say, as the prosecution invite you: 'We cannot see that it could be anybody else.' Now let us look to see whether it is proved that it is the defendant.

'We cannot see that it could be anybody else.' On the evidence presented to the jury, that was a fair conclusion. There seemed to be no other conceivable explanation for the death of Jonathan Lewis than that he was killed by Colin. What little the jury heard of Jonathan's business difficulties could hardly explain his killing. Mr Y, as the judge said, did give evidence, and it did not appear either from his demeanour or from the history of the commercial problems of the Lewis family and their antiques business that there was anything there which remotely suggested that Jonathan should be rubbed out. It might well have been that he was having some secret liaison with a woman, as Mrs Bradbeer's evidence suggested. No one ever found the woman with whom, according to Mrs Bradbeer, he may have been sitting in his car in the week before he

died. Maybe he was attending some illicit rendezvous in those mysterious visits to the swimming pool car park. But if so, so what? Jonathan Lewis would not have been the first married man to meet another woman in secret surroundings, and there was nothing in that faint suggestion which smacked of murder or manslaughter.

It was not of course necessary for the defence to suggest another scenario for Jonathan's killing. Mr Kennedy did so, if only to prove that the evidence did not necessarily point to his client's guilt. Mr Kennedy suggested that Jonathan may have been walking by the river bank by the sluice gate, when he was attacked and left unconscious by the riverside. Gaining consciousness, perhaps he staggered to the river's edge and attempted to urinate. Losing his balance, he fell in, and was unable to stop himself drowning.

It was an ingenious theory which fitted some of the evidence every bit as much as the prosecution story. The watch and the keys could well have ended up where they were found if Jonathan had been attacked. The zip of the dead man's fly was undone, and his penis protruded from it. This suggested that he was in the act of trying to urinate when he lost consciousness.

But so many things about the theory were implausible. To start with, what was Jonathan doing on the river bank by the sluice gate so far from his car – about a mile away? How did he get there either from the centre of Arundel, where Colin said he dropped him off, or from the Golden Goose, where Amanda Metcalfe said she saw him?

All the evidence on Jonathan's habits suggested that he was unwilling and unlikely to walk any distance at all from his car unless accompanied by his dog, and even then he always walked the other way up the Arun, towards the Black Rabbit.

Secondly, what would have been the motive of these chance assailants? Did they want money? There was at least £200 in notes in his trouser pocket, which was found on his dead body? Why would they choose such a populated part of the river bank for their attack? If Jonathan was conscious when he went into the river, how was he unable to reach some kind of safety when he was, as everyone testified, such a powerful man and such a strong swimmer? If anything, the Kennedy theory was even more implausible than the prosecution story. It provided no motive for the killing, while the prosecution provided a very good motive.

However weak the prosecution case seemed, therefore, the jury were driven back to the question: who in the world was likely to kill Jonathan Lewis? The only sensible answer was Colin Wallace.

The defendant was the only person likely to have done the deed. Once that was established, it shaped the attitude of anyone observing the trial. Evidence inevitably became assessed according to whether or not it fitted the only possible scenario for Jonathan's killing. If there was evidence which didn't fit that scenario, it could be leaped over, as if it were an obstacle on the journey to the truth. These cars fitted Colin's drive – they should be taken seriously. These cars did not fit Colin – they should not be taken seriously. A witness sees Colin's car at the swimming pool at 6.30 – she is a serious witness, because it fits the story. Another witness sees Jonathan in the Golden Goose at some time after seven – that doesn't fit, so it can be turned aside. Above all, there was the fear that a guilty man might go free. In this case, there was only one possible guilty man – Colin Wallace. No one else, as far as anyone could see, could have done it. Therefore to respond to the contradictory evidence by concluding that Colin was Not Guilty was to run a very real risk of unleashing a killer on society – and on the Council offices into the bargain. The danger of convicting an innocent man had to some extent been softened by the direction of the judge that Colin was not guilty of murder. Was it worth running the risk of allowing a killer free, when all that he faced was a smallish sentence for manslaughter?

These thoughts ran through the mind of anyone who attended the court. The rails along which they ran were laid down firmly from first to last. 'Look at Jonathan Lewis' went the message. 'Who would have wished this man wrong? Only Colin Wallace. We cannot see that it can be anybody else.' Thoughts like these led inevitably to a conclusion that the evidence which did not fit should be cast aside.

Was there an alternative, however? *Was* there any other way of looking at the mystery?

One starting point, where no one at the trial started, was that two things happened when Jonathan was killed. He died, and Colin Wallace became a suspect. Instead of hunting for anyone else who might have had a grudge against Jonathan Lewis, it might have been profitable to ask: could Lewis's killer have been trying to do damage to Colin Wallace? Was Wallace the real target of the killing, not the man who was killed?

If Jonathan Lewis was killed so that Colin Wallace could be framed for his murder, much of the evidence which didn't fit the prosecution story at the trial immediately fits.

Amanda Metcalfe, who gave such decisive evidence within days of Jonathan's death, and who spoke up so firmly at the trial, did not fit. She 'did not even start' in the judge's words. To find Colin guilty, the jury were effectively directed that they had to discount this highly credible witness altogether. But if Jonathan *was* in the Golden Goose on the night he died, if he *was* with a strange man with whom he had never been seen in the pub before, there is suddenly a new suspect, and a new story which unfolds around him.

The car sightings were hopeless evidence for the prosecution. They proved nothing except that more than one *Knockout* car was on the road in the late afternoon, evening and night of 5 August. Once again, the judge told the jury effectively to discount the car evidence altogether – and especially the cars which did not fit the journeys laid out for Colin by the prosecution. Another problem for the prosecution was that no one saw a *Knockout* car down the narrow Gasworks Lane at the end of which Colin was meant to have dumped the body. The car evidence was therefore *inexplicable*. The jury simply had to remove it from their minds.

The theory that someone may have 'framed' Colin Wallace changes all that. It immediately provides an explanation for the large number of cars which, in the judge's words, were 'popping up all over the place', all along the River Arun from Littlehampton to the Black Rabbit. It provides a motive for someone to get hold of another *Knockout* car – or even to create their own *Knockout* car, a relatively simple exercise – and drive it up and down the river with one purpose: to suggest that Colin Wallace, the only man known to be driving a *Knockout* car on that evening, was closely associated with the River Arun on the evening his friend died in it.

If there was such a 'frame-up', there was no better day to do it than 5 August: the very last day Colin had his distinctive car, after almost all the other similar cars had been taken back to their dealers.

What about the evidence in the river, and on the river bank?

One inescapable difficulty for the prosecution was the suggestion that Colin dumped his friend's body in the river at one of its most conspicuous and public places. No one saw him do it. No one saw his car down Gasworks Lane.

Yet the place where the body was supposed to have gone in, the closest point of car access to the river from Colin's home – was strikingly signposted by Jonathan's keys and watch, carelessly jettisoned in different directions from the body.

Would Colin have planted these clues exactly where he dumped the body, and where he would be so clearly implicated?

There were no answers to any of these questions. The best Mr Hollis could do was to suggest that the keys and watch must have dropped from the body accidentally, and been picked up and dropped some yards away by passers-by. No one knows how this suggestion went down with the jury. They were obliged once more to cast aside the difficulties of the evidence of the watch and keys.

The 'frame up' theory points to a way out of these difficulties. What if Jonathan's body did not go into the river at the sluice gate? What if someone intended to point to the sluice gate as the place of the dumping, when in fact the body went in somewhere else? What if the watch and keys were *placed* at the sluice gate, the nearest point of access by road to the river from Colin's house, to identify it as the place the body went into the river?

Other evidence from the river which didn't fit the prosecution theory fits this one. Andre Buller, the river expert, said that in his view the body went in the river much further downstream. If it had gone in at Arundel, he said, it would not have reached the Ford Marina where it was found, in the three days that had elapsed since it entered the river.

PC Cannon, the police diver, admitted in court that the 'scuff marks' on the stones on the bank by the sluice gate did not indicate a body going in, as the prosecution suggested. Rather, it suggested someone stepping in (or out) of the river up the bank. The bass fisherman, Douglas Hart, had seen someone with a light in the river under the sluice gate at midnight. Could this have been someone making marks and leaving evidence to suggest that the body did go into the river there? Despite police appeals, no one came forward to explain what Hart had seen.

If Colin Wallace was framed, who wanted to frame him? One answer was the 'ultras' in the security services. They had every reason to do Colin damage. What would discredit him more than his conviction for murder? To kill Colin, when his record was spotless, would be to invite all sorts of awkward questions. To get Colin convicted for a vile and jealous murder would shut him up, literally, for life.

Other pieces fit into this ugly jigsaw. The curious story of the pictures taken for Kaymar Studios is suddenly explained. If people were to believe that Colin was a violent man, he should be seen in the newspapers in uniform. More importantly, journalists could be 'reminded' that Colin had a propensity to do damage to the men who loved or married his girlfriends. The ludicrous but damaging smear about the Ulster Citizens Army and Ron and Joan Horn began to circulate during the trial.

Who knows whether any member of the jury heard on the grapevine, as did one witness I have interviewed, that Colin had 'done this before, you know, long ago in Ireland'?

The prosecution story at Lewes did not fit the facts. One scenario which does fit the facts is the murder of Jonathan Lewis by a professional team of killers, who planned the exercise over a long period with the single intention of shutting up Colin Wallace.

This seems hideous and fantastic beyond belief. As the trial ended at Lewes, it was not even considered. The judge finished his summing-up just before lunch, and the jury went out just afterwards. After about three hours they returned to say they were undecided. The judge urged them to reconsider.

They returned soon afterwards with a unanimous verdict: Guilty.

The judge added the accustomed homily about the awful nature of the crime: 'the worst case of manslaughter I have ever come across,' he called it. He sentenced Colin to ten years in prison.

'My first thought,' remembers Eileen, 'was that he would never see the dog again.'

CHAPTER SEVEN

The Secret State

Wormwood Scrubs on a freezing wet March night. The wind was whistling in the barbed wire and the looming towers of the Scrubs reached up like ghostly sentinels into the sky. Dazed by despair and shock, Colin sat through the three hours of 'reception'. He accepted a set of prison clothes which didn't fit, tolerated a medical in which no one looked at him, and endured long hours of waiting and answering questions, fingerprints, photographs and a trudge over to D wing, which held the 'lifers'. He was banged up in a cell all by himself. The plaster was falling off the walls and in the corner was a filthy mattress on a green metal bed. Somehow, perhaps because he was exhausted, Colin fell asleep. In the morning a prison officer brought him a copy of the *Daily Telegraph* and urged him: 'Read about yourself.' Gloomily, he fought his way through a long diatribe by Kenneth Clarke, the former Northern Ireland correspondent in Belfast who had in the past made great use of Colin's information. It was Clarke, for instance, who had 'floated' the story about communist influence in the extremist Protestant organisations during the Ulster Workers' Council strike. The poster which 'proved' that influence had been planted on him by his favourite information officer whom he was now, in accordance with new priorities, subjecting to sarcastic indignation.

In the gloom which closed in on him in those early days, Colin was comforted greatly by the attitude of his fellow prisoners. He was astonished by the general knowledge among the prisoners about his case; and warmed by the way in which long-term prisoners immediately sympathised with a new inmate.

Before long, he was moved into a cell with two other people where he would spend twenty-three hours a day in prison conditions which are, by any standards, intolerable. Once again the only relief was the humour of his constantly changing companions. The joke had got around A wing, where he now was, that he had something to do with the Duke of Norfolk (who had stood bail for him soon after his arrest). One prisoner was convinced by the others that Colin was the Duke of Norfolk and had been convicted of poaching.

The constant anxiety was that he would have to share a cell with one of the many prisoners who found it impossible to cope. One night, one of his cellmates slashed his wrists in a suicide bid. On another, a man who had killed his wife started conversations with her through the cell wall.

After about three months, he was shifted to a self-contained unit of thirty cells where the atmosphere was unrecognisably more civilised. Into this unit came prisoners with long sentences, whose behaviour had been singled out by prison staff as reliable. One such was Martin Bendelow, Conservative Parliamentary candidate and a former assistant to a Secretary of State for Health and Social Security in the Conservative government, Sir Keith Joseph. Bendelow had served on a government committee on drug abuse, but had himself been convicted of cocaine smuggling. Colin liked him – they stayed in contact after leaving prison – and thought he detected a common background in Intelligence. There were also a couple of former soldiers in the unit with whom Colin immediately struck up a friendship, and a fraudsman who came from Magherafelt, not far from Colin's home town. Colin got on well with pretty well everyone in the unit, including the officer in charge.

As the worst of his despair lifted, he was able to concentrate on preparing his appeal. He was visited from time to time by James Morgan-Harris, and by Michael Kennedy, both of whom were anxious to expose the judge's summing-up. Colin had kept the copious notes he had taken in the dock, and the 500 pages of depositions. He wrote a constant stream of letters to his solicitor. He still has many of the diagrams and special analyses he made of different aspects of the case, such as the mysterious journeys of the *It's A Knockout* cars.

Apart from the occasional visits of his lawyers Colin saw no one from outside the prison except Eileen, who was allowed one visit a month. He had written almost as soon as he got to the Scrubs to Jane Lewis, assuring her that he had had nothing whatever to do with Jonathan's death and apologising for all the wretchedness she had had to go through at the trial. The letter ended up with Detective Superintendent Harrison (who had been promoted immediately after Colin's conviction), who gave strict instructions that Colin was not to be allowed to write to Jane again. Jane resigned her job at Arun and returned to her native Norfolk, where her parents lived, to try to start a new life.

Eileen's life had collapsed. She and Colin had settled down in their comfortable house in Sussex with a relaxed life style based on Colin's acceptable local government salary. That had suddenly disappeared. Eileen was left with the small salary she earned as a secretary at Arundel Castle. She made an early decision to keep the house, and was therefore, for six years, keeping up mortgage and rate payments which amounted to three-quarters of her after-tax income. Somehow she always found the money for the expensive trip to London every month to visit Colin. Unlike many other prisoners' wives, none of her life was subsidised by Social Security payments. She and Fred (the dog) kept going, and they were helped by most of the neighbours, who were consistently supportive. However, most of the circle of friends in which she and Colin had moved now believed that Colin had killed Jonathan, and were therefore not at all keen to keep in contact. She never again saw the Muggeridges or Jill Belt or any of their circle.

Eileen's courage and persistence throughout that period was based on her absolute certainty that Colin had not killed Jonathan. This was not merely a standard wifely reaction, indeed Eileen had every reason to be annoyed about Colin's infatuation with Jane. During the weeks of June and July when the affair with Jane flared up, she struggled, without much success, to hold on to his affection. During the early months in which Colin was in prison on bail, and especially at the trial, she had to endure all the humiliation of a wife whose husband has fallen for someone else.

On the face of it, she had every reason to doubt Colin's story. He had deceived her, too, about his meeting with Jonathan. Her certainty that there had not been any struggle between the two men was based on an assessment of their character and her personal knowledge of much of what happened on the night of the dinner party. 'They would both have been so *embarrassed*,' she explains. 'Neither of them would have wanted to have talked about it for a moment. Colin would have ducked away from it as quickly as he could. He would have seemed cool, but he would have been eager to change the subject. The very idea that either of them would start a fight with each other is just too ridiculous to anyone who knew them.' This intrinsic gentleness, affability and anxiety to avoid anything embarrassing is confirmed by everyone else I have spoken to who knew Colin well (and it is confirmed about Jonathan by the evidence of his family).

Colin had been in the Scrubs for almost a year when his application for leave to appeal was summarily dismissed in February 1982.

The disappointment had hardly sunk in when another dramatic development plunged him back into the past.

He was by this time a charge hand in the prison workshop, which was manufacturing double-glazing units for the Home Office. He and his team of three fitted the metal window frames to shape, according to plans. The most outstanding member of the team was a millionaire and company director, who had been convicted of conspiracy to cause grievous bodily harm for hiring a man to beat up a neighbour who, in an argument over the drive, had sowed the millionaire's lawns with weedkiller.

One afternoon (in February 1982) Colin was in the workshop when the phone rang. This usually meant that a prisoner was being called to a visit or an interview. The phone was answered by a civilian instructor in a small office behind a glass window. Colin saw him look up, startled, from the telephone and tap the window and beckon to Colin to come over.

The instructor had his hand over the mouthpiece, and said to Colin 'There's a policeman here called Harris who says he knows you and wants to talk to you.'

Colin immediately started to back away. 'I don't know any policeman called Harris,' he said, nervously.

The instructor spoke again, and came back once more to Colin. 'Harrison,' he corrected himself. 'And he wants to talk to you about something called Kincora.'

Colin was startled.

'I certainly won't speak to *him*,' he said. 'He's the man who put me in here. He knows who my solicitor is, and he can speak to him whenever he likes.'

Kincora! A foul ghost from the past. Back at his work, Colin puzzled about this new mystery. What were they up to now? What on earth had Harrison, the chief instigator of Colin's prosecution and conviction, who was based in Chichester, West Sussex, to do with a boys' home in Belfast? Colin's fear was that this was some new set-up, some new attempt to discredit him and perhaps to associate him with charges even more grotesque than the one for which he had already been convicted.

He had no answer to any of these questions until a letter from Eileen arrived a few days later. She had heard Colin's name mentioned by Gerry (later Lord) Fitt on the BBC Radio 4 summary *Yesterday in Parliament* in connection with a new inquiry which had been ordered into the Kincora Boys' Home scandal.

Unknown to Colin there had been striking new developments in the Kincora story. In January 1980, as we have seen, the *Irish Independent*, the morning paper with the largest circulation in Ireland, dramatically exposed the scandal at the Kincora Boys' Home which Colin had tried to persuade the Press to expose in 1973 and again in 1974.

The paper revealed some of the facts which were in Colin's last memorandum to his colleagues in Information Policy at Lisburn six years earlier. It named William McGrath, Joseph Mains and Raymond Semple, and gave currency to the allegations of one of the inmates of Kincora that he had been sexually abused. The *Irish Independent* exposé was followed by a short flurry of articles in the Irish newspapers. There was a very rapid investigation by the Royal Ulster Constabulary. Detailed investigation or comment was quickly doused when McGrath, Semple and Mains were charged with sexual assaults on boys at the Home. The law of contempt of court, which bans press speculation pending criminal trials after named people have been charged, came into effect.

After the charges in April 1980, therefore, there was a respectful silence. For some time, McGrath indicated that he would plead not guilty. When first confronted with the statements of the young men he had humiliated and abused, he denounced the boys as liars. For a time, it seemed that there would be a long and juicy trial in which the full facts about the horrors of Kincora could be revealed without fear of libel or contempt to a fascinated public.

William McGrath in due course changed his mind. No doubt the dangers of pleading not guilty when the evidence against him was so overwhelming were made clear to him. Perhaps, as so often in these cases, he was helped in his decision by assurances that his sentence, if he pleaded guilty, would be considerably less than anything he might have to serve after the full horror of what he had done had been brought home to the public. Whatever the discussions behind the scenes, however, the result was that McGrath, Mains and Semple appeared in a Belfast court on 16 December 1981 and pleaded guilty to twenty-eight specimen charges of sex offences over twenty years. The case lasted half a day. McGrath was sentenced to four years, Mains to six and Semple to five. Later in 1982, when he heard about the sentences, Colin wondered how it was that McGrath, by far the worst offender, should have got the lowest sentence.

The three officers at Kincora were not the only men convicted of sex offences that day. Peter Bone, a chief architect for the North-Eastern Education and Library Board in Northern Ireland, was convicted on eight charges of sexual abuse of young boys, one of whom was in care at another local authority home, Bawnmore in Newtownabbey. Bone was a Boy Scout commissioner, who had visited the Home to do community work, and had taken the boy out in his car where he had committed the offences.

A fire safety officer for the Northern Health and Social Services Board of Northern Ireland, Robert Dewer, also pleaded guilty to two charges of gross indecency with the same boy from Bawnmore.

These two less publicised convictions indicated that a sex scandal involving boys in care in Northern Ireland spread beyond Kincora.

The convictions lifted the threat of contempt on journalistic comment and unleashed a powerful investigation by two journalists on the *Irish Times*, Ed Moloney and Andrew Pollak. On 17 December 1981, the day after the convictions, Moloney published an article which struck a sensitive nerve:

> The real scandal of the Kincora Boys' home, as the Lord Chief Justice Sir Robert Lowry indicated in court yesterday, was the fact that the activities of Joseph Mains, Raymond Semple and William McGrath apparently went undetected by the authorities since the home was established twenty years ago.' (*Irish Times*, 17 December 1981.)

The article went on to list several occasions when boys had made complaints to social workers or welfare departments. It disclosed that these had been passed on to police and other authorities without any action being taken.

The immediate response of the authorities was cautious. On the same day, 17 December, the Northern Ireland Eastern Health and Social Services Board set up a committee of inquiry into the management of Kincora and associated matters. As the press and television exposed more and more facts about Kincora, the committee of inquiry took on more responsibilities. Its Chairman was the former North of Ireland Ombudsman, Mr Stephen McGonagle, and its members were Dr Stanley Worrall, headmaster of the Methodist College, Belfast, Professor Olive Stevenson of Keele University, and Professor Norman Tutt of Lancaster University.

The allegations continued. In the *Irish Times* of 13 January 1982, Ed Moloney and Andrew Pollak told a bloodcurdling story about a suicide pact between two former inmates of Kincora. One of them, Stephen Waring, ran away from the home, escaped to Liverpool, was picked up by the police there and put back on the ferry to Belfast without an escort. Halfway over, he jumped from the ferry. His body was never found, nor was there an inquest. Stephen Waring, the article alleged, had made a number of allegations against the officers at Kincora before his suicide.

All this happened in 1977, three years before the scandal was exposed.

As the revelations poured out, mainly from the *Irish Times*, public indignation grew. All sections of both communities in the North were united in disgust at what had happened at the Kincora Home.

The McGonagle Committee met on 12 January 1981 and established an all-time record for the shortest committee in history. On the day it met, three of its five members (Worrall, Stevenson and Tutt) resigned. The three told the press that they had been given assurances about the scope of their inquiry which turned out at its first sitting to be incorrect. They had been assured, they said, that all matters connected with Kincora were open to them for their inquiry. But on the first day they were abruptly told that the police were still investigating certain criminal matters, and that therefore anything covered by criminal charges, in the future or in the past, was closed to them. The suggestion that there had been a cover-up of Kincora, therefore, could not be investigated by the committee.

The collapse of the committee left the Secretary of State, James Prior, with an awkward problem. Prior had taken on the Belfast job reluctantly after his resignation from the Thatcher government on grounds of disagreement with its policies had been widely predicted. Once in office in Stormont Castle, Prior seemed singularly reluctant to rock any boat at all. After the collapse of the McGonagle Committee, he was urged by politicians on both sides of the religious divide to set up a full judicial inquiry, with no boundaries to its investigation. Anyone giving evidence to such an inquiry would be protected by privilege, and could not be prosecuted under any section of the law, such as libel or the Official Secrets Act.

True to his political reputation, however, Prior funked the bold decision. On 18 February, he told the House of Commons:

> It is being urged that a public judicial inquiry should investigate these and similar rumours. If such an inquiry did disclose new criminal offences, it would in the process have made it impossible for any offenders to be prosecuted either because immunities had to be given, or because the publicity which the disclosure would have received when the evidence was given in a public inquiry would make it impossible to find a jury which would not be seen as prejudiced. It is essential to hold to the principle that allegations of criminal activities are investigated by the police and that offenders are dealt with by the courts.

Instead of an independent court of inquiry, then, the police investigation would continue. Further, Prior announced, a chief constable of another police force would be appointed to 'investigate allegations about the way in which the police had conducted their inquiry, and in addition to have general oversight of the continuing investigation'.

The name of this chief constable was not disclosed that day.

The timid announcement by James Prior was not challenged by the opposition spokesman for Northern Ireland, Don Concannon, or anyone else. The Rev. Ian Paisley, the extremist Protestant leader, who had put down a motion on the House of Commons Order Paper calling for a full-scale judicial inquiry, was overcome by an uncharacteristic silence. The general view was one of widespread relief that this nasty business was being wrapped up once again and deposited in the safe and secret hands of the Royal Ulster Constabulary and an unnamed chief constable. Only one critical voice was raised: that of Gerard Fitt, MP for West Belfast, leader of the Social Democratic and Labour Party in Northern Ireland, who had played a considerable part in the original exposé of Kincora in 1980.

After referring with some sarcasm to Paisley's motion on the Order Paper, Mr Fitt asked:

> Is the Right Hon gentleman aware of the need for the police investigations to come to a conclusion as quickly as possible so that the idea is not implanted in people's minds that time may erase the matter from the memories in Northern Ireland?

Mr Fitt then went on to ask specific questions about the law governing the inquiry which Prior had promised to set up after the police inquiries were completed.

> Would it enable Mr Colin Wallace, a former British Army security spokesman, who gave an interview to journalists in 1975 and made them aware

of all the aspects of Kincora, to be brought before the inquiry or the courts?

There was no reply.

Since Mr Fitt's voice was the only one raised in opposition to the postponement of any judicial inquiry, he was asked to expand on his views in the BBC's current affairs programme, *PM*. He repeated the question about Colin Wallace: could he give evidence or could he not? As in the House of Commons, no clear answer was forthcoming.

Gerry Fitt had made a slight mistake. Colin Wallace's briefings of journalists about the scandal at Kincora had been in 1973 and 1974 and not, as Fitt said, in 1975.

The effect of Fitt's intervention was to name Colin Wallace, and Colin Wallace alone, as a witness who could testify that the authorities knew perfectly well for at least eight years that boys were being abused while they were in the care of the local authority. This unexpected naming of Wallace must have had considerable impact in the Northern Ireland Office and in the higher echelons of the Royal Ulster Constabulary and in MI5.

The following day came an announcement with strange overtones. The name of the chief constable 'with general oversight' into the police inquiries into Kincora was Sir George Terry, Chief Constable of Sussex, the adopted home county of Colin Wallace. Even more surprising was the name of the Detective Superintendent whom Terry promptly appointed to take charge of the Kincora inquiry: Gordon Harrison, the man who only twenty months earlier had taken charge of the prosecution of Colin Wallace.

Thus it was that Mr Harrison telephoned the next day to Wormwood Scrubs for a friendly word with his old acquaintance, only to be brusquely referred to Thomas Eggar and Sons, solicitors.

A few days later, Colin was in the workshop once again when he was called to the visiting room for an 'official visit'. He was taken inside a cubicle where two large gentlemen in plain clothes and full of good cheer introduced themselves as Detective Superintendent George Caskey and Detective Sergeant Elliott of the Royal Ulster Constabulary. They said they had come to ask a few questions on Kincora. Colin immediately persuaded the prison officer who had brought him down, and who was making as if to leave the cubicle, to stay. He then told Mr Caskey that he had already made it quite clear that he would discuss nothing without his solicitor present. On Kincora, he said, he could say nothing at all without written authority from the Ministry of Defence. The officers made an attempt to persuade Colin that there was nothing very awkward about their questions. Colin was adamant that he would not talk to them on any basis without his solicitor and the MOD authority. The officers left.

In April, to his intense relief (and to Eileen's) Colin was moved out of Wormwood Scrubs (which had just been described in a letter to *The Times* by the Governor as a 'penal dustbin', a protest which resulted in the Governor's instant resignation). He was taken to Lewes prison, where the conditions were much better and the regime much more relaxed. He still worried about the Kincora questions. His main feeling was that this was another attempt to get him into trouble, and that his priority if the questions continued was to avoid any possibility of prosecution under the Official Secrets Act.

He had hardly settled down at Lewes before the RUC were back again, this time in the office of the chief prison officer. These were two different officers from the RUC whose names Colin does not recall. Once again Colin refused to answer any questions without a letter of authority, and his solicitor. Once again the officers sought to ask him questions anyway, and once again he explained that he would not even listen to the questions. Once again, they left.

The officers then visited James Morgan-Harris in Chichester and corresponded with him. He confirmed his advice to Colin that he should not proceed with any interviews in the Terry inquiry without an assurance from the Ministry of Defence that there would be no prosecution under the Official Secrets Act in respect of anything which Colin told the investigating officers. Morgan-Harris also insisted that he should be present at any interview.

Nothing happened for a month or two, after which Colin wrote to his Member of Parliament, Michael Marshall (Conservative), and asked him if he could help in getting the necessary authority from the Ministry of Defence. In this case, as in many others in the next few months, Colin took the initiative. He was anxious to talk about Kincora. On the other hand he was worried about breaking the Official Secrets Act. He had, of course, technically broken the Act in the past, in his conversations with Airey Neave, for instance, or with David McKittrick or David Blundy. But he had done so in confidence – and as a free man. Now he was in prison for a crime for which he thought he had been framed. He could not escape the fear that he was being 'set up' once more – to provide information publicly which would render him liable to yet another prosecution. He wanted to help; but he wanted to be absolutely sure that he was safe in doing so.

His letter to his MP produced a reply from James Prior, Secretary of State for Northern Ireland. The letter gave this assurance:

> The Director of Public Prosecutions for Northern Ireland has given an assurance that Mr Wallace will not be prosecuted for any breach of the Official Secrets Act in respect of any information which he communicates of this kind.
>
> My department is concerned with the points which Mr Wallace has

made concerning the investigation into alleged homosexual offences against those in care in homes and hostels for young children and persons in Northern Ireland, including the Kincora home. The police are anxious that Mr Wallace should give them any information in his possession about such offences.

Mr Prior's letter ends by dealing with Colin Wallace's request that James Morgan-Harris's costs while advising Colin on the Kincora inquiry should be met by public funds. He thought it 'unlikely' that they would be, and concluded his letter with the remarkable sentence:

> The most helpful point I can make at this stage on that point is to repeat that the questions which the police would like to put to him are of quite a limited nature.

This was the first 'assurance' in writing that Colin had received from anyone in authority and he acknowledged in another letter to Marshall that he was glad to have got it. However, as he also pointed out, the assurance was limited. Prior's letter referred to an investigation 'into alleged homosexual offences'. Colin knew little about such offences. He had no idea, for instance, whether there were any Belfast boys' home officials who had been involved in such offences, or what such offences might have been. The only information he had was that the Army and Intelligence services knew from the early 1970s that homosexual offences were being committed at Kincora. His knowledge, which sprang from official secrets, was about what the authorities knew up to eight years before the scandal was exposed. He wanted to know if he could avoid prosecution if he passed on secrets about that state of knowledge. To that question, Prior's letter gave no answer. Moreover, it was precious little use to Colin to be assured that he would not be prosecuted in Northern Ireland, when he was sitting in a jail in England. What he wanted was an assurance either from his previous employers, the Ministry of Defence, or from the Attorney-General.

In October 1982, it seemed at last that his difficulty had been cleared up. Detective Superintendent George Caskey of the RUC came once again to Lewes prison with a Detective Inspector Cook. This time Colin was prepared to talk to them partly because James Morgan-Harris was there (unpaid) to advise him; and partly because the policemen said that they had with them the crucial assurance from the Ministry of Defence. They produced it at once. It read as follows:

> Under the terms of the Official Secrets Act Declaration which you signed upon your appointment with the Ministry of Defence you undertook to seek authorisation from this Department before discussing with anyone information gained in the course of your employment. It is now necessary for the police to

investigate fully allegations of criminal offences involving homosexual conduct in or connected with the Kincora Boys Home in Belfast. The purpose of this letter is to confirm that you may disclose to Supt G A Caskey and Inspector S E Cooke, of the Royal Ulster Constabulary, the information that is in your possession which is directly relevant to the investigation – including where necessary information which you gained in the course of your employment with the MOD and which is security classified.

You will of course appreciate that the responsibility for safeguarding information not related to the police investigation remains unchanged and you must therefore be careful not to divulge any information other than that which is directly relevant to them.

The letter, which was dated 25 October 1982, was written by Colin's old colleague Len Garrett who had been Chief of Staff at Lisburn barracks in Colin's heyday, and was now a general.

It was if anything even more useless to Colin than the 'assurance' from James Prior. It made the same specific reference to homosexual offences in boys' homes as the only subject of the police inquiry. There was no mention of any investigation of a cover-up as promised by James Prior. It carried with it the clearest possible warning that any classified information outside this specific area could be divulged only on pain of prosecution. All Colin's fears that he was being set up flooded back to him as he read the letter. He handed it glumly to Morgan-Harris. Morgan-Harris at once declared that it took the matter no further, and that in no way did it give the assurance his client needed. He advised Colin in the strongest possible terms to leave the interview. The officers protested in vain.

Morgan-Harris wrote to Colin a few days later, on 25 November 1982:

After you had left, the senior officer informed me that he felt that nothing further would take place and the matter would be concluded as he thought the authorities were not likely to go so far as to grant legal aid or make any provision for legal representation.

It appears that they are trying to close their case without your evidence on the basis that you are unwilling to assist – as I believe was the general tenor of the interview. In the circumstances no doubt you would like to continue your representations with your present correspondents, and if I can be of assistance please do not hesitate to contact me.

Colin wrote again to General Garrett in conciliatory terms asking for a definition of what was 'directly relevant' to the inquiry, and what wasn't, and who was to decide. Obviously the police officers could not decide, but what criteria was he to use when giving information? Garrett replied on 13 December:

The relevance of any information you may have to criminal activity in the

Kincora Boys Home is a matter that, in the first instance, only you can judge in the light of the police questions.

This was no use whatever. Colin's information was about a cover-up; about the state of knowledge of the military and intelligence authorities of homosexual offences, not about the offences themselves. If the inquiry was restricted to the offences themselves, Colin had nothing to say which could help it.

He replied to Garrett two days after Christmas (1982):

I have not seen the precise terms of reference for the current police investigation, and I believe that it is therefore unrealistic to expect me to determine what information if any in my possession is 'directly relevant' to those investigations, particularly in a situation where I am unable to receive proper legal advice.

For example:-

a). May I disclose information about homes other than Kincora?

b). May I disclose information about the death of Brian McDermott?

c). What is the position regarding disinformation material based on Kincora but used for other projects?

d). How much information may I disclose to the RUC to explain how I came to be in possession of Kincora material and how such material was used?

e). The RUC have in their possession some unattributable documents produced by official sources for use in Information Policy activities. May I please be informed if they have been given full access to all Kincora-related material held at HQNI and Stormont Castle?

f). May I identify members of the Secret Intelligence Service and the Security Service to the RUC?

g). If you consider that your letters of 25 October and 13 December give me authority to disclose information which I consider relevant to the terms of reference for the police investigation, may I please see a copy of those terms of reference?

These were the crucial questions. If the answer to them all was 'yes', then Colin could disclose to the RUC the full details of the Kincora cover-up.

So sensitive were his specific questions that they ushered into the correspondence no less a person than the Prime Minister. On 27 January 1983, Margaret Thatcher wrote to Michael Marshall, Colin's MP:

Mr Wallace has been assured that he will not be prosecuted for any breach of the Official Secrets Act in respect of any communication by him to members of the RUC in connection with their investigations into allegations of homosexual offences in Northern Ireland or any information which was obtained by him in the course of his employment in the Ministry of Defence and which relates or is relevant to the subject of the investigation. It remains Mr Wallace's duty not to disclose to those conducting the investigation confidential information obtained by him in the course of his employment in the Ministry of Defence and which is unrelated or irrelevant to the investigation.

As she makes clear in her letter, Margaret Thatcher had read the correspondence between General Garrett and Colin Wallace. However, only one of the six specific questions asked by Colin in his letter of 27 December is answered by the Prime Minister. She indicated (though not specifically) that he could give information on homes other than Kincora. The other questions remained unanswered both by Mrs Thatcher and in a further letter (on 29 March) from General Garrett. The Prime Minister, like her officials in the Ministry of Defence, had defined the police inquiry very strictly as dealing with allegations of homosexual conduct, and had not indicated whether or not this included a cover-up of such offences by the police, the military and intelligence.

Colin's position, entirely supported by his solicitor, was unchanged. He could not risk giving information to Caskey and Cooke which could lead to a prosecution under the Official Secrets Act, or forfeiting his chances of parole, because it was held to be not 'directly relevant' to the inquiry, whose terms of reference he never saw.

A further matter worried Colin. James Morgan-Harris, without ever a word of complaint, had been advising him since his conviction without getting a penny for his work. Colin and Eileen had no money. Mr Morgan-Harris had travelled frequently to Wormwood Scrubs and to Lewes to discuss Kincora. Colin had insisted from the outset that any interviews he had about Kincora should be attended by his solicitor, who should be paid for his time out of public funds.

He wrote letter after letter – to Lord Hailsham, Lord Chancellor, to the Northern Ireland Law Society, to the Attorney-General and to others with this entirely reasonable demand. It was first deflected, and then turned down. The final letter from General Garrett insisted that if there were any interviews at all which involved classified information, no third party could be present.

The police inquiry into Kincora was therefore completed without too much haste, and without Colin's assistance.

No report was ever published either in Sussex or in Northern Ireland or anywhere else. Instead, on 28 October 1983, RUC Chief Constable Sir John Hermon and Sir George Terry, Chief Constable of Sussex, held a press conference in Belfast. They released only the 'conclusions' of the Terry report. Sir George Terry was keen to denounce those who had criticised the police or any other authority. He had some mild criticism for the Royal Ulster Constabulary for not acting on information received about Kincora in the mid-1970s. 'But he excuses this,' reported the *Guardian*, 29 October 1983, 'by arguing that this was a time of intense terrorist activity which placed an excessive strain on police resources and undoubtedly dictated priorities.'

If the police were marginally to blame, however, no blame whatever attached to the Army or the intelligence services. Said Sir George: 'Military sources have been frank, and I am satisfied there is no substance to allegations that Army intelligence had knowledge of homosexual abuse at Kincora.'

This breathtaking conclusion, which was, as has been established here many times, entirely false, could have been corrected by Colin Wallace. When Colin finally saw the reports of the press conference, he could not believe them. Again and again during the past year he had written letters to people in authority in the Ministry of Defence, the Northern Ireland Office, the Attorney-General and the Lord Chancellor's office, to his MP, his solicitor, to Sir George Terry himself and to the RUC. Each time, his question was the same. Was the police inquiry concerned with information about a cover-up of Kincora, or was it only concerned with the homosexual offences themselves? If the first was the case, Colin had a lot of information which was secret, but directly relevant. If the second, he had no relevant information and to disclose classified material on something else would have laid him open to prosecution.

He never got a straight answer to this question. In so far as the question was answered, every authority repeated that the inquiry was about homosexual offences. No letter or statement from anyone in authority even indicated that a cover-up of the Kincora scandal was 'relevant' to the police inquiry. Colin therefore concluded that it was not relevant, and decided that it was better both in his own interests and in the interests of classified information, which he strongly believed should remain secret, that he should not give evidence.

When the inquiry was completed, however, and when its conclusions were published, it became clear that the question of cover-up *had* been investigated by the Terry inquiry, and that the conclusion of Sir George was the precise opposite of what he knew for certain (and could prove) was the truth.

In the Northern Ireland Assembly which had been set up by James Prior, but which was boycotted by the main opposition party, and effectively by the entire Catholic minority, there was nothing but outrage and ridicule.

John Cushnan, a spokesman for the non-sectarian Alliance Party, was indignant:

He found one of the most disturbing aspects of Sir George's conclusions was the complete dismissal of any possibility that military circles knew about the scandal. He then referred to a number of people – including Mr Garland, an active politician, a professional man and an evangelical preacher in Belfast – as having been interviewed by British Army people for British military intelligence about McGrath and Kincora. Mr Cushnan concluded by saying that it was misleading and blatantly dishonest for Sir George Terry to claim that the whole matter had been fully ventilated. (*Irish Times*, 10 November 1983)

The Unionists were also angry. Robert McCartney QC, Official Unionist, said that the report 'looks as if it were ghost-written by someone in the Northern Ireland Office'. (*Irish Times*, 11 November 1983.)

The notion that the Kincora scandal was being swept under the carpet gathered strength over the next few weeks. The Unionist Parties started to demand that the Secretary of State should order a full judicial inquiry, in public.

Mr McCartney was indignant that the police had not acted on information in 1974.

The horrible and awful truth was that the RUC did absolutely nothing in the period between 1974 when it was alleged that they first heard about offences at the home and 1980 when they opened their inquiry. In that six years children continued to be abused, sodomised and buggered. (*Irish Times*, 10 November 1983.)

Mr McCartney produced an interesting example to back up his demand for a full judicial inquiry.

He produced a letter and a four-page document sent to him by Colin Wallace the former British Army Press Officer who had leaked information to journalists about McGrath in the early 1970s. Mr McCartney said Wallace had been willing to give evidence to the police but had been refused legal representation with investigating detectives. He said this was just 'one small aspect to show why a full judicial enquiry should be held into the whole affair'. (*Irish Times*, 11 November 1983.)

Mr Prior did not agree. On 18 January 1983 he rose in the House of Commons to announce yet another inquiry into Kincora. After fulsome tribute to Sir George Terry, Mr Prior said he did not favour a full inquiry under the Tribunals of Enquiry (Evidence) Act 1921, which would have scope to range over any matter it liked and would also have protected any witness giving any evidence. Instead, he set up a much less prestigious inquiry under the Health and Social Personal Services (Northern Ireland) Order, 1972. He announced that Judge Hughes, a retired circuit judge, would be Chairman. Witnesses, he assured the House, would be protected. But what was the scope of the inquiry? Peter Archer, Labour spokesman on law, asked:

Will this committee have a duty and power to investigate previous enquiries, whether they were misled and how? As this is at least the fourth investigation into the events at Kincora, does the Rt Hon Gentleman recognise that this is his last opportunity to allay public disquiet, if it can properly be allayed, and that this time he had better get it right?'

The Rev. Martin Smyth, Unionist MP for Belfast South, Grand Master of the Orange Order, was even more inquisitive. 'I query whether the terms of reference are too narrow to deal with the problem.'
Mr Prior had no time for such doubts:

It will be up to the enquiry and the eminent judge who will preside over it to examine anything which is relevant to the particular boys home, or to the other five boys homes, and the circumstances which led up to the problem.

Then he gave a specific assurance:

I believe that it would be within the enquiry's terms of reference to examine why no enquiry was instigated before 1980. This goes to the heart of much of the concern expressed in Northern Ireland. (House of Commons Official Report, 18 January 1984.)

A rather different 'belief' was voiced by Judge Hughes when he opened the committee of enquiry in Belfast on 4 May 1984. Commenting on its terms of reference, the judge said it would inquire into and make recommendations on 'the administration of boys homes':

It would not involve itself in the criminal investigations already undertaken in the RUC and would not investigate the allegations carried in the newspapers and on television that there was any cover-up of the Kincora affair, or that there was a vice ring in operation.
There have also been allegations that there has been an establishment cover-up of homosexual activities involving boys in care, and that British military intelligence were aware that homosexual offences were being committed by a member of the staff of the Kincora boys hostel. The committee's approach to these matters is straightforward. It will not engage in hypothetical discussion of them. (*Irish Times*, 4 May 1984.)

The committee's position was clearly demonstrated when they failed to interview any of those convicted of offences against the inmates. Even more inexplicable was their refusal to call Roy Garland who, by his own admission, had alerted the security forces to the affair as early as 1972.
In an understandable outburst of frustration, Mr Robert McCartney QC, who represented the inmates at the inquiry, told the committee: 'Are my wits leaving me? A man who detonated an entire police enquiry and

put the finger at a fairly early stage on the man subsequently convicted for some of the most brutal acts of sodomy is not a relevant or material witness?' (*Irish Times*, 24 November 1984.)

Mr Reg Weir QC, who represented the Eastern Health Board, supported McCartney on this issue. 'It seems astonishing that no attempt has been made on behalf of the Committee to ascertain what this witness might say,' he said. (*Irish News*, 24 November 1984.)

Perhaps the reason for the committee's refusal to interview Roy Garland can be found in a report in the *Irish Times* on 3 November 1983 which claimed that Roy Garland and a 'well known Belfast Protestant evangelical preacher' had been interviewed by Army Intelligence officers at Army Headquarters in Lisburn on a number of occasions during an eighteen-month period in 1974/75.

The evangelical preacher told the *Irish Times* that he was contacted by British Army intelligence around 1974. He was asked if he could arrange a meeting with Mr Garland. The *Irish Times* report (3 November 1983) said:

> Both he [the preacher] and Mr Garland say that two intelligence officers attended that meeting, at the former's house outside Belfast, and that one of them was a Scotsman called Mr Brian Gemmill. The officers produced military identification.

The preacher told the *Irish Times* he met at least six and perhaps more intelligence officers at his house over the next eighteen months to two years. He said he was asked questions about McGrath's paramilitary involvement with TARA and political involvement with the Young Union-ists and the Democratic Unionist Party, as well as his homosexual activities. Towards the end of this series of meetings – between three and five in all – he remembered them talking about monitoring McGrath. 'I got the impression they were keeping a very close watch on him, and there is no doubt that at this stage they knew he was working in a boys home,' he was quoted as saying. The *Irish Times* report went on to say that Roy Garland confirmed the preacher's account of what had happened. He himself had met British Army Intelligence Officers on two occasions:

> He said that at the first meeting, in the house of a prominent Belfast evangelical, the intelligence officer called Mr Gemmill had expressed concern at McGrath's activities in both the Kincora home and elsewhere.
>
> Mr Garland said that a couple of weeks later he received a telephone call from the other intelligence officer present at the meeting asking him to come to the Army headquarters at Thiepval barracks in Lisburn. This officer called for him and drove him to the barracks.
>
> The whole tone was different from the first meeting. He was less concerned

about sexual abuses, and more about Tara. He asked particularly about the involvement of a man prominent in Belfast life, who was also a part-time officer in the UDR.

The *Irish Times* concluded that this testimony 'would appear to cast doubt on the claim by the former Sussex police chief, Sir George Terry, that he found no evidence of any awareness of goings-on at Kincora in military circles'.

The metamorphosis from the 'belief' of the Secretary of State in January 1983 that the terms of reference of the inquiry which he set up *did* include investigating a Kincora cover-up into the bland assertion of the committee Chairman that no such matter would be investigated has never been explained by anyone. Nor did the Orange Order or the Save Ulster From Sodomy campaigners kick up too much of a fuss. As with the Terry inquiry, Hughes said he would limit himself strictly to the offences themselves, and not to the way in which they became known to the authorities, and were covered up by them for eight years.

Colin remembers greeting the news of the Hughes inquiry and its new terms of reference with some scepticism. After his experience with Terry and the RUC, he did not imagine for a moment that the cover-up he knew about would ever be officially exposed.

His life in prison had become more tranquil. He had been working during 1982 and some of 1983 transcribing old baptismal certificates for Sussex County Council Archives to facilitate the computerisation of their records. He was then promoted from the archives to the important post of education orderly, where he was responsible for keeping records of prisoners who attended classes, allocating prisoners to classes, and administering them. He bceame an adult literacy teacher and helped many of the prisoners to learn to read and write.

Between 1983 and 1985, Colin wrote three long petitions insisting that he had not killed Jonathan Lewis. The petitions produced little new evidence, but they did complain for the first time about the press briefing given by the police during the trial, the conversation James Morgan-Harris had seen between a journalist and a juror, and witnesses to car sightings who had not been called. Colin also asked the Home Secretary to arrange for Jane Lewis to be interviewed again about the cleaning labels on Jonathan's brown suit. Had they been taken off the suit on 5 August? If so, they provided proof that Jonathan had not worn the suit for several days before the night of his death, and further confirmed that Amanda Metcalfe had seen him in the Golden Goose on 5 August.

The petitions were all summarily dismissed. Colin asked his MP, Michael Marshall, to seek more detailed explanations. Marshall had a long correspondence with the Parliamentary Secretary at the Home Office, David Mellor. Mellor's letters made it clear that, in his opinion, there was no case for re-opening the trial or the appeal, since there was no new evidence. He refused any inquiry into the press briefing of the juror. But he did assure Mr Marshall that police interviews with Jane Lewis had established that the cleaning labels had come off the brown suit on the day Jonathan died.

A further matter about the trial worried Colin. He had always wondered why it was that the police had gone to such trouble to take samples of water from the hot and cold water tanks in his house. During conversation with DCI Harrison shortly before he was charged (on 18 September 1980), Harrison had said that the police did not know where Jonathan had been drowned. 'It could have been in your bath,' he had added.

Colin had always suspected that Jonathan may have been drowned somewhere else than the Arun, and thrown in the river not just after he had been knocked out, but after he had been forcibly drowned elsewhere. He believed the injuries to Jonathan's body, especially to his arms and shoulders, suggested a forcible drowning.

He has therefore always been interested in the report of Dr William Wilson from the Scotland Yard forensic laboratory on the diatoms in the water found in Jonathan's stomach and lungs. Diatoms are small organisms in water which vary in size and character in different types of water. The nature of the diatoms would disclose, for instance, whether a water sample comes from the River Arun, which is tidal and salty; from a lake; or from a domestic water tank (which might not contain any diatoms at all). Evidence was given at the trial that there were diatoms in the water in Jonathan's body consistent with his drowning in a river – but no details were disclosed.

Dr Wilson had done tests on the amount of alcohol in the blood and urine which might help to solve a crucial mystery at the trial: the time of death. One forensic expert had estimated that Jonathan had died only an hour and a half after drinking alcohol – which made the prosecution story impossible. If he had died only an hour and a half after drinking, he could not have been unconscious, as the prosecution suggested, all the time Colin was at the Avisford Park Hotel from 8 p.m to around 10.30 p.m.

Where was Dr Wilson's full report? James Morgan-Harris wrote in August 1985, and again in November, asking for it. Dr Wilson wrote back saying he had written to the Sussex Police asking for permission to disclose his findings and had not yet had a reply. Morgan-Harris promptly wrote to Detective Superintendent Harrison.

On 7 March 1986, Mr Harrison replied: 'The Metropolitan laboratory have refused to supply further information and I do not propose to intervene in what must be a decision for them.'

In vain did James Morgan-Harris and Colin complain that the forensic laboratory had always agreed to make the report available, but needed only police permission to do so. Back and forth went the letters through the spring and summer of 1986. It was not until 3 December that year that the Metropolitan Police wrote back with a brief summary of some of Dr Wilson's findings, none of which revealed what sort of water the diatoms had come from. A few more exasperated letters from Colin and his solicitor produced nothing more. Dr Wilson's report remains entirely secret and the mystery of the diatoms, and the type of water in which Jonathan Lewis drowned, is still unsolved.

In May 1984, Colin got a rare boost. One of the worst aspects of his position was its isolation.

Apart from Eileen there seemed to be no one who could see any connection between his conviction and his past life in Northern Ireland. His petitions had emphasised this connection, but he realised that to most people in civilian life, it seemed like fantasy. The idea that he might be right and everyone else wrong was difficult to sustain amid the dull routine of Lewes prison.

One day, a prisoner dropped into his cell a cutting from the *Guardian* which referred to a series of articles in the *New Statesman* and a television programme about allegations of dirty tricks in Northern Ireland. The man making the allegations, the article disclosed, was Fred Holroyd.

Fred Holroyd! Colin remembered meeting Fred in the company of an SAS major in the top secret intelligence corridor in Lisburn in 1974. Holroyd, a Yorkshireman who had started his military career in the Royal Corps of Transport, was then an officer in Special Military Intelligence. He 'ran' sensitive agents in the IRA and in the Protestant organisations both in Northern Ireland and the Irish Republic. He was always close to the front line of the battle against both.

Colin got a home address for the journalist who had written the *New Statesman* articles – Duncan Campbell. The address, which came from a fellow prisoner who was also writing to the journalist, turned out to be wrong. There are, as contemporary modern journalists are always finding out, two Duncan Campbells, both investigative journalists. At any rate, in the long run Colin's letter got through to the right Duncan Campbell, at the *New Statesman*.

It consisted of a few lines, including code names of Northern Ireland agents which Fred Holroyd would recognise. Fred wrote in reply at once and before long found himself on a train to Lewes where he was to spend a lot of his time over the next two years.

Fred has told his own story in his own disturbing book, still to be published.

What connected him to Colin is that he too felt he had been forced out of the Army because he crossed his intelligence masters. Like Colin, his life had been turned upside down by the experience. As part of the campaign against him, he argued, the Army had tried to classify him as emotionally unstable and had even tricked him into going into a mental hospital.

Like Colin, he had not been able to find anyone who believed his story. The two men suddenly became allies. Both of them had found someone else who believed anything was possible in the intelligence community.

Remarkably, they had both worked for and with the same people at the same time in the same place, and their experiences kept on overlapping. Colin had been convinced at the time that Fred had been badly treated, and had told his lawyer and his friends of the victimisation. Fred, on the other hand, was not so sure about Colin. The first months of their relationship were largely taken up with Colin explaining his case to a fascinated former fellow-soldier. Very quickly, Fred became absorbed in the Jonathan Lewis killing.

'I believed him when he protested his innocence,' Fred wrote. 'But I had to be absolutely sure, or I could risk losing all the hard-fought ground I had won. I decided the whole matter had to be investigated.'

Fred went to Arundel. He returned again and again in 1984 and the first part of 1985, pacing out the paths by the Arun, and interviewing anyone who would speak to him. At Arundel police station, he saw Detective Superintendent Gordon Harrison and Sergeant Kent, who called him 'Major Holroyd' when he described himself as 'Mr Holroyd' and seemed strangely well informed about him, though he had neither seen nor heard of either of them in his life. The attitude of the police officers prompted him to write later: 'If anything convinced me of Colin's innocence, that interview did the trick.'   (From the manuscript of Fred Holroyd's book Fighting on Two Fronts.)

By far the most important witness whom Fred saw was the former barmaid of the Golden Goose, Amanda Metcalfe. The hotel had been sold by the Metcalfe family, and Amanda was now a full-time riding instructress at Patching just outside Arundel. She was very keen to talk about the case, explaining to Fred that she felt that she had not given as full an account to the court as she should have done.

Fred stayed in touch with Amanda. As late as 1 February 1987, she wrote to him:

In reply to your letter including the statements (which I am afraid I really can't remember what was taken down at the time as it really was a long time ago). The only thing I can say is the same as I said to you in person that many of the things I said to the police at the time were not taken down at all because the police kept saying that unless I was absolutely certain not to include it in my statement. I'm still sure to this day that the man wasn't Wallace, and I still have fixed in my mind's eye somebody totally different.

When you're faced with a situation of giving a statement to the police of pure certainties one starts to wonder if anything is such, but having been over and over that night I can only say that to the best of my knowledge the first time I have ever seen Colin Wallace was in Lewes courtroom.

The letter seems to end there, but there was another piece of paper in the envelope, in which Amanda Metcalfe wrote:

I have steamed open the envelope containing the main letter in order to add this as a postscript, hopefully to ease my conscience a little. It is very difficult to explain how one feels in a situation like this. Firstly, I must say that after the Lewes court fiasco I ended up in tears twice that day which is totally out of character for me. It was through a feeling of pure cowardice and frustration. The frustration at only being allowed to say Yes or No to any questions asked and not to give any more detailed evidence, and cowardice that I didn't say then and there that I had never seen Wallace before.

This was because local opinion was that he had done it and I didn't want him to get off the charge if he had, just in case I had made a mistake. Therefore, on the next sheet, I have put down what I can remember of that night.

On the next sheet, she had written:

I remember Lewis being in the Goose that night, mainly for two reasons: one that he was dressed differently than his usual casual wear. That night he had a light-coloured beige/fawn suit on, he had a chocolate brown tie and I think chocolate brown socks with light coloured shoes. I did not serve them their first drinks, and my first sighting of Lewis was as I carried a tray of either glasses or crockery through from the Somerset bar direction towards where they were sitting. As I did so, Lewis turned in my direction and looked at me with what I would describe as a hang-dog expression on his face. Unfortunately, this is something which has stayed on my mind since, because he looked so miserable. He had his right leg crossed over his left ankle.

Secondly, he was not with his usual companion, which was a dark-haired woman. He was with a man who I would age in his fifties, with thinning grey hair combed back over the top of his head. At some point I was stood directly opposite the two men. I was by the glass washing machine behind the bar, and I remember Lewis was turning a glass in his hand and looking down at it. The glass was a 6-ounce Paris goblet which again would have been unusual because I think he normally drank halves of bitter. After this he turned and made a comment to the man with him. From his movement I would not have thought that they were having a friendly conversation – it was too sharp a movement. I think the man with him had a dark suit on – possibly grey.

The significance of this letter was chiefly in its tone, and its reference to 'conscience'. The details of the man in the Golden Goose whom she had seen with Lewis don't add much to the description she gave in February 1981 to private detectives shortly before the trial. The detail about the goblet was new. Amanda Metcalfe was unlikely to have known that according to Colin's evidence, he had given Jonathan a gin and tonic in his house at about 7 p.m., and that Jonathan was unlikely to mix his drinks. Nor would she have known the forensic evidence that Jonathan had drunk about three tots of gin before he died.

The chief addition to her evidence at the trial, however, is her certainty that the man with Lewis was not Colin. It was clear from the whole tone of the letter, which was repeated in conversation with Fred on more than one occasion, that Amanda Metcalfe had grown more and more certain as she thought about it that the man in the Golden Goose was not Colin Wallace, and that she had seen Jonathan Lewis alive after Colin did.

Fred's meetings with Amanda Metcalfe, and his other investigations (which were not the work of an amateur, but of a trained Army Intelligence officer who was attached to the RUC Special Branch) convinced him quickly that Colin had had nothing to do with Jonathan Lewis's death.

Nor was he alone in this conclusion. In some of his visits to Arundel he had been accompanied by James Campbell, a journalist employed by *The Times Literary Supplement*. Campbell had been commissioned by Weidenfeld and Nicolson to write a book about life inside a prison and was granted access to Lewes. The book, *Gate Fever*, was published in 1986. One chapter was entitled: 'The Case of Colin Wallace'. James Campbell concluded:

> My own feelings about the case were and remain a tangle. The prosecution case, as I studied it, only confused them further. Whoever killed Jonathan Lewis it was surely not done in the alleged way. Finally, I have to admit that the case was intellectually inscrutable. Trying to penetrate it was like attempting to answer the question of God's existence. Every argument in favour produced a counter-argument against, and in the end one was thrown back on faith.
>
> I myself believed in Colin's innocence, but knew that no-one could be certain, finally, that he did not kill Jonathan Lewis, except Colin himself.

After convincing himself, Fred Holroyd set himself to galvanise his new friend to action. Colin was allowed three visits a month. Two visiting orders went to Eileen, who came every two weeks. Fred used the other one. Every month, he hitch-hiked to Lewes from Southend, where he was living in some poverty. Colin used one of his two letters a week to write to Fred with more information. In this correspondence and meetings, the two men put together a vast dossier. In more than two hundred pages, it outlined the stories of the two men's careers in the Army and afterwards. Fred's story of his victimisation was set out at length. Colin's told in detail of the Clockwork Orange project, the attempt to discredit the Labour government, the knowledge of what went on in the Kincora Boys' Home and his argument that he was wrongly convicted of killing Jonathan Lewis. The pages were interspersed with documents to prove the stories, including the Clockwork Orange notes and the Kincora memoranda, the forged bank statements, the letters from Airey Neave, and fifty-seven varieties of documents and statements.

When the document was complete, all beautifully typed by Eileen, or in James Morgan-Harris's office, Fred Holroyd collected it and, without taking a copy, sent it by recorded delivery to the Prime Minister at 10 Downing Street, marked 'in confidence'.

Colin wrote a covering letter, dated 1 November 1984.

Dear Prime Minister,

I have gone to very considerable lengths during the past nine years to avoid causing any undue embarrassment to successive Governments or to the Security Forces in Northern Ireland, in the hope that the relevant authorities would act reasonably and deal with the matter fairly and expeditiously. Having read the file, I hope you will agree that I have done everything that could be expected of me in the circumstances to achieve that aim. In that context there are two points that I would stress most strongly: firstly, I have not asked for any special consideration or treatment, only that the quite bizarre chain of events be investigated impartially and with determination; secondly, although I understandably feel bitter about what has happened to me, I am not seeking any form of revenge on those responsible and, even at this late stage, would be quite content for the matter to be resolved with the minimum of fuss.

After nine fruitless years, it has become very clear to me from the apparent lack of interest shown by the authorities concerned that no-one 'wants to know' about what has happened, let alone accept any form of responsibility for the situation. In submitting this file to you, I have now exhausted every legitimate channel of communication known to me to obtain a proper examination of all the relevant matters, without causing undue difficulties to the various members of the security authorities who played no part in the events recounted in my narrative, or without giving the various terrorist groups and their supporters a propaganda weapon with which to impede the work of the Security Forces in Northern Ireland. In so doing, however, I would ask you to understand that from my point of view I am now serving a prison sentence for an offence which I did not commit and that I was forced to resign my appointment with the Ministry of Defence in circumstances which were quite scandalous and, indeed, unconstitutional by the standards of any democratic society. I have no alternative, therefore, but to continue to press for a proper examination of my case and to have the matter rectified satisfactorily. I realise that by doing so I will exclude myself from obtaining parole and that the relevant authorities can ensure that I will not 'win'. Clearly they have both the resources and the ability to effect a total cover-up of the matter and to make life even more difficult for me in the future, but I also have a duty to myself and to a number of other people who have been seriously hurt by what has happened to ensure that the matter is not allowed to go by default.

Neither Capt Holroyd nor myself can be regarded in any way as 'politically motivated'. Neither can it be said that we are anti the security services, the Army or the forces of law and order in general – our respective records speak for themselves. It is therefore with very great sadness that we find ourselves driven into such a situation.

There was a note from Downing Street the following day, acknowledging receipt of the letter.

On 21 November, David Barclay, Mrs Thatcher's Private Secretary, wrote a brief note to Fred, returning the dossier. 'Mr Wallace's case has also been the subject of the most thorough consideration,' he wrote. On Kincora, 'Mr Wallace has been given every opportunity to make his views known.'

Colin replied in great indignation on 14 December. He said it was certainly untrue that the material he had sent her had been subject to 'thorough consideration'. Much of the material was classified and could not by its nature have been part of his petitions or his previous letters to anyone at all. He had been able to include this material, he explained, because the Prime Minister was 'head of the Intelligence and Security Services'.

His pent-up frustration burst out in his concluding paragraph.

If my suspicions are correct then the situation is quite iniquitous. For the relevant authorities to ignore the facts or pretend that they are untrue is at best hypocritical, at worst dishonest. If those employed in the service of the Crown use their position or knowledge to manipulate the democratically elected Government agencies, then they should be regarded as a risk to our democracy in the same way as those who resort to the gun or bomb. To do nothing about such a situation is to do a very great injustice to all those who have been killed or crippled in the fight against terrorism. Having said that, I would be quite content to be proved wrong in my suspicions, but I have very serious doubts about the effectiveness of any 'routine' investigation into such matters. For example, between 1975 and 1978, Capt Holroyd made a number of unsuccessful attempts to get several police forces to investigate his allegations. In each case the police said that they had been instructed by MI5 not to process his allegations, and in one instance he was even threatened with prosecution under the Official Secrets Acts if he pressed his complaint. I hope you will agree that it would be a very sad reflection on the state of law and order in this country if a single Government body, particularly one that is not directly answerable to Parliament, could decide what allegations of criminal activity the police could or could not investigate. You and the members of your Government have constantly stated that 'no-one is above the law' and that 'the rule of law is paramount'. Captain Holroyd and I heartily endorse those sentiments and we hope that you will therefore understand why we feel so frustrated by the treatment that we feel we have been subjected to at the hands of those whose job it is to uphold the law.

I do not intend to trouble you with further correspondence on this matter and I thank you for at least considering these two letters.

In his indignation, Colin did not mention one aspect of the Prime Minister's secretary's reply which had puzzled him and Fred. The 'file' sent back with Mr Barclay's letter was not the file which they had sent to the Prime Minister. It was a copy of it, and it was annotated in pencil. Neither Colin nor Fred thought this was peculiar. They both assumed that the original of the dossier had been kept at Downing Street, or at least passed on to the Ministry of Defence, the Northern Ireland Office or some other relevant body.

There was, perhaps predictably, no answer to Colin's angry letter. The correspondence with Downing Street seemed to be closed. But it was opened again as a result of another letter Colin received in prison from a most unexpected source: the Hughes inquiry into the Kincora affair.

Mr S. Quinn, secretary to the inquiry, wrote to say that the Royal Ulster Constabulary had passed to the inquiry certain information which came from Fred Holroyd. This included nine allegations that Colin, while serving as an information officer for the Army in Northern Ireland, had known that homosexual assaults were being carried out on boys at the Kincora Home, and had known that others in authority were aware of it. He asked if Colin would be prepared to talk to representatives from the inquiry.

It seemed like a repeat performance of what had happened with the Terry inquiry. Colin felt as though he was going through familiar contortions when he wrote, wearily, to James Morgan-Harris on 21 April 1985:

> Of course I am still willing to assist the enquiry – if this were not the case then I would not have spent a considerable part of the last three years in protracted correspondence with various individuals in Whitehall. Before doing so, however, I would like to be absolutely certain in my own mind that the current enquiry is genuinely determined to get at all the true facts of the matter and that it is not being used simply as a means of preventing the full story from emerging. Indeed I find it rather disturbing that Mr Quinn and the members of the Committee do not appear to be aware of the efforts we have made to assist them during the last three years.

Colin rehearsed the same old problems of the Official Secrets Act and of legal aid for James. Towards the end of his letter he proposed a solution to the secrets problem. He had, he said, written the whole story out and submitted it to the Prime Minister, head of the Intelligence and

Security Services. His dossier to her had pulled no punches and contained all the classified information. Colin went on:

> I am amazed that she has not provided the enquiry with the relevant information, and I would therefore ask Mr Quinn if he would, as a matter of urgency, contact the Prime Minister's office for a copy of my file – or such parts of it as she may decide to release.
>
> If the Prime Minister will release the contents of my file to the enquiry, and provide me with authority to discuss the relevant parts of its contents with the committee, then I am quite prepared to answer any questions relevant to the disclosed information.

In July, Colin got a letter, dated the 16th, from his old colleague General Garrett. It was like the ringing of an old bell.

> The purpose of this letter is to confirm that you may disclose to members of the Committee any information that is in your possession which is directly relevant to the investigation – including, where necessary, information which you gained in the course of your employment with the Ministry of Defence and which may be security classified.
>
> You will of course appreciate that your responsibilities for safeguarding information not related to the inquiry remain unchanged and you must therefore only divulge information which falls within the scope of the Committee's terms of reference, a copy of which is attached.

The terms of reference however did not clear up the eternal problem: was it relevant to disclose what Colin and his colleagues knew about Kincora in 1973 and 1974? The committee had already confirmed that it was not empowered to inquire into the performance of the police or Military Intelligence. It looked like the same Catch 22 which had prevented him giving evidence to Terry. This time, however, he had hit on a solution. If the Prime Minister herself passed on his information to the Committee, she would do so as head of the intelligence services and would thus provide Colin with the ideal authority to disclose what he knew.

The solution did not last for long.

On 6 August, Mr Quinn wrote again with the surprising information:

> The Committee has been informed that the file of papers submitted to the Prime Minister on 1st November 1984 was returned to Mr Frederick Holroyd on 21 November.

Colin replied at once (August 12) to the Prime Minister.

> That statement is quite untrue. Your office copied the file which Capt Holroyd submitted to you on my behalf, and retained the original. Indeed, you will note that the documents retained by your office have plastic reinforcing rings affixed

to them; the ones returned to Capt Holroyd do not. Those rings were fixed to the documents in my file by Capt Holroyd before he submitted the file to you. Also, you will note that someone in your office added small pencil ticks to the top of certain documents before they were photocopied.

If the Northern Ireland Office reply is correct then I think it is quite disgraceful that someone in your office should have lied to the Committee about the file in this way.

To this shocking allegation, there was no reply.

On 27 August James Morgan-Harris wrote to the Hughes inquiry saying that his client's letter to the Prime Minister 'remains unacknowledged for the time being'. He repeated that his client was prepared to give evidence to the committee if he could satisfy himself that he was authorised to tell what he knew.

The reply to this offer of assistance was an ultimatum. Mr Quinn wrote on 29 August:

The Committee has instructed me to inform you that unless your client indicates, by 13th September at the latest, an unconditional willingness to be interviewed by its staff on the basis of the existing authorisation, it will be deemed that he is not prepared to assist this enquiry.

This was greeted with a blistering reply (9 September) from the Chichester solicitor: 'Our client is not unwilling to assist the enquiry and indeed he never has been so.' The problem was one of authority to disclose matters which could result in a further prosecution. The solicitor concluded:

The matter would be greatly simplified if the papers at present with the Prime Minister were to be made available to you by her so that you could see the content and extent of the information available to our client. This would also, in our view, give him the authority to make the evidence available.'

At last, the message seemed to have sunk in. On 8 November 1985, Colin got a letter from Mr Simon Routh, Private Secretary to Lord Trefgarne, Minister of State at the Ministry of Defence. All the letters Colin had written to Downing Street had been passed to Trefgarne. Mr Routh confirmed that some of the papers sent by Colin and Fred to Downing Street had been copied and sent to the Hughes inquiry. These papers, he wrote, 'include the document entitled "Political and Security Implications Regarding the Disclosure of Security-Classified Information to assist in the Investigation of the Allegations Relating to the Kincora Boys' Hostel in Belfast".'

At last, Colin had the assurance he wanted. Although he knew perfectly well that the entire document he had sent to Downing Street had been copied – he had the copy to prove it – he was no longer in the mood to quibble. He had it on excellent authority that the crucial document in the dossier which gave chapter and verse of all he knew about Kincora and Clockwork Orange had been passed to the Hughes inquiry from 10 Downing Street. Attached to the document were all the memos and briefings on Kincora which Colin wrote in Lisburn in 1973 and 1974. As far as he was concerned he now had carte blanche to discuss with the Hughes inquiry the matters in the documents. He wrote to James Morgan-Harris as soon as he saw Routh's letter saying he was now willing to meet the Hughes inquiry, to answer any questions 'relevant to the disclosed information'. The offer was plainly restricted to information sent to, and released by, the Prime Minister.

The offer was accepted, and on 13 December 1985, shortly after lunch, Colin was called from his cell to the legal visits room where James Morgan-Harris was waiting for him with a Mr David Mercer, a lawyer carrying out investigations for the Hughes inquiry.

It was agreed by all three men that Colin was prepared to talk about the documents released from 10 Downing Street. As Mr Mercer started to ask his first question, Colin asked if he could see the released document. Mr Mercer promptly produced from his brief case what he described as 'the document'.

It was, however, not the document, nor any document sent by Colin to Downing Street, nor anything like any such document. It was a memorandum Colin had produced at Wormwood Scrubs in 1982 for his solicitor in response to the request from the RUC for information for the Terry inquiry. It had presumably found its way to the Hughes inquiry via Fred Holroyd and the Essex Police.

For a moment Colin could not believe it. Somehow finding his voice, he asked his solicitor to confirm to Mr Mercer that this was not one of the documents submitted to the Prime Minister. Nor were the vital memos and briefing papers of 1973 and 1974 attached. Angrily, Morgan-Harris confirmed what Colin said, and immediately advised him to have nothing further to do with the interview. He asked Mr Mercer to leave at once.

Colin made his way back to his cell and sat down to write to his solicitor:

> I can only apologise for today's quite unbelievable meeting . . . and say that had I known how it would turn out I would never have agreed to the interview in the first place. It is quite beyond belief that after four years of wrangling over evidence a lawyer for the enquiry should come here today with a document which the Committee must have known was not the one sent by me to the Prime Minister . . . Mr Mercer freely admitted that it had not been supplied by the Prime Minister's office and that the Committee had obtained it in February or March this year, i.e. nine months before Lord Trefgarne claimed it had been sent to the Committee.

Six weeks later, at the end of January 1986, the Hughes inquiry report was published. A short passage in it, seventeen paragraphs long, refers to Colin Wallace.

The report suggests that Colin Wallace was of no interest to them until they received via Fred Holroyd and the Essex Police his documents about Kincora, in particular the four-page memo, dated 8 November 1974, which listed Colin's growing concern about the Kincora Boys' Home. The Hughes report could hardly fail to accept that this document, if genuine, 'would be directly relevant to the enquiry'. It suggested in forthright terms that the abuse at Kincora had been covered up for at least eight years since 1967, and that the cover-up extended from Social Services to the Army and to Intelligence.

After summarising the document, the report devotes several paragraphs to its authenticity. 'We investigated as far as we could certain aspects of the document which we had seen.' (Hughes Report, 4.80.) The inquiry referred to the journalists who agreed that Colin had briefed them about TARA and about McGrath in 1973 and 1974. David McKittrick agreed he had been handed a document by Wallace in 1974. 'The document alleged,' said McKittrick, 'that McGrath was a homosexual. Wallace did not tell me McGrath worked with children and it was not until McGrath was charged that I realised this was the case.' (*ibid.*)

This was not the only time McKittrick had declared that he had information from Colin on Kincora. In an article in the *Irish Times* in March 1981, just after Colin was convicted, McKittrick had written:

> He told me what he knew about the small loyalist group TARA. My notes which I still have show that he gave the name, address and telephone number of its commanding officer . . .
>
> For example, a document from Wallace on the TARA group described one of its leaders in the following terms: 'He is said to be homosexual and has conned many people into membership by threatening them with revealing homosexual activities which he has himself initiated.'

These exact words appear in the press briefing on Kincora which Colin circulated in 1974, and which includes the information: 'and also runs a home for children on the Upper Newtownards Road, Belfast (Tel: 657838)'.

After interviewing a few other journalists who said they had not been told anything by Colin Wallace about Kincora, the Hughes inquiry blandly suggested the four-page memo of 8 November might have been forged.

The RUC investigation attempted, inter alia, to validate the authenticity of the document dated November 1974. The statements of MOD personnel,

including purported addressees, did not establish its authenticity. A forensic
report raised the possibilities that the first page had been tampered with and that
two typewriters had been used but was inconclusive as to authenticity.   (Hughes
Report, 4.85.)

In March and April 1989, I tried to discover from the RUC which
forensic experts had examined the document, and concluded that there
was a possibility that two typewriters had been used on it. No answer
was forthcoming.

I consulted two top experts in Britain. Mr Derek Davis of Hemel
Hempstead, Hertfordshire, wrote to me on 29 March 1989:

I cannot find any evidence of more than one typewriter having been used,
as alleged. All four pages are consistent.

Mr Robert Radley of Reading wrote to me on 11 April 1989:

I have been unable to find any significant differences in design or spacing
characteristics nor have I found any significant differences in typographical
layout features which would suggest more than one typewriter or more than
one typist has been involved in its production.

The key to all these questions of course was held by Colin Wallace
himself. Several paragraphs are devoted to the committee's explanation of
how they tried to interview Colin Wallace and failed. 'The purpose of our
approach to him . . . and subsequent correspondence with him . . . was
to remove all obstacles which might discourage him from volunteering a
contribution to this enquiry.'

The report quoted the assurances given in the letter to Colin by
General Garrett, and declared: 'We were satisfied that the authorisation
was sufficient for the purposes of the inquiry . . . '

The report also stated:

We pursued the file of papers which Mr Wallace had sent to the Prime Minister
on lst November 1984 . . . We subsequently examined the very limited number
of documents which the NIO informed us had been retained by the Government.
This did not advance our inquiries.   (Hughes Report, p. 52.)

This was extraordinary. In November 1985, Mr Routh from the
Ministry of Defence had written to Colin about the papers which had
gone from the Prime Minister to the Hughes inquiry. 'I should also add,'
he wrote, 'that the Committee have a copy of the index to the file . . . '

This index included a list of personalities involved in the Kincora scandal, the Army's unattributable press briefing on TARA, and 'The Kincora Inquiry – Summary of Events'.

None of this, apparently, could 'advance the enquiries' of the committee.

Mr Routh in his letter to Colin had singled out one document which had gone from Downing Street to Hughes. It was sixteen pages long. It included a huge section on the Kincora Boys' Home and the role of McGrath in the intelligence and security network. It states quite clearly how much Colin and his colleagues knew of the Kincora scandal at the time. Yet this document, according to the Hughes report, 'did not advance our enquiries'.

The mystery deepened as the Hughes report attempted to explain the curious incidents in Lewes prison the previous December:

> Early in December 1985 we were made aware that Mr Wallace had, in correspondence with his solicitor, indicated that he was prepared to answer questions from the Committee on one document in the file of papers submitted to the Prime Minister's office.

This was of course the document mentioned above. The next sentence in the report, therefore, is difficult to credit. It reads:

> This appeared to be the document mentioned in paragraph 4.75. (Hughes Report, 4.86)

The document in paragraph 4.75 was the 1982 memorandum which Colin had written to his solicitor. This document was *not* sent to the Prime Minister. It could not possibly have been the one Colin referred to when he agreed to give evidence. Yet it was this document, which Mr Mercer took with him to Lewes prison, thus ensuring that Colin would not give detailed evidence to the committee.

After promising to ask questions based on a document which had been sent to and from the Prime Minister, the Hughes inquiry proceeded to try to ask questions based on another document which never went anywhere near the Prime Minister. The response from Colin and his lawyer was predictable.

Having ensured by deceit and double-talk that Colin did not respond, the inquiry then proceeded to denigrate him on the grounds that he had voluntarily refused to respond. Their final paragraph on this section read:

> Since Mr Wallace declined . . . to answer our questions . . . he has never authenticated or repudiated the papers which we have seen. They have therefore no probative value to this enquiry. (Hughes Report, 4.87.)

The cover-up was complete. As after the Terry inquiry, politicians in Northern Ireland, usually so hostile to one another, came together in unaccustomed unanimity to denounce the Hughes report.

Mr Cedric Wilson, for the extreme right DUP, described the report as a 'whitewash'. Alliance Party leader John Cushnan said: 'Only a full judicial enquiry could have resolved the matter.' Dr Joe Hendron for the SDLP said: 'The enquiry has been hampered by its excessively restricted terms of reference. No investigation into Kincora can be considered complete until the role of those more widely involved such as government officials, military intelligence, police, administrators and others with political responsibility is considered.' (*Belfast Telegraph*, 5 February 1986.)

If, in the wake of the Hughes inquiry, anyone had been in any doubt about which documents did go to the Prime Minister, there was at least some proof. There was no doubt that Fred Holroyd had received a copy of the dossier, and it was complete. He had handed the copy, stressing the fact that it was the only one in circulation, to Edward Taylor, Tory MP for Southend East. Mr Taylor showed great interest in Fred's story, and determined to read the file from cover to cover. He kept it in the most secure place he could think of: a locked cupboard in his office in the Norman Shaw buildings, which are reserved for MPs and House of Commons staff, and are guarded by police twenty-four hours a day. In the first week of April 1986, Mr Taylor decided to consult the file. To his horror, it had vanished.

The theft was reported, via Fred Holroyd, to Duncan Campbell of the *New Statesman*, who published the news that Taylor had reported the theft of the file to the police 'after his research assistants had carried out several extensive searches'. 'I don't know whether they've simply been lost or removed,' Mr Taylor was quoted as saying. 'Or whether I've mislaid them.' (*New Statesman*, 10 April 1986.) He said it was the first time anything of the kind had happened to him in a parliamentary career of twenty-one years. Speaking to me about it a year later Mr Taylor assured me that he, his wife and research assistants had looked not only in the House of Commons office but also in his home and in his constituency office in Nelson Street, Southend. (*Daily Mirror*, 30 April 1987.)

Fred was furious. So was Colin when he heard about it. On 14 April he fired off letters to the leaders of the four political parties of the time: Mrs Thatcher for the Conservatives, Mr Neil Kinnock (Labour), Mr David Steel (Liberals) and Dr David Owen (SDP). All except Kinnock replied. David Owen took the matter further on the basis that there had been an unexplained burglary in the House of Commons and if Teddy Taylor's office wasn't safe, whose was?

The result was dramatic. A fortnight after the loss of the file was reported to the police, and only a day or two after Colin's letters had reached their destination, Teddy Taylor walked into his constituency offices in Nelson Street, Southend, and saw the large red file squatting obtrusively on his desk. He has never resolved the mystery of its reappearance. Colin believes that the burglars had gone too far; and that when a bit of stink was made by MPs about the sanctity of Parliament, they were told to put the file back at once. Nearly a year later Colin wrote to the Commissioner of Metropolitan Police to ask what police inquiries had been carried out into the theft and whether or not there had been any report to the Director of Public Prosecutions. The Commissioner replied that police inquiries were 'confidential'.

Colin made one last attempt from prison to raise his case through official channels. In May 1986 he read newspaper accounts of a report by the Parliamentary Select Committee into the Duties and Responsibilities of Civil Servants and Ministers. He wrote on 26 May to the Chairman of the committee, the Rt. Hon. Terence Higgins, a former minister, who was Conservative MP for Worthing. He congratulated Mr Higgins on a 'very constructive report' and went on to tell the story of what had happened to him in the Civil Service.

> Much of my day-to-day work involved the tactical leaking or planting of highly sensitive and security-classified information in the Press on an unattributable basis because the authorities did not want the source of the information traced back to them.
>
> During the 1973–4 industrial unrest in Britain elements within the intelligence services began a planned political warfare campaign with the following objectives:
>
> a) to prevent the election of a Labour government in the spring of 1974;
> b) to prevent a coalition between the Labour and Liberal parties or to prevent any deal being struck between two parties to keep a minority Labour government in power, as had happened in the 1960s;
> c) to prevent the re-election of a Labour Government in October 1974;
> d) to bring about a change of leadership in the Conservative Party.

The point of his long letter was to ask whether his employment on such work as a Crown servant was ethical. He enclosed the documents which showed that he had been employed on a secret job description to do something very different from what he was formally employed to do.

He got an acknowledgement from the clerk of the Committee promising a 'substantive reply' as soon as possible. Nine months later, Colin wrote again wondering about the substantive reply. On 5 March 1987, Mr Higgins wrote that his committee did not think it appropriate to deal with the matters Colin had raised.

A month later a curious story of what happened at the committee was told by one of its members. In a letter to the *Guardian*,
Brian Sedgemore, Labour MP for Hackney South and Shoreditch,
wrote:

> The papers were not circulated to members of the Committee but were kept
> under lock and key despite the fact that one member of our committee, Austin
> Mitchell MP, had been sent copies in his own right. Mr Mitchell's personal copies
> disappeared, presumed stolen.
>
> Members of the Committee decided at one of their secret meetings
> to allow themselves individual access to the papers by reading – but not
> copying – them in the office of one of the committee clerks. Subsequently
> the Committee decided at another secret meeting that it could not usefully
> do anything with the papers – a decision with which I concurred - although it's
> not clear if all the members of the Committee who took the decision had read
> the papers.
>
> The Committee then formally decided to send the papers to the Prime
> Minister where it seems they've either found a shredder or the dust shelf. To be
> more precise, the Prime Minister is once again – pace Oman, Westland, Wright
> – failing to investigate what must now be regarded as serious constitutional
> improprieties which involve the commission of crimes.
>
> This incident speaks volumes for the way in which Parliament in Britain in
> the last quarter of the 20th century under a Tory Government preserves our
> freedoms and checks the abuse of power by the executive.

In July (1986), only a month after he wrote to the Select Committee, Colin got some good news from the Parole Board. He was
granted parole. The bad news was that he was not to be released
until the following December. For most of those long six months
Colin was intrigued by the biggest spy story ever to have been told in
Britain.

In 1976, soon after Prime Minister Harold Wilson had unexpectedly
resigned, an undistinguished scientific officer called Peter Wright retired
from MI5. He used his small pension to buy a stud farm in Tasmania and
retired there in poverty and obscurity.

In August 1980 (the month when Jonathan Lewis was killed) Wright
got an unexpected letter from Lord Rothschild, a millionaire and former
boss of Edward Heath's 'think tank'. Rothschild offered to pay Peter
Wright's first class fare to London, and said he had a proposition to
put to him. Wright agreed at once. In London, Rothschild introduced
him to Chapman Pincher, the *Daily Express* 'spy journalist'. Pincher
agreed to write an 'inside story' about MI5 based on Wright's account
of his activities there. The journalist travelled to Tasmania in the early
winter of 1980. The book, *Their Trade Is Treachery*, argued that the

former Director-General of MI5, Sir Roger Hollis, had been a Soviet spy. It was written in a trice and published in January 1981, after a letter from the Cabinet Office gave it immunity from prosecution. In Parliament, Mrs Thatcher denounced the theory that Roger Hollis had been a spy and refused any further investigation. Pincher accepted this with good grace – he and Wright had pocketed £30,000 each from the advance for the book and it was a bestseller. Back in Tasmania the irascible and fanatical Wright fumed with rage. He had not got the inquiry which he believed would justify a lifetime's activity snooping against his own colleagues in the certain belief that most of them were agents of the Soviet Union. He started to think of writing his own account to set the record straight.

In 1984, Wright appeared on *World In Action*, a Granada TV current affairs programme in which he repeated his allegations against Roger Hollis and gave some account of the curious life of a British Intelligence officer. There was no reaction from the government. No one prosecuted Granada Television. A reporter on the programme, Paul Greengrass, persuaded Wright to help him to 'ghost-write' his story. Before long *Spycatcher* – the inside story of an untalented man who never caught a spy – had been written.

The British government decided at once to ban the book and to demand that it be banned in Australia. A legal case was mounted against Heinemann, who planned to publish there. In June 1986, the *Guardian* and the *Observer* published an outline of Peter Wright's allegations. These had moved a long way from the sectarian in-fighting within MI5. Wright's book, it was now widely reported, was alleging that a gang of ultra-right fanatics in MI5 had been plotting against the Wilson government in 1974 and 1975. The allegations which Colin Wallace had been making for ten years and more were now being made by an MI5 veteran.

Who would take any notice of the coincidence? Locked up in Lewes, Colin had very few contacts in the outside world. The only journal to take him seriously (apart from the *New Statesman*) was a curious rogue publication with the irresistible name of *Lobster*.

In early 1985, Colin read in *Private Eye*, for which he had a special affection, an advertisement for a magazine called *Lobster*, which was publishing a special feature on Kincora. Fred got him a copy of *Lobster* and the two men sent off their detailed criticisms of the article. To Colin's surprise the reaction to the letter was a visit from one of the two editors, Stephen Dorril.

Stephen Dorril and Robin Ramsay had started *Lobster* in 1983, after discovering their joint fascination with what they called 'para-politics'. They wrote, typed and published the little magazine and established for it a small circulation and rather larger respect among the few people who read it.

Stephen Dorril travelled to Lewes in May with Fred Holroyd and immediately afterwards Colin and Robin Ramsay started writing to each other. One result was an enormous issue of *Lobster*, which was launched in the House of Commons with a cautious foreword by Ramsay's MP, Labour frontbencher Kevin McNamara.

> Brutally summarised, our thesis is this. Mrs Thatcher and Thatcherism grew out of a right-wing network in this country with extensive links to the military-intelligence establishment. Her rise to power was the climax of a long campaign by this network which included a protracted destabilisation campaign against the Labour and Liberal Parties – chiefly the Labour Party – during 1974–1976.

Fifty pages followed, much of it based on Colin's papers. The introduction gave generous tribute to its source. 'In our view Colin Wallace is the most important source on the British state's covert activities to have appeared since World War Two.'

This was published in the summer of 1986, and in spite of its rather grand launch went down like a lead balloon. No one seemed remotely interested in the allegation that the Wilson government was subject to a 'destabilisation campaign' by the same secret state which promoted Thatcher for high office in the Conservative Party. When Peter Wright's allegations hit the headlines the following year, however, Ramsay and Dorril were besieged. Everyone wanted to plunder their material. They too found themselves being accused of 'cashing in' on the Wright allegations about a Wilson plot which they had published in much greater detail, with much better authority and in a much more readable style than anything written by Peter Wright, and long before him. In particular, they had realised what very few journalists in the mainstream press had realised, that the convicted manslaughterer in Lewes jail had more information about the government than all the government information departments rolled into one.

Shortly before *Lobster* was published, there was further support for the theory that the intelligence services were engaged in something very nasty in 1974. Cathy Massiter, a former officer in MI5, was so disturbed by what she had been asked to do in the interests of Queen and country that she had resigned and made an hour-long programme on Channel Four's *20/20 Vision*. The programme exposed the extent of surveillance on British dissidents by MI5. Cathy Massiter showed on the programme how phone taps were ordered on anyone who was engaged in organised dissent, including the leaders of the Campaign for Nuclear Disarmament whose policies were supported by half the population. Her exposé pointed to 'the mid-1970s' as the starting point for the structural changes in MI5 which led to the political surveillance to which she objected. Thus, quite independently of each other, three people who were working in or with the intelligence community in 1974 – Wright and Massiter as full-time MI5 officers, and Colin in 'psyops' – made the same allegations about MI5's dirty tricks against the left. All three, incidentally, had worked in Army Headquarters in Northern Ireland.

All through the second half of 1986, the government pursued Peter Wright relentlessly through the Australian courts. The main case was heard in November. The Government lost and, in spite of notice to appeal, *Spycatcher* began to circulate. The Wright affair had fascinated the press and public. So when Colin Wallace at last walked out of Lewes prison on 5 December 1986, he found himself in great demand.

Colin left many good friends behind. They gave him a handsome send-off, an engraved wall plaque, an engraved tobacco box made out of stainless steel and a cake. The road outside the prison was packed with journalists and the Governor had to arrange a 'photo facility' at the gate. He had been a model prisoner. In September 1986, the prison nominated him for the 1986 Butler Trust Award, whose patron was Princess Anne. This was the only such nomination of a prisoner, and caused the award panel a lot of anxious discussion. Eventually Colin was turned down for the award on the grounds that it had to be restricted to prison staff.

A lot of people were interested in the early release of the former 'psyops' man from Northern Ireland. Those that had read or heard of *Lobster* knew that this was no common or garden manslaughterer, but a man of high intelligence with a strange story to tell. Other scandals in Northern Ireland were in the news. John Stalker, Deputy Chief Constable of Greater Manchester, had just left office after being suspended and 'inquired into' by a senior policeman from another force. The suspension had its roots in Northern Ireland and the Royal Ulster Constabulary into whose alleged 'shoot-to-kill' policy John Stalker had been conducting a rigorous investigation.

Colin had some foreknowledge of the tremendous media interest in his case. In September 1986, he had been visited twice by a team from Yorkshire Television's *First Tuesday* programme. They were quickly fascinated by his story. They planned two programmes, one on the Jonathan Lewis killing, the other on dirty tricks in Northern Ireland. The researcher was Julian Hendy, who spent several weeks making inquiries in Arundel even before Colin came out of prison.

Colin felt committed to the Yorkshire venture. For some weeks after his release he put off inquiring journalists who wanted to write long features or make programmes, by saying he owed it to Yorkshire to give them 'first bite'. YTV filmed extensively about the Lewis killing and Julian Hendy started to make inquiries in Northern Ireland about dirty tricks. Then, suddenly, the project was stopped. The producer wrote to Colin to say that so much of the story had now been made public that the 'exclusivity' of the programme was in doubt.

Because of his self-imposed commitment to YTV, Colin had had little contact with other journalists. On his release, he issued a press statement reaffirming his innocence of Jonathan Lewis's killing and announcing his determination to clear his name. He was interviewed that first day by Southern Television, who broadcast what he said, and by BBC South, which did not. The experience with the BBC was repeated in March, when Julian O'Halloran went to Arundel to record an interview with Colin for BBC 2's *Newsnight*. The *Newsnight* team were in Colin's house all afternoon filming a huge interview. Later that week Julian O'Halloran rang Colin with the bad news that the interview would not be broadcast.

A member of the *Newsnight* staff told Barrie Penrose of the *Sunday Times* that the interview had been censored. When Penrose rang the BBC, he was told: 'No footage had been shot for this programme.' (*Sunday Times*, 5 April 1987.)

This contrasted rather sharply with Colin's experience, so Penrose asked the same question of the BBC Director-General's office. They agreed reluctantly that several cans of footage had been shot and that the Director-General had himself stopped the interview being broadcast. A BBC spokesman, referring to the growing rift between the BBC hierarchy and the current affairs department based at Lime Grove, said: 'The difficulty with the children at Lime Grove is that they don't understand that they actually have to have proof before they run some stories.'

In the first few weeks after his release, therefore, the government and media authorities had some success in stopping any major inquiry into Colin Wallace's case. The dam was broken, as so often, not in Britain but in Ireland where there was not the same squeamishness about criticism of British Intelligence matters. In March 1987 Radio Telefis Eireann broadcast a fifty-minute programme in their *Today/Tonight* series called, simply, 'MI5'.

The programme triggered off a series of articles in Ireland and radio programmes for BBC Northern Ireland. Ulster TV, the commercial channel in Northern Ireland, broadcast a discussion between Fred Holroyd, Colin, Merlyn Rees, Dale Campbell Savours, a backbench Labour MP who was asking questions about Intelligence, and Gerry Fitt, now Lord Fitt, who had played such a prominent role trying to uncover the Kincora scandal. Merlyn Rees confirmed on the programme that Roland Moyle, his junior minister at the Northern Ireland Office, had come to him with Colin's allegations in 1975, when Colin was living in Moyle's London constituency. Merlyn Rees had told Mr Moyle to take it up with the 'appropriate authority' – MI5 – but had no idea what happened after that.

The programmes in Ireland had an immediate impact on the British media. The Press Association in Ireland sent a précis of the programme on the wires to British newspapers. From that moment, press interest seemed to take off and the phone at Colin's house never stopped. Investigative journalists (myself included) were filling the long, slow trains to Arundel.

Meanwhile, Colin was making some headway in the political world. Humphry Berkeley, a former Tory MP and Labour candidate, was the SDP candidate for Southend East, Fred Holroyd's constituency, in the 1987 general election. Berkeley had been shocked to discover that he himself was on the list of politicians in the 1970s who had been marked down for 'dirty tricks'. He travelled to Arundel to meet Colin and later introduced him to Laura Grimond, a former Liberal MP. Lady Grimond took the papers to Alex Carlile, MP, legal affairs spokesman for the Alliance, as the Liberals and SDP then called themselves. Colin was summoned to the House of Commons for a long meeting with Carlile, which resulted in an extraordinary press release on 2 March:

> It is clear that Colin Wallace, a principled man, knew too much about the Kincora Boys' Home scandal. Since his trial and conviction in 1981 for manslaughter of antique dealer Jonathan Lewis, facts have emerged which suggest that Mr Lewis may well have been killed by some person or persons other than Colin Wallace, in a successful attempt to frame Wallace.
>
> These facts suggest a link may exist between the Kincora affair and the fate of both Wallace and Lewis. I have asked the Home Secretary to refer Mr Wallace's conviction to the Court of Appeal. This is a case in which justice may have been foiled by intrigue.

The release was printed in the small-circulation *Today* newspaper (3 March 1987), but nowhere else in the British media. Carlile put down his question to the Home Secretary, which was deflected, and asked for an adjournment debate, which was refused because the House was about to rise for Easter. Two and a half months later Mr Carlile made another even more extraordinary statement in *Sunday Today* (17 May 1987.):

> I believe there are many people in high places and within the security services who feel ill-will towards Wallace for exposing their activities. The question is that if MI5 was prepared to kill to get even with Wallace, why not kill him? It may be that Wallace's allegations about MI5 officers being involved in activities verging on the treasonable were widely known – so if any harm came to him the finger would point directly at them. I have tried repeatedly in the House to get an adjournment on the conviction and will continue to do so.

The rest of the media were unwilling to go as far as Alex Carlile, but by the end of March 1987 any reluctance or shyness about telling the Wallace/Holroyd story was vanishing. In the next four months Colin could not keep pace with the tremendous demand on his services from the media. He featured in a long *20/20 Vision* documentary on Peter Wright in December 1986. He was twice interviewed by David Frost on TV-am's Sunday morning current affairs round-up in April and May 1987, and again, when Frost was away, in June. He was interviewed by Anne Diamond of TV-am and by Jonathan Dimbleby on *This Week* (which devoted a whole programme to the subject). He appeared as one of the guests on the first edition of *After Dark*, a late-night discussion programme, on 1 May. A special half-hour programme on Channel Four's *Diverse Reports* challenged his conviction. In April, Bob Parker of *Channel Four News* approached Colin and suggested a series of programmes to be fitted into the popular seven o'clock bulletin. When Colin agreed, a delighted Robin Ramsay was taken on as a researcher.

In the press, the interest was even more widespread. Journalists who kept in constant touch with Colin during this period (apart from myself) were Barrie Penrose of the *Sunday Times*, Richard Norton-Taylor and David Pallister of the *Guardian*, Howard Foster of *Today*, Ian Macaskill of the *News of the World*, Paul Lashmar of the *Observer*, Lewis Chester of the *News on Sunday* – all ran reports and substantial features on his case. For none of these appearances and articles was Colin paid a penny. Desperately poor as he was, he insisted that he must not be paid.

The main reason for this flourish of interest was the Peter Wright case and the appetite for any information about MI5. When Mrs Thatcher said in public that she had set up a special inquiry under the Director-General of MI5, Sir Anthony Duff, into Peter Wright's allegations, and that all the allegations had been proved to be without substance after a thorough investigation, Colin went on television to recount his experiences with 'full investigations' from Number 10 Downing Street. These investigations, he said, had a peculiar quality. The person making the allegations and anyone who supported the allegations were never contacted by the 'investigators'.

From this welter of journalism it is worth picking out one or two vital revelations, which pushed Colin's story further on.

Barrie Penrose of the *Sunday Times*, whose sensitivity to Colin's allegations dated back to his 1978 book on Harold Wilson and MI5, wrote a sympathetic article about Colin and Fred in early March. Penrose got a phone call from a man called James Miller who said he knew Colin's name from his time as an MI5 agent in Northern Ireland in the 1970s. Miller then told Penrose that he had for three years infiltrated the UDA for MI5, and one of his jobs had been to help inspire the Ulster Workers Council strike of 1974:

I could never understand why my case officers, Lt Col Brian X* and George X, wanted the UDA to start a strike in the first place. But they specifically said I should get UDA men at grass-roots to 'start pushing' for a strike. So I did.

Barrie Penrose wrote:

Miller said his MI5 case officers told him Harold Wilson was a suspected Soviet agent and steps were being taken to force him out of Downing Street. (*Sunday Times*, 22 March 1987.)

When Miller first contacted him, Barrie Penrose was not inclined to believe him. Miller explained that he'd been forced to leave Ireland when the UDA started to suspect him of being a spy. MI5 had brought him back to England, provided him with a house in North Devon and set him up with a small business. He cheerfully gave Penrose the names of his current MI5 'minders'. Penrose rang one of them up. When he said he was inquiring about James Miller, the 'minder' asked resignedly: 'What's the problem with him now?' and grumbled that Miller was never satisfied. When Penrose, slightly embarrassed, said he was a reporter from the *Sunday Times* there was a shocked silence and the phone went down.

Penrose confirmed with MI5 that Miller had been working for the security forces in the 1970s. He was promptly rung up by Admiral William Higgins, Secretary to the D-Notice Committee, and asked not to publish Miller's whereabouts or the identity of his case officers.

Liam Clarke, a tenacious investigative journalist in Belfast, who was working with Penrose on Northern Ireland matters, phoned Miller a day or two later.

In a much longer interview, Miller disclosed that before he played such an important role in industrial subversion as an agent for the security services, he had, as his first mission in Northern Ireland for MI5, infiltrated the small Protestant sect, TARA. One of the men he trailed was TARA's leader, William McGrath. He had built up a dossier on McGrath's sexual activities at Kincora Boys' Home and submitted it to MI5, who took no action. Miller told Clarke:

My case officer told me to leave McGrath to them and I have always believed they used the information [on his sexual activities] to recruit him as an informer.

When he left TARA, Miller joined the UDA and rose to the rank of intelligence officer. He was a man of some mischief and resource. When the IRA denounced him as a British spy he approached and befriended

---

* Lieutenant Colonel Brian X is dead now. His name was Dixon.

Ivor Malachy Bell, an IRA leader, complaining that he, Miller, a mere
lift engineer and working-class innocent, was being wrongly hounded by
Bell's troops. Bell promptly took him into his house and protected him.
Miller told Clarke that he had contacted Penrose after reading about Colin
Wallace but he too was disgusted by the behaviour of the security services
in the mid-1970s. He said:

> It is like layers of an onion, and the more you peel them away, the more
> you feel like crying. There are two laws running this country: one for them
> (the security services) and one for the rest of us.

Miller's extraordinary intervention very quickly ceased. He changed
his phone and moved from the area.

Liam Clarke uncovered another former member of Army Intelligence
who knew about Kincora. In a report in the *Sunday World* on 10 May
1987, Liam Clarke wrote:

> In 1976 a field intelligence non commissioned officer who had recently
> started collating intelligence for East Belfast after his predecessor was posted
> to Cyprus became aware of Tara and passed a report on the matter to senior
> officers – it came back marked no action, a colleague recalls.
>   Within weeks the situation became clear to the officers. McGrath was
> an agent whose first experience of spying had come in the 1950s when he
> smuggled bibles into Russia as a front for intelligence gathering by MI6.
>   His handler was an MI5 officer based in the Old Holywood Road who
> was later charged with an offence against a young boy. A Tara member recalls
> McGrath boasting at meetings that he could get information from the Security
> Service (MI5) and had friends within it.
>   John McKeague, another well known homosexual who was killed in
> mysterious circumstances, was also an agent whose information was routinely
> collated in the restricted corridor at military headquarters in Lisburn.

Confirmation of many of the allegations which Colin had been
making about his work in 'psyops' in the 1970s came with a programme
in the Thames Television current affairs series, *This Week*, foreshadowed
by another article from Barrie Penrose. Penrose had got from Colin's
solicitors the forged bank account in the name of Ian Paisley, referred to
earlier here. He published an article on 26 April 1987 entitled HOW MI5
FORGED BANK ACCOUNTS TO SMEAR MPS. He quoted from, and
reprinted, the forged accounts in the names of Paisley and John Hume,
and quoted an anonymous English former Intelligence officer as saying
he had handled and circulated the forgery.

'I assumed MI5 had intercepted Paisley's accounts by normal intelli-
gence-gathering,' the officer was quoted as saying. 'Only later did I realise
that the security forces had manufactured them.'

The following Thursday, 30 April, Paisley and Colin appeared on *This Week*. Confronted with the forged share certificates, the Rev. Paisley was most amused.

'I've got no shares anywhere,' he said. 'But I mean it's common knowledge put out by the dirty tricks department that I have ranches in Canada and ranches in Australia. That has been common parlance for years.'

Paisley went on to argue that this smear campaign was part of a plot to assassinate him, about which he had publicly complained in 1976. Paisley claimed at the time that he was tipped off about the proposed assassination by an Army Intelligence officer. He told the programme that the officer said he was far more likely to be assassinated by the British security services than by the IRA.

A few weeks later came powerful proof that the allegations of Wallace and Holroyd were disturbing the authorities even before the two men knew each other. Clive Ponting had been a senior civil servant at the Ministry of Defence before he disclosed to Labour backbencher Tam Dalyell some awkward secrets about the government's decision to sink the Argentinian cruiser *General Belgrano* in 1982. Ponting eventually confessed to leaking the material, was prosecuted under the Official Secrets Act and, in February 1985, triumphantly acquitted.

It was Barrie Penrose once again who first disclosed that Ponting had some interesting things to say about Colin and Fred. In the *Sunday Times* on 17 May 1987, under a headline which referred to the likelihood of Peter Wright's book *Spycatcher* being published in Ireland, Penrose disclosed that Ponting had taken part in meetings at the ministry whose sole purpose was to discuss Wallace and Holroyd. Ponting was quoted as saying:

> By 1983 the cases of Wallace and Holroyd had been a long-running internal problem and a great effort had gone into contingency action if and when Holroyd got the story into the Press. The task was to try to ensure their stories were contained.

The main immediate problem was Fred's allegations about sectarian assassinations inspired by the security services, and about the role of the Military Intelligence agent Robert Nairac who was murdered by the IRA in 1975. Ponting also said that Wallace was a greater problem. 'They were genuinely worried that Wallace had far worse things to say.'

A few weeks later, Clive Ponting appeared on television in one of the outstanding series of programmes on the Holroyd/Wallace affair which was broadcast on Channel Four News. Ponting, who was head of the legal department of the Ministry of Defence at the time, said he remembered a meeting in 1983 with two MI5 officers in which the Wallace problem was discussed. No one, he said to camera, for a moment questioned what Colin was saying:

> There was never any suspicion that Wallace was making these stories up or that it was totally unfounded and very easy to rubbish. It was very much a matter that, OK the story was being contained at the moment because he was in jail, but that in a few years' time he would be back out again and could be expected to start making the allegations again and then that would be a serious problem. (*Channel Four News*, 25 June 1987.)

The same *Channel Four News* programme in which Clive Ponting had appeared provided still further proof of the truth of Colin's story. The originals of the Clockwork Orange notes had been submitted to Dr Julius Grant, a handwriting expert. As we have seen, his report firmly placed the documents in the mid-1970s. This Channel Four scoop was followed up in the *Observer* on 5 July under the heading TESTS BACK MI5 'DIRTY TRICKS PLOT' ALLEGATIONS. David Leigh and Paul Lashmar wrote: 'Wallace's notes are explosive.'

They showed how Dr Grant's report confirmed that the notes were almost certainly not written after 1976, and therefore were unlikely to be forgeries. For some reason, however, and without offering a word of proof, the *Observer* authors broke off to cast doubt on Colin's credibility. Colin was described as a 'self-confessed fantasist and convicted killer'. Many journalists had referred to Colin's conviction but had usually prefaced it with Colin's fervent and consistent denial of guilt. As for the charge that he was a self-confessed fantasist, Colin still wonders where and how he is meant to have confessed such a thing; or why such a charge should be made when he has never confessed to anything of the kind. He wrote to the editor of the *Observer*, and got a phone call from David Leigh who rather lamely suggested that the words referred to his work in disinformation.

Fantasist or not, Colin's allegations about Clockwork Orange got a great boost from Dr Grant's report. The next, and final, *Channel Four News* item went on to matters which were even more controversial.

Undoubtedly the most vigorous journalism in support of Colin and Fred were Bob Parker's five programmes for *Channel Four News*. The then editor of *Channel Four News*, Stuart Purvis, strongly supported the programmes against considerable opposition. Peter Sissons, *Channel Four News* presenter, was very supportive. But inside the ITN network, from which *Channel Four News* works, there was considerable hostility. None of the items broadcast on *Channel Four News* appeared on *News At Ten*.

The last programme in the series, broadcast on 13 July 1987, six weeks after the Conservative Government had been returned in a general election with a big majority, concentrated on Colin's association in 1976 with Airey

Neave, the former wartime Intelligence agent who had master-minded Mrs Thatcher's election as Tory leader in 1975. Neave had spoken from the Tory front bench on Northern Ireland from the moment Mrs Thatcher took office to his assassination in 1979. The programme dealt in detail with Colin's meetings with Neave and the very close connection between what Neave said in speeches in September 1976 and the McCarthyite hysteria which characterised the Clockwork Orange notes.

In a hard-hitting report, Bob Parker hinted that Neave may have been connected with the right-wing ultras in MI5. He scoffed at any possible denial from 10 Downing Street on this matter, in view of the discredited denials which had come from that quarter over Colin's 1984 allegations. Parker did not know and could not have known that his hints about Neave could well have been supported from a knowledgeable source. In the original manuscript for *Spycatcher*, Peter Wright described meetings which he had with Airey Neave during the 1970s. These extracts and all references to Neave were carefully removed from the finished version.

A few days after the Neave programme, David Mannion, acting news editor at Channel Four, wrote to Stuart Purvis under the heading COLIN WALLACE. He said he had had a letter dated 21 July from Paul Wilkinson, Professor of International Relations at Aberdeen University. Wilkinson specialised in terrorism, had written several books on the subject and was ITN's 'consultant in terrorism'.

The letter is given in full below:

Dear David,

Herewith the interesting letter I received from one of our researchers on the Colin Wallace Affair. I think you and members of your team will find this of interest. It certainly raises major question marks about the extent to which one can rely on his version of events in Northern Ireland and elsewhere.

I have had a word with Robert Parker who rang me after I spoke to you and I know he would be keen to see a copy.

I have also spoken to the leading journalist mentioned in the letter and although he is not willing to talk about it or write about it publicly at present, he confirmed the main thrust of the letter's interpretation of events.

As promised, I am having a word with the researcher who wrote the letter and will try to persuade him to talk with you and your colleagues on a confidential basis. I cannot promise anything because his home is in Belfast and he is naturally rather reticent and nervous of possible repercussions. However, I will do my best.

With best wishes,
Yours sincerely,
Paul

The letter from the 'researcher', who was of course anonymous, read as follows:

Dear Prof Wilkinson,

You have probably been watching the unfolding revelations of Mr Colin Wallace (ex MI5) concerning the late Airey Neave and Peter Wright's allegations. To say the least I am surprised that anyone would give Colin Wallace houseroom.

If you are better briefed on this matter than I am, may I apologise for wasting your time. However, you may recall that on one of our first meetings I told you the story of the Ulster Citizens Army. Colin Wallace (in 1973) was posing as a journalist (while also an officer in the UDR and working for MI5 and the Army Information Department) and was engaged in some maverick (I stress maverick and not 'deniable' operations) operations.

Wallace was having an affair with a Mrs. Horne and was also trying to discredit the U.D.A. Wallace produced posters and sent anonymous press statements to various journalists about the Ulster Citizens Army. The statements were along the lines that socialist and class-conscious elements in the U.D.A and U.V.F. had formed a new left-wing group in protest at gangsters having taken over the other two groups.

Wallace phoned up the UDA and said that he had met the head of the Ulster Citizens Army, a Mr. Horne of such and such address, could they confirm that this was the head of the Ulster Citizens Army?

Considering that the Ulster Citizens Army press statements threatened to kill the UDA leadership along with various capitalists and businessmen, this was tantamount to setting up Mr. Horne for killing. So Mrs. Horne would have been missing a husband. The UDA leaders and a journalist David McKitterick (of the *Irish Times*) managed to pin Wallace down and followed him to Magheralave Barracks Lisburn.

McKitterick met Wallace and put it to him that he was the Ulster Citizens Army and was trying to set up Mr. Horne. Wallace was then pulled out of Northern Ireland. Wallace was then jailed for killing the husband of an 'It's a Knockout' hostess in England after having an affair with her.

Concerning Wallace's link with Airey Neave, rather than a fantasy about destabilising the Wilson government, it is more likely that Wallace was trying to ingratiate himself with Neave in order to get to Neave's friend Lt-Col Brush, the head of Down Orange Welfare.

Neave had much better contacts on Communist infiltration in Northern Ireland than Colin Wallace such as his links, that went back to his post-war work, with the Security Services.

Are the British (mainland) press not aware of Wallace's past in Northern Ireland? Are they not aware that he was trying to recruit informers left right and centre in Northern Ireland and that the man had James Bond fantasies. He had done skydiving and fancied himself as a womaniser and superspy.

You can check the information on Wallace from the UDA leaders such as Tyrie, McMichael or Duddy or from David McKitterick. If you feel this information would be of any use to a reliable journalist to expose that charlatan please feel free to use it. Traitors do not deserve to get away with this kind of behaviour never mind to defame the reputation of a real hero like Airey Neave.

> I hope that this note is of some use
> Best wishes

This was the old Horn smear which has been analysed comprehensively earlier in this book.

Colin didn't see a copy of the letter until May 1988, nine months later. At once, he fired off a furious letter to George McNichol, Principal and Vice Chancellor of Aberdeen University, demanding to know why such false and malicious lies should be passed to the media on Aberdeen University notepaper. He demanded a 'full and unqualified retraction' of the letter from the university and a public retraction and apology for its circulation.

He got both immediately. On 9 June 1988, Professor Wilkinson grovelled low. He wrote to the editors of all the national newspapers as follows:

> The claims made in the letter regarding the letter are totally untrue. I therefore offer Mr Wallace a full apology . . . and I would give the widest possible circulation to this complete retraction.

The only circulation which the retraction gained was in the magazine *Private Eye* and the local papers in Aberdeen.

Soon after the mysterious 'researcher's' letter quoting so favourably from David McKittrick, the Belfast journalist was to come into the story again and make an even greater impact.

One of the new MPs elected in June was Ken Livingstone, the former Labour leader of the GLC. Livingstone, who represented Brent East, a constituency with a large Irish population, had always retained a deep interest in Irish affairs. He was shocked by the fifty-minute programme on Colin and Fred Holroyd which had been broadcast by Radio Telefis Eireann. His maiden speech on 9 July 1987 was devoted to the Wallace/Holroyd allegations. He mentioned the contacts between Colin and Airey Neave, and the latter's close liaison with the ultras in Intelligence. Livingstone was interrupted by a furious Ian Gow, MP, who had understudied for Neave from the Tory front bench on Northern Ireland in the days of the Labour government, and had done a long stint as the Prime Minister's Parliamentary Private Secretary. Livingstone was bitterly attacked in the House and outside for his speech.

The speech was further proof of the growing credibility of both Wallace and Holroyd. On his own, with the honourable exception of the *New Statesman* and Channel Four's *Diverse Reports*, Fred Holroyd had had little success in penetrating the media. When Colin came out

of prison, considerable efforts were made at the outset to keep his story
away from the public.

But in the spring and early summer of 1987 the media coverage of
both their stories rose to a crescendo. More and more journalists were
believing what Colin and Fred had to say and exploring the dark avenues
to which their accounts pointed. They were joined by politicians of all
persuasions. A petition of MPs calling for a public inquiry was circulated
to MPs. In July 1987, on the prompting of Humphry Berkeley, a formidable
trio of politicians decided to set themselves up as an informal committee of
inquiry into what Fred and Colin were saying. They were Roy Jenkins of
the SDP, a former Home Secretary, Merlyn Rees from the Labour Party,
a former Home Secretary and the former Prime Minister, Edward Heath.
Berkeley himself had appeared on Radio Telefis Eireann, where he stated
his unequivocal view that Colin had been framed for Jonathan Lewis's
killing by the intelligence services.

The counter-attack started during this period – not always successfully.
Richard Norton-Taylor, an investigative journalist on the *Guardian*, for
instance, was approached by the Cabinet Office, off the record, and
warned of the unreliability of Wallace and Holroyd. Similar approaches
were made without much success to other independent-minded journalists
and editors.

In early July, shortly after the Livingstone speech, there was a more
determined initiative from the Belfast correspondent of the *Sunday Times*,
Chris Ryder. Ryder had to leave his native Northern Ireland in 1973 after
'breaking' a story in the *Sunday Times* on embezzlement in the higher
reaches of the IRA. The story was planted by Information Policy, under
the guidance of Colin Wallace. It forms the basis of the excellent novel
Interface Ireland (published by Barrie and Jenkins (London) in 1979), by
Kevin Dowling, another correspondent in the North of Ireland at the time.
Ryder and his large family were housed in Butlin's at Bognor Regis and
then went to work in Manchester for the *Sunday Times*. From there he
kept up his contacts with the security forces in Belfast and effectively ran
the coverage from Northern Ireland.

In April 1987 Ryder wrote a story in the *Sunday Times* about
Maurice Oldfield, the former head of MI6. It disclosed 'an incident in a
public house' in 1980 in which Oldfield had allegedly followed a man into
the lavatory and propositioned him. The police had been called, Ryder
alleged, and the whole matter hushed up.

The 'story' was comprehensively destroyed by Bob Parker on Channel
Four News, whose team tracked down every member of the staff of the
pub in 1980, all of whom said that the incident had never happened. The
police, locally and nationally, denied it hotly.

At the time, MI5 and MI6 were engaged in one of their customary
fratricidal quarrels. MI5 had detested Oldfield ever since he had been

chief of MI6 in the 1970s when he had denounced MI5 and their gang of
extremists under Peter Wright to the Prime Minister himself. The campaign
against Oldfield at that time is very well documented in 'C', his biography
by Richard Deacon. MI5 were dismayed when Oldfield was brought in
by Mrs Thatcher in 1979, immediately after she was first elected, to sort
out the growing chaos of Intelligence operations in the North of Ireland,
particularly the involvement of Intelligence in assassinations and 'shoot to
kill' operations, both of which he specifically forbade.

In 1987, beleaguered as they were by the allegations from Peter
Wright, the Stalker affair and the growing political discontent about
the irresponsibility of the security services, MI5 re-opened their campaign
against Oldfield, leaking facts about his homosexual youth which Mrs
Thatcher was forced, much against her will, to admit in the House of
Commons. The Chris Ryder article complemented these allegations. Its
effect was counter-productive, however, not just because it was annihil-
ated by Channel Four News but also because many of Oldfield's former
MI6 associates, especially Anthony Cavendish and G. K. Young, were so
disgusted at the campaign that they demanded a halt.

In late July, Chris Ryder got on to the *Sunday Times* with yet
another scoop. He sent them, in the strictest confidence, a photograph
of a dead IRA man, John Green, who, Fred Holroyd alleged, had been
assassinated by a group of Protestant extremists led by Robert Nairac,
a British Army officer attached to the SAS. Fred said that Nairac had
given him the Polaroid photograph which he had taken immediately after
the shooting and Fred had given it to the Royal Ulster Constabulary, in
the shape of Superintendent George Caskey, who at the same time was
leading the police inquiry into Kincora.

Ryder's accompanying article to the *Sunday Times* denied that Nairac
had had anything to do with the photograph and alleged it had been taken
by the Gardai, the Irish police, the morning after the killing.

There followed an argument in the *Sunday Times* offices as to whether
the Ryder article should be used. Barrie Penrose, who had written many
articles about Fred and Colin, argued strongly that this was just 'black
propaganda' to discredit Fred Holroyd and that the piece should not be
used without some form of corroboration. He referred his editor back to
the Oldfield catastrophe the previous April.

The article was not used. Ryder, who was furious at the decision,
demanded that the photograph should be sent back to him at once and
that it should not be copied. The *Sunday Times* complied.

A few weeks later the picture appeared again in another editor's
office in London. The *Independent*, a new national newspaper, had been
launched the previous year and had covered itself in glory, not just because
it had survived in a difficult market without the backing of a rich proprietor,
but also because it had maintained the highest journalistic standards. The

paper's editor, Andreas Whittam Smith, whose experience was chiefly in city and commercial journalism, had surprised the newspaper world with his paper's breadth of coverage and willingness to contradict officialdom.

The *Independent*'s correspondent in Northern Ireland was David McKittrick, whom we have met many times before in this story, chiefly as reporter for the *Irish Times* when Colin was at Lisburn. McKittrick was born and bred on the Shankhill Road, the centre of the Belfast Protestant working class. He was and is a resourceful and able journalist. Though generally supportive of the state of Northern Ireland and its Protestant majority, his reporting was in no way sectarian and he had built a reputation for following up good stories regardless of whom he offended.

This made the articles which he published on 2 September all the more remarkable. They covered the whole of page four and were 'signalled' by a strong piece on the front-page. This was perhaps the most important newspaper article published on Colin Wallace and Fred Holroyd. It had the effect of rolling back the tide of credibility and concern which had been rising steadily in the media and the public ever since Colin had been released from prison nine months previously.

The thrust of the articles was to cast doubt and suspicion on the two men and what they were saying. Fred Holroyd has told his own story and has defended himself admirably. What follows concentrates, therefore, on the sections dealing with Colin Wallace.

David McKittrick's front page article consisted of fourteen paragraphs. In full, with appropriate comments, they went like this.

Allegations made by two former intelligence personnel that the security forces carried out undercover assassinations in Northern Ireland have not been borne out by an investigation by 'The Independent'.

The claims by Colin Wallace and Fred Holroyd have received widespread publicity in newspapers and on television. Mr Wallace also says that he knew of a plot by MI5, the security service, to overthrow the Labour government in 1975.

Colin's allegations were about 1974 – not 1975 – as McKittrick claimed. Colin was posted from Northern Ireland in 1974.

Our enquiries have revealed major discrepancies, inconsistencies and inaccuracies in their stories which cast serious doubt on the reliability of their version of events.

That remained to be proved. The article went on (in full):

Many of their claims appear incapable either of being proved or disproved, not least because many of the figures accused of misbehaviour are now dead. But the weight of evidence goes against the allegations.

Part of the importance of the two men's claims lies in the fact that they appear to confirm, and indeed extend, some of the allegations made by Peter Wright, the former MI5 officer and author of Spycatcher, the book whose publication the British government is trying to ban.

The Wallace/Holroyd allegations form the basis of claims that there were smear operations directed against the Wilson government. The two men have also produced documents showing that they were in touch with Airey Neave, Margaret Thatcher's confidant, who was assassinated by the Irish National Liberation Army in 1979.

The Wallace/Holroyd claim of having discussed smears on Labour politicians with Mr Neave formed the basis of allegations made by Ken Livingstone, the Labour MP, in his maiden speech in the House of Commons on 7 July. Mr Livingstone, guided by the Wallace/Holroyd version of events, linked Mr Neave with dirty tricks and suggested the Prime Minister might have known of that.

The theme of these paragraphs is that Colin *and* Fred were making allegations about Wilson, Neave and so on. In fact, from the outset, Fred had nothing to do with any of this. He knew nothing of the political information which Colin had. He had never written to or met Airey Neave. He had not made any of these allegations. Apart from their brief introduction at Lisburn, the two men had not met until 1984, ten years after the events of which both complained, from very different angles. This imprecise term 'Wallace/Holroyd allegations' set the tone for the rest of the article. Then came the first serious charge:

It is a fact that many of the Wallace/Holroyd allegations dovetail neatly with those of others, but many well-informed sections of opinion in Ulster suspect that their accusations have been constructed to do so.

Such a process was unwittingly described by Mr Livingstone when he said, in a radio interview after his speech: 'We have to take the Peter Wright book and jigsaw that in with what Holroyd and Wallace and others have been saying. And what's interesting about all these allegations is that none of them is contradictory. It's not the whole jigsaw yet, but it's a lot of it and it all fits in quite nicely. If a lot of it was fabrication or invention by now there would have been things that were mutually exclusive or contradictory and there's none of that here.'

Had Colin 'constructed' his allegations about Wilson, Clockwork Orange and MI5 to 'dovetail neatly' with those of Peter Wright? Ken Livingstone had said that Colin's allegations fitted Wright's. He did not say, or even suggest (since he does not believe) that Colin was deliberately making up stories to fit in with those of Wright.

There was one journalist in the British Isles who knew better than any other that Colin's allegations about MI5 and the Wilson government had not been made specially to fit those of Wright. His name was David McKittrick. As we have seen, McKittrick himself, throughout Colin's time as Information Officer in Lisburn, kept in touch with Colin and printed information he received from him. In 1980, before anyone had heard of Peter Wright, he had travelled twice to Britain to meet Colin, once in London and once in Arundel. As a result of these meetings, he had written three articles, most of which relied on what Colin told him. In those articles, for the first time in print in Britain or Ireland, came the allegation from someone inside the system that there had been a campaign to discredit the Labour government by Intelligence officers.

Neither in his meetings with Colin nor in the articles he wrote was there the slightest sign from David McKittrick that Wallace was not to be trusted. On the contrary, he accepted everything he was told and printed most of it. The real significance of the 1980 articles was that they prove that Wallace was making his allegations about MI5 and the Wilson government long before Peter Wright even thought of writing a book.

There was plenty of other evidence that Colin was complaining about MI5 and Wilson even before that. *Channel Four News* had broadcast a long interview with the Blackheath solicitor Graham Dodd, who represented Colin in his attempts to sue the Ministry of Defence in 1975 and 1976. Dodd had recalled on television that Colin had said he knew of a dirty tricks campaign against Harold Wilson. I myself had published in the *Daily Mirror* the response of Roland Moyle to the suggestion that Colin and Graham Dodd had approached him in 1976, when he was MP for Blackheath, and asked him to take up Colin's case. Moyle had said to me: 'He [Colin Wallace] was telling me about some dirty tricks operation designed to blacken the names of Northern Ireland politicians.' (*Daily Mirror*, 9 April 1987.)

There was other evidence that Colin had been making these allegations for twelve years. He had, for instance, written to Harold Wilson in 1977, as Lady Falkender, Wilson's political secretary, could confirm.

In 1984, as anyone who asked him would have known, Colin had set out his story in the most meticulous detail and sent it to the Prime Minister as the Head of the Intelligence and Security Services. The Clockwork Orange programme, with all the smears against elected politicians, and the forgeries, were included in that dossier, long before *Spycatcher* was published, and even before Peter Wright had gone on *World In Action*. The point about Peter Wright's book which Ken Livingstone was making was that it confirmed what Colin Wallace had been saying for twelve years. He could prove he had been saying these things. A single phone call to Graham Dodd or Roland Moyle (or even to Colin) would have established this. Yet the suggestion that the allegations were being 'constructed' to 'dovetail' with Wright was purveyed to the readers of the *Independent*.

The article went on to deal with some more 'specific' charges against Colin Wallace.

Some of Mr Wallace's statements are clearly untrue. A profile of him in a South of England newspaper describes him as a graduate of Queen's University Belfast, but the university says he does not hold one of their degrees. He once claimed to have been a member of the Widgery Tribunal, which reported on the Bloody Sunday killings in 1972, but he demonstrably was not. He has said that he was three times recommended for decorations, but there is no record of this.

This paragraph makes three allegations. How did they match the facts?

A few days after his article appeared, I rang McKittrick in Belfast and questioned him closely about his article. We had two conversations, both long ones. I published a small critical article in my *Mirror* column on 9 September.

I was specially interested in the three allegations in this paragraph. I asked McKittrick for the identity of the 'South of England' newspaper which published the 'profile' of Colin Wallace in which he was alleged to have claimed that he was a graduate of Queen's University. I was interested because Colin had never made such a claim to me, nor in anything I had ever seen published about him.

McKittrick was at once forthcoming. The 'South of England newspaper', he said, was the Bognor Regis *Observer* for 23 September 1976. I would find the reference on the front page.

I hunted down the article and the man who wrote it, Philip Colley, who was still working as a journalist in the south of England. The article is a very short five paragraph news item which does not quote Colin at any stage. It refers to the fact that a new man had been taken on as Information Liaison Officer for Arun District Council, whom it identifies as 'John Wallace, a graduate of Queens University'.

Confronted with this article, Mr Colley was able to recall how it came about. There had, he said, been some resentment in Arun Council that an outsider had applied for the job of information officer. On the day of Colin's interview at Arun, 23 September 1976, when he was told he had got the job, someone anonymously phoned Colley with the 'leak' that the post had gone to an outsider, and an Irishman at that! The *Observer* were just able to squeeze the piece in.

How did the reference to Queen's University get in? Philip Colley thought that the leaker had read the item out of the curriculum vitae which Colin had supplied to the Council. This CV did refer to Queen's University. Colin included in it the fact - which was perfectly true - that he had helped to train cadets there as part of his military duties in Northern Ireland. Colley suspects that the reference to the university caught the eye of the 'leaker' of the story, and that it had been passed on to him as fact though John Wallace was a graduate. Another possibility was that the CV had been read out hurriedly on the phone and the information garbled in the process. This theory was supported by the term 'John Wallace'. John is Colin's first Christian name and appeared as such on his CV, though no one who spoke to him would so describe him.

On one point Colley was absolutely clear. He had not got the information from Colin Wallace. Indeed, he remembers trying to get hold of Colin to interview him about his new appointment, but could not find his London address or telephone number.

Colin had returned to London immediately after the selection interview and had not supplied any information about himself to any journalist anywhere.

The matter was not over there, however. There remained a mystery, which is still unsolved. In general, during our conversations, a close record of which I have kept, David McKittrick was very forthcoming and had a quick and easy answer to my questions. One question, however, did cause him difficulties. 'How,' I asked him, 'did you get hold of a tiny clipping about Colin Wallace in a Bognor Regis newspaper?'

There was a long and embarrassing silence. At the end of it the journalist muttered: 'I can't remember.'

No one doubts that McKittrick is a hard worker and has a reputation as a relentless investigator. He did, of course, know Colin Wallace in Ireland, though their association was not specially close. It is possible that McKittrick (though he did not claim this) may have kept a file on Colin Wallace after the latter left Northern Ireland. That file might have rendered up one or two cuttings from national newspapers, though there was nothing written or spoken in the media about Colin until the *It's A Knockout* murder fascinated Fleet Street in 1980 and 1981.

Was it conceivable, however, that a five-paragraph story in the Bognor Regis *Observer* about Colin's appointment as information officer to the local Council in 1976 would have come into McKittrick's hands by any normal method of investigation or filing? It was not. In the rest of his replies to my questions on this, he did not even claim it. I thought that some secret serviceman might have been collecting anything that was ever published about Colin. So I put it to David McKittrick that he got the clipping from a police or intelligence file and he denied it. He did not provide any explanation of how he came by the cutting.

No one has ever been able to explain how an obscure and irrelevant cutting from a small-circulation newspaper, eleven years old, ended up as front page news in the *Independent*.

The second claim in this paragraph dealt with Colin's 'claim' that he was 'a member of the Widgery Tribunal'. 'He demonstrably was not,' wrote David McKittrick. 'Demonstrably', if it means anything, means 'can be demonstrated'. David McKittrick failed to demonstrate his demonstrable assurance. After damning Colin as a liar in this respect, he passed on, without a word of proof, to the next point.

The Widgery tribunal, in the simplest and strictest sense, consisted of

Lord Widgery. He sat in sole judgement, and was solely responsible for the conclusions which he wrote. He was, however, assisted in his work on the tribunal by a substantial team from the British Army, headed by three counsel for the Ministry of Defence (who later became judges), Brian Gibbens and Michael Underhill; Colin Overbury, then a lieutenant colonel in the Army Legal Services, and a staff major from the Life Guards, all of whom were sent over from London. Colin Wallace was seconded from Lisburn to this team as were a major and a staff sergeant from the Special Investigation Branch. Tony Staughton the head of the Army Information Services at Army Headquarters in Lisburn confirmed this to me in a personal interview. (Major Staughton, incidentally, described the *Independent* article as 'disgraceful'.)

He made the point that David McKittrick knew him and could easily have contacted him on this or any other aspect of Colin Wallace's career in the Army. He did not do so. In case there remains any doubt about it, I had lunch in February 1989 with one of the members of the Army team who remembers Colin Wallace very well as an everyday member of the team at the tribunal, and who every night stayed in the barracks at Derry, then occupied by a battalion of the Royal Greenjackets.

What then is left of McKittrick's claim that Colin was 'demonstrably' not a member of the Widgery tribunal? Colin was (which is all he ever claimed) a member of the Army team assisting and administering the tribunal. If McKittrick did not know this, he could easily have found it out.

The third allegation in the paragraph pooh-poohed Colin's claims that he had three times been recommended for decorations, with the single sentence: 'there is no record of this'.

There was, however, a record of it. Tony Staughton, head of the MOD Information Office in 1972, told me on the telephone and in interview that he had twice recommended Colin for the MBE and was so certain he would get it that he went out and bought champagne to celebrate. He wrote this down in a letter of recommendation of Colin to Arun District Council: 'I twice recommended him for an award for his exceptional services, and felt it was most unfair that he was not so recognised.' Colin was recommended a third time for the honour by Peter Broderick, Staughton's successor.

Tony Staughton confirms that he would have given McKittrick access to this document if McKittrick had contacted him. Anyone bothering to check whether there was any record of such a recommendation would have turned automatically to Staughton, who was the man in charge. McKittrick did not do so.

All three pieces of 'proof', then, that 'some of Mr Wallace's statements are clearly untrue' can be proved not to be proof.

McKittrick's front page article went on:

Former colleagues and a number of journalists who had contact with him in Belfast, regard him as a Walter Mitty figure. Mr Wallace started making his allegations after his removal from Ulster in 1975, after he was discovered to have leaked a classified document to a journalist.

The expression 'Walter Mitty figure' had been used to describe Colin after his conviction in 1981. The three most prominent journalists at the trial were Kenneth Clarke of the *Daily Telegraph* (who had been in Northern Ireland when Colin was there), Tim Miles of the *Daily Mail* and Roger Beam of the *Daily Mirror*. On the day of his conviction, all three wrote substantial articles on him.

Roger Beam's article was headlined: COLIN WALLACE, THE ARMY WALTER MITTY WHO WAS HYPNOTISED BY INTRIGUE AND VIOLENCE.

It quoted an Army officer who worked with him as saying: 'I had to watch out for the Walter Mitty side of his character . . . '

After Colin's appointment as Arun Information Officer, Beam wrote: 'His Walter Mitty life resumed.' (*Daily Mirror*, 21 March 1981.)

Tim Miles wrote: 'Wallace was something of a Walter Mitty character, given to invention both in the course of his work and his personal life.' (*Daily Mail*, 21 March 1981.)

And Kenneth Clarke, in by far the longest of these profiles, wrote: 'Wallace was a Walter Mitty, who was handed the role in which to live his fantasies.' (*Daily Telegraph*, 21 March 1981.)

One journalist who did not use the expression at that time was David McKittrick. His long article in the *Irish Times* on Colin after his conviction did not in any way cast doubt on Colin's credibility.

Walter Mitty was a character in a Danny Kaye film who lived in a world of fantasy. Such a characterisation of Colin Wallace is not shared by people who worked with him in the Army Information Office in Lisburn, nor by his colleagues at Arun Council. Neither Tony Staughton, nor Mike Taylor nor Tony Yarnold from the Army, nor any of the Council officers at Arun I spoke to recognised this fantasist as their former colleague. Nor did any journalist before 1981 describe Colin Wallace in this way. The 'Walter Mitty' image, then, was created during Colin's trial, at some time close to, or at, police and Special Branch 'briefings' of reporters about Colin Wallace's background. It persevered for several years and was used by David McKittrick in his *Independent* article.

The second half of the paragraph contains a glaring error. Colin was *not* removed from Ulster after he had leaked a classified document to a journalist. He was removed from Ulster in December 1974 for reasons which have never been satisfactorily explained either to him or to anyone else. The ostensible reason was that his life was in danger. His 'leaking' in February 1975 of the 'classified' (and entirely false) document led to his dismissal from the Ministry of Defence, not his removal from Northern Ireland. The point is important, because it smoothes over the authorities' failure to explain Colin's initial removal from Lisburn.

> In 1981 he received a ten-year jail sentence for the manslaughter of his girlfriend's husband in the South of England. Mr Holroyd, in turn, has waged a campaign against the authorities ever since he spent a month in a mental hospital in 1975.

This paragraph is true about Wallace (though of course it does not refer to any of the questions about the conviction) but not about Fred Holroyd. The centrepiece of Fred's campaign was that he was obliged against his will to spend a month in a mental hospital, and that he was put there deliberately to discredit him and any allegations he might later make. To refer to the visit in the mental hospital without including Fred's reply was simply to suggest that Fred was barmy.

> Many Press and television reporters have given promincncc to Mr Wallace's allegations, which contain many attractive stories. But the two television programmes which have researched his claims most exhaustively – the BBC's *Panorama* and Yorkshire Television's *First Tuesday* – both concluded they were unhappy with the evidence.

A letter to Colin from Grant McKie, the producer of the Yorkshire Television programme, makes quite clear that the YTV programme was dropped ostensibly because the revelations it intended to make had already started to appear in the newspapers, and their 'exclusivity' to the television programme had therefore been removed. Grant McKie told me: 'If anyone said we dropped the programme because we were unhappy with the evidence, that would not be correct.' (Interview with author, 27 March 1989.) Julian Hendy, YTV's researcher, confirms to me that he and his superiors were never for a moment put off by the unreliability of what Colin said. On the contrary, Julian Hendy has always been convinced of Colin's trustworthiness and credibility; and that he was framed for Jonathan Lewis's killing.

What about BBC *Panorama*? In the spring of 1987, the veteran investigative reporter Tom Mangold, and Gordon Carr, who had produced some of Mangold's investigations in the 1970s, approached *Panorama* with an idea for a programme which would deal extensively with Colin Wallace's allegations about dirty tricks against the Wilson government. The original brief was very friendly to Wallace and what he was saying. A new recruit to *Panorama*, John Ware, put up a different prospectus, which was much more hostile to Colin. Ware was chosen as the reporter, and Mangold and Carr were sent packing. Ware spent four days with Colin and took some of the originals of his documents (which later went missing). In the end, the idea of a programme based on Colin's allegations was shelved.

Ware wrote a long article for the *Listener* on 'the *Spycatcher* affair' entitled 'A Wilderness of Mirrors'. 'I would suggest,' he wrote, 'that focussing any more attention on Wallace is a waste of time.' He offered this example for his theory that Wallace was a 'Walter Mitty'. Colin, wrote Ware, claimed to have written a document in 1976 about the suicide of a policeman which had happened in 1981. (*Listener*, 6 August 1987.)

He repeated this claim in greater detail in the *Listener* three weeks later (27 August) naming the police officer as Superintendent Fairweather of the Thames Valley police.

As Robin Ramsay pointed out in a letter to the BBC, this proved only that John Ware had not properly read the documents he cited in evidence. There are, in fact (as anyone who reads Colin's papers can quickly establish), three different papers on the same subject. The first is written in 1976, and does not mention Superintendent Fairweather at all. The second is written in 1984 from prison, and does mention Superintendent Fairweather. The third was written later in 1984, after Colin had compared notes with Fred Holroyd, and was sent to the Prime Minister.

The Ramsay/Ware controversy transferred itself from the *Listener* to *Tribune*, the small left-wing weekly which gave space to Robin Ramsay's furious attack on Ware's *Listener* articles. In his reply, John Ware openly accused Colin of forging an important part of the Clockwork Orange notes: the reference to Dick Vaygauskas, the KGB officer who played chess with Harold Wilson's friend Lord Kagan.

Ware wrote:

> The problem is that Vaysgaukas' name is written in pencil which, unlike ink, cannot be dated. It also first surfaced in the *Sunday Times* in December 1980, which just happened to be within a few days of Wallace being released on bail and committed for trial. The possibility that these so-called Clockwork Orange notes were actually written up as part of Wallace's long-term preparation for his defence, seems to have been dismissed by the uncritical and unsceptical Mr Ramsay. (*Tribune*, 3 September 1987.)

Vaygauskas's name in the Clockwork Orange notes appears three times, twice in pencil and once in ink. Both ink and paper in the notes had been tested by Dr Julius Grant, who found them consistent with being written in the early 1970s. The first public reference in Britain to Dick Vaygauskas, moreover, was not in 1980 but in 1974, in John Barron's book *KGB*. (Hodder and Stoughton, 1974, p. 411.)

This was the journalist whose investigations had concluded that Wallace was not to be believed, and therefore should not be taken seriously by the programme for which John Ware worked, *Panorama*. When citing *Panorama* in support of his stand in the *Independent*, David McKittrick did not mention that he had been joined in his investigation by the same John Ware.

By citing *Panorama* as an ally, he was citing his own fellow-investigator. McKittrick's last paragraph, for the record, read as follows:

> Significantly, the IRA does not believe the two men. According to a senior Republican source: 'There's probably bits of truth scattered among it all, but it's all been so embellished.'

In these fourteen paragraphs on the front page of a respectable newspaper there were at least three verifiable mistakes of fact (Colin's alleged claim about Queen's University, the time he was removed from Northern Ireland, his recommendation for honours), and nothing at all of substance which backed up the article's basic thesis: that Colin was a liar and a Walter Mitty.

This approach was maintained in the huge article which David McKittrick published on page 4.

There were four main allegations against Colin on the page.

The article complained that Colin suggested 'that the Army may have been involved in as many as 28 murders in two months in 1974. These claims are not supported by the statistics or by the experience of the past 18 years of violence.'

Colin had suggested, to the reporters of the Radio Telefis Eireann programme *Today/Tonight* (by far the most thorough account in one programme ever produced on this subject) that in November 1974 there was a sudden rash of sectarian assassinations on both sides, which may well have been promoted by the security services who were anxious to wreck government talks with the IRA and the Protestant paramilitaries.

Sectarian assassinations in October and November 1974 reached a horrific crescendo. In November alone there were twenty-six sectarian killings – thirteen each of Protestants and Catholics. The next highest monthly figure in the year was ten, in October. There was also, in subsequent years at least, plenty of evidence of Army involvement in sectarian killings. In 1976, for instance, two members of the UDR, a regiment in the British Army, had been sentenced to life imprisonment for their parts in the massacre of the Miami Showband, a pop group dedicated to peace between the two communities.

McKittrick alleged that Colin 'did not co-operate' with the Kincora inquiry. We have seen how Colin refused to give evidence either to Terry or to Hughes after he tried again and again to get an assurance from higher authority that he could speak about the knowledge of the Army and the security services of Kincora in 1972, 1973 and 1974. A phone call to Colin's solicitor would have established that this allegation was quite groundless and that, on the contrary, Colin and James Morgan-Harris had gone to great lengths in order that Colin should give evidence.

Turning to the memorandum about Kincora, which Colin said he wrote in 1974, McKittrick had this: 'A forensic science report on the document raised doubts about its authenticity: two different typewriters were used . . . '

This appears to be derived from the Hughes Report (para 4.85) which stated that a forensic report 'raised the possibilities' that two typewriters had been used. The possibility (Hughes) had become the fact (McKittrick). As we have seen, however, two named experts in Britain take the view that only one typewriter was used.

Under the emotive heading LEAFLETS THAT ENDANGERED LIFE, McKittrick hauled out the story of Ron Horn and the Ulster Citizens Army. The article started: 'In 1974 an innocent man was put at grave risk when Colin Wallace's girlfriend left Mr Wallace and married another man.'

As we have seen Joan Horn did not 'leave Colin Wallace and marry another man'. Her relationship with Colin was always low key – nor was it exclusive to her or to him. I have traced the Horn story, using as a main source McKittrick's own articles of the time. It started not with Colin, as was suggested, but with elements in the UDA who were anxious to prove that the left-wing splinter group, the UCA, was 'founded' by British Army propagandists, chiefly Colin Wallace. Thus the Horn story was started in order to discredit Colin. Colin himself had secured a denial as soon as McKittrick came to see him about it, had denied it himself and had asked McKittrick to contact him again if he planned to publish anything about it. This was not the reaction of a man who was out to smear a rival.

Perhaps the most remarkable item on the page was a section down in the bottom right-hand corner, entitled PARACHUTIST WHO WAS ALL WAFFLE AND NO ACTION. This was written not by David McKittrick, but by his fellow investigator John Ware of *Panorama*.

The gist of Ware's article was that Colin was a braggart over his claims to be an experienced parachutist. In fact, Ware alleged, he was nothing of the kind.

This extraordinary article had the same sort of pedigree as the 'Walter Mitty' tag. After Colin's conviction in 1981, Tim Miles had written in his *Daily Mail* 'profile' of Wallace:

> He said he was a qualified free-fall parachutist. He showed his friends photographs of himself in paratrooper's combat jacket . . . Colleagues at the Army HQ in Lisburn treated the stories with scepticism. One told how he used to walk round the HQ with a parachute, leaving it on his desk. 'But we knew him as the man on the ground who lit the smoke cannons,' said a colleague.　(21 March 1981.)

This notion, that Colin had never been a real parachutist as he claimed, was 'fed' to Bob Parker of Channel Four News while he was investigating the affair. Parker thought nothing of it, but Colin became concerned. Perhaps because he placed no limit on the lengths to which his detractors might go, he asked me to try to establish that he had been an experienced parachutist in case the propaganda that he wasn't was used at a later date.

As proof of his experience Colin produced his membership card for the British Parachute Association. He told me that he had been awarded a D Licence, the highest grade in the Association, on 5 June 1974, but could not be sure of his number. He thought it was 1516 or 1615.

In July 1987, as the Channel Four series came to an end, I telephoned the British Parachute Association and asked about the D Licence for a man called Wallace who was then serving in Northern Ireland. The initial response was depressing: there was no such licence. The Association confirmed that they had records of all the licences awarded that year, but there was none for the whole year (or 1973 or 1975 for that matter) for a man called Wallace, or anything which could have been mistaken as such. For the first time in the three months since I had known him, I had come across something which directly contradicted what Colin had told me, and indeed suggested that he had fabricated documents to improve on his credibility. For the first time, the shadow of Walter Mitty loomed large over my typewriter.

I was determined to do what I could to be sure that Colin's information did not check out. I telephoned the BPA again and again and eventually won grudging respect for persistence from a secretary there. She promised to do what she could to make absolutely sure that there was nothing in the records to suggest membership of the BPA by what to her was 'this mysterious Captain Wallace'.

After a day or two, she rang me back, triumphant. The records of the BPA membership, she told me, were duplicated at the international parachutist association (FAI) to which the BPA was affiliated. She had checked with them, and yes, sure enough, there had been a D Licence for a Captain Wallace, No. 1615, taken out on 5 June 1974. She could not explain how the records of this had somehow vanished from the BPA files, and another name had been inserted alongside Colin's number. But there was no doubt about the main point: Colin had got a D Licence in 1974. A D Licence could only be obtained by someone who had done 300 jumps. These jumps all had to be recorded in a book, each signed by another jumper, and counter-signed by a senior official of the BPA.

I passed this information on to Colin who was relieved yet concerned by the apparent loss of his licence record at the BPA. There was nothing for us to publish at the time and I remember laughing a little with him, both about my immediate feelings that he had sought to deceive me and about his absurd suggestion that the records of the BPA might have been tampered with by someone who wanted to prove him a fantasist.

The joke dried up on 2 September, as I read John Ware's article. The following section puzzled me:

> Mr Wallace claims to have completed more than 200 free-fall jumps. The proof, he says, can be found at the headquarters of the British Parachute Association in Leicester. Journalists have accepted his story because BPA files do indeed show that he was granted the highest parachutists' certificate – a D Licence, No 1615 on 5 June 1974. But several display parachutists active in the early seventies say that the D Licence system was open to abuse until it was tightened up by law under the Air Navigation Order of 1984.

The innuendo was that Colin had falsely acquired his D Licence by forging his jumps, or by some other deceitful method. This was bitterly rejected by officials of the BPA. Ware's article quoted Jeff Page, a former Phantom parachutist in Northern Ireland saying:

> He organised the flares for the drop zone and he often did the ground commentary. He loved doing that. He always used to arrive in full jumping gear as if he was going to jump with us. He was what we call a 'Woofo' - all waffle and no action.

Proving that Colin Wallace was an experienced free-fall parachutist seemed to Colin and some of his former colleagues like proving that the world goes round the sun. It was the most obvious fact to anyone who had known Colin in Northern Ireland. It was such an obvious fact, so widely known that he was one of the most consistent parachutists in the Six Counties that it seemed absurd to try to prove it.

Colin produced various magazines and bulletins from the parachutists' world in Northern Ireland to prove he was a team leader and a constant jumper. The most persuasive of these was a memorandum from Major Edward Gardener of the 3rd Battalion of the Parachute Regiment who was the Safety Officer for the Army Parachute Association. The memo, dated 22 April 1974, discussed a near-fatal accident which had taken place in one Army jump, and proposed plans to tighten the regulations about free-fall jumping in Northern Ireland. The final paragraph read:

> The man chiefly responsible for promoting parachuting among servicemen in Northern Ireland and for getting the sport properly organised is Mr Colin Wallace who works in the Press Office at HQNI. He is himself a keen and fairly experienced parachutist with about 300 jumps.

Major Gardener went on to say that Colin Wallace was a very busy man who could not co-ordinate all the jumps and he recommended a new instructor who would 'take care of a lot of the day to day problems under the overall direction of Mr Wallace'.

Major Gardener had since been promoted to colonel and was by 1987 the Regimental Colonel of the Parachute Regiment. I phoned him at Regimental Headquarters in Aldershot. He was happy and interested to talk to me, though intrigued about the reason. He at once confirmed that he knew Colin Wallace and had jumped many times with him. He told me that he had filled in Colin's books about his jumps, just as Colin had filled in his. He said he had kept his books and would gladly make them available to Colin. Colin's own book recording his jumps had been among the papers he had lodged with his solicitor before going to prison. In March 1982, the solicitor's office was burgled. Nothing of value was taken. Most of the top-secret papers had been stored away elsewhere by James Morgan-Harris. Years later, after his release, Colin found that his parachutist's log-book was missing.

I published Colonel Gardener's remarks and his memo in the *Mirror* of 20 September 1987. No one ever again made any allegation that Colin was not an experienced parachutist. However, when Colin wrote to Gardener asking for the confirmation from his books, he got no reply.

Colin and Fred read the *Independent* articles of 2 September with a mixture of fury and disbelief. What could they do? Colin wrote at once to Andreas-Whittam Smith (14 September) pointing out some of the worst errors. Two days later, Whittam-Smith replied: 'If it can be shown that our original story contained mistakes, we shall correct them, and if it appears that we have been unfair, we would want you to exercise a right of reply.'

There was no correction and no space offered Colin for a reply. Instead, as Colin continued to complain, Andreas Whittam-Smith offered both men a meeting with himself and McKittrick to sort out the problems. Colin was advised that such a meeting might prejudice any further legal action he took against the paper. He had also got a new job and was anxious not to be absent in the first few days he was working. Fred Holroyd did go to the meeting and wrote down his feelings about it in a letter to Colin:

Whittam-Smith then suggested I go through the article piece by piece to identify my complaints. The first couple I raised, quite minor issues, he just said 'Well, we disagree and we are not going to change it'. That was enough for me. It was the old story all over again, extreme politeness while completely refusing to address the issues – no, worse than that pretending there was no issue. It was a shame, really, my cup of tea had just arrived and I was parched. But the whole thing had become pointless. I asked him directly whether or not he was prepared to accept that McKittrick had got his story wrong. He did not answer that openly but did the lawyers' weasel trick of answering a question with a statement. He said he stuck by everything McKittrick had written. I never got to drink that bloody tea, as I left then. They seemed a bit put out by my exit, probably not used to plain use of the English language.

Colin wrote another long letter, but this time got no reply. On 24 January 1988, he sent a twenty-seven-page complaint to the Press Council. The Council for a long time would not accept the complaint, though all the necessary procedures (writing to the editor and getting no correction published) had been scrupulously followed. After over a year's prevarication, the Council insisted, on prompting from the editor of the *Independent*, that Colin's complaint could only be heard if Fred Holroyd gave an undertaking that he would not sue for libel. Fred saw no reason why he should give such an undertaking and a prolonged correspondence followed. In the meantime not a single word of apology or correction has been published by the editor of the *Independent* or David McKittrick.

It is very much easier to make an allegation than to refute it. Once the mud of rumour sticks, it is a mammoth task to wash it off. The effect of the *Independent* articles was far more devastating than anything Colin or Fred had imagined. All over the media, journalists who had taken Colin and Fred seriously began to shy away from them and their story. The unofficial inquiry by Rees, Heath and Jenkins never got off the ground. There were no further programmes on *Channel Four News* – indeed (with the exception of one magnificent edition of *After Dark* in which Robin Ramsay excelled himself) no more television programmes at all. The credibility which Fred and Colin built up in the first nine months after Colin's release from prison suddenly collapsed. Everywhere I went and discussed the case, I was met with a reference to the *Independent*. Why, I was asked, would such a distinguished paper and such a distinguished correspondent engage in a smear campaign?

The articles by McKittrick and Ware, however, had another, perhaps unexpected, effect. Those very few of us who bothered to dig deep and compare their every line and allegation to the facts became convinced of the credibility of Colin and Fred. Robin Ramsay wrote a magnificent tirade in his *Lobster*, though he could only find another publisher in the small-circulation Labour left paper, *Tribune*, which had consistently published his material.

I published a short article in my column in the *Mirror*, attacking the *Independent*'s articles. No reply was forthcoming from Whittam-Smith or McKittrick.

This book was for a brief moment threatened by the *Independent* article. The publishers argued with some reason that if the *Independent* allegations were accurate, I and they might be made to look foolish with a book which boosted a couple of hoaxers and Walter Mittys. When the articles were examined thoroughly, the publishers too determined to proceed.

One influential man in public life was not convinced by the *Independent*. Ken Livingstone knew enough about Northern Ireland to realise that what Colin and especially Fred were saying was highly credible. He had observed the John Stalker scandal and the way in which one of the country's most senior and respected policemen was hounded, smeared and eventually pushed into resignation because he dared to question the assassins' role of the security services in Northern Ireland. If the authorities could do that to John Stalker, how much more easily could they discredit a couple of men with no influence, no money and (in Colin's case certainly) no reputation. Livingstone, to the dismay of almost everyone who supported him, embarked on a long Parliamentary campaign to get to the root of the Wallace/Holroyd stories. Almost every week he put down questions based on information from the two men. Once he drew question No. 1 to the Prime Minister. His colleagues begged him to ask about a London hospital which was to close down. He asked instead about Kincora.

The Ministry of Defence, irritated sometimes beyond endurance by these questions, stuck resolutely to the same theme: Colin Wallace had never worked in a psychological operations unit; he was an ordinary Information officer; he was not sacked, he resigned. He was not a captain in the UDR (as his military identity card had him) but a lieutenant. There was no Clockwork Orange project, no warning about Kincora in 1974, not even a raid on Aldergrove Airport in 1973.

A good example of the way in which ministers dealt with Ken Livingstone's questions was this exchange on 6 May 1988:

> *Mr Livingstone*: To ask the Secretary of State for Defence on how many occasions members of the Army Information Services have planted hoax bombs between 1973 and the current date; and whether such services were subsequently dismantled by an Army explosive ordnance disposal team.
> *Mr Freeman* (Parliamentary Under-Secretary, Ministry of Defence): I am aware of none. Such an act would not have been part of the duties of a member of the Army Information Services and would have been illegal.

Ken Livingstone's question referred to the spoof 'raid' on Aldergrove Airport and its surrounding areas which was organised by Colin Wallace in 1973 in order to test airport security. The story, which is in Chapter One, was told to me in detail not only by Colin, but also by Mike Taylor, his associate in Army Information Services at the time, from whose house the extraordinary exercise started.

When Bob Parker wrote from Channel Four News to the Ministry of Defence asking about the incident, the Director of Army Public Relations Major William Rous said he could not remember any such incident. This astounded Colin, since Rous was in nominal charge of the exercise.

After reading Freeman's denial, I checked the story out a second time. Colin had said that one of the people who took part in the exercise was Wendy Austin, who worked at the time for the East Antrim *Times*, and is now on the staff of the BBC in Belfast. She at once cheerfully recalled the 'raid' on the airport, and her role in it. She and another of Colin's recruits, Chris Whitehead, had driven in an Escort estate through three road blocks, pretending that they were heading for an illicit weekend. 'We had a rocket launcher under the back seat of the Escort,' Wendy Austin recalls with a laugh. 'We acted as weekend lovers, giving a nudge and wink to the soldiers that we wanted to get through quickly, and they just waved us through. When we wound up at the UDR headquarters I remember wondering what would happen if they wouldn't believe our story.' Wendy Austin confirmed every other aspect of Colin's story.

The most consistent answer to Ken Livingstone from ministers high and low was that Colin's allegations had been 'fully investigated' and there was 'not a shred of evidence' to support any of them. These were the favourite phrases of the Prime Minister whenever Ken Livingstone approached her on the subject. When he sent her a long letter from Colin in May 1988, which exposed many of the Parliamentary answers as at best shallow and at worst false, Mrs Thatcher wrote back (23 June): 'The allegations by Mr Wallace have been fully and carefully investigated and Mr Wallace himself failed to take the opportunity to contribute to these investigations.'

This brand of answer infuriated Colin. Since he and Fred had sent their vast dossier to the Prime Minister in 1984, not a single person had approached either of them to investigate what they were alleging.

On 10 August 1988, Ken Livingstone sought to pin the Prime Minister down. In another letter, he asked:

> I am not prepared to accept answers which only state that 'full and careful' investigations have occurred without knowing their precise nature. For example:
> 1. Who carried out such investigations?
> 2. What were the terms of reference?
> 3. On what dates did investigations begin and end?
> 4. Who was interviewed?
> 5. Were any reports submitted or any documents produced?'

To these entirely reasonable questions there was *no reply*.

Margaret Thatcher did reply, however, to another letter from Ken Livingstone written about the same time (12 August). This drew her attention to the unquestionable links between Colin Wallace and Airey Neave, Mrs Thatcher's former campaign leader and close friend. Neave, Ken Livingstone reminded her, had approached Colin and used material from his essay 'Ulster - A State of Subversion'. This essay had been written while Colin was a Ministry of Defence Information officer, and was put together from information which he claimed came from the security services. Livingstone's letter ended:

> Given that Airey Neave was a key member of your Opposition team, will you explain:

1. How a Shadow Spokesman actually knew such material existed?
2. What links did Members of your Opposition have at that time with plans to undermine the then Labour Government?
3. To what extent were other Conservative Members of Parliament involved in these activities?
4. Were you personally aware of Airey Neave's working relationship with Colin Wallace?

The remarkable reply to this letter was dated 29 September 1988.

Thank you for your letter of 12 August.

You say that the material enclosed with your letter entitled 'Ulster – A State of Subversion' was written by Mr Wallace as part of his official duties while employed by the Ministry of Defence in Northern Ireland. In fact such a document could under no circumstances have formed a part of any official duties undertaken by a civil servant.

You also allege, without foundation, that Airey Neave contacted Colin Wallace after he left Northern Ireland and asked him to provide official information. This attempt to blacken Airey Neave's name is deplorable. I am aware of no such evidence to show that Mr Wallace had contact with Mr Neave before he left Government service. On the contrary, the evidence rejects this allegation. Moreover, the material provided by Mr Wallace was obviously provided freely as his own work and not presented anywhere as a product of his employment with the Ministry of Defence. The note at the bottom of the letter from Airey Neave of 31 August describes the material as 'your own resume'.

I repeat that any new evidence in your possession relating to the commission of criminal offences should be given to the appropriate authorities.

Mrs Thatcher's assertion that 'such a document' as 'Ulster – A State of Subversion' 'could under no circumstances have formed part of the official duties undertaken by a civil servant' exactly summarised Colin Wallace's main point. It was a point he had made with increasing vehemence over the years, and had emphasised, in particular, to the Parliamentary Committee on the Civil Service the previous year. It was true that documents such as 'Ulster – A State of Subversion' *should* under no circumstances have formed part of the official duties of a civil servant. It was also true that he, as part of his duties as a civil servant, had written it. That was the central feature of his complaint. It was precisely because his role as servant of a government had been twisted into a role which was subversive of the government that he had baulked at Clockwork Orange, and refused to carry out any further similar duties without ministerial clearance. Yet no sooner had he been chucked out of the Army than he was approached by a leading Conservative politician who asked for the information he had put together with the specific purpose of further assaulting the elected government.

It was no use Mrs Thatcher writing: 'I am aware of no such

evidence to show that Mr Wallace had contact with Mr Neave before he left Government service.' No one, least of all Ken Livingstone, had suggested he had. Neave met Wallace after Colin had left the Ministry of Defence. But when Mrs Thatcher referred to Wallace's essay 'Ulster – A State of Subversion' as 'his own work', she was skipping over the truth. Handwriting experts dated the essay to 1974, when Colin was an active civil servant. Parts of the essay and of the Clockwork Orange notes could not have been put together by a freelance conservative collecting published material. The allegation was that Airey Neave had sought out Wallace precisely because he knew that Colin had special information which he had gleaned when working for the Ministry of Defence.

In a wry reference to the Peter Wright affair, Ken Livingstone replied (16 January 1989):

> It appears somewhat disingenuous to insist that former Crown servants have a life-long duty of confidentiality when one of your closest advisers encouraged another Crown servant to break that duty.

To that letter, too, there was no reply.

Apart from Ken Livingstone's lone campaign, the authorities, with the help of the *Independent*, succeeded in stifling the rising concern and interest in what Colin and Fred had to say. There is however no guarantee that either of them will shut up or go away. In both cases, loyal and amiable men have been toughened by years of smears and snubs. Both men feel threatened. Like the smears and snubs, this succeeds only in stiffening their resolve.

Colin Wallace's charge against the authorities starts with the way he has been treated. He is outraged that his MOD career was so abruptly cut short, and with the way he has been hounded and smeared ever since. But there is much more at stake here than the unjust treatment of two men, disgraceful though that has been. Colin's story suggests that his removal from the army was engineered because he refused to take part in political dirty tricks against the Ministers he was meant to be serving; and because he urged action against a child abuser whose activities were tolerated long after they were discovered. He believes that when he continued to protest about his treatment, and eventually to make public some of the fearful things he learned when he was a black propagandist for the British Army in Ireland, he was framed by the security services or their agents for the murder of his close friend.

Far more than Peter Wright, Colin Wallace has exposed the 'state within a state'. He suggests that by the middle of the 1970s sections of the security services were completely out of control. They were running their own operations without anyone with democratic responsibility knowing about them, let alone controlling them. The chief victim of these campaigns was not 'the enemy' as it is widely known – foreign powers, perhaps, who threaten invasion – but 'the Left' in general and in particular; in this particular the elected government of the country. So powerful was this secret state that it was, if Colin is right, able and keen to operate *against* that part of the state for which elected people have to answer. In the hothouse atmosphere created by irresponsibility to the outside world, those sections of the Intelligence services tried to change the outside world to their best taste: a taste which by the very nature of the type of organisation, and the secrecy with which it worked, was inevitably of the most bizarre and terrifying variety. The politics of these people in Intelligence with whom Colin was working were invariably extreme right-wing. Some of them openly flaunted fascist views; others were more subtle about it. Their hatred of all forms of democracy revealed itself at its nastiest when that process elected Labour governments committed to some form of change in the social order to the benefit of people who have nothing, and to the disadvantage of the people who have everything.

Peter Wright wrote that none of his colleagues in MI5 (by which he probably meant none of his own right-wing gang in MI5) felt themselves loyal to Parliament. They all, he said, felt loyal to the Queen. They never met the Queen, and were certainly never called to account by her. So the expression 'loyalty to the Queen' was a fiction; a mere excuse to be loyal to nothing except themselves.

If a secret state like this is allowed to grow unchecked, all democratic politicians are at risk. It is no use right–wing politicians imagining that they themselves will be safe from the secret state, perhaps because they have more in common with each other politically. The monster, once fed, will grow hungrier. The upholders of the secret state regard all democratic politicians as traitors to the true cause, and will attack them just as readily as they attacked Harold Wilson or Merlyn Rees in the past. Early on in the miners' strike of 1984, a vile rumour about the personal behaviour of the Home Secretary, Leon Brittan, started to circulate among journalists. The information was, as I eventually discovered, completely untrue. But it had about it just enough of the 'ring of truth' to make it sound credible. Anyone who believed it for an instant would have wanted Leon Brittan removed from office at once. After checking that the information was wrong, I then strove for many days to try to find its source. It was nowhere to be found. Everybody had 'heard it from someone else'. Sometimes they could remember where they heard it, but that source would prove as maddeningly vague about *his* source – and so on, endlessly to nothing. Fortunately for Mr Brittan, the rumour never got into print. But where did it come from? So untrue was it that it could not have originated in that part of Britain where the 'event' was said to have taken place. It must have been entirely made up. But who could or would have made it up, save those same operators in the Intelligence service who, perhaps, did not want a Jew with a faintly liberal reputation to be leading the government offensive against the miners and in nominal control of MI5. This was by no means the first time that anti-semitic propaganda against the large number of Jews in Mrs Thatcher's circle has insidiously circulated among journalists and politicians.

This is why the cavalier approach of Mrs Thatcher and her ministers to Colin Wallace and to Fred Holroyd has been so extraordinary. The phrases 'fully investigated' and 'not a shred of evidence' seem to have stuck in their throats. The plain fact is that what Colin and Fred sent to Mrs Thatcher in 1984 in such detail and with such courtesy has not been investigated at all. Proof of that is easy. Colin Wallace and Fred Holroyd have not been interviewed by a single investigator appointed by Downing Street, the security services or anyone else. If there has been no inquiry of the people making the allegations, how can anyone say that there is not a 'shred of evidence' of what they are saying? And does not the contempt with which these very serious charges have been greeted demonstrate precisely the overweening power and influence of the security services which Colin is trying to curb?

Are Colin's allegations perhaps too ridiculous for serious consideration? Is it really credible that intelligent, rational and responsible people in the security services could go round forging leaflets to discredit ministers, or could overlook child abuse on a horrifying scale or frame an innocent man on a murder charge?

If anyone imagines that the world of the intelligence services is sane, rational or responsible, they need recall only one story; that of Michael Bettaney. Michael Bettaney was educated at the University of Oxford. While he was there, however, he annoyed or amused his fellow undergraduates (depending on their point of view) by strutting around pretending he was one of Hitler's stormtroopers. Fellow drinkers in Oxford pubs, where Michael Bettaney spent a great deal of his time, would be interrupted in their conversations or their reveries by a sudden clicking of heels from the young Bettaney, who would at once address the assembled company, his arm raised aloft in a Heil Hitler salute, about the evils of modern democratic society and the urgent need to replace it with what Hitler and Goering thought was best for Britain in 1940.

With that sort of background, Michael Bettaney had no difficulty getting into MI5. He climbed steadily up its hierarchy, despite occasionally being stopped by policemen for being drunk in charge of motor cars he was driving. Most of the time he was 'spy-catching' Michael Bettaney was completely off his rocker, but no one in Intelligence seemed to notice.

It wasn't very long before the undergraduate fascist developed into what he thought was a full–blown communist. As a communist, he reckoned he ought to be passing MI5 secrets to the Russians. Gathering up some secrets, then, he tried to make contact. After failing to do so, he dropped a bundle of secret documents through the letterbox of the Russian Ambassador. The Russians were so terrified by what they found that they immediately told MI5, who finally caught their colleague *in flagrante* when he tried to do 'the drop' again. Michael Bettaney went to prison for the best part of the rest of his life. Everyone to do with the secret services hopes that he will be forgotten. He is, after all, living proof that there is no limit to the insecurity, lunacy and chaos into which a bunch of entirely irresponsible men with vast powers and megalomaniac intentions can lead us.

In the light of the Bettaney case, therefore, can it any longer be said that the allegations of Colin Wallace are to be believed only by wild men of the Left, such as Ken Livingstone (or the author), who are wedded to notions of conspiracies in the state machine? It is worth recalling in this context that many people in the centre of British politics – Humphry Berkeley, Alex Carlile, Laura Grimond – who have studied the case carefully are inclined to believe what Colin says. One final voice may be called in evidence: a voice from the far Right, which has some authority in the world of intelligence. Anthony Cavendish, a former MI6 officer and a close friend of the late MI6 chief Sir Maurice Oldfield, talked with Colin on many occasions. He concluded that the story Colin tells, although 'frightening and disquieting' fitted closely with what he had heard and discovered about the intelligence community in the 1970s and 1980s. In particular, he believed Colin because much of what Colin told him about the MI5 smear campaign against Oldfield matched closely the information which Cavendish had heard from the mouth of Sir Maurice himself.

On all sides, the evidence mounts up in support of Colin Wallace's central charge: that from the early 1970s onwards, and particularly in Ireland, the British secret state stepped for beyond any line which should be tolerated by a democratic and civilised society; and that if such things, once exposed, are ignored or covered up by the authorities, the one certainty is that they will continue, to excesses even more horrific than anything which has been recounted here.

Chronology

06.06.43	Colin Wallace (JCW) born at Randalstown in Northern Ireland
1955–60	Attended Ballymena Academy
1960–68	Employed by a firm of manufacturing pharmaceutical chemists
27.09.61	Commissioned into the Territorial Army Volunteer Reserve (TAVR) General List
05.10.68	Riots in Londonderry following Civil Rights march
01.05.68	JCW appointed Assistant Command Public Relations Officer, Army HQ Northern Ireland
02.03.70	JCW promoted to Information Officer
18.06.70	General Election – Edward Heath becomes Prime Minister
05.02.71	First British soldier shot dead in Northern Ireland
18.01.72	JCW commissioned into the Ulster Defence Regiment
30.01.72	Bloody Sunday
13.03.72	Harold Wilson meets IRA delegates in Dublin
24.03.72	British Government announce Direct Rule in Northern Ireland
07.07.72	Secretary of State William Whitelaw has secret talks with IRA delegates in London
14.10.72	Ulster Citizens Army (UCA) manifesto issued
07.12.72	Ernie 'Duke' Elliott of the Ulster Defence Association (UDA) assassinated
c1.08.73	JCW briefs journalists about William McGrath and TARA
14.09.73	UDA leader Tommy Herron kidnapped
16.09.73	Tommy Herron's body found near Lisburn – he had been assassinated
06.12.73	Sunningdale conference begins
01.01.74	Northern Ireland Power Sharing Executive takes office
28.02.74	General Election – Labour victory but no overall majority
10.05.74	'Doomsday Plan' found at Malone Road, Belfast
15.05.74	Ulster Workers Council (UWC) strike begins
28.05.74	Northern Ireland Executive collapses – UWC strike ends

27.09.74	JCW promoted to Senior Information Officer
c1.10.74	JCW declines to undertake further work on the 'Clockwork Orange' project
10.10.74	General Election – Labour victory
16.10.74	JCW offered a post at the Northern Ireland Office
30.10.74	JCW visited by journalist David McKittrick at Lisburn saying he had been told by the UDA that a man called 'George Horn' was the leader of the UCA
08.11.74	JCW writes Kincora memorandum complaining about lack of action by the police
20.12.74	IRA announce ceasefire in Northern Ireland
24.12.74	JCW told by Tony Chinneck at Ministry of Defence (MOD) that he is to be moved from Northern Ireland because his 'life is in danger'
30.01.75	Commander Land Forces Study Day at Army HQ Lisburn
04.02.75	JCW deposits Study Day script at home of *Times* reporter and leaves Army HQ Northern Ireland that evening for his new appointment at Army HQ near Preston
11.02.75	JCW suspended from duty at HQ North West District near Preston, Lancashire
18.02.75	Airey Neave appointed Conservative Northern Ireland Spokesman
25.06.75	JCW sent notice of dismissal from the MOD
17.10.75	JCW Appeal Board hearing
25.11.75	JCW reinstated pending resignation from MOD
27.11.75	JCW briefs Blackheath solicitor, Graham Dodd, about his allegations
31.01.76	Peter Wright retires from MI5
15.01.76	JCW and his solicitor see Roland Moyle MP about his allegations
16.03.76	Harold Wilson tenders his resignation to the Queen – James Callaghan succeeds him
12.05.76	Harold Wilson invites Barrie Penrose and Roger Courtiour of the BBC to his London home and tells them that during 'the last eight months' of his term in office he did not know 'what was happening, fully, in Security'
02.08.76	Letter from Airey Neave to JCW suggesting a meeting at the House of Commons
04.08.76	First meeting between JCW and Airey Neave
10.09.76	Airey Neave uses JCW's 'Ulster – A State of Subversion' material in a speech at Seaton Delaval, Northumberland
13.03.77	*Sunday Times* report – 'Ulster's Dirty War' – about psychological operations in Northern Ireland

05.08.77	Letter from JCW to Harold Wilson about 'dirty tricks' against Labour Government
30.03.79	Airey Neave killed by bomb near Parliament
03.05.79	General Election – Conservative victory
c1.08.79	'Kaymar Studios' request pictures of JCW in SAS/parachute kit
02.10.79	Sir Maurice Oldfield appointed Intelligence Co-ordinator at the Northern Ireland Office in Belfast
24.01.80	Kincora story exposed in the *Irish Independent*
22.04.80	First of three stories by David McKittrick in the *Irish Times* about British Intelligence in Ireland
05.08.80	Jonathan Lewis goes missing
08.08.80	Body of Jonathan Lewis found in River Arun – police say foul play not suspected
10.08.80	JCW first interviewed by police
18.09.80	JCW charged with murder
01.12.80	JCW committed for trial at Arundel Magistrates Court
16.12.80	McGrath, Mains and Semple sentenced for sexually assaulting inmates of the Kincora Boys' Home
03.03.81	JCW's trial begins at Lewes Crown Court
20.03.81	Trial ends: JCW convicted of manslaughter and sentenced to ten years' imprisonment
11.02.82	Leave to appeal refused
18.02.82	Secretary of State James Prior announces an independent police investigation into allegations of a cover-up of the Kincora scandal. JCW named in House of Commons as a 'key witness'
19.02.82	Sir George Terry appointed to head Kincora investigations
04.03.82	Detective Superintendent Harrison telephones Wormwood Scrubs to speak to JCW
14.04.82	JCW transferred to Lewes prison
09.06.83	General Election – Conservative victory
28.10.83	Findings of Sir George Terry's investigations published
18.01.84	James Prior announces the setting up of the Hughes inquiry into Northern Ireland Boys' Homes
03.05.84	Fred Holroyd's story on Channel 4's *Diverse Reports* programme
16.07.84	Peter Wright interview on *World in Action*
01.11.84	File sent to Mrs Thatcher
05.02.86	Hughes inquiry report published
24.06.86	JCW granted parole by Home Secretary
05.12.86	Released on parole

07.07.87   Ken Livingstone's maiden speech in Parliament deals with Irish TV programme about JCW's allegations and those of Fred Holroyd

13.07.87   *Channel Four News* broadcast a report about Airey Neave's contacts with JCW

06.08.87   John Ware of *Panorama* publishes an article in the *Listener* about the *Spycatcher* affair and suggests that focusing 'attention on Colin Wallace is a waste of time'

02.09.87   David McKittrick and John Ware publish a lengthy report in the *Independent* saying the allegations made by Colin Wallace and Fred Holroyd are false

Appendix: Colin Wallace's File

This appendix reproduces facsimile copics of notes kept by Colin Wallace dated 1974 (pp. 282–91). He says they were compiled by him mainly from information supplied by security service intelligence officers for 'Clockwork Orange', a 'dirty tricks' disinformation project directed at leading British politicians. Neither the author nor the publishers believe the allegations contained in these to be true; they are included merely to show the absurd and dangerous lengths to which those responsible were prepared to go.

It also reproduces documents forged by the security services in order to discredit the Labour Party and various politicians.

(p. 292) Colin Wallace's briefing memorandum to the press on TARA, 1973. Note initials on top left-hand corner.

(p. 293) Forged letter to Merlyn Rees, MP, from the American Congress for Irish Freedom.

(p. 294–5) Two leaflets advertising a demonstration in 1973 to commemorate 'Bloody Sunday'. One is real, one forged, adding the names of five Labour politicians.

(p. 296) Forged Labour Party leaflet calling for revolutionary struggle against the Northern Ireland 'client regime'.

(p. 297) Forged poster advocating Protestant and Catholic working class unity 'against the capitalist state machine'. Contents printed in the *Daily Telegraph*.

(p. 298) Two forged bank accounts, for the Rev. Ian Paisley, and for Edward Short, MP (now Lord Glenamara).

1970 GENERAL ELECTION — PARTY STRATEGIES.

LABOUR	CONSERVATIVE
LOW KEY	HIGH PROFILE
PARTY'S RECORD IMPROVEMENTS ON THE ECONOMY	HW COMPLACENT ABOUT INFLATION + STRIKES

NOTE. The mass media 'presidentialise' the campaign by projecting the issues in PERSONAL terms particularly the party leaders.
SEE ENOCH POWELL who attracted up to twice as much in some papers as the entire Liberal party — and on Radio / TV the Powell issue took about 20 per cent of all election coverage.

THIS WILL NO DOUBT BE THE CASE ON THIS OCCASION !!

(1) INVESTIGATE BACKGROUND INFORMATION
(2) FEASIBILITY STUDY
(3) RECOMMENDATIONS

OPINION POLLS showing WILSON rated much higher than HEATH as a personality leader. NOTE: 30% of all lead stories on the election in major dailies and Sundays in the three weeks before polling day [illegible] a clear Labour victory and led to speculation about Heath's future.

RELATIONSHIPS / FRICTION ETC
WILSON / CALLAGHAN / WILLIAMS
FOOT / BENN / HATTERSLEY
MELLISH / SCANLON / JONES
HEATH / THORPE / MAUDLING
HEIRS APPARENT ???

Given the foregoing, it is clear that the campaign for the next General Election will be largely dominated by the personality factor and any effort should be made to exploit character weaknesses in 'target' subjects, and, in particular: —

   (a) Financial misbehaviour
   (b) Sexual misbehaviour
   (c) Political misbehaviour.

Heath
Maudling (T Dan Smith)
Pym
Gilmour
St Jon Stevas
Von Stankyon
Lubbon
Rees [Sockie]
Benn – MIKARDO
Owen D + Owen W
Hart / Stonehouse
Driberg etc.

There is little doubt that the Labour Party are very vulnerable to the allegation of Communist or left wing infiltration. It is estimated that between 20 and 30 Labour MPs are members of the Communist Party and that Wilson has bound to this premise by removing the embargo on CP membership for members of the Labour Party.

T. Dan Smith
Short. (also Rowse)
Thorpe / Bessell / Smith
Foot
Thomas
Wedgbenford, Helfer
Castle

Scanlon, McGahey

It can be shown that both Wilson and Heath are under Soviet control through Dick Vargannies (?) and Lord Rothschild. It can also be shown that Wilson + Lee received approx /60,000 from East German sources for Company funds and that he Lee → fund in the Soviet Government.

See also KGB officers
Victor Louis [Lui]
Yuri Ustimenko
Nicholas Glawotsky
Yuri Yazwov
IRA Links .
~~Minor intelligence~~ (?)

HW's pro Israeli stance — impact on Britain through Arab terrorism : —

Cyprus now centre for mounting various espionage missions against Israel .

Cyprus now one of the main KGB HQs in the Middle East (+ over 100 staff in Soviet Trade Mission)

FNU Mikoyan

Heath – Yon Kippur
Julian Amery

AL FATAH — YASSER ARAFAT
THE PFLP — Dr GEORGE HABBASH
PDFLP — NAIF HAWATMEH
PALESTINE ARAB ORGANISATION — AHMED ZAAROR
POPULAR FRONT GENERAL COUNCIL — AHMAD JIBRIL
BLACK SEPTEMBER — PART OF AL FATAH
~~BLACK ARAB SECURITY — ATIF NATSHE~~

Danger to British aircraft

See 'Times'
14-7-72

CHINA was the first country to recognise Al Fatah and provides training for Palestine guerrillas at Nanking Military Academy. USSR have now taken over from China who are keen to counteract Soviet interests. China also has a strong influence in YEMEN — Chinese Islamic Association etc.

GR Young
G Howarth   SIF
F Bennion
G. Stewart-Smith.

ABU MAHIR
'Rent Resistance' HOLLAND
AUDRE and CISCA FERKEN — 'Red Help' HOLLAND.
DAVID TINNIN

ATHENS BOMBING 27-11-69
Weapons used in
         2 x AK-47
         8 x Handgrenades USSR
         4 x Thermal bombs Czech
         3 x sticks of 'Vitezit - Spezial (Jugoslavia)

AIR FRANCE FLIGHT 132 30-5-72
weapons used
         Czech M435 (7.62) ~~Stag~~

Civil unrest, political violence and industrial disputes in Britain engineered and coordinated by Soviet Union through Labour Party activists and Left wing organisations. Role of Labour MPs in CDU and TOM.

Soviet plan to ruin Britain's economy aided by Labour Government.

NUM strike to bring down Heath Govt funded by USSR.

USSR anxious to turn Britain out of NATO and being about the removal of US bases in UK.

Corrupt our MPs — homosexuals and other blackmail   See also Driberg and
      Heath   Berkeley. BARCLAY
      St John Stevas
      Van Straubenzee   Floyd (died 1967?)
      Cudlipp
      Wilson — who entered relationship with
Marcia Williams.

                               Lord Salisbury
Link a homosexual story via Zeppo McElligott,   Joseph Josten
McGrath etc.   John Wilkinson
                               John Slessor
Factors keeping terrorism in N. Ireland.   Leonard Schapiro

1. Release of Internees.

2. Talks with Sinn Fein and UDA etc.

3. Cut-backs in Defence Budget.

4. Meetings between Unionists and IRA.

UWC Strike
14 MAY 1974 — Begins
     Jun 1973 — Assembly election
     Dec 1973 — Sunningdale conference
     Jan 1974 — NI Executive taken over
   28 Feb 1974 — Heath comes to power.

INCOS LIMITED (SWISS BRANCH OF GEWARDS), DIRECTOR:
ROGER SIMONET

GUNTHER LEINHAUSER — 'ELMSTADT' LATER RENAMED   LINK TO WILSON'S
'CLAUDIA' BY HAMBURG   PRO ISRAELI STANCE
HALLER CONTACTED LIBYAN MISSION TO THE UNITED   BUT BEWARE OF CONFLICT
NATIONS IN GENEVA WHEN THEIR FUNDS RAN OUT.   WITH SOVIET/ISRAELI
LIBYAN CONTACT WAS: MINISTER TARTARIN DJERBI   ATTITUDES.
WHO PASSED HALLER'S REQUEST TO GADAFFI

HALLER WAS INVITED TO LIBYA ONE WEEK LATER AND   LIBYA LINKS WITH
STAYED AT THE AFRICA HOTEL TUNIS WITH JOE CAHILL   USSR — KGB'S ROLE
DAVID O'CONNELL   IN THE AFFAIR — LINKS
CLAUDIA LEFT TUNIS ON 12 MARCH AND SAILED TO   WITH UDA
TRIPOLI WHERE SHE LOADED 5 TONS OF ARMS
ELECTRONIC HOMING DEVICE PLANTED ON BOARD — TRACKED
BY RAF NIMROD — INFO PASSED TO IRISH AUTHORITIES
HALLER FLEW FROM TUNIS TO ROME ON 7 MARCH —
TELEPHONE TO O'FARRELL ASKING TO STAY AT HER
ADDRESS.
SEEN IN MILAN IN AUGUST WITH GIORGIO PERETTI
    "   " DUBLIN IN OCTOBER
[~~xxxxxxxxxxx~~]

KGB PLOT TO LEAK RADIOACTIVE WASTE NEAR POLARIS   1 DIRECTORATE
SUBMARINE BASES — TO CAUSE PUBLIC CONCERN IN UK   3 DEPARTMENT
AND SUPPORT LABOUR'S ANTI-NUCLEAR STANCE → STOP TRIDENT

MURDER OF HUGH GAITSKELL TO ASSIST WILSON TO POWER?   LINK DISCLOSURES MADE
    BY OLEG ADOLFOVICH
WILFRED OWEN - CZECH INTELLIGENCE AGENT AND CLOSE   ~~LEW~~ LYALIN
CONFIDANT OF WILSON   "PLANS TO INFILTRATE
    SABOTAGE AGENTS INTO UK
FEMALE KGB AGENT/PROSTITUTE'S LINKS WITH LABOUR MPs   TO WORK INSIDE TRADE
IN LONDON. COVER-UP BY HOME SECRETARY   UNIONS"

MICHAEL FOOT — A CLOSE FRIEND OF TOM DRIBERG WHO   DRIBERG - access to current
WAS AN ASSOCIATE OF GUY BURGESS.   secrets?? TONY

Stonehouse — Shielded by Wilson for his own "protection"?

Information passed to Wilson by security authorities not
acted upon or action delayed — why?" Wilson
had refused to take action against the KGB officers
already identified by security authorities.
✠ RICHARD KONSTANTINOVICH VAYGAUSKAS   ~~xxxxxxxxxxxxxxx~~
KGB OFFICER IN LONDON 1968-'71   ~~xxxxxxxx~~

DESMOND McCARTNEY   GR 951894   BALLYMAGUIGAN
TONY McCARTNEY   GR 953883   "
EDDIE BATESON   GR 952891   16 ROSS ROAD
FINBAR BATESON   GR 952891

CONSERVATIVE LEADERSHIP CHANGE — LIKELY KEY FIGURES

WHITELAW, NEAVE, ST JOHN STEVAS, PYM, WALL, MATHER,   STEVAS — the 'unknown'
KNIGHT, MITCHELL, BOYSON, GOODHART, BIGGS-DAVIDSON   quantity! The inclusion
CHURCHILL, MAUDE, FOX, SOAME, AMERY, CARLISLE, ONSLOW   of PYM is also odd ??
BUCK, BLAKER AND POWELL, ALSO ROTHSCHILD CPRS

                   Shake WALKER, LONGO

ULSTER VOTING PATTERNS 1970 – 1974

1970		1974	
UNIONIST	54.1	UUUC	50.8
LABOUR	12.6	FALK U	12.1
LIBERAL	9.6	SDLP	22.2
INDEP	4.8	ALL	3.1
P. UNIONIST	4.6	LABOUR	2.1
R. LABOUR	3.9	REP. CLUBS	1.7
NAT	3.4	OTHER PARTIES	6.4
LIBERAL	1.5		
NAT DEM	1.3		
OTHER PARTIES	3.7		

POLL: 779,192   TOTAL POLL 722,282

IMPACT OF UNIONIST AND LIBERAL PARTIES ON THE LABOUR GOVT

(1) The Unionists (anti Power Sharing) will clearly be 'mavericks' and vote   20 SEATS REQUIRED BY CONS
according to what suits them best

(3) The election has shown a re-emergence of Liberal popularity ie 19.5%
of the vote this time against 7.5% at the previous election. There
appears to have been a key figure and most of the votes gained came
from the Conservatives.

Q: What would happen to the part of the vote of the Liberals became
unpopular?

Q: If both Labour and Liberal lost public confidence simultaneously
would the votes go to the Conservatives or just be lost by people
not turning out in the election? How would this situation
alter under a different Conservative leader?

A split could be engineered in the Liberal party over the   SUPPORTERS OF
role in power sharing with either Labour or Conservative.   Thorpe, Steel, Grimond
                                                    (Partly or amenable to share power)

It is unrealistic to expect much change in Unionist voting patterns but the Liberals are very vulnerable under certain circumstances and the Cons could recapture their lost ground.

FINANCE, HOMOSEXUALITY, PERSONALITY CLASHES e.g. HOOSON / THORPE / STEEL

(3) INDUSTRIAL UNREST:

   (a) UNION POWER — WHOLE COMMUNITY SUFFERED DURING THE 3 DAY WEEK.

No BLACKS — LIBERAL OR

   (b) LACK OF DETERMINATION BY HEATH — WHY?

LABOUR

   (c) SOVIET INFLUENCE / CONTROL AND FINANCE

RIGHT/LEFT SPLIT WITHIN LABOUR

   (d) IDENTITY OF THE 'FIFTH' MAN

   (f) SOVIET LINK WILSON / HEATH

   (G) HOMOSEXUAL LINK HEATH / THORPE

(adopted children?)

   (H) HOMOSEXUAL (BLACKMAIL) LINK THORPE / WILSON — ALSO FINANCE

   (·) FINANCIAL ASSOCIATIONS SMART / MAUDLING / T.D. SMITH etc.

(2) SECURITY CONCERNS

   (1) NATO — WITHDRAWAL BY USA

   (2) ANTI-NUCLEAR STANCE — LOSS OF US SUPPORT

   (3) SOVIET INFILTRATION OF GOVT

   (4) ANTI VIETNAM DEMOS / CND DEMOS — KGB INSPIRED

   (5) ARAB TERRORISM ETC LINKS WITH IRA, CUBA, YEMEN, LIBYA ETC (RED BRIGADE ETC ANT. NATO)

(3) FINANCIAL CONCERNS

   (1) DEVALUATION

CONTRAST: POULSON, SMITH, FIELD

   (2) UNEMPLOYMENT

AND SMART etc — LINK THORPE.

   (3) INFLATION

Possible legal action against WILSON concerning former PS

(4) POLITICAL

LABOUR POLITICIANS WHO ARE BELIEVED TO BE COMMUNISTS AND WHO HOLD POSITIONS OF INFLUENCE: —

CREATE / EXPAND RIFT WILSON / REC ROLE OF LEVER?

Despite assurances in the Commons

   (a) BENN

that he would not speak with

   (b) MIKARDO

"men of violence", Wilson,

   (c) HEFFER

accompanied by Rees, met —the

   (d) OWEN D

IRA twice in 1972

   (e) HART

   (f) DRIBERG

   (G) CASTLE

   (H) FOOT

   (·) STONEHOUSE (FORMER MINISTER)

1973 PERSONALITIES

JAMES BROWN	BELFAST BDE PARA	MALACHY McGURRAN
IVOR BELL	" " "	BILLY McMILLAN
FRANCIS FOX	" " "	CATHAL GOULDING
LIAM ADAMS	32 WESTROCK DRIVE OC 'F'COY 2 PIRA	Meet in London after
BRENDAN COUSINS	OC/ADJ 'F' COY 1 PIRA	WILSON KILLED.

<u>Political Appreciation — General Notes</u>

The results of the February General Election indicate that unless there is a dramatic change in the fortunes of the Conservative Party it cannot win the next election under Edward Heath's leadership. The key issue, therefore, is whether there should be cosmetic treatment to keep-elect a weak Government under Heath or major surgery to bring about a change of leadership before the next election. <u>If Heath goes willingly before the next election who would be his successor?</u>

① WHITELAW : Popular with the senior members of the Party. Has attracted quite a lot of sympathetic following his time in Ulster. His new job at the M of L may, however, tarnish his image. It is believed that he would attract the support of the pro Paisley Unionists (He argued with Heath that they have a place at the Sunningdale Conference). Also, it would appear that Paisley offered Heath the support of the anti-Sunningdale Unionists subject to a 'deal' on Assembly elections etc. Heath is very anti-Paisley and would not accept support from him or Bill Craig.

② SOAMES : Strong contender. No seat in Parliament at the moment — in Brussels at EEC.

③ POWELL : Has annoyed senior Tories by his 'Vote Labour' call at the last election. May not stand as a Conservative next time and future, therefore, uncertain.   RIPPON ?

④ PRIOR : Lacks experience but well liked

⑤ Du CANN : Possible financial skeletons in his cupboard

⑥ RIDLEY : Too close to Powell

⑦ BIFFEN : Too close to Ridley & Powell

⑧ CARRINGTON : A strong contender but not far enough to the Right if Heath went after the next election.

If Heath loses the next election and is forced to give up the leadership then the field is wide open and one of the 'new' faces may come to the fore to depose the 'Old Brigade'. In that case too, there will certainly be a marked swing to the Right. Indications are that Whitelaw would then play a key role in the 'selection' of the new leader and

his relationship with the new leader would be crucial vis a vis
the co-operation of the pro-Paisley unionists.
In essence, Paisley and his fellow MPs would not support
Wilson or Heath. If Wilson 'falls', he would support
Callaghan but not Rees. Callaghan could be a good
choice because of his rôle as Police Federation representative
but he also has 'financial skeletons' relating to the Welsh
banking matters in his cupboard. Roy Jenkins is the
unknown quantity but his 'liberal' policies at the Home
Office have not helped his cause with the establishment —
he is also very close to Wilson and could therefore be discredited
with him.

    Healey: SA arms
    Communist nucleus etc.

VULNERABILITIES

	FINANCE	MORAL	POLITICAL	MAY 'D'EVANS'
WILSON	✓	✓	✓D	(POULSON / SHORT)
HEATH		✓	✓D	17 JUN 'NL'
THORPE	✓	✓		DOCS ON UDA/IRA funds found
CALLAGHAN	✓	—		
PAISLEY	✓	✗D		
MAUDLING	✓	✓		
STEEL		✗D		
{ SLATER	✓			
{ WALKER	✓			
FOOT			✓	
BENN			✓	
SHORT	✓			

CDU / AIL / TOM

Mikardo, Foot, Orme, Miller, Rose, Byers, Stallard, Maynard,
Litterick, Tinn, McNamara, Walden, Owen, Mellish, Heffer,
Prentice, Hattersley etc. See also Pardoe. (See 145)

    Misuse of Party Funds
    by Thorpe — see
    details of LP accounts
    in JT's name.

'Northern Ireland — The Way Ahead'

Any democracy is only threatened by revolutionary
terrorism when there is a general withdrawal of
popular support from Government, or when Government
appears entirely unable to deal with the problems
that face it. Most people believe that this is
now the situation in Northern Ireland.

    The liberties of a democratic society are
ultimately dependent upon the maintenance
of the rule of law. Terrorism is the most

system will remain unstable because it tends to unite
all Ulster politicians against a system of government that is
no longer accountable to them. In turn this offers the
initiative to the paramilitary groups to use violence to
resolve disputes and settle old scores.

The major weakness of Westminster policy is that it is
addressed to the wrong problem and it assumes conditions
that do not now exist in the Province.

Labour's New Left in Northern Ireland

CAMPAIGN FOR SOCIAL JUSTICE (Dr. + Mrs J McCLUSKEY, DUNGANNON)	IMG
CAMPAIGN FOR DEMOCRACY IN ULSTER	97 CALEDONIAN RD
BRITISH WITHDRAWL FROM NI GROUP	NI
TROOPS OUT MOVEMENT	INT SOCIALISTS
ANTI INTERNMENT LEAGUE	
IRISH POLITICAL HOSTAGES RELEASE COMMITTEE	

The most prominent activist in the above groups is Paul Rose   Manchester's 'Left Club'
(MP Blackley in Manchester) who was appointed Chairman   M+D's 'Young Socialists'
of the CDU and has involved various other Left wing Labour   CND
MPs in its activities. Rose is a Lawyer who studied   'Democratic Defence'
at Manchester University and was a key member of
the university's Communist Controlled 'Socialist Society'.
He is a former contributor to the Communist youth   'Young Communist'
newspaper and his wife was born in the Soviet Bloc.
He was elected to Parliament in 1964. Born 1936.
Other relevant key personalities: ORME, OGDEN, OWEN, DELARGY,   ~~Sinclair~~ (Comm)
HEFFER, MILLER, BROCKWAY, NEWENS, ALLAUN, CUNNINGHAM
He could become a source of embarrassment to the Party
Leadership because of his independent views on a number
of matters eg he supported Heath in the 1971 RTZ split.   ~~Michael Foot~~
He is also a member of the 'League for a Democratic Greece'   ~~Wedgwood Benn~~
or League for Democracy in Greece.
Most of his close associates are on the left of the Party and
his role in the Party could be a key one in the event
of a change in leadership. A potential/possible
Soviet agent he appears to be much liked by Wilson!!
His close liaison with Stan Orme at the NIO are important
and it may be significant that Orme was promoted   Joan Maynard
to the NI post by HW. Thought to be pro Israeli   Albert Booth 'Puritan'
and strongly anti South Africa — see Anti-Apartheid   Jock Stallard.
Movement and Labour's row over the 'Arms to South
Africa' issue.
PPS to Barbara Castle. Election majority approx 7,000

'ULSTER — A STATE OF SUBVERSION'

An analysis of Soviet influence on Labour Party policies in Northern Ireland.

The Irish scene has fascinated the Communists for many years. Lenin learned from Marx and Engels, and often repeated, that British rule in Ireland was bad not only for Ireland but also for the British working class. While writing his article on 'The Right of Nations to Self Determination', in 1914, Lenin took particular note of a letter from Marx to Engels, dated 2nd November 1867:

"I used to think that the separation of Ireland from England was impossible. Now I think it is inevitable, although the separation there may come as a federation."

It is remarkable, therefore, that some sixty years later during the present unrest, both Loyalist and Republican groups have put forward federation proposals as a possible solution.

Communist views of the events in Northern Ireland are governed among the West and East European Communist Parties by the degree of their dependence on the Soviet Union and, in the case of the British and Irish Parties, by the need to consider the tactical implications for themselves. Thus the Communist position on Northern Ireland ranges from the extreme of Moscow's over-simplification and distortion designed to fit the issue into a colonial mould, to the more balanced and factual coverage of Rumania and Yugoslavia, which have avoided attempts to make propaganda capital out of the Irish tensions.

In the face of such propaganda government information policy in Northern Ireland has been weak, ineffective, un-co-ordinated and defensive — like their security policies as a whole. Public confidence in government determination to defeat terrorism and the credibility of British political policies are now regarded with much scepticism, if not disbelief. A direct result of this political and security vacuum is the spread of acquiescent violence of the mind. People who would never have advocated the use of violence have now turned to preaching about the end justifying the means, and about the use of force being an acceptable evil.

Such a psychological climate is ripe for exploiting by the terrorist's propaganda machine. The terrorists constant policy has been the undermining of any individual, activity or organisation that threatens their survival. Abuse is heaped upon any politician, civil servant, prisoner or soldier whose efficiency and tenacity lead to effective counter-terrorist measures

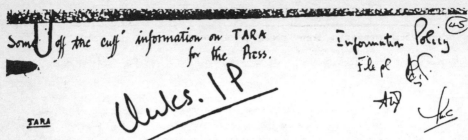

Some off the cuff information on TARA for the Press.

Information Policy File pl

TARA

TARA first came to police in the late sixties when the group issued a statement to the press claiming to be "the hard core of Protestant resistance", and it is thought that the organisation was set up as a counter to the civil disturbances associated with the NICRA marches.

The name TARA is derived from the place where the ancient high kings of Ireland were crowned and is, therefore, an unusual choice of title for a Loyalist paramilitary group.

Operating from its HQ at Clifton Street Orange Hall, Belfast, as 'The Orange Discussion Group', TARA was organised initially into platoons of 20 or so men and run on military lines not unlike the old Ulster Special Constabulary ('B' Specials). Membership is drawn almost exclusively from the Orange Order and each platoon has a Sgt/QM (Quartermaster) and 10 (Intelligence Officer). Contributions: 50p per month – half to a central fund – half at pln level. Plns are able to draw on the central fund if the opportunity to buy stores arises. Training includes radio, weapons and guerrilla tactics.

The OC is William McGRATH. He is a known homosexual who has conned many people into membership by threatening them with revealing homosexual activities which he himself initiated. He is a prominent figure in Unionist Party politics and in the Orange Order.

McGRATH uses a non-existent evangelical mission as a front for his homosexual activities and also runs a home for children on the Upper Newtownards Road, Belfast (Tel: B'fast 657838). Also at ██████ Newtownards Road (B'fast ██████).

he said he resigned

The TARA 2 i/c is Roy GARLAND, a close personal friend of McGRATH and his former employer.

McGRATH's 'ADC' is Frank MILLER who comes from the Shore Road area of Belfast and who is also an active member of the Unionist Party. He is the author of a number of political pamphlets including one called 'Dangers and Sinister Realities'.

TARA's 'Intelligence Officer' is Clifford SMITH who lives with McGRATH, and the group's 'Admin Officer' is David BROWN from Bangor Co Down. BROWN is Deputy Editor of Rev PAISLEY's 'Protestant Telegraph'.

Other people closely associated with McGRATH and aware of his activities are Thomas PASSMORE, Rev PAISLEY, Rev Martin SMITH, James MOLYNEAUX and Sir Knox CUNNINGHAM QC MP.

✱ 'ULSTER'S children of conflict'. New Society 15. Apr 71

DR M. FRASER ?
RUH

?? Samuel Doenan or William Wilson

AMERICAN CONGRESS FOR IRISH FREEDOM

326 WEST 48TH STREET • NEW YORK, N. Y. 10036

October 3, 1971

Mr Merlyn, Rees MP
The House of Commons
Parliament Buildings
London
England

Dear Mr Rees:

Thank you for your generous donation on behalf of the British
Labour Party for relief in the Occupied Six Counties of
Ireland. We in the Congress are very grateful for the support
you and your Party colleagues have given us during the past
two years and we join with you in looking forward to the day
when, under a Labour government, Britain will end its
repression in the Occupied Six Counties and disengage both
politically and militarily from Ireland.

With all good wishes.

Respectfully yours,

James C. Heaney
President
760 Ellicott Square Bldg
Buffalo 3, N.Y.

JCH:hs

3.55pm.
Derry, Bloody Sunday

DERRY BLOODY SUNDAY COMMEM-ORATION VIGIL

BDCC
37 Middle Lane
London N.8

On Sunday, January 28th, 1973, the people of Northern Ireland will be commemorating BLOODY SUNDAY 1972, when highly trained soldiers of the British Army, under official orders, shot and killed 13 unarmed civilians peacefully marching for their civil rights. English, Scots and Welsh people of many different political opinions will be visiting Derry on Saturday, January 27th, to hold an ALL-NIGHT VIGIL at Free Derry Corner in order to dis-associate ourselves from the outrage that was committed by "our" Govern-ment in "our" name. NICRA (the Northern Ireland Civil Right Association) welcome this action. I's important that a large body of Scots, English and Welsh participate — both as individuals and as delegates from organisations. WHAT ABOUT YOU? Participants will be going from all parts of Britain. There is a Heysham-Belfast boat Friday night returning Sunday night (£6.60 return). BEA flies London-Belfast Saturday, returning Sunday evening (after the Commemoration Ceremony) at £13.20 return. It is hoped to organise cheap coaches from Belfast to Derry. Please return form as soon as possible.

Sponsors

FENNER BROCKWAY	ERNIE ROBERTS	JOAN GABRIEL
GWYNFOR EVANS	JOAN MAYNARD	CHRIS FARLEY
DONALD SOPER	BILL JONES	TONY SMYTHE
GORDON McLELLAN	BRIAN NICHOLSON	MALCOLM CALDWELL
DIGBY JACKS	STAN NEWENS	JOHN BERGER
PETER HAIN	KEN COATES	ADRIAN MITCHELL
LOUIS EAKS	COLIN SWEET	MARY HOLLAND
	PAT ARROWSMITH	

Printed by The Russell Press Ltd.

TO: British Derry Commemoration Committee, 37 Middle Lane, London N.8.

I am/ . . . . of us are/interested in joining the Derry Commemoration Vigil. Please send further information. I enclose a stamped self-addressed envelope and £. . . . . . .p as a contribution to the organisation expenses. I intend to travel as follows:

....

NAME (S) ....

ADDRESS ....

....

PHONE; day .... eve/weekend .... Organisation ....

Please send . . . . . . further leaflets to me/the following:

**3.55pm.
Derry, Bloody Sunday**

DERRY BLOODY SUNDAY COMMEM-ORATION

VIGIL

BDCC
37 Middle Lane
London N.8

On Sunday, January 28th, 1973, the people of Northern Ireland will be commemorating BLOODY SUNDAY 1972, when highly trained soldiers of the British Army, under official orders, shot and killed 13 unarmed civilians peacefully marching for their civil rights. English, Scots and Welsh people of many different political opinions will be visiting Derry on Saturday, January 27th, to hold an ALL-NIGHT VIGIL at Free Derry Corner in order to dis-associate ourselves from the outrage that was committed by "our" Govern-ment in "our" name. NICRA (the Northern Ireland Civil Right Association) welcome this action. It's important that a large body of Scots, English and Welsh participate — both as individuals and as delegates from organisations. WHAT ABOUT YOU? Participants will be going from all parts of Britain. There is a Heysham-Belfast boat Friday night returning Sunday night (£6.60 return). BEA flies London-Belfast Saturday, returning Sunday evening (after the Commemoration Ceremony) at £13.20 return. It is hoped to organise cheap coaches from Belfast to Derry. Please return form as soon as possible.

Sponsors

FENNER BROCKWAY	ERNIE ROBERTS	PAUL ROSE
GWYNFOR EVANS	JOAN MAYNARD	CHRIS FARLEY
DONALD SOPER	BILL JONES	TONY BENN
GORDON McLELLAN	BRIAN NICHOLSON	MALCOLM CALDWELL
DIGBY JACKS	STAN ORME	JOHN BERGER
PETER HAIN	KEN COATES	ADRIAN MITCHELL
LOUIS EAKS	COLIN SWEET	MARY HOLLAND
MERLYN REES	PAT ARROWSMITH	DAVID OWEN

Printed by The Russell Press Ltd.

TO: British Derry Commemoration Committee, 37 Middle Lane, London N.8.

I am/ . . . . of us are/interested in joining the Derry Commemoration Vigil. 'Please send further information. I enclose a stamped self-addressed envelope and £. . . . . . .p as a contribution to the organisation expenses. I intend to travel as follows:

....

NAME (S) ....

ADDRESS ....

....

'PHONE; day .... eve/weekend .... Organisation ....

ULSTER IS BRITISH

INTERNMENT

SPECIAL POWERS

DISCRIMINATION

INTIMIDATION

ASSASSINATION

British capitalism has long exported its violence to its imperial possessions: it does so in full measure to its nearest vassal territory—the police state which it maintains in Northern Ireland. Irish workers and peasants have, however, a revolutionary heritage, both of class struggle and of combat against British imperialism. This tradition has powered the civil rights association in the North, a movement whose radical component—People's Democracy—is attempting to transform a sectional fight for elementary civic rights on the part of the Catholic population into a class assault of both Protestant and Catholic workers, peasants and students against their exploiters. Such a development threatens not merely the maintenance in power of the Northern Irish client régime— it menaces the equally reactionary 'independent' régime in the South.

The struggle in Northern Ireland has attained a higher level than on the English mainland. The Left there has traditionally failed to win any important section of the working class to anti-imperialist positions, even where it is subjectively anti-capitalist. The situation in Northern Ireland highlights the urgency of doing so. If effective solidarity action is to be achieved, a considerable work of propaganda and demystification in Britain will be needed.

VOTE LABOUR

7 Carlisle Street, London, W.1

WORKERS UNITE

PROTESTANT AND CATHOLIC WORKING
PEOPLE HAVE THE SAME **COMMON** ENEMY
— THE IMPERIALIST RULING CLASS —
EVERY BLOW STRUCK AGAINST THE CAPITALIST
STATE MACHINE IS A BLOW FOR A FREE
AND INDEPENDENT ULSTER

FREE THE PEOPLE

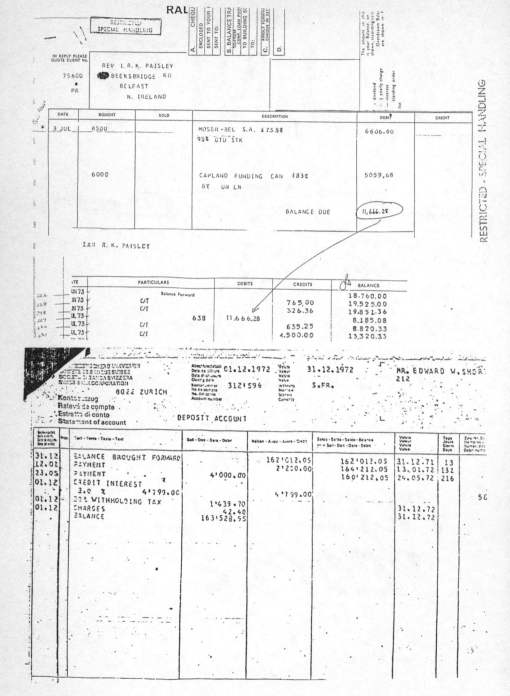

Index

Picture Acknowledgements

All the pictures come from Colin Wallace's own collection except the following: the Sussex police appeal and the River Arun (*Portsmouth News*); William McGrath (Allan McCoulough, Belfast); Colin in parachute gear (James Clevett, Littlehampton); Fred Holroyd and Colin after his release from prison (*Daily Mirror*).